# ASIAN ECONOMIC INTEGRATION REPORT 2025

## HARNESSING THE BENEFITS OF REGIONAL COOPERATION AND INTEGRATION

ASIAN DEVELOPMENT BANK

ADB

6 ADB Avenue, Mandaluyong City, 1550 Metro Manila, Philippines
Tel +63 2 8632 4444; Fax +63 2 8636 2444
www.adb.org



ISBN 978-92-9277-251-2 (print); 978-92-9277-252-9 (PDF); 978-92-9277-253-6 (ebook)
Publication Stock No. SGP250106-2
DOI: http://dx.doi.org/10.22617/SGP250106-2



Notes:
In this publication, "$" refers to United States dollars, "€" refers to euros, "B" refers to baht, "NZ$" refers to New Zealand dollars, "SLRs" refers to Sri Lanka rupees, "SUM" refers to sum, and "Tk" refers to taka.

ADB recognizes "China" as the People's Republic of China, "South Korea" as the Republic of Korea, "USA" as the United States, and "Vietnam" as Viet Nam.

Cover design by Erickson Mercado.

All masthead photos are from ADB.

# CONTENTS

# TABLES, FIGURES, AND BOXES

## TABLES



## FIGURES

## BOXES

# FOREWORD

Asia and the Pacific is expected to continue its relatively strong economic performance despite waning global growth momentum post pandemic. Nonetheless, the region must continue to adjust to changes in the environment for international trade and investment caused by evolving geopolitical tensions.

While forecasts vary by subregion and economy, continued strong domestic demand has been supplemented by the semiconductor upcycle, in particular strong demand for higher-end products associated with artificial intelligence. Shifts in supply chain structure will likely continue to be fueled by political shifts and trade policies in advanced economies. The region's ability to attract new foreign investment (including intraregional) remains high.

The *Asian Economic Integration Report 2025: Harnessing the Benefits of Regional Cooperation and Integration* explains and analyzes how regional integration has deepened over the past 2 decades, influenced by both long-term trends and recent global events. It examines changes in cross-border activities in trade and global value chains, foreign direct investment, finance (or portfolio investment), migration, remittances, and tourism. While trade integration in the region now rivals that of the European Union plus the United Kingdom, foreign direct investment and people mobility remain steady with financial integration lagging behind.

Among subregions, Southeast Asia continues to lead in regional integration, with East Asia relatively strong as well. The People's Republic of China, despite its own domestic economic issues, continues to expand its economic integration across the region, particularly with Southeast Asia and South Asia. The region continues to shift toward more resilient, regional supply networks, particularly in upgrading its supply and value chains. Rising geoeconomic fragmentation due to continuing global policy shifts, while posing growing challenges, nonetheless offers new opportunities for the region to strengthen integration by facilitating intraregional flows of goods and services, capital, people, and knowledge. Unlocking the great potential economic integration holds for the region requires further efforts to strengthen regional economic cooperation and partnerships in the areas of trade, investment, macroeconomic and financial stability, and cross-border connectivity.

This report hopefully will stimulate dialogue and discussion on how deeper regional cooperation and economic integration can help the region navigate challenges posed by the evolving geopolitical landscape without losing sight of the long-term vision of a more green, inclusive, and sustainable Asia and the Pacific.

**Albert Park**
Chief Economist and Director General
Economic Research and Development Impact Department
Asian Development Bank

# ACKNOWLEDGMENTS

The Asian Economic Integration Report (AEIR) 2025 was prepared by the Regional Cooperation and Integration Division (ERCI) of ADB's Economic Research and Development Impact Department (ERDI), under the overall supervision of ERCI Director Jong Woo Kang. Kijin Kim coordinated the overall production, assisted by Mara Tayag. ERCI consultants under Technical Assistance 10136: Asian Economic Integration: Building Knowledge for Policy Dialogue, 2023–2025 (Subproject 3) contributed data compilation, research, and analysis.

Contributing authors include Sanchita Basu-Das, Rolando Avendano, Paulo Rodelio Halili, Lovely Ann Tolin, and Rainiel Aquino, with data support from Pilar Dayag (Chapter 1: Overview); Neil Foster-McGregor, Pramila Crivelli, Joshua Anthony Gapay, Carlos Cabaero, and Pia Medrano (Chapter 2: Trade and the Global Value Chains); Rolando Avendano and Clemence Fatima Cruz (Chapter 3: Cross-Border Investment); Alexander Raabe and Rainiel Aquino, with data support from Carlos Cabaero and Clemence Fatima Cruz (Chapter 4: Financial Integration); and Kijin Kim, Sanchita Basu-Das, Ma. Concepcion Latoja, and Ma. Veronica Domingo, with data support from Zemma Ardaniel (Chapter 5: Movement of People).

The section on "Regional Cooperation Initiatives in Asia" in Chapter 1 was consolidated by Paulo Rodelio Halili based on contributions by regional departments in ADB: Lyaziza Sabyrova, Dorothea Lazaro, and Carmen Maria Garcia Perez of the Central and West Asia Department; Thiam Hee Ng, Dongxiang Li, Masato Nakane, Pia Reyes, Lani Garnace, and Esnerjames Fernandez of the South Asia Department; Alfredo Perdiguero, Maria Josephine E. Duque-Comia, Jason Rush, Asadullah Sumbal, and Sophia Castillo-Plaza of the Southeast Asia Department; Hsiao Chink Tang of the East Asia Department; and Kaukab Naqvi, Rustam Ishenaliev, Maria Melei, and Kayleen Gene Calicdan of the Pacific Department. Melanie Pre of the RCI and Trade Division, Climate Change and Sustainable Development Department provided data on RCI-related commitments.

Background papers were provided by Manuel Albis, Mara Tayag, and Jong Woo Kang for Chapter 1: Overview; Emily Blanchard, Will Olney, Amelia Santos-Paulino, Claudia Trentini, and Rolando Avendano, with data support from Camille Reverdy for Chapter 3: Cross-Border Investment; Josef Yap as well as Daniel te Kaat and Alexander Raabe for Chapter 4: Financial Integration; Isaacs Leon, Jon Capal, and Maria Cherry Lyn Rodolfo for Chapter 5: Movement of People. The report benefited from comments and suggestions provided by the participants of "AEIR 2025 Workshop: Harnessing the Benefits of Regional Cooperation and Integration" held on 20 September 2024. Helpful comments were also provided by ADB's regional departments. The overall guidance and comments of ADB Chief Economist Albert Park are gratefully acknowledged.

Guy Sacerdoti and James Unwin edited the manuscript. Joseph Manglicmot typeset and produced the layout. Erickson Mercado created the cover design and assisted in typesetting. Tuesday Soriano proofread the report. Clemence Fatima Cruz, Rainiel Aquino, Carol Ongchangco, and Joshua Anthony Gapay assisted in proofreading and page proof checking. Support for AEIR 2025 printing and publishing was provided by the Printing Services Unit of ADB's Corporate Services Department and by the Publishing and Dissemination Unit of the Department of Communications and Knowledge Management. Carol Ongchangco, Amiel Bryan Esperanza, Angel Love Roque, Nanette Lozano, and Arielle Fajardo provided administrative and secretarial support and helped organize the AEIR workshops, launch events, and other AEIR-related webinars and briefings.

# ABBREVIATIONS

| | |
|---|---|
| ADB | Asian Development Bank |
| ABF | Asian Bond Fund |
| ABMI | Asian Bond Markets Initiative |
| APEC | Asia-Pacific Economic Cooperation |
| ARCII | Asia-Pacific Regional Cooperation and Integration Index |
| ASEAN | Association of Southeast Asian Nations |
| BIMSTEC | Bay of Bengal Initiative for Multi-Sectoral Technical and Economic Cooperation |
| BLA | bilateral labor agreement |
| CAREC | Central Asia Regional Economic Cooperation |
| CMIM | Chiang Mai Initiative Multilateralisation |
| CPIS | Coordinated Portfolio Investment Survey |
| PRC | People's Republic of China |
| EU | European Union |
| FDI | foreign direct investment |
| FTA | free trade agreement |
| GCAP | green city action plan |
| GDP | gross domestic product |
| GMS | Greater Mekong Subregion |
| GMSKN | GMS Knowledge Network |
| GVC | global value chain |
| HS | Harmonized System |
| ICT | information and communication technology |
| IFD | Investment Facilitation for Development |
| IMF | International Monetary Fund |
| IMT-GT | Indonesia–Malaysia–Thailand Growth Triangle |
| KYC | know-your-customer |
| M&A | merger and acquisition |
| MFN | most-favored nation |
| MNE | multinational enterprise |

| | |
|---|---|
| MOU | memorandum of understanding |
| MRA | mutual recognition arrangement |
| MTR | midterm review |
| OECD | Organisation for Economic Co-operation and Development |
| PNG | Papua New Guinea |
| PPP | public–private partnership |
| PRIF | Pacific Region Infrastructure Facility |
| PSDI | Private Sector Development Initiative |
| PTA | preferential trade agreement |
| RCEP | Regional Comprehensive Economic Partnership |
| RCI | regional cooperation and integration |
| RoO | rules of origin |
| RTA | regional trade agreement |
| RVC | regional value chains |
| SAARC | South Asian Association for Regional Cooperation |
| SASEC | South Asia Subregional Economic Cooperation |
| SDG | Sustainable Development Goal |
| SMEs | small and medium-sized enterprises |
| TA | technical assistance |
| UK | United Kingdom |
| UN | United Nations |
| UNCTAD | United Nations Trade and Development |
| US | United States |
| WTO | World Trade Organization |

# HIGHLIGHTS

**Economic integration has been pivotal in Asia and the Pacific's remarkable economic growth and rapidly rising global clout over the past 2 decades.** Asian Development Bank (ADB) estimates indicate that the degree of Asia's trade integration is comparable to that of the European Union plus the United Kingdom (EU+UK).[1] Regional integration in foreign direct investment (FDI) has also advanced significantly, although less than trade integration. Migration, remittances, and tourism—or "movement of people"—have remained steady. Financial integration has been the lowest, being lower than in trade, investment, and movement of people, and has lagged behind that of the EU+UK. This progress in regional integration has been supported by various projects, programs, and policy dialogue. Cooperation through trade facilitation, along with the development of transport and economic corridors, has helped advance integration across the region. Expanding digital connectivity and efforts to address climate change—supported by shared national and regional commitments—are strategic areas for future cooperation and integration in regional public goods.

**Although the expansion of preferential trade agreements (PTAs) across the region underscores its strong commitment to regional integration and global connectedness, its PTAs remain relatively narrow and shallow and have had limited impact.** The significant rise in PTAs, now comprising 45% of all global PTAs, underscores Asia's drive for expanding market access and deepening economic partnerships—even amid slow multilateral progress. However, estimated average exports increased by 3% among Asian PTA members compared with 20% in the more comprehensive agreements outside Asia. PTAs primarily intensify existing trade flows (intensive margin) without significantly broadening the diversity of traded goods (extensive margin). This trend is seen across intra-Asian PTAs, where the impact on manufacturing is modest compared to agreements outside Asia. Consequently, trade gains under Asian PTAs tend to be concentrated in specific sectors, particularly primary sectors, rather than producing broad-based trade expansion. The low utilization rates across PTAs often result from complex administrative requirements, stringent rules of origin, and limited understanding of PTA benefits, particularly for small and medium-sized enterprises.

**Services, digital, and green industries have become major areas for foreign investment in Asia, while economies should embrace policy options to mitigate the impact of geopolitical risks.** Asia continues to show strong intraregional linkages, with FDI among Asian members accounting for an average 52% of regional FDI from 2013 to 2023. FDI in services is now the main driver of foreign investment in Asia—its average share grew to 58% during the past decade from 46% over the previous decade. Digital and green FDI continues to redefine Asia's investment landscape. Climate-related greenfield investments as a share of regional greenfield investment rose from 8% in 2013 to 27% in 2023. This was in part possible due to the expansion of renewable industries and deployment of electric vehicle supply chains across Southeast Asia. Global investment patterns have been influenced by geopolitical tensions as well as major industrial developments and changing policy environment in host economies. ADB estimates suggest that greenfield investments in trade-exposed sectors experienced sharper declines than other sectors during periods of increased geopolitical tensions, while ASEAN economies attracted significantly higher FDI primarily driven by the PRC. Regional economies need to continually work to improve the overall business climate and ease restrictions to FDI.

---

1 Asia refers to the 49 members of ADB in Asia and the Pacific, which include Australia, Japan, and New Zealand in addition to 46 developing economies.

**Global monetary easing could increase capital inflows into the region, bringing with it important macroeconomic and policy implications.** The global monetary easing since mid-2024 can help strengthen capital inflows due to smaller policy rate differentials between the US and the euro area on the one hand, and Asian economies on the other. While this also expands room for monetary policy easing across the region, each economy must remain vigilant against the risks of potential swings in capital flows and exchange rate volatility in case of unexpected economic shocks. It is vital to use regional cooperation to boost financial integration and maximize its benefits while minimizing costs due to vulnerabilities from any negative regional spillovers. Stronger regional cooperation can also harmonize disclosure standards and promote targeted financial instruments to help develop regional capital markets and promote sustainable finance when coping with the risks of climate change and environmental degradation.

**The growth and ease of Asian labor migration has benefited from increased regional cooperation.** The increasing use of digital platforms in channeling remittances enhances access to the formal financial system and promotes financial inclusion. The region's bilateral labor agreements are increasingly being used to provide access to work opportunities for low-skilled and semiskilled migrant workers. In addition, regional trade agreements, along with mutual recognition arrangements, have supported high-skilled labor mobility. However, these have had limited impact on high-skilled Asian migrants due to their minimal coverage for developing Asian economies, narrow occupational scope, and high implementation costs. Digital remittances, supported by an efficient regulatory environment, can help bring down remittance costs, which currently average 5.9% per transaction in Asia—above the 3% target of the United Nations 2030 Sustainable Development Goals. Regional cooperation should focus on leveraging digitalization in cross-border payments while narrowing the digital divide. Continuous financial and digital education, alongside best practice exchanges, would also help reduce barriers to financial access and enhance digital financial literacy.

**Accelerating regional cooperation on improving physical and institutional connectivity will increase tourism competitiveness and resilience, unlocking the industry's potential for economic development.** International arrivals in Asia grew at an average annual rate of 7.6% from 2010 to 2019, outpacing the global annual average of 5.1%—increasing the intraregional tourism share from 73.1% to 77.3%. As at least 60% of tourists to Asia arrive by air, good infrastructure and logistics are essential to support the flow of tourists. Land transportation is important for destinations that share common international borders. For institutional connectivity, visa policies are strongest in Southeast Asia, followed by Central Asia and East Asia. ADB research shows the important role connectivity plays in promoting tourism. Transportation infrastructure, in addition to other tourism infrastructure, positively influences international tourist flows and boosts the attraction of Asian destinations. Regional connectivity can help attract long-haul travel from outside the region and strengthen intraregional tourism as well. Priority investments in airport infrastructure and logistics, along with liberalizing and harmonizing policies on cross-border travel requirements, are crucial to increase tourist flows and foster the industry's contribution to growth.

# EXECUTIVE SUMMARY

**Regional integration across Asia and the Pacific has progressed steadily over the past 2 decades, led by integration in trade and investment.** The Asian Development Bank (ADB) estimates indicate the degree of Asia's trade integration is comparable to that of the European Union plus the United Kingdom (EU+UK).[2] Regional integration in foreign direct investment (FDI) has also advanced significantly, although less than trade integration. Migration, remittances, and tourism—or "movement of people"—have remained steady. Financial integration had the lowest level of integration among the four dimensions, also lagging behind the level in the EU+UK. Economic integration varies across Asian subregions. Southeast Asia leads with greater integration in trade, finance, and movement of people, while East Asia is strong in FDI and movement of people, with the Pacific and Oceania well integrated in trade and FDI. Over the past 2 decades, the People's Republic of China (PRC) has become a key driver of regional integration on cross-border trade and a significant partner in investment and financial flows with Southeast Asia and South Asia. In addition, FDI and financial flows have driven closer connectivity between Asian and non-Asian economies.

ADB's Asia-Pacific Regional Cooperation and Integration Index (ARCII) highlights the dynamics of integration across Asian subregional initiatives. These efforts to deepen regional integration among members have grown through various projects, programs, and policy dialogues. Cooperation through trade facilitation, along with transport and economic corridor development, have helped advance integration across the region. Expanding digital connectivity and the increased efforts to address climate change and environmental issues—supported by shared national and regional commitments—are strategic areas for future cooperation in strengthening cooperation and integration in areas of regional public goods.

## Trade and Global Value Chains

**Asia's increasing integration into regional value chains (RVCs) underscores a shift toward more resilient, regionally focused supply networks.** RVCs have gained importance across the region as economies rely more on regional sourcing to enhance supply chain resilience and mitigate global trade risks. Asia's intraregional trade value also increased by an annual average of 8.2% from 1990 to 2023, faster than the growth of extraregional trade at 6.8%. As of 2023, Asia's intraregional trade share stood at 56.1%, lower than in the European Union but substantially higher than in Africa and Latin America. An indicator of RVCs, which measures the share of trade in value-added attributed to regional trade, reveals a high dependency on RVCs for backward global value chain integration in economies like Bhutan, Cambodia, the Lao People's Democratic Republic (PDR), Malaysia, Nepal, the Philippines, and Viet Nam—all with RVC shares above 70%. By contrast, economies like the PRC, India, and Kazakhstan have RVC shares below 40%, indicating a lower degree of regional integration. This pattern of RVC dependence also extends to forward linkages, where economies such as Bhutan, Brunei Darussalam, Indonesia, the Lao PDR, Malaysia, and Mongolia maintain high RVC shares. Between 2000 and 2023, RVC integration generally increased, with forward linkages growing faster,

2 Asia refers to the 49 Asia and Pacific members of the Asian Development Bank (ADB), which includes Japan and Oceania (Australia and New Zealand) in addition to 46 developing Asian economies.

suggesting a gradual shift toward regionalization. In particular, the PRC has become a leading supplier of intermediates within Asia, with its forward RVC share rising from 0.31 in 2016 to 0.47 in 2023, a shift likely influenced by heightened geopolitical tensions.

**The expansion of preferential trade agreements (PTAs) across the region underscores the region's strong commitment to regional integration and global connectedness.** The number of intra-Asian PTAs surged from 4 in 1990 to 77 by 2023. In addition, there were over 100 agreements with economies outside the region. This significant rise in PTAs, comprising 45% of all global PTAs, underscores Asia's drive for expanding market access and deepening economic partnerships even amid slow multilateral progress. Several factors contribute to the increase in PTAs in Asia. While high most-favored nation (MFN) tariff rates decrease the likelihood of forming PTAs—reflecting complementarity between multilateral and preferential trade liberalization—the relationship is nonlinear. When trade volumes are substantial, very high MFN tariffs can increase the likelihood of negotiating PTAs, reflecting efforts to mitigate trade barriers. Trade volume between partners positively correlates with PTA formation, driven by motives to stabilize and formalize existing trade ties. This effect initially decreases as MFN tariffs rise, while extremely high MFN rates combined with high trade volumes increase the likelihood of PTA formation.

**Asian PTAs now include emerging areas such as services and investment, but they remain narrower than non-regional agreements with shallower goods-related commitments, limiting their impact on trade flows and diversification.** Although intra-Asian PTAs increasingly cover areas such as trade-related investment measures, visas and asylum, investment, education and training, and consumer protection, they remain narrower than the agreements outside Asia. Holding the (average) level of gross domestic product (GDP) per capita and distance between trade partners constant, an intra-Asian agreement is expected to include 10% less of the 18 core PTA provisions relative to agreements signed between non-Asian economies. While Asian PTAs cover services, investment, and movement of capital relatively well—reflecting the region's focus on deepening economic integration—many agreements remain shallow in areas directly impacting goods trade market access such as rules of origin (RoO), export restrictions, technical barriers, and trade facilitation. In terms of intra-Asian PTAs, 36% include comprehensive trade-facilitating RoO provisions compared to 48% in agreements involving non-Asian economies. PTAs between Asian economies also tend to have fewer members than those signed by the economies outside of the region. These lead to differences in the impact of PTAs, with average exports estimated to increase by 3% among Asian PTA members compared with 20% in more comprehensive agreements outside Asia. PTAs primarily intensify existing trade flows (intensive margin) without significantly broadening the diversity of traded goods (extensive margin). This trend is seen across intra-Asian PTAs, where the impact on manufacturing is modest compared to agreements outside Asia. Consequently, trade gains under Asian PTAs tend to be concentrated in specific sectors, particularly primary sectors, rather than producing broad-based trade expansion.

**The growing network of agreements has created significant complexity and administrative challenges.** The rapid expansion of PTAs across Asia shows a strong commitment to regional integration. But their overlapping "noodle bowl" effect increases complexity and administrative burdens. Compliance requirements, particularly for small and medium-sized enterprises and the developing members in agreements at various levels of economic advancement, limit PTA utilization, especially where multiple agreements overlap. The Regional Comprehensive Economic Partnership (RCEP) is a good example. Only 0.67% of Vietnamese exports to RCEP members were covered by an RCEP certificate of origin in 2022, as opposed to 34.7% for the Association of Southeast Asian Nations (ASEAN)–Japan and Viet Nam–Japan Economic Partnership Agreements combined. Low utilization rates across PTAs often result from complex administrative requirements, stringent RoO, and limited understanding of PTA benefits, particularly for small and medium-sized enterprises. Strengthening negotiating capacities, especially in plurilateral agreements covering many partners and non-trade areas, can help increase the depth of commitments and provide better clarity in legal texts, reducing ambiguity in interpretation and implementation. Targeted technical assistance—particularly in new areas such as digital trade and sustainable trade, along with streamlined RoO and reduced nontariff barriers—can further improve utilization rates, unlocking greater trade benefits, and supporting global value chain resilience.

## Cross-Border Investment

**Services, digital and green industries have emerged as main areas for foreign investment in Asia.** The region continued to show strong intraregional linkages, with FDI among Asian members accounting for an average of 52% of regional FDI from 2013 to 2023. As in other emerging regions, FDI in services is now the main driver of foreign investment, with its average share growing to 58% in the past decade from 46% in the previous decade. The expansion of FDI in digital industries has also been a major shift, with investments in digital infrastructure, e-commerce, and digital services expanding rapidly. Regional investments in telecommunications and IT industries, particularly in South Asia, have stood out. Green FDI continues to redefine the investment dynamics in Asia. Climate-related greenfield investments as a share of total greenfield investment rose from 8% in 2013 to 27% in 2023. This is supported by major industrial developments, such as the expansion of renewable industries and deployment of electric vehicles supply chains in Southeast Asia. While Asia's position as a global manufacturing hub has favored foreign investment, regional efforts remain important. Various subregional initiatives are driving investment facilitation efforts, such as the ASEAN Investment Facilitation Framework and investment facilitation mechanisms in the Brunei Darussalam–Indonesia–Malaysia–Philippines East ASEAN Growth Area (BIMP-EAGA) and the Central Asia Regional Economic Cooperation (CAREC) Program.

**Asian economies should strengthen policy efforts to mitigate the impact of geopolitical risks.** Despite persistent shocks, FDI inflows to Asia have remained resilient. Investments from multinationals remained robust, with the value in greenfield projects growing on average by 14% from 2013 to 2023 and mergers and acquisitions by 16% over the same period. Global investment patterns have been influenced by geopolitical tensions as well as major industrial developments and changing policy environment in host economies. ADB estimates suggest that greenfield investments in trade-exposed sectors experienced sharper declines than other sectors during periods of increased geopolitical tensions, while ASEAN economies attracted significantly higher FDI flows driven primarily by the PRC. Strengthening regional trade linkages through free trade agreements and other policy measures could support regional FDI flows, in particular efficiency-seeking investments.

**Ensuring investment policy coherence—whether international, regional, or domestic—is critical for economies to benefit from FDIs and support broader development objectives.** Investment policies continue to develop across the region at all levels of government. Internationally, the modernization of Asia's investment treaty network is gradually moving forward, with economies terminating or upgrading old agreements to introduce stronger provisions on the definition of investment, public interest obligations, and dispute mechanisms, and including more robust investment chapters or provisions in trade agreements. Investment facilitation has gained traction as an effective FDI inducement strategy. However, according to the German Institute of Development and Sustainability (IDOS) and the World Trade Organization (WTO) Investment Facilitation Index, Asia's investment facilitation score remains on average 14% lower than Europe's and 23% lower than North America's, suggesting much room for improvement. Ensuring coherence across investment policy instruments and convergence with other policy areas will be critical for enhancing the quality of FDI in the region. Regional economies need to continually work toward improving the overall business climate along with easing restrictions to FDI.

## Financial Integration

**Global monetary easing will likely increase capital inflows into the region, bringing with it important macroeconomic and policy implications.** Cross-border assets increased from 55% to 83% of regional gross domestic product (GDP) from 2010 to 2020 before settling at 75% in 2023. Cross-border liabilities followed a similar path. Over the same period, intraregional asset and liability exposures rose from 27% to 36%, and from 30% to 37%, respectively. On balance, the intraregional share of cross-border exposures remained unchanged over 2022–2023. Specifically, on the asset side, the intraregional share of the inward portfolio equity and debt stocks fell slightly to 21% each, while the intraregional shares for FDI rose to 51%. On the liability side, the intraregional shares of the portfolio debt stock were 30%, and the stock of portfolio equity and bank liabilities were 20% and 44%, respectively. The global monetary easing since mid-2024 can help strengthen capital inflows due to larger policy rate differentials between the US and the euro area on the one hand, and Asian economies on the other. While this also expands room for monetary policy easing in the region, each economy in the region must remain vigilant against the risks of potential capital flow swings and exchange rate volatility in the case of unexpected economic shocks.

**Regional financial cooperation has been a key driver of economic stability and prosperity in Asia.** Cross-border financial flows benefit growth and prosperity in Asia through lower cost of capital, expanded resource pools for investment, and enhanced international risk sharing, helping reduce income and consumption volatilities. Increased openness supports economic competitiveness, with knowledge transfers nurturing regional capital markets. Regional cooperation was paramount following the 1997–1998 Asian financial crisis in driving integration as it led to major advances in deepening the region's capital markets, expanding safety nets as buffers against global shocks, and creating effective communication channels during crises. The Chiang Mai Initiative Multilateralisation (CMIM) and the ASEAN+3 Macroeconomic Research Office (AMRO) grew to become the institutional backbone of regional financial stability. Several other initiatives launched under the auspices of the ASEAN Economic Community solidified ASEAN as the key anchor for financial cooperation in Asia.

**Reinvigorating regional cooperation can help realize the full potential of regional financial integration.** Financial integration in Asia has decelerated over the past decade, both relative to other regions and other integration dimensions such as trade. It is vital to harness the potential of regional cooperation to boost integration and maximize its benefits while minimizing costs due to vulnerabilities from negative regional spillovers. Primarily, this includes strengthening regional financial safety nets in addition to prudent domestic macroeconomic and financial management. Key steps include (i) increasing the pool of emergency funding available from the CMIM, (ii) broadening the scope of its lending instruments such as the new Rapid Financing Facility, (iii) improving governance of regional financing arrangements in association with "(i)" and "(ii)", and (iv) continuously improving regional surveillance. In addition, regional cooperation must live up to new policy challenges, such as geoeconomic fragmentation, technological innovations, public health emergencies, climate change, and biodiversity loss. These new frontiers require improved macroeconomic surveillance, smooth cross-border payments, and innovative financing to help cope with structural challenges. Stronger regional cooperation can also harmonize disclosure standards and promote targeted financial instruments to help develop regional capital markets and promote sustainable finance.

## Movement of People

**Migration has been integral to Asia's development, with Asians accounting for one in every three cross-border migrants.** The number of out-migrants from the region reached 94.6 million in 2021 from 49.5 million in 1990. Led by migrants from South Asia and Southeast Asia, they have increasingly sought more opportunities beyond the region—65% in 2021, up from 53.6% in 1990—notably in the Middle East and North America. Meanwhile, persons from Oceania, East Asia, and Southeast Asia actively migrate within the subregion. The overall intraregional migration share remained at an average of 39.5% during the period.

**Increased cross-border mobility of Asian labor migrants has benefited from increased regional cooperation over the last 2 decades.** In particular, Asian economies actively participated in bilateral labor agreements, serving as at least one of the parties in 58% of such agreements from 1990 to 2020, underscoring Asia's growing role as both a source and destination for low- and semiskilled migrant workers. In addition, regional trade agreements, along with mutual recognition arrangements, have supported high-skilled labor mobility. However, these measures have had limited impact on high-skilled Asian migrants due to minimal coverage for developing Asian economies, narrow occupational scope, and high implementation costs. To maximize migration's development impact, models like Skills Mobility Partnerships, designed to benefit all stakeholders—migrant workers, origin and destination economies—could promote net gains from labor migration. Incorporating development aspects, such as remittance facilitation, into bilateral labor agreements could lead to more positive outcomes, including greater financial inclusion, in source economies. National and regional migration policies, for both source and host economies, could take guidance from the Global Compact for Migration to promote safe, orderly, and regular migration.

**Remittance inflows to Asia, bolstered by out-migration, have gained increasing economic significance, rising from 19% of the global total in 1990 to 43% in 2024.** During the same period, these inflows increased thirty-five-fold, making remittance inflows the largest and most stable source of external financing for many migrant-sending Asian economies, with inflows to Asia reaching $392.1 billion in 2024. Overall annual growth in remittances to Asia in 2024 increased to 7.5% driven by the recovery of the job markets in major Organisation for Economic Co-operation and Development migrant host economies, particularly the US. By subregion, remittance inflows continued to grow in South Asia (11.8%) and Southeast Asia (3.6%) as migrant outflows from these subregions continued their prepandemic pace.

**Channeling more remittances using digital platforms could enhance access to the formal financial system for migrants and their families, paving the way for financial inclusion.** With improved financial system and institutional capacity, remittance-dependent developing economies can leverage remittance facilitation to drive further financial inclusion. Digital remittances, supported by efficient regulatory environments, can help bring down remittance costs in the region, which currently average 5.9% per transaction, above the 3% target of the United Nations 2030 Sustainable Development Goals. Asia is rapidly adopting digital payments and remittances, driven by financial technology and enhanced digital infrastructure. Improved interoperability enables seamless cross-border remittances, such as between India's UPI and Singapore's PayNow, with more economies getting on board. Regional cooperation should focus on leveraging digitalization in the cross-border payment ecosystem while narrowing the digital divide. Continuous financial and digital education, alongside best practice exchanges, would also help reduce barriers to financial access and enhance digital financial literacy.

**Amid steady growth in international tourism in Asia, Southeast Asia and East Asia led the region's recovery.** International arrivals to Asia grew by an average annual rate of 7.6% from 2010 to 2019, outpacing the global annual average of 5.1%, with the intraregional tourism share increasing from 73.1% to 77.3% during the period. Southeast Asia and East Asia collectively accounted for at least 80% of Asia's arrivals before the pandemic. Although severely affected by the pandemic, by the end of 2023, East Asia welcomed 38.9% of Asia's tourists while 37.6% visited Southeast Asia. Southeast Asia's relatively liberal policies toward cross-border connectivity (e.g., air transport and visa policies) have helped boost tourism flows to the subregion. Meanwhile, other subregions retain more restrictive policies, with many lacking the domestic infrastructure needed to support tourism development.

**Accelerating regional cooperation to improve physical and institutional connectivity will increase tourism competitiveness and resilience, unlocking the industry's potential for economic development.** As at least 60% of tourists to Asia arrive by air, good infrastructure and logistics are essential to support tourism flows. Land transportation is important in destinations sharing common international borders, such as Singapore–Malaysia and Georgia–Türkiye. For institutional connectivity, while visa policies are strongest in Southeast Asia, followed by Central Asia and East Asia, air service agreements are becoming more liberal across Southeast Asia. Other subregions can adopt these policies to help boost their tourism industries. ADB research shows the important role connectivity plays in promoting tourism. Transportation infrastructure, in addition to other tourism infrastructure, positively influences international tourism flows and increases the attractiveness of Asian destinations. Regional connectivity can help attract long-haul travel from outside the region and strengthen intraregional tourism as well. Priority investments in airport infrastructure and logistics, along with taking a subregional approach to liberalize policies on cross-border travel, are crucial to increase tourism flows and foster the industry's economic contribution to growth.

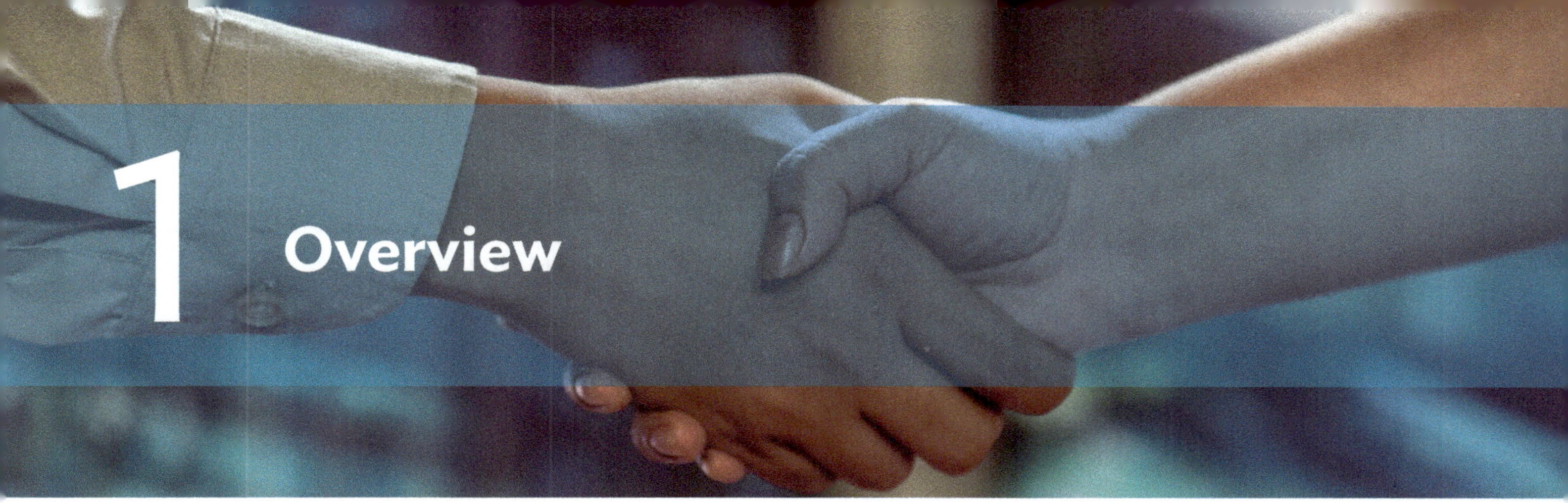

# 1 Overview

## Trends in Regional Integration in Asia and the Pacific

**Asia and the Pacific has made significant progress in regional integration, surpassing other regions in most dimensions of the new Regional Integration Index of the Asian Development Bank (ADB).**

Over the past 2 decades, Asia has significantly tightened its regional economic integration, surpassing other regions in foreign direct investment (FDI) and the "movement of people" (Figure 1.1).[1] For trade in goods and services, Asia led in 2005 but came in a close second to the European Union (EU) plus the United Kingdom (UK) in 2023. While the EU+UK continued to lead in financial integration, Asia is a close second. Latin America has advanced but still remains behind in financial integration. Despite improvements, Africa remains the least integrated in terms of trade, FDI, and movement of people. The methodology and data used to measure regional integration is based on ADB's Bilateral Economic Integration Index framework (Box 1.1).

**Figure 1.1: Regional Integration Index by Dimension—Asia and the Pacific Versus Other Regions**

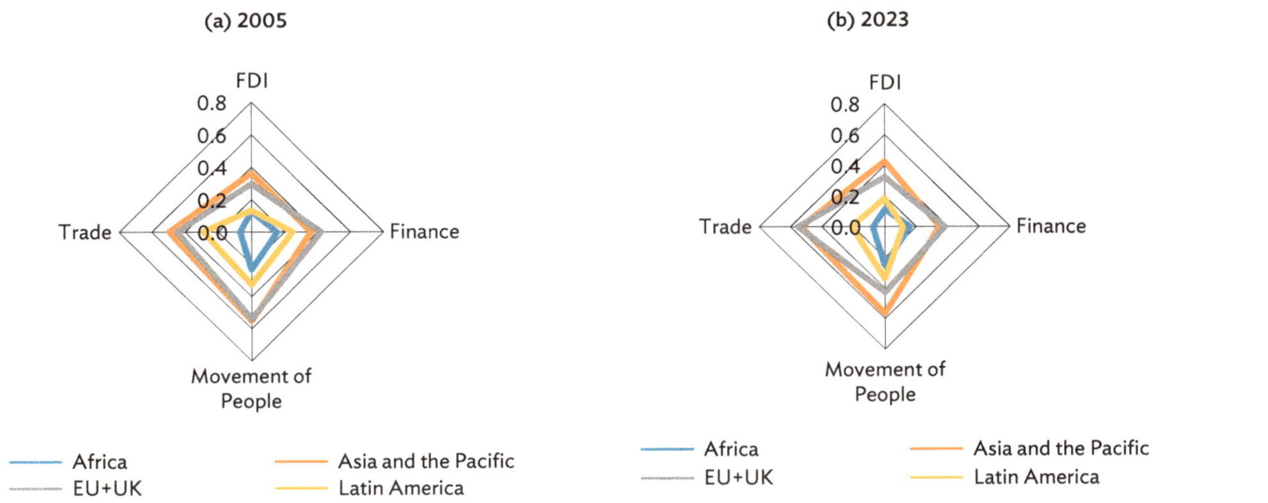


EU = European Union (27 members), FDI = foreign direct investment, UK = United Kingdom.

Notes: Based on ADB's Regional Integration Index estimates, the values for each dimension represent the ratio of the number of strong intraregional connections at the bilateral level relative to the sum of strong intraregional and extraregional connections. For the detailed methodology, indicators used per dimension, and data sources, see Box 1.1.

Source: ADB calculations using data from ADB. Bilateral Economic Integration Index Database.

[1] Asia refers to the 49 members of the Asian Development Bank (ADB) in Asia and the Pacific, which include Australia, Japan, and New Zealand in addition to 46 developing economies.

**Box 1.1: Methodology and Data in Estimating the Regional Integration Index Based on ADB's Bilateral Economic Integration Index**

The Bilateral Economic Integration (BEI) Index is a new metric introduced by the Asian Development Bank (ADB) to measure regional integration. It adds on to ADB's existing measures by using a fully bilateral data structure to clarify economic relationships. This bilateral approach provides a clearer and more detailed picture of how economies are integrated with each other, both within and outside their regions. The index also focuses on de facto flows, meaning the actual market-based interactions between economies. It does not cover regional cooperation efforts between economies.

The methodology for estimating regional integration closely follows that of Rayp and Standaert (2017), which follows a two-step sequence. First, the degree of integration between two economies, the BEI, is estimated using the dynamic factor model (DFM) in state-space representation. Then the regional integration indexes are generated from the BEI estimates.

**Estimation of Bilateral Economic Integration**

A BEI is derived from four dimensions: trade, foreign direct investment (FDI), finance, and movement of people. A high BEI from economy A to B indicates a large flow from economy A to B, or vice versa, with respect to the total flows of economy A, implying that B is an important economic partner for A (box figure). The BEI from economy A to B is extracted from a pool of bilateral flows between A and B that are normalized relative to the total flows and size of economy A (gross domestic product or population). In contrast, the BEI from economy B to A is extracted from the same set of bilateral flows but is normalized by the total flows and size of economy B. This allows for the BEI to be not commutative, such that economy A may be more integrated to B than B is to A, which can be the case when B is a large economy.

**Network Representation of Two Economies**

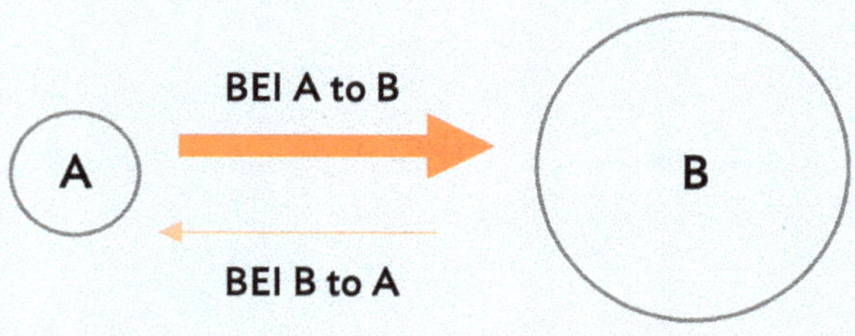


BEI = bilateral economic integration.

Source: ADB, based on Albis, Tayag, and Kang (2023).

The DFM is used to extract the BEIs from the normalized bilateral flows. Let $y_{it}^{(j)}$ be the $j^{th}$ integration indicator $j = 1, \dots, k$ for the $i^{th}$ directional economy-pair $i = 1, \dots, n$, at time $t = 1, \dots, T$. The $y_{it}^{(j)}$, in equation 1, can be expressed in linear regression form being explained by a constant term $C^{(j)}$, the integration index $BEI_{it}$ with its corresponding coefficient $Z^{(j)}$, and a random fluctuation $\epsilon_{it}^{(j)}$. Only $y_{it}^{(j)}$ is observed, and the regressor $BEI_{it}$ is a latent variable.

$$y_{it}^{(j)} = C^{(j)} + Z^{(j)} BEI_{it} + \epsilon_{it}^{(j)} \quad (1)$$

where $\epsilon_{it}^{(j)} \sim N(0, H^{(j)})$, $Cov\left(\epsilon_{it}^{(j)}, \epsilon_{i^*t}^{(j^*)}\right) = 0$ for all $i \neq i^*$ and $j \neq j^*$. The $C^{(j)}$, $Z^{(j)}$, and $H^{(j)}$ are parameters to estimate one set for each $j$. The equation for $BEI_{it}$ is assumed to follow a Markovian structure, given in Equation 2.

$$\underline{BEI_{it} = T^{(i)} BEI_{i,t-1} + v_{it}} \quad (2)$$

where $v_{it} \sim N(0,1)$, $Cov(v_{it}, v_{i^*,t}) = 0$ for all $i \neq i^*$, and $BEI_{i0} = 0$. $T^{(i)}$ is an autoregressive parameter that ranges from [-1,1], allowing inherent autocorrelations and stochastic trends. Equation 1 is the measurement equation while Equation 2 is the state equation of the DFM in state-space form.

The parameters $C$, $Z$, and $H$ are restricted to be fixed across $i$ and $t$ to allow BEIs to be compared across directional economy pairs and time. Because of this parameter restriction, which would be difficult to implement using common approaches such as the least-squares method, the Bayesian approach is used (refer to Koop (2003), and Chan et al. (2019) for a discussion of the Bayesian estimation). In particular, Gibbs sampling was repeated to get 100,000 sets of parameter estimates; the earliest 70,000 iterations were dropped as burn-in. Due to the linear and Gaussian form of the state-space model, a Kalman filter was applied to generate the BEIs for each of the remaining 30,000 sets of model parameters. This allows the BEI estimate to be the posterior mean of the Kalman filter results and calculate its confidence intervals for significance tests.

**Regional Indicators and Data Used to Estimate Bilateral Economic Integration**

As mentioned, the regional integration data are categorized into four dimensions: trade, FDI, finance, and movement of people. Trade data, including manufactured goods, primary commodities, and services, are sourced from the United Nations (UN) Commodity Trade Database and the World Trade Organization–Organisation for Economic Co-operation and Development Balanced Trade in Services

*continued on next page*

*Box 1.1: continued*

dataset. FDI data come from ADB's Asian Economic Integration Report FDI Database. Finance data, covering short- and long-term portfolio investments in debt securities and equities, are sourced from the International Monetary Fund's Coordinated Portfolio Investment Survey. The movement of people includes data on migration (UN International Migrant Stock), tourist arrivals (UN Tourism), and remittances (World Bank). All indicators are bilateral or at the economy-pair level.

**Estimation of Regional Integration Indexes**

The Regional Integration Index (RII) measures the interconnectedness of economies in a region. Using this approach, a strong connection between two economies exists for a particular year if the corresponding BEI value belongs to the top 10% of the BEIs across all economy pairs from 2000 to 2023. The results using the 10% cutoff are similar and comparable to applying a significance test to check if the BEI is greater than that of an economy pair with zero or negligible flows using a 1% level of significance.[a]

The RII for Asia and the Pacific is the ratio of strong intraregional connections relative to the sum of strong intraregional and extraregional connections:

$$RII = \frac{strong\ connections\ intraregion}{strong\ connections\ intra\ and\ extraregion} \quad (3)$$

Regional integration for other regions was also calculated: Africa, the European Union (EU) plus the United Kingdom (UK), and Latin America (for each economy's composition per regional grouping, see Annex 1a). A high RII implies that the economies within the region are more connected than to economies outside the region. Integration indexes for Asian subregions—Central Asia, East Asia, the Pacific and Oceania, South Asia, and Southeast Asia—were also calculated and are defined as:

$$RII_{sub} = \frac{strong\ connections\ of\ subregional\ economies\ to/from\ Asia}{all\ strong\ connections\ of\ subregional\ economies} \quad (4)$$

where a high $RII_{sub}$ implies higher integration of the subregion to Asian economies than to non-Asian economies.

[a] The economy pairs that have mostly zero transactions or a low share of flows to total flows with few missing values from 2000 to 2023 are selected as comparison pairs. A BEI is significant if its 99% confidence interval does not overlap and is greater than that of the comparison pair. As a robustness check, several base pairs were used and gave similar results. Examples of the base pairs used for robustness checks are Czech Republic–Fiji for trade, France–Kyrgyz Republic for FDI, the Republic of Korea–Argentina for finance, and Romania–Mongolia for the movement of people.

Sources: ADB, based on the methodology in Albis, Tayag, and Kang (2023); Chan et al. (2019); Koop (2003); and Rayp and Standaert (2017).

The trend of all four regional integration index dimensions over the 2005–2023 period shows Asia leading in trade integration until 2015, the year coinciding a global economic slowdown (Figure 1.2a). Since then, the EU+UK have led in trade integration, with Asia following closely behind. Latin America has a moderate trend with a pronounced decline from 2015 to 2020, with Africa having the lowest trade integration and minimal changes over time.

Asia's FDI integration has risen steadily, showing the highest regional integration index estimates through 2023 (Figure 1.2b). This underscores Asian investors' increasing preference to invest within the region. Nonetheless, Asia's degree of FDI integration remains below its trade integration. By contrast, for example, FDI integration in Latin America remains moderate with some fluctuations over the years. Africa's FDI integration has declined since 2009, although it has remained fairly stable over the past 5 years.

The EU+UK region held the highest level of financial integration throughout the period, given its well-established intraregional financial markets and regulatory frameworks that ease cross-border financial transactions, particularly among eurozone economies (Figure 1.2c). Importantly, 7 of the 27 EU members along with the UK do not use the euro as they are not in the eurozone. While financial integration in the EU+UK remains relatively stable, Asia has been steadily improving, especially since 2015, and is catching up quickly. Despite this, Asia's own regional integration on financial flows remains lowest among the four dimensions. Latin America and Africa show relatively low levels of financial integration with minimal changes over time.

In terms of the movement of people (covering migration, remittances, and tourism), all four regions remained relatively stable until the drop during the coronavirus disease (COVID-19) pandemic (Figure 1.2d). The movement of people indexes have recovered since but remain below prepandemic levels. Asia leads in the movement of people with the highest levels throughout

**Figure 1.2: Trends in Regional Integration Index by Dimension—Asia and the Pacific Versus Other Regions**

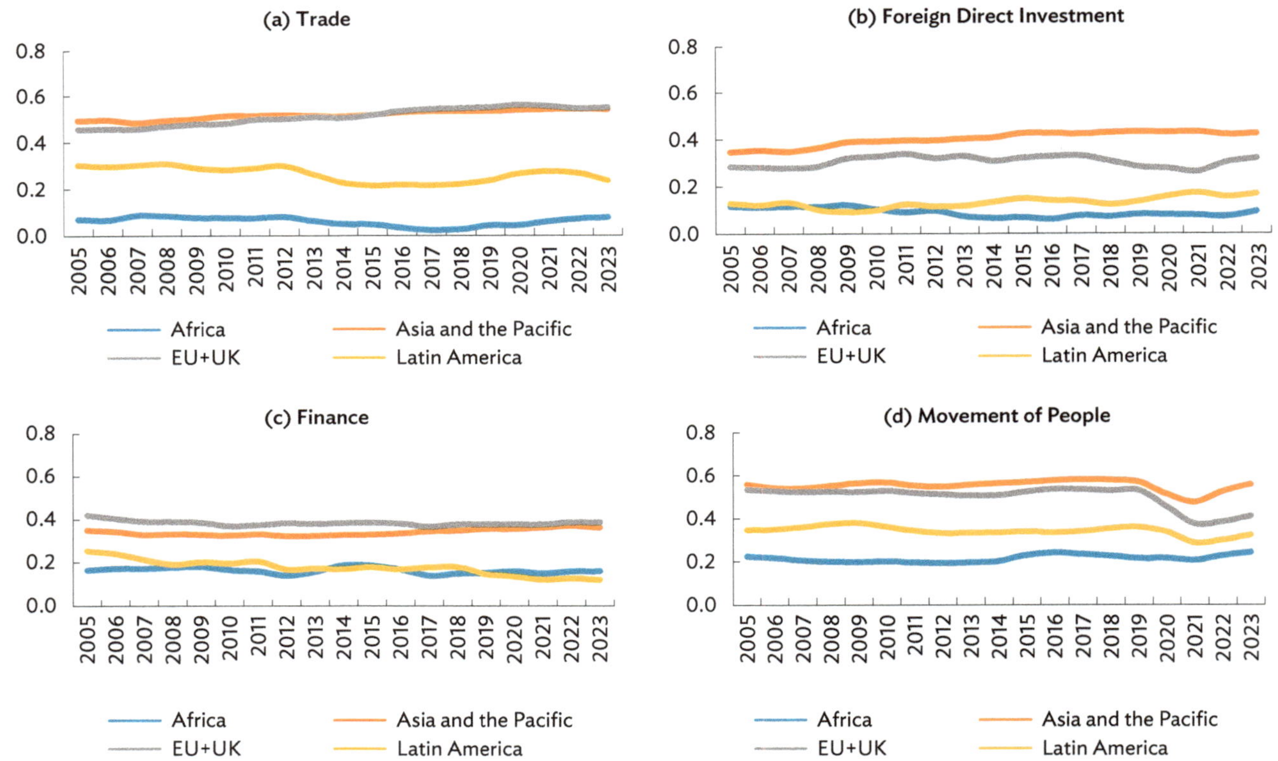


EU = European Union (27 members), UK = United Kingdom.

Notes: Based on ADB's Regional Integration Index estimates, the values for each dimension represent the ratio of the number of strong intraregional connections at the bilateral level relative to the sum of strong intraregional and extraregional connections. Values are presented as a 3-year moving average, with a higher weight given to the most recent periods. For the detailed methodology, indicators used per dimension, and data sources, see Box 1.1.

Source: ADB calculations using data from ADB. Bilateral Economic Integration Index Database.

the period and sharpest increase since the pandemic. The EU+UK follows, with Latin America and Africa at the lower end.

## Asian economic integration remains uneven across subregions.

By subregion, Southeast Asia is most integrated within Asia across all but the FDI dimension (Figure 1.3). This strong integration overall comes from Southeast Asia's robust trade networks, solid financial linkages, and substantial movement of people across the Asian region. East Asia, along with the Pacific and Oceania, also showed substantial integration. East Asia has strong trade and investment flows and is well-integrated financially. The Pacific and Oceania benefits from active trade and people traveling and working in other Asian economies.

In contrast, Central Asia and South Asia recorded the lowest integration indexes. These subregions are challenged by underdeveloped infrastructure and smaller markets—which limit economic diversification. Central Asia's landlocked geography and reliance on a limited range of export commodities reduce natural opportunities for integration. While South Asia is showing some progress, it still lags as development remains uneven across the subregion, particularly in terms of trade, openness to FDI, and advancements in financial markets.

## Key pairs of economies are driving Asia's integration both within and outside the region and can be identified through network analysis—relevant subregional clusters can be highlighted.

**Figure 1.3: Regional Integration Index by Dimension—Asian Subregions**

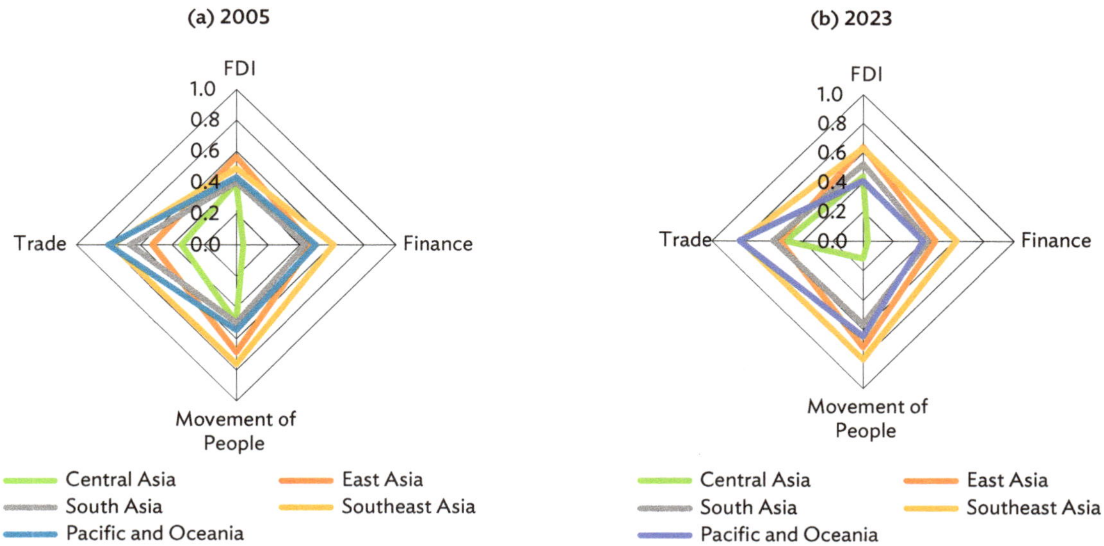


FDI = foreign direct investment.

Notes: Based on ADB's Regional Integration Index estimates, the values for each dimension represent the ratio of the subregion's strong connections with Asia and Pacific economies at the bilateral level relative to the subregion's total strong connections with the world. For the detailed methodology, indicators used per dimension, and data sources, see Box 1.1.

Source: ADB calculations using data from ADB. Bilateral Economic Integration Index Database.

Network graphs can be created for Asia's intraregional and extraregional linkages (Figure 1.4). In reading the graph, the node size corresponds to the economy's gross domestic product (GDP) in logarithm; node color intensity shows the number of strong connections pointing to the economy (indegree); and line color intensity indicates the strength of integration between the two economies (the value of the Bilateral Economic Integration Index). Orange lines represent Asia's intraregional links, and blue lines represent its non-Asia linkages.

Trends vary across dimensions. In 2005, several Asian economies had high trade integration with Australia, Japan, and the People's Republic of China (PRC) (Figure 1.4a). There were clusters within and between East Asian and Southeast Asian economies. By 2023, these clusters had strengthened, with more intersubregional linkages forming, especially between the PRC and Central Asia and South Asia, centering the Asian network around the PRC. Bilateral pairs have strengthened considerably from 2005 to 2023—for example, the Kyrgyz Republic and the PRC, and the PRC and Viet Nam. The number of extraregional linkages also grew—particularly with some economies in the EU, Africa, and Latin America.

Since 2005, Asia's FDI integration within the region has increased, but its integration with non-Asian economies grew relatively stronger with advanced economies such as Canada, the EU, and the United States (US) as major non-Asian partners for FDI (Figure 1.4b). The PRC has become an important FDI partner for some African economies. Within Asia, new intersubregional links have formed between Singapore and several South Asian and Pacific economies as well as between Japan and several Southeast Asian economies.

Asia is more extraregionally integrated in finance than even FDI (Figure 1.4c). Outside the region, the UK, Ireland, Canada, and the US are the main financial partners of many Asian economies. Within Asia, Australia; the PRC; Japan; Hong Kong, China; and Singapore remain key partners.

For the movement of people, Asian economies are more integrated within the region than with extraregional economies (Figure 1.4d). Within Asia, new intersubregional connections have formed for Australia and the PRC with some economies in South Asia and Southeast Asia, while Fiji and the Republic of Korea have also established links with several Southeast Asian economies.

**Figure 1.4: Network Representation of Intraregional and Extraregional Integration Linkages—Asia and the Pacific**

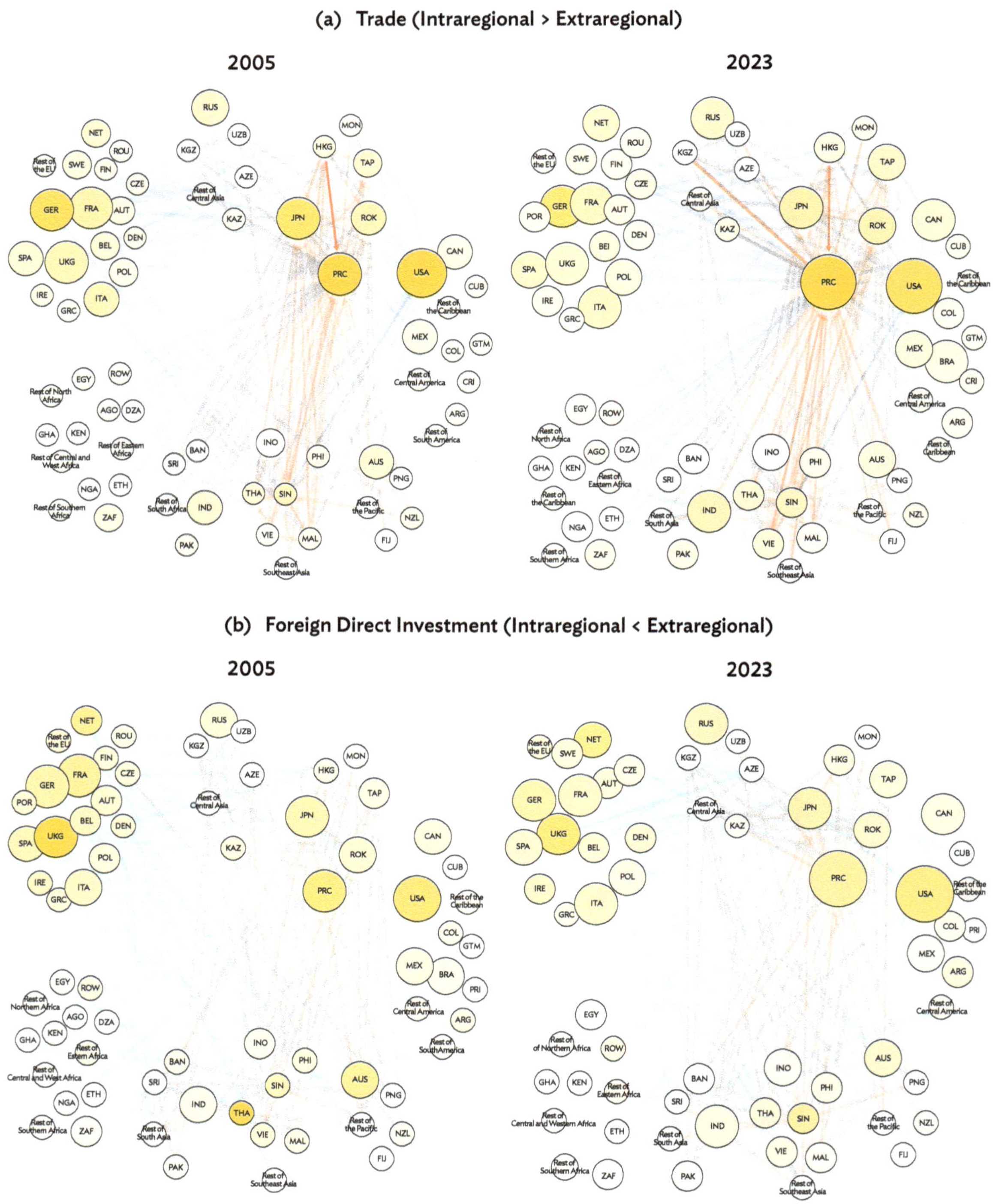


*continued on next page*

*Figure 1.4 continued*

### (c) Finance (Intraregional < Extraregional)

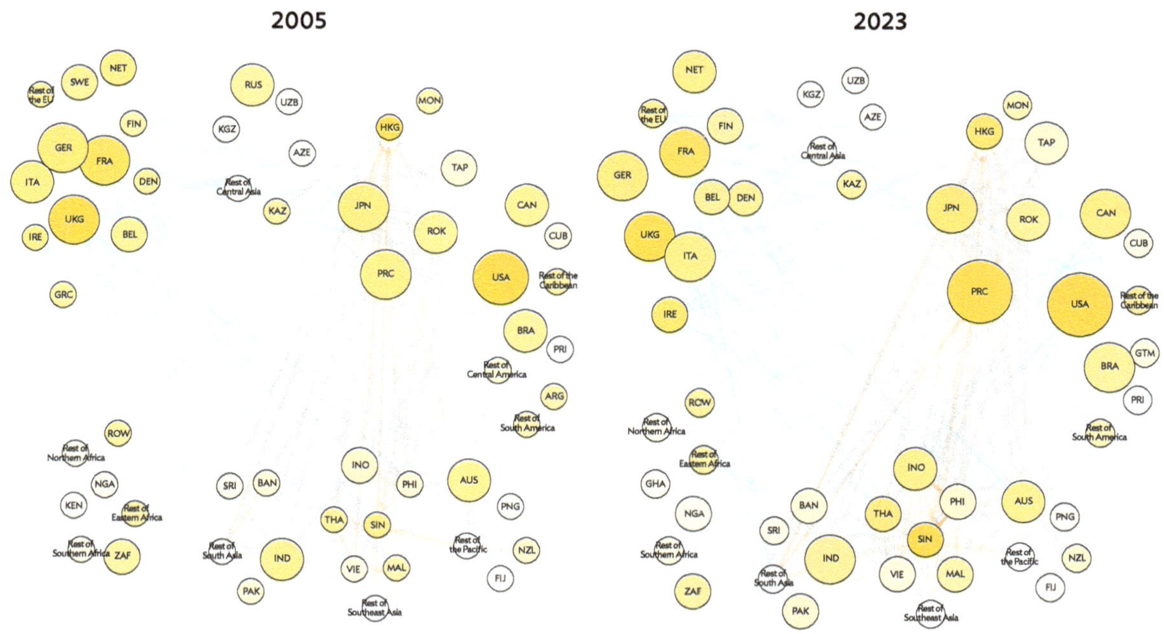


### (d) Movement of People (Intraregional > Extraregional)

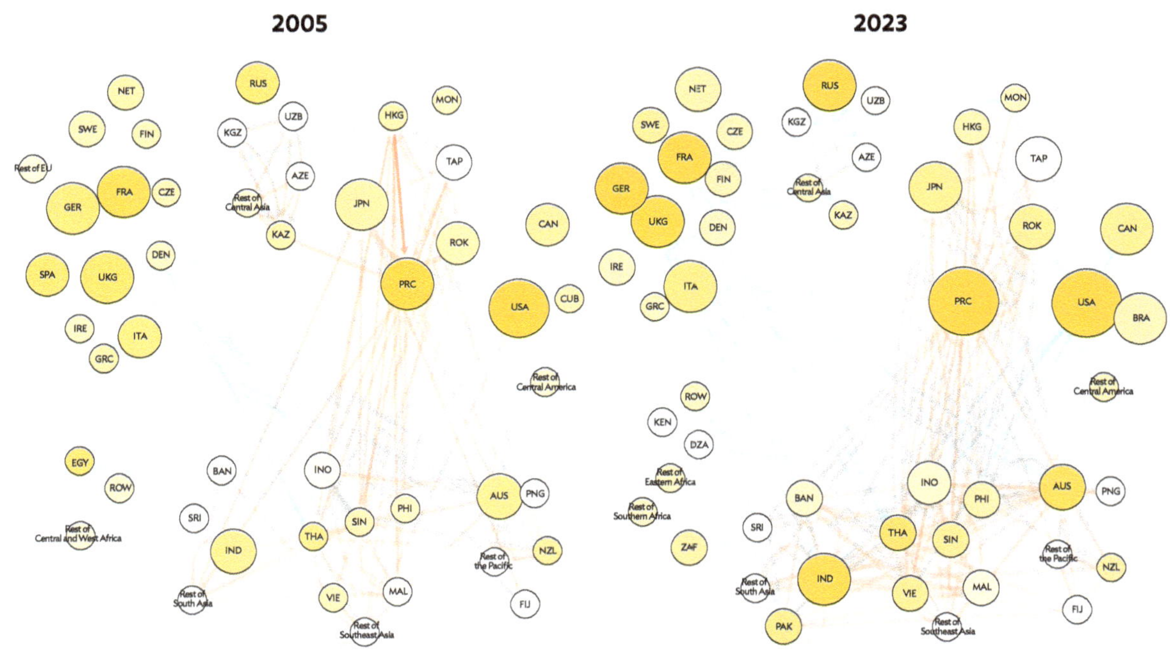


> = greater than; < = less than; AGO = Angola; ARG = Argentina; AUS = Australia; AUT = Austria; AZE = Azerbaijan; BAN = Bangladesh; BEL = Belgium; BRA = Brazil; CAN = Canada; PRC = People's Republic of China; COL = Colombia; CRI = Costa Rica; CUB = Cuba; CZE = Czechia; DEN = Denmark; DZA = Algeria; EGY = Egypt; ETH = Ethiopia; EU = European Union (27 members); FIJ = Fiji; FIN = Finland; FRA = France; GER = Germany; GHA = Ghana; GRC = Greece; GTM = Guatamela; HKG = Hong Kong China; IND = India; INO = Indonesia; IRE = Ireland; ITA = Italy; JPN = Japan; KAZ = Kazakhstan; KEN = Kenya; KGZ = Kyrgyz Republic; ROK = Republic of Korea; MAL = Malaysia; MEX = Mexico; MON = Mongolia; NET = Netherlands; NGA = Nigeria; NZL = New Zealand; PAK = Pakistan; PHI = Philippines; PNG = Papua New Guinea; POL = Poland; POR = Portugal; PRI = Puerto Rico; ROU = Romania; ROW = rest of the world; RUS = Russian Federation; SIN = Singapore; SPA = Spain; SRI = Sri Lanka; SWE = Sweden; TAP = Taipei,China; THA = Thailand; UKG = United Kingdom; USA = United States; UZB = Uzbekistan; VIE = Viet Nam; ZAF = South Africa.

Notes: The node size corresponds to the size of the economy as measured by its gross domestic product in logarithm. The node color intensity shows the number of strong connections pointing to the economy (indegree). The color intensity of the lines and arrows corresponds to the directional Bilateral Economic Integration Index values. The more intense the color of the lines, the higher the economic integration between economy pair. The orange lines refer to Asia's intraregional links, while the blue ones are to its non-Asia linkages. For detailed methodology, indicators used per dimension, and data sources, see Box 1.1.

Source: ADB calculations using data from ADB. Bilateral Economic Integration Index Database.

## Asia-Pacific Regional Cooperation and Integration Index: Subregional Initiatives

### Asian subregions are growing more integrated.

Flows in trade, investment, finance, and movement of people provided by the Bilateral Economic Integration Index provide a benchmark of regional integration in Asia. However, other important aspects, such as institutional arrangements, digital connectivity, or environmental sensitivity can also help assess regional cooperation and integration (RCI) progress in the region. One can look deeper into the dynamics of economic integration in Asian subregional initiatives using the Asia-Pacific Regional Cooperation and Integration Index (ARCII), which tracks progress using a broader set of dimensions. The ARCII framework is also used in assessing trends in global integration, or globalization (Box 1.2).

The regional integration estimates for subregional initiatives highlight some differences in integration within subregions (intrasubregional integration) and integration of subregions with the rest of Asia (intersubregional integration) (Figure 1.5). Intrasubregional integration in the Greater Mekong Subregion (GMS) has increased over the past decade due to stronger cooperation among its members. While the Central Asia Regional Economic Cooperation (CAREC) program shows more moderate levels of integration, both intrasubregional and intersubregional linkages have gradually increased, more consistently since 2020. The South Asia Subregional Economic Cooperation (SASEC) highlights the subregion's increasing contact and transactions with other Asian economies.

Overall, these trends suggest different forces at work in terms of integration from Asia's subregional initiatives, both among members and with the rest of Asia. While GMS is strongly anchored on subregional integration, Central Asian economies have enhanced linkages over time both within and outside the CAREC region, while SASEC economies maintain strong linkages with other Asian economies.

**Figure 1.5: Overall Regional Integration by Subregional Initiative**

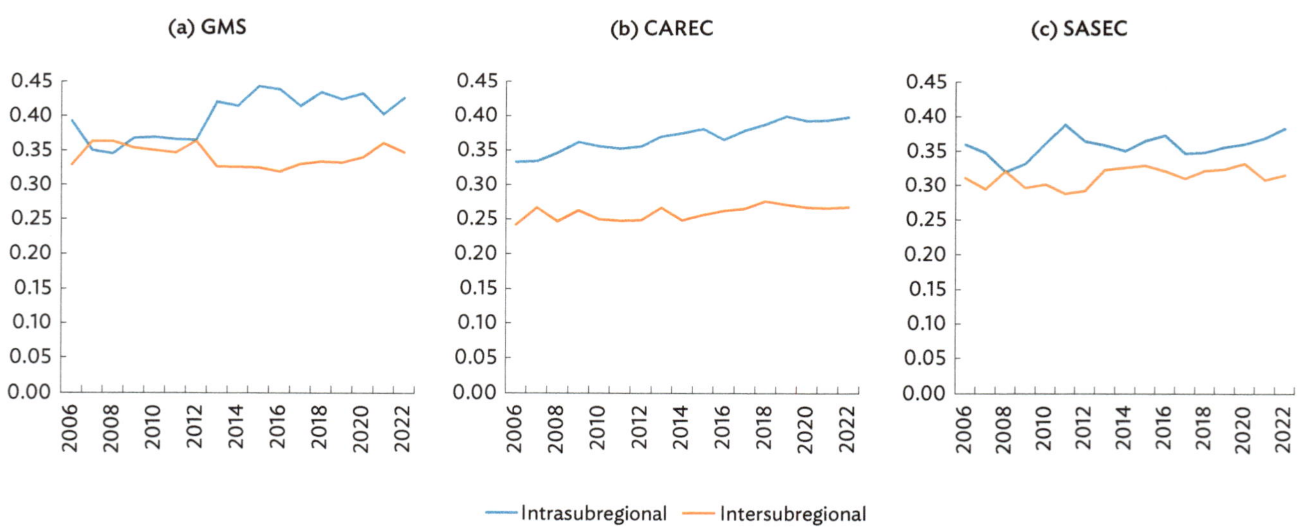


CAREC = Central Asia Regional Economic Cooperation, GMS = Greater Mekong Subregion, SASEC = South Asia Subregional Economic Cooperation.

Notes: Based on ADB's Asia-Pacific Regional Cooperation and Integration Index estimates. Higher index estimates denote greater regional integration. Intrasubregional integration is measured within members of the same subregional initiative. Intersubregional integration is measured with other Asian economies outside each subregional initiative.

Source: ADB. Asia-Pacific Regional Cooperation and Integration Index Database. https://aric.adb.org/database/arcii (accessed November 2024).

**Box 1.2: Connecting Regional Integration to a Global Integration Framework**

The Asia-Pacific Regional Cooperation and Integration Index (ARCII) framework allows analysis of subregional patterns, defining differences between intrasubregional and intersubregional integration. These trends indicate how certain subregions prioritize internal connectivity ahead of broader, cross-Asia linkages, which develop more gradually. By extending the ARCII framework to include both regional and extraregional linkages, the resulting global integration index (GII) can offer further insights on intraregional and extraregional integration across regions.

The GII, closely patterned on the ARCII methodology, is a comprehensive, multidimensional tool for assessing global integration. Initially developed in 2021 as the Global Economic Integration Index (Huh and Park 2021), the GII helps analyze global and regional linkages simultaneously. It includes 43 indicators spread across eight dimensions—trade and investment, money and finance, global value chains, infrastructure and connectivity, people and social integration, institutional arrangements, technology and digital connectivity, and environmental cooperation.

GII estimates suggest that global integration has increased overall and most prevalent among high-income economies. Among regions, the European Union (EU) leads in most dimensions, although other regions have progressed from 2006 to 2022. Among regions, global integration in Asia and the Pacific has improved, with some economies such as Singapore highly integrated, but with higher dispersion among other economies, showing they are heading in different directions (box figure 1). Other emerging regions, such as Latin America and Africa show generally lower global integration and greater variability.

While, regional, extraregional, and global integration strengthened across most economies from 2006 to 2022, each regional contribution differs (box figure 2). The EU and North America, generally high-income economies, have stronger regional linkages than extraregional ones. In Asia, both regional and extraregional linkages are equally important, with a relatively narrow gap between the two. By contrast, other emerging regions such as Latin America remain more integrated with external partners than those within the region. These patterns highlight the close linkages between development outcomes and economic integration and the importance of assessing both regional and extraregional linkages.

**1: Global Integration Index, by Region**

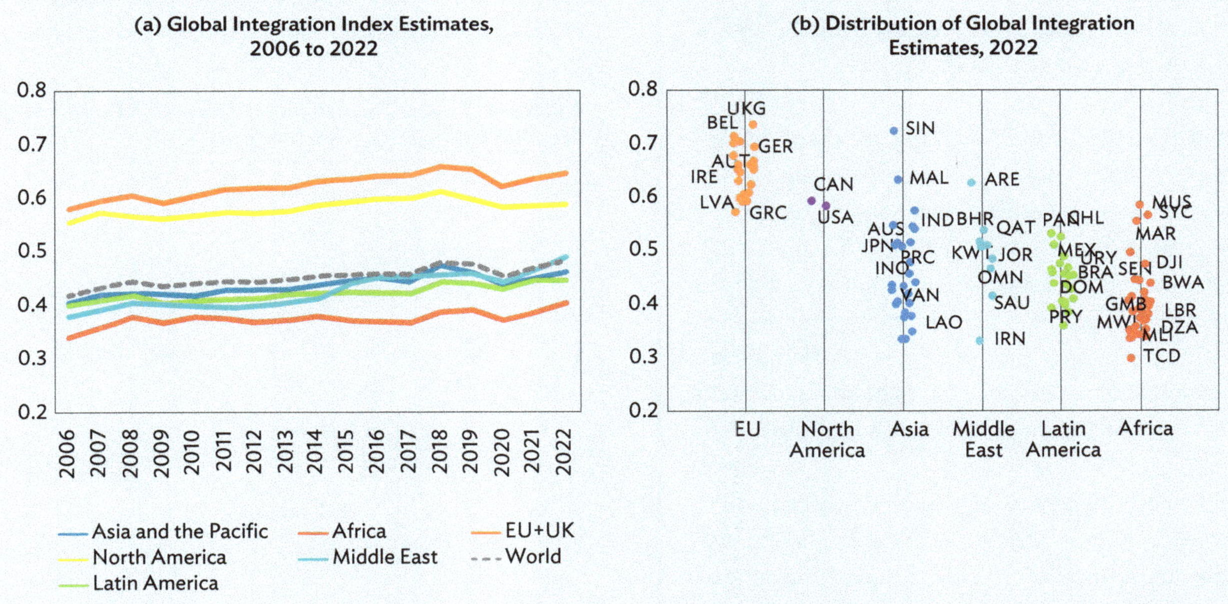


AUS = Australia, AUT = Austria, ARE = United Arab Emirates, BEL = Belgium, BHR = Kingdom of Bahrain, BRA = Brazil, BWA = Botswana, CAN = Canada, CHL = Chile, PRC = People's Republic of China, DJI = Djibouti, DOM = Dominican Republic, DZA = Algeria, EU = European Union (27 members), GMB = Gambia, GER = Germany, GRC = Greece, IND = India, INO = Indonesia, IRE = Ireland, IRN = Iran, JPN = Japan, JOR = Jordan, LAO = Lao People's Democratic Republic, LBR = Liberia, LVA = Latvia, MAL = Malaysia, MEX = Mexico, MUS = Mauritius, SYC = Seychelles, MAR = Morocco, MLI = Mali, MWI = Malawi, PAN = Panama, PRY = Paraguay, QAT = Qatar, SAU = Kingdom of Saudi Arabia, SIN = Singapore, TCD = Chad, UKG = United Kingdom, USA = United States, URY = Uruguay, VAN = Vanuatu.

Source: ADB. Asia-Pacific Regional Cooperation and Integration Index Database. https://aric.adb.org/database/arcii (accessed November 2024).

*continued on next page*

*Box 1.2: continued*

**2: Regional, Extraregional, and Global Integration Indexes, by Selected Regions**

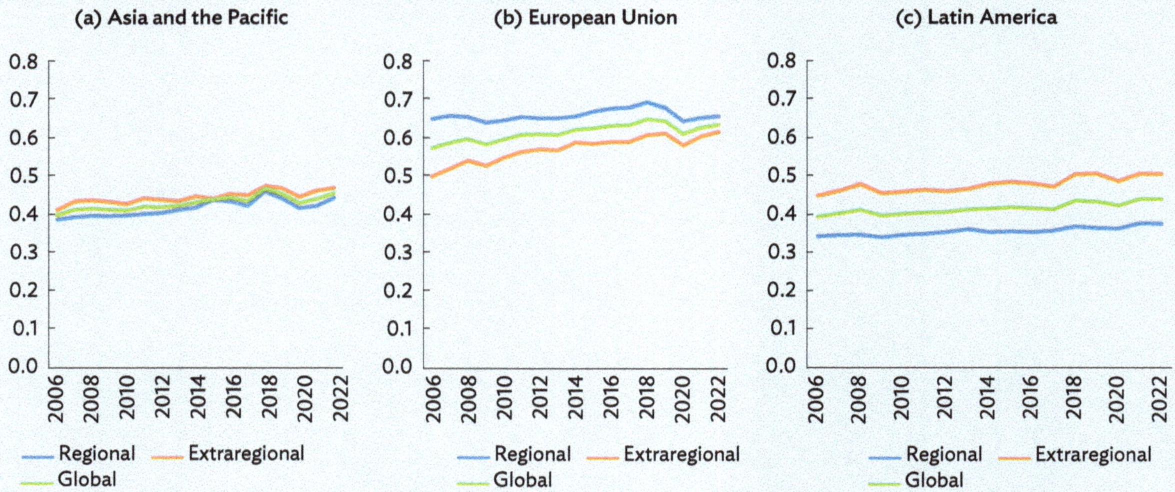


Note: European Union includes 27 members and the United Kingdom.

Source: ADB. Asia-Pacific Regional Cooperation and Integration Index Database. https://aric.adb.org/database/arcii (accessed November 2024).

## From 2006 to 2022, RCI across subregional initiatives was based on institutional arrangements, infrastructure and connectivity, regional value chains (RVCs), and money and finance.

During the period, the CAREC region was primarily driven by institutional connectivity, for example, by a large number of bilateral investment treaties and more embassies among members. Progress in value chain integration came from growth in intermediate goods trade, while advances in technology and connectivity were marked by sustained increases in information and communication technology (ICT) goods trade and a higher share of people using the internet (Figure 1.6).

In South Asia, initiatives such as the Bay of Bengal Initiative for Multi-Sectoral Technical and Economic Cooperation (BIMSTEC), SASEC, and the South Asian Association for Regional Cooperation (SAARC) grew from improvements in regional value chains and better institutional arrangements (Figure 1.7). Notably, the average trade concentration among SAARC economies declined over the years, meaning a wider variety of goods were traded, and therefore higher integration among members. Financial linkages have improved moderately, seen in the steady rise in cross-border equity liabilities in some initiatives since 2019. Digital transformation showed robust progress, contributing to improved connectivity.

**Figure 1.6: Central Asia Regional Economic Cooperation Program Intrasubregional Integration**

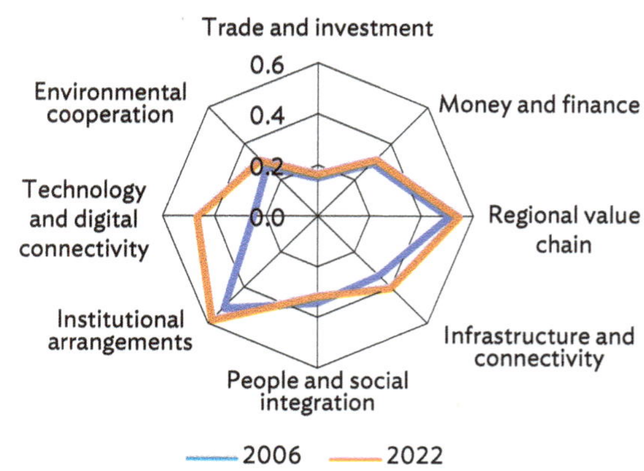


Notes: Based on ADB's Asia-Pacific Regional Cooperation and Integration Index estimates. Higher index estimates denote greater regional integration. Intrasubregional integration is measured within members of the same subregional initiative.

Source: ADB. Asia-Pacific Regional Cooperation and Integration Index Database. https://aric.adb.org/database/arcii (accessed November 2024).

**Figure 1.7: Intrasubregional Initiatives—South Asia**

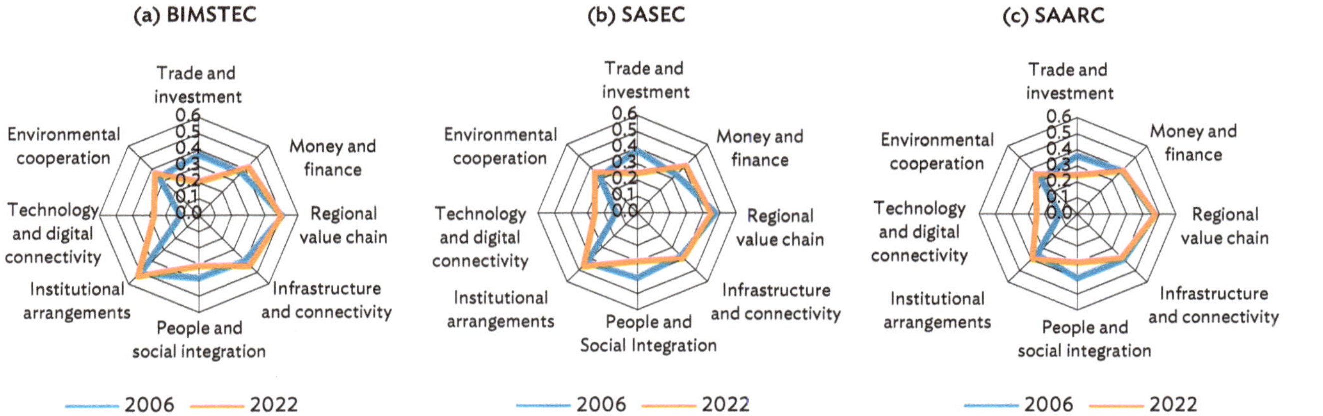


BIMSTEC = Bay of Bengal Initiative for Multi-Sectoral Technical and Economic Cooperation, SAARC = South Asian Association for Regional Cooperation, SASEC = South Asia Subregional Economic Cooperation.

Notes: Based on ADB's Asia-Pacific Regional Cooperation and Integration Index estimates. Higher index estimates denote greater regional integration. Intrasubregional integration is measured within members of the same subregional initiative.

Source: ADB. Asia-Pacific Regional Cooperation and Integration Index Database. https://aric.adb.org/database/arcii (accessed November 2024).

Southeast Asia's subregional programs—GMS, the Indonesia-Malaysia-Thailand Growth Triangle (IMT-GT), and the Brunei Darussalam–Indonesia–Malaysia–Philippines East ASEAN Growth Area (BIMP-EAGA)—have also integrated more deeply. From 2006 to 2022, integration was largely driven by infrastructure connectivity, institutional arrangements and technology, and digital connectivity. For instance, lower trade costs and improved liner shipping connectivity contributed to stronger regional linkages. Integration momentum was further sustained by joining regional value chains, improving trade complementarity, and importing intermediate goods (Figure 1.8).

Deepening regional integration between subregional initiative members occurs through various projects and programs. Most subregional initiatives prioritize projects that improve trade and supply chain linkages, transport and infrastructure connectivity, and the movement of people. These are usually included in strategic documents such as the GMS Economic Cooperation Program Strategic Framework 2030, the CAREC 2030 Strategic Framework, and the SASEC Vision (Figure 1.9). Large investments also support these, with $34.3 billion and $12.7 billion allotted for transport and energy projects in the CAREC region, and $34.5 billion mobilized to support BIMP-EAGA infrastructure projects (CAREC 2025; BIMP-EAGA 2023). Beyond these traditional links, subregional initiatives have also begun to sharpen their focus on supporting newer channels of connectivity, such as digital transformation and environmental cooperation initiatives. For instance, GMS developed a Digital Economy Cooperation Initiative in 2022 to promote inclusive digitalization and advance technology use.

## Technology sharing and digital connectivity have been engines of RCI in all subregional initiatives, while environmental cooperation has only seen slight progress.

Based on International Telecommunication Union Statistics data, internet penetration in Asia rose sharply from 18% to 73%, alongside substantial growth in mobile subscriptions, from 2006 to 2022. This established a strong foundation for technological and digital connectivity across the region (Figures 1.6, 1.7, and 1.8). Subregional efforts have also reinforced digital

**Figure 1.8: Intrasubregional Initiatives—Southeast Asia**

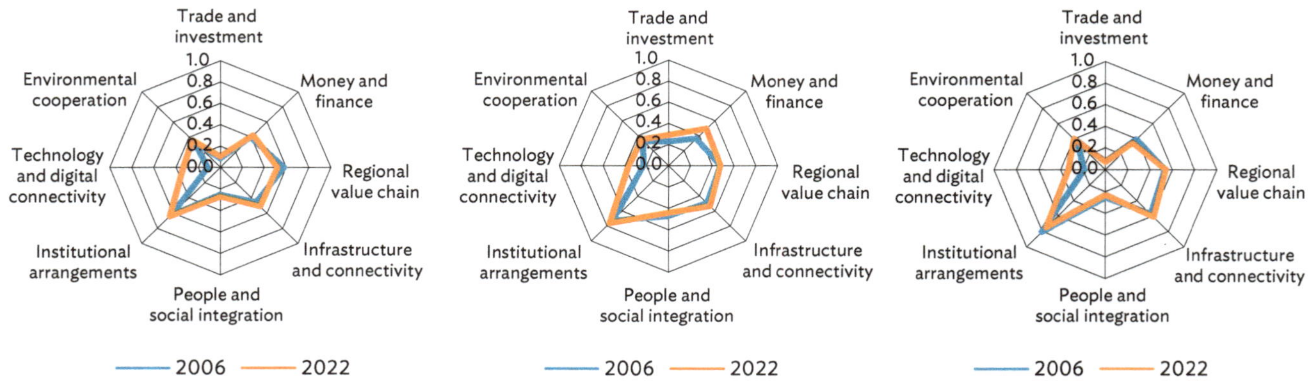


BIMP-EAGA = Brunei Darussalam–Indonesia–Malaysia–Philippines East ASEAN Growth Area, GMS = Greater Mekong Subregion, IMT-GT = Indonesia-Malaysia-Thailand Growth Triangle.

Notes: Based on ADB's Asia-Pacific Regional Cooperation and Integration Index estimates. Higher index estimates denote greater regional integration. Intrasubregional integration is measured within members of the same subregional initiative.

Source: ADB. Asia-Pacific Regional Cooperation and Integration Index Database. https://aric.adb.org/database/arcii (accessed November 2024).

**Figure 1.9: Relevant Operational Regional Cooperation and Integration Areas of Subregional Initiatives**

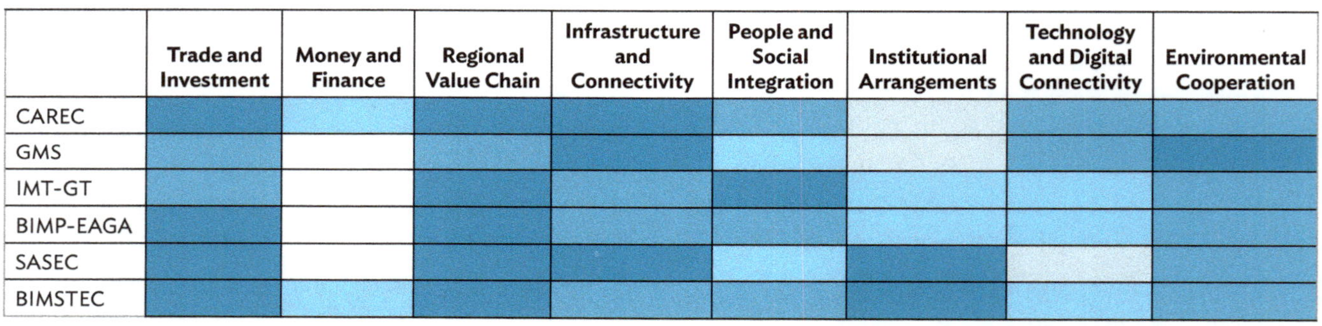


BIMP-EAGA = Brunei Darussalam–Indonesia–Malaysia–Philippines East ASEAN Growth Area, BIMSTEC = Bay of Bengal Initiative for Multi-Sectoral Technical and Economic Cooperation, CAREC = Central Asia Regional Economic Cooperation, GMS = Greater Mekong Subregion, IMT-GT = Indonesia-Malaysia-Thailand Growth Triangle, SASEC = South Asia Subregional Economic Cooperation.

Note: The colors represent the degree of prioritization placed by subregional initiatives on different regional cooperation and integration (RCI) areas. Darker shades denote high prioritization, lighter shades indicate less prioritization. The criteria used for determining subregional priorities was based on: (1) if the RCI dimension is explicitly mentioned as a priority based on the program's long-term plans or agenda; (2) if a dedicated working group is created for the RCI dimension; (3) if funds are allocated for certain RCI-related projects and activities; and (4) if there are recent events, documents, or work plans launched for the RCI dimension.

Source: ADB. Asia-Pacific Regional Cooperation and Integration Index Database. https://aric.adb.org/database/arcii (accessed November 2024).

integration, with GMS leading in ICT goods trade, accounting for an average 51% of ICT trade within the subregion in 2022 based on the UN Commodity Trade Statistics Database. GMS also showed the highest level of regional research collaboration, with 28% of international collaborations occurring within the subregion, nearly doubling between 2006 and 2022 (Clarivate 2024). CAREC had remarkable progress, with intrasubregional integration nearly doubling or even tripling.

Environmental cooperation across Asia's subregional initiatives showed modest gains, such as their environmental health score. BIMP-EAGA and Indonesia–Malaysia–Thailand Growth Triangle (IMT-GT) recorded the highest estimates in this area, noticeably ahead over other initiatives. Across subregions, the average number of environmental agreements increased slightly, showing a stronger commitment to environmental protection. However, significant challenges remain. For instance, the environmental footprint per capita has increased, and environmental goods represent a very small share of intrasubregional trade—only about 1% or less across initiatives, according to the UN Commodity Trade Statistics Database—suggesting there remains ample opportunity to intensify growth.

## Subregional Cooperation Initiatives in Asia and the Pacific

Each subregion discussed here describes the key cross-border initiatives and progress made so far under subregional cooperation initiatives within the past 5 years. It also substantiates ADB support and investment in these initiatives and shares some of the next steps to strengthen cooperation in the subregions.

### Central and West Asia, East Asia, and the Caucasus

The CAREC program has been a cornerstone for regional cooperation and integration in Central Asia, South Caucasus, East Asia, and South Asia since its inception in September 2001.[2] The program continues to generate substantial investments in transport, energy, and trade facilitation; and helps reduce travel times, lower trade costs, facilitate safer movement of goods and people, and generate other economic activity in the region. Under CAREC 2030: Connecting the Region for Shared and Sustainable Development (CAREC 2030 Strategy) endorsed in 2017, the program's scope expanded from three sectors (transport, energy, and trade) to five operational clusters:

- **Economic and financial stability**—to support macroeconomic policy coordination, promote financial stability, and strengthen investment climate;
- **Trade, tourism, and economic corridors**—to expand the region's trade and tourism potential and develop economic corridors. The CAREC Integrated Trade Agenda 2030, endorsed in 2018, supports CAREC members to integrate further into the global economy by expanding trade from increased market access, greater diversification, and stronger trade institutions. The CAREC Tourism Strategy 2030 endorsed in 2020 aims to develop sustainable, safe, and inclusive tourism;
- **Infrastructure and economic connectivity**—two strategies were endorsed under this cluster in 2019. The CAREC Transport Strategy 2030 works in conjunction with the 2030 trade agenda to enable the efficient movement of goods and people through a safe multimodal corridor network of roads, railways, aviation services, ports, multimodal logistics hubs, and improved border crossing facilities and services, both within the region and with the rest of the world. The CAREC Energy Strategy 2030 is inspired by the vision of achieving a reliable, sustainable, resilient, and reformed energy market in the CAREC region by 2030, where the electricity network and gas pipeline system allow energy to be traded across borders at competitive prices;
- **Agriculture and water**—to develop productive, resilient, and sustainable agriculture guided by the Cooperation Framework for Agricultural Development and Food Security in the CAREC Region endorsed in 2022; and
- **Human development**—to improve the quality of human capital and promote labor mobility through cross-border education. The CAREC Health Strategy 2030 endorsed in November 2021, among others, aims to enhance a member's capacity to respond effectively to transboundary health risks.

The CAREC 2030 Strategy also includes three cross-cutting themes:

- **Climate change.** In November 2023, members endorsed the Regional Action on Climate Change: A Vision for CAREC (CAREC Climate Change Vision). The vision aims to help members implement their

[2] CAREC members include Afghanistan; Azerbaijan; the People's Republic of China's Xinjiang Uygur Autonomous Region and Inner Mongolia Autonomous Region; Georgia; Kazakhstan; the Kyrgyz Republic; Mongolia; Pakistan; Tajikistan; Turkmenistan; and Uzbekistan. ADB placed on hold its regular assistance to Afghanistan effective 15 August 2021.

commitments under the Paris Agreement and achieve the Sustainable Development Goals (SDGs) by promoting regional action on the energy transition, decarbonization, innovative financing solutions, and climate-resilient infrastructure and policies.[3]

- **Information and communication technology.** In 2021, the CAREC Digital Strategy 2030 was endorsed as a catalyst for regional cooperation on digital technologies.
- **Gender.** The CAREC Gender Strategy 2030 endorsed in 2020, provides strategic guidelines for mainstreaming gender into CAREC operations.

### *Progress so far*

During the first half of the CAREC 2030 Strategy (between 2018 and 2023), 78 projects valued at over $14.7 billion were approved and financed by ADB and other CAREC development partners.[4] A large portion of these investments focus on enhancing connectivity, efficiency, and sustainability of transport and energy infrastructure, followed by trade facilitation aimed at enhancing regional economic competitiveness.

A total of 33 transport projects valued at $8 billion were approved from 2018 to 2023, contributed to the $34.7 billion cumulative investments in transport since the program started. ADB–financed projects led to improved regional connectivity along the six CAREC corridors, with over 12,863 kilometers (km) of roads built or improved, 1,995 km of railway tracks built, and 4,152 km of railways rehabilitated from 2008 to 2023. Increasing transport and logistics costs, geopolitical uncertainties, and emerging challenges including supply chain disruptions and threats due to climate change require a review of corridors and priority projects.

Energy is the second-largest share of the CAREC portfolio with 16 new energy projects amounting to $3.5 billion in 2018–2023. These include those promoting physical connectivity for power transmission among the Central Asia Power System economies. A project approved for Tajikistan in 2018 will allow power trade between Tajikistan and Uzbekistan and the reconnection of Tajikistan with other power system economies. The completed Kyrgyz Republic Power Sector Improvement Project, rehabilitated 118 substations and linked major substations improving efficiency and reliability of power supply.[5]

Five trade-related projects valued at $759 million were approved between 2018 and 2023, including the Border Efficiency for Sustainable Trade Project, the Developing Economic Cooperation Zone Project (both in Mongolia), and the Inner Mongolia Sustainable Cross-Border Development Investment Program for the PRC. The Regional Improvement of Border Services projects supported the Kyrgyz Republic, Mongolia, Tajikistan, and Pakistan in upgrading their border infrastructure, facilities, and systems, and in establishing a national single window system.

Beyond physical infrastructure development, substantial progress has been made in improving capacity and supporting reforms to align with international standards and best practices. A key aspect is support to World Trade Organization accession of three remaining CAREC members (Azerbaijan, Turkmenistan, and Uzbekistan). The CAREC program also supports economies in implementing the World Trade Organization Trade Facilitation Agreement and in acceding to international agreements that are crucial for trade.[6] CAREC members also started leveraging global technology to facilitate trade and digitize trade processes. Uzbekistan and Pakistan have successfully integrated into global ePhyto solutions, while Georgia is piloting robotic process automation or artificial intelligence for import procedures.

---

3 With their agreement, the ministers also adopted a Joint Ministerial Statement on promoting regional disaster risk financing solutions and improving the resilience of public sector budgets to disaster events through regional collaboration.

4 Other partners include the Asian Infrastructure Investment Bank, European Bank for Reconstruction and Development, International Monetary Fund, Islamic Development Bank, United Nations Development Programme, and the World Bank Group.

5 ADB. 2020. *Project Completion Report: Kyrgyz Republic Power Sector Improvement Project* (Grant 0218).

6 Azerbaijan, the PRC, the Kyrgyz Republic, Mongolia, Tajikistan, Turkmenistan, and Uzbekistan already signed or acceded to the UN Framework Agreement on Facilitation of Cross-Border Paperless Trade in Asia and the Pacific; while Azerbaijan, Mongolia, and the PRC are parties to the UN Convention on the Use of Electronic Communications in International Contracts.

**Economic corridor development.** The CAREC program has been piloting the Almaty–Bishkek Economic Corridor since 2014.[7] The corridor will unify the two city regions of Kazakhstan and the Kyrgyz Republic into a single economic space, fostering the rapid exchange of ideas and the seamless movement of goods and people.[8]

**Mainstreaming climate action.** To operationalize the CAREC Climate Change Vision, the CAREC Working Group on Climate Change was established in April 2024 and the Climate Change Action Plan 2025–2027 was endorsed in November 2024. The action plan prioritizes regional climate adaptation and mitigation projects and initiatives across CAREC clusters and focuses on four areas of intervention: (i) climate risk, preparedness, and health; (ii) water–energy–food security nexus; (iii) low carbon growth; and (iv) a CAREC climate platform.

## *ADB's support and investment in these initiatives*

**Acting as CAREC secretariat.** As an honest broker of regional cooperation, ADB is supporting the various CAREC committees, sector working groups, and expert groups—from advisory to technical support in prioritizing activities, preparation of investment projects and initiatives, monitoring of activities, and reporting the progress to the ministerial conference through the senior officials or national focal points meeting.[9]

**Mobilizing financing and technical assistance (TA) resources.** A total of 71 TA projects worth $113.0 million were approved, mostly financed by ADB. In line with the *"projects++" approach* under the CAREC 2030 Strategy, most TA projects focus on capacity building, policy dialogue, project preparation, and knowledge products and services.[10] Recently approved ADB TA projects supporting new CAREC 2030 areas/sectors include TA 9977: Developing the CAREC Water Pillar ($1.6 million, approved May 2020); TA 6535: Addressing Health Threats in CAREC Countries and the Caucasus ($4.3 million, approved July 2020); TA 6806: Strengthening Regional Cooperation on Skills Development under the CAREC Program ($2 million, approved October 2021); TA 6947: Supporting CAREC Regional Capital Market Regulators Forum ($0.7 million, approved August 2022); TA 10258: Resilient and Inclusive Agricultural Development and Food Security in the CAREC Program Member Countries ($3 million, approved December 2023); and TA 10390: Developing a Disaster Risk Transfer Facility in the CAREC Region (Phase 2) ($ 3.1 million, approved November 2024).

**Supporting project preparation.** Projects with regional implications require a high level of cooperation and collaboration among participating economies. ADB is implementing a $1.4 million technical assistance facility to support the preparation of follow-up regional infrastructure and connectivity projects within the CAREC region and the Caucasus. It supported the detailed engineering design and procurement of equipment and recruitment of consultants for ensuing work and development of pipeline projects under the CAREC Water Pillar.

In October 2024, ADB established the CAREC Climate and Sustainability Project Preparatory Fund (CSPPF). The CSPPF is a multi-partner trust fund—with the Republic of Korea and the PRC as founding financing partners—to help address and narrow CAREC economies' financing gaps in achieving climate change goals and the SDGs by supporting the preparation of bankable climate- and SDG-related regional projects. The CSPPF offers CAREC economies a streamlined mechanism to identify, prepare, structure finance, and implement regional climate- and SDG-related projects aligned with their commitments to address climate change.

7 See Independent Evaluation Department. 2024. *Validation Report: Almaty-Bishkek Economic Corridor Support (TA 9487)*. ADB.

8 Initiatives include modernization of priority border crossing points between the two economies; preparation of a tourism master plan connecting Almaty, Kazakhstan with Lake Issyk-Kul, the Kyrgyz Republic; cooperation in health laboratories to prevent future pandemics; and support for the Clean Air Action Plans for Almaty and Bishkek, with the installation of air quality monitoring sensors to allow officials to effectively measure the impact of air quality improvement initiatives.

9 As of June 2024, there are 4 CAREC sector coordinating committees, 3 thematic working groups (WGs), and 14 WGs/sub-WG/experts group, with ADB acting as the CAREC secretariat.

10 "Under the *"projects++" approach*, CAREC's historical emphasis on regional projects will be complemented with a framework for policy dialogue and knowledge cooperation on the one hand, and promoting people-to-people contacts on the other, as part of a holistic and encompassing strategy to deepen regional integration."

### *Next steps to strengthen cooperation*

The rapidly evolving global and regional landscape requires review, adaptation, and reform to ensure the CAREC program's continued relevance, effectiveness, and responsiveness to the needs and priorities of its members and to pursue its regional objectives. In November 2024, the 23rd CAREC Ministerial Conference endorsed the program's midterm review (MTR), which assessed the progress of implementing the CAREC 2030 Strategy and offers forward-looking options to revitalize regional cooperation. The program will prioritize economy-driven activities, pursue regional impact and innovation, strengthen partnerships, and adopt robust monitoring and evaluation to help build a more prosperous, integrated, and resilient future for the CAREC region.

Specifically, the program will implement 10 recommendations from the MTR:

- **Streamline scope for enhancing the impact of CAREC initiatives.** The program will adopt a more targeted approach and establish a multiyear rolling pipeline for regional programs, projects, and technical assistance that are demand-driven and linked with economy programming. It will assess and direct resources to projects with the highest impacts and benefits and optimize resource allocation through subregional cooperation (2+X principle), and cross-sectoral initiatives for greater specialization and in-depth engagement.
- **Review and recalibrate sectoral strategies.** The CAREC program will conduct midterm reviews of sector strategies to make them more responsive to emerging needs and requirements (CAREC Transport Strategy 2030, CAREC Energy Strategy 2030, CAREC Integrated Trade Agenda 2030, and CAREC Digital Strategy 2030). As it plays a pivotal role in linking CAREC members to global value chains, a strategy for CAREC Corridor 2 (which broadly relates to the Trans-Caspian International Transport Route or the Middle Corridor) is being developed to coordinate the hard and soft infrastructure investments in the corridor. In helping members transition to clean and sustainable energy, the focus will be on developing transformational regional energy projects such as the Rogun and Kambarata-1 Hydro Power Plant or the Caspian Undersea Cable Project to help secure the region's energy future. As a cross-cutting theme, the CAREC program must leverage digitalization and the use of information and communication technology (ICT) to promote innovation while simultaneously catalyzing solutions to achieve climate priorities. This includes digitalization of trade processes and cross-border paperless trade, low-carbon mobility and logistics solutions, and technological transfer in energy.
- **Pursue regional public goods to address common issues.** The program will continue to promote regional public goods in combating communicable diseases, promoting environmental sustainability and climate change, water resources management, and sustainable energy transition. It will develop a multi-hazard early warning system for detecting, forecasting, and communicating diverse hazards. It will promote cross-border sustainable energy projects and transboundary water management systems.
- **Reinvigorate regional ownership for sustaining outcomes.** The CAREC program will engage with all stakeholders to foster ownership and sustainability of TA projects while tailoring the program to address each economy's unique needs, priorities, and capacity. It will improve its communication by telling impact stories and tangible benefits, highlighting the impact on beneficiaries, aligning national interests with regional objectives, and strengthening stakeholder engagement in business, civil society, and local communities.
- **Promote integrated and climate-smart development.** This includes integrating CAREC climate change, digitalization, and trade initiatives under the declaration on CAREC Partnership on Climate, Innovation, and Trade signed at the 29th Conference of the Parties (COP 29) in Baku in November 2024. The CAREC program will also enhance capacity and coordination among relevant institutions to mainstream climate change action across CAREC sectors such as the Water–Energy–Agriculture nexus or a "One-Health" approach. It will promote innovative and green finance initiatives to mobilize investments for renewable energy, energy efficiency, climate-smart agriculture, regional disaster risk transfer solutions that leverage international

reinsurance and capital markets, and sustainable urban development.

- **Strengthen engagement with development partners and the private sector.** The CAREC program will involve development partners in the proposed multiyear project pipeline and climate action plan, impact assessment of projects, robust project monitoring, and evaluation framework. It will explore innovative financing options to support critical regional infrastructure projects and leverage private sector expertise and investment through public–private partnerships.
- **Improve program effectiveness and monitoring.** The program will develop a real-time operational dashboard to track project progress, monitor key performance indicators, improve transparency, and inform evidence-based decision-making. It will facilitate knowledge exchange programs and develop communities of practice for regional experts to collaborate and share best practices in partnership with the CAREC Institute.
- **Strengthen the CAREC secretariat.** The program will integrate CAREC and regional cooperation and integration (RCI) activities into national programs and pursue regional projects by enhancing coordination with economy teams, including ADB resident missions. It will strengthen its field presence to enhance regional collaboration, bridge the distance to regional partners, and address the program's expanding roles and needs.
- **Enhance the CAREC Institute.** As a strategic partner for knowledge-driven development and regional cooperation, the CAREC program will leverage the CAREC Institute's established expertise in research, capacity building, and knowledge sharing.
- **Prepare an MTR implementation action plan.** The CAREC secretariat will prepare a comprehensive action plan with defined timelines, deliverables, and accountabilities to implement the recommendations outlined in the MTR.

By implementing these recommendations, the CAREC 2030 Strategy can significantly strengthen its role as a driving force for positive change within the CAREC region, fostering a more integrated and resilient future in 2030 and beyond.

## South Asia

ADB serves as secretariat for the SASEC program. It helps SASEC gain greater acceptance and a broader constituency among SASEC members and promotes intersubregional cooperation between South Asia and Southeast Asia. ADB supports BIMSTEC and SAARC in research and knowledge outreach, institutional capacity building, and promotion of policy dialogue. It seeks to develop a greater partnership with SAARC and BIMSTEC through technical assistance and dialogue with their respective secretariats and members.

### *Key initiatives as well as projects and plans under SASEC, SAARC, and BIMSTEC in the past 5 years*

**BIMSTEC.** ADB's partnership with BIMSTEC began in 2005 as it supported the preparation of the BIMSTEC Transport Infrastructure and Logistics Study. This partnership has expanded to cover institutional strengthening and regional policy dialogue on a wide range of areas, including trade, tourism, financing, and energy. Through technical assistance, ADB continues to support BIMSTEC in preparing studies and research, convening knowledge-sharing events and policy dialogues, and strengthening capacity of the BIMSTEC secretariat and member states through training and workshops. In response to the request of BIMSTEC members and secretariat, ADB has done analytical studies on transport, trade, tourism, transport financing, and energy. These have been discussed by BIMSTEC members and endorsed for implementation.

**SAARC.** At the request of SAARC, ADB has recently conducted various studies. These include Updating the SAARC Regional Multimodal Transport Study with a chapter on connectivity between South Asia and Central Asia; Study on Implementation of the Thimphu Statement on Climate Change; Study on Contextualization of Sustainable Development Goals (SDGs) and to Revisit the SAARC Plan of Action on Poverty Alleviation; and Study on Harmonization of 8-Digit Harmonized System (HS) Tariff Lines of SAARC Member Countries. ADB also assists the SAARC Council of Experts of Energy Regulators (Electricity), which is creating a road map to implement the SAARC Framework Agreement on Energy

Cooperation. Also, informal meetings of SAARC finance ministers are organized annually on the sidelines of ADB annual meetings. The 17th Informal Meeting of SAARC Finance Ministers was held in Incheon, Republic of Korea on 5 May 2023.

**SASEC.** Over the past 5 years, SASEC has supported key initiatives in the following areas:

- **Transport.** The program has focused on enhancing subregional connectivity by developing multimodal transport networks and upgrading seaport infrastructure. Major projects include railway modernization, the construction of new airports, and better seaport operations.
- **Energy.** Priority has been given to developing transmission infrastructure and incorporating cleaner energy, such as renewable energy. The subregional power market and cross-border electricity trade have been strengthened, contributing to more energy security and sustainability.
- **Trade facilitation.** SASEC has prioritized reducing trade bottlenecks and modernizing customs procedures. Key initiatives include a national single window customs system and electronic cargo tracking to streamline trade processes.
- **Economic corridor development.** Economic corridors, such as the Visakhapatnam–Chennai Industrial Corridor, have been developed to enhance economic linkages and promote subregional growth and diversification.

### *Progress on projects and plans*

**BIMSTEC.** Progress has been made on preparing analytical studies that shape discussions during BIMSTEC meetings. These include

- **Leveraging Thematic Circuits for BIMSTEC Tourism Development.** This study identifies ways to revive tourism in the region through "thematic circuits." It should lead to a comprehensive strategy for developing tourism in the subregion. Some of the study's recommendations were adopted during the Second Meeting of BIMSTEC Tourism Working Group held in February 2024.
- **BIMSTEC Trade Facilitation Strategic Framework 2030.** This framework aims to promote intraregional trade by reducing nontariff barriers from (i) soft infrastructure, (ii) hard infrastructure, (iii) logistics, and (iv) building institutional capacity and promoting cooperation among members.
- **BIMSTEC Master Plan for Transport Connectivity.** The plan presents a comprehensive 10-year strategy and action plan for improving the subregion's transport and trade linkages. It was formally adopted at the Fifth BIMSTEC Summit held in Colombo, Sri Lanka, on 30 March 2022. BIMSTEC leaders would like it to be implemented soon, so that improved connectivity can bring better integration, better trade, and better people-to-people relations.
- **Financing Transport Connectivity in the BIMSTEC Region.** This study assesses the financing landscape for infrastructure in the subregion and analyzes various ways of financing transport infrastructure, including public–private partnerships.

There were two capacity-building activities organized for BIMSTEC. The first training was on trade facilitation in May 2023 together with the Ministry of External Affairs of India, and the Indian Council for Research on International Economic Relations. The second was on authorized economic operator programs held in June 2024 in New Delhi. The goal was to strengthen the capacity of BIMSTEC customs administrations to design and implement effective authorized economic operator programs based on India's experience.

**SAARC.** Good progress has been made on agreed areas of cooperation but more could have been done at the national level. Recent developments in SAARC–ADB Cooperation include

- The 10th Meeting of SAARC Sub-Group on Customs Cooperation, held at the SAARC secretariat, Kathmandu, Nepal, to consider the Draft Final Study on Harmonization of 8-Digit HS Tariff Lines of SAARC Member Countries on 1–2 October 2024 with a timeline agreed for implementation. A consultation workshop was held in Colombo, Sri Lanka on 11–12 September 2023 with customs and HS experts from SAARC members to review the study.

- SAARC–ADB 5th Meeting of SAARC Council of Experts of Energy Regulators (Electricity) was held in Islamabad, Pakistan on 13–14 November 2023 to review implementation of the SAARC Framework Agreement on Energy Cooperation. The Sixth Meeting of the SAARC Council will be held once the road map for implementing the agreement has been updated to include members' comments, and the SAARC Framework Agreement on Energy Cooperation has been ratified by all members.
- The Consultation Workshop on Climate Change was held in Thimphu, Bhutan on 10–11 July 2024 to review the implementation of the Thimphu Statement on Climate Change. ADB described its current status. Further actions were discussed and finalized during the Meeting of the Inter-Governmental Expert Group on Climate Change held in Colombo, Sri Lanka on 3–4 December 2024.
- Informal meetings of SAARC finance ministers are usually held on the sidelines of the ADB annual meeting. The 18th Informal Meeting is expected to be held in May 2025. These meetings, attended by ADB senior management and experts, provide a platform for SAARC finance ministers and ADB to exchange views on specified themes, enhance understanding of macroeconomic and contemporary RCI issues, and reach consensus on what needs to be done.

**SASEC.** Progress has been made on various fronts. These include:

- **Transport.** ADB has supported SASEC economies in developing a multimodal transport network across the subregion. The SASEC corridors have been revised to better support regional cooperation objectives, facilitating multi-economy trade and improving access to gateways for landlocked economies. The updated corridors are: (i) Nepal/Bhutan–India Corridor; (ii) Sri Lanka–India–Bangladesh–India–Myanmar Corridor (aligned with economic corridors); (iii) Nepal–India–Bangladesh Corridor; (iv) Bhutan–India–Bangladesh Corridor; (v) Nepal–India–Myanmar Corridor; and (vi) Myanmar–Bangladesh–India–Sri Lanka–Maldives (Maritime) Corridor. These corridors are served by multiple transport modes, including road, rail, and waterways, and are complemented by trade facilitation and economic corridor initiatives. ADB has provided loans for the construction of roads along these corridors, support for the development of railway systems in Bangladesh, India, and Sri Lanka, as well as the construction of new airports in Bhutan and Nepal. For maritime transport, ADB has helped improve seaports, including Chattogram in Bangladesh, Visakhapatnam and Chennai in India, Kulhudhuffushi in Maldives, and Colombo in Sri Lanka. In addition to ADB support, several economies have developed transport infrastructure with domestic resources or assistance from other development partners.
- **Energy.** Energy supply has increased significantly in recent years, with ADB supporting several economies to increase their power generation capacity by building new power plants and upgrading existing ones. ADB has supported their increasing use of natural gas and renewable energy sources, such as solar, hydro, and wind power. ADB has also supported electricity transmission upgrades and tariff structure reforms. Power trade runs through bilateral arrangements between India and Bangladesh, Bhutan, Nepal, and Myanmar.[11] A notable milestone is the Bangladesh–India Electrical Grid Interconnection Projects, which created the first international transmission lines in South Asia. Installed electricity capacity in the subregion increased from 417 gigawatts to 550 gigawatts between 2017 and 2023.
- **Trade facilitation.** In May 2019, ADB approved a $10 million Asian Development Fund loan and/or grant to develop the Maldives' National Single Window, an electronic platform designed to enhance the speed and efficiency of cross-border control procedures using advanced technology. ADB also approved $1.5 million in technical assistance to prepare Bangladesh's SASEC Integrated Trade Facilitation Sector Development Program. This was included in ADB's 2021 pipeline for $200 million to improve the economy's border infrastructure and trade facilitation environment. ADB supported the continuation of reforms in Nepal through the implementation of the Customs Reform and Modernization Plan 2021–2026 and the improvement of trade logistics through the preparation and

[11] As of February 1, 2021, ADB has placed a temporary hold on sovereign project disbursements and new contracts in Myanmar.

implementation of a new Trade Logistics Policy 2022 under the SASEC Customs and Logistics Reforms Program (Subprogram 1).

- **Economic corridor development.** ADB has been instrumental in supporting India's East Coast Economic Corridor through the development of the Visakhapatnam–Chennai Industrial Corridor. It strengthened economic linkages across industries and sectors through policy reforms, institutional development, and high-quality infrastructure investment, contributing to regional GDP growth and better living standards. Following its success, economic corridor studies have been done in Bangladesh, northeastern India, and Sri Lanka to identify opportunities for growth centers and investment. In 2023, the SASEC corridor was updated to reflect evolving needs. The revised corridors include (i) the Nepal/Bhutan–India Corridor, (ii) the Sri Lanka–India–Bangladesh–India–Myanmar Corridor, (iii) the Nepal–India–Bangladesh Corridor, (iv) Bhutan–India–Bangladesh Corridor, (v) the Nepal/Bhutan–India–Myanmar Corridor, and (vi) the Myanmar–Bangladesh–India–Sri Lanka–Maldives Maritime Corridor. For Nepal, ADB conducted an urban corridor development study to analyze industrial development. Economic corridor development support helped create regional value chains in tourism and food supply. It also increases competitiveness by reducing constraints on the movement of goods and services and improving market access across borders.

### *ADB support and investment in these initiatives*

**BIMSTEC.** Since 2019, ADB has offered two technical assistance grants amounting to $2.0 million. This helped ADB prepare analytical studies for BIMSTEC meetings. Consultation workshops were conducted to obtain members' views on the directions and contents of the studies. Dissemination workshops were conducted to present study findings and discuss the next steps for implementation. ADB supported capacity building for the BIMSTEC secretariat and members.

**SAARC.** Since 2019, ADB has provided $950,000 in technical assistance to support the development of analytical studies discussed during SAARC meetings. Consultation workshops were conducted to validate the initial study findings and obtain additional input from members. Thereafter, the final reports with policy recommendations were presented and adopted in SAARC meetings.

**SASEC.** As of 30 June 2024, a total of 87 SASEC projects valued at $20.8 billion, of which $12.8 billion is financed by ADB, are either ongoing or completed across the six member economies. Additionally, 155 technical assistance projects worth $224.78 million have been implemented to support project preparation, strategic planning, and capacity building.

### *Strengthening cooperation in South Asia*

**BIMSTEC.** The signing of a memorandum of understanding (MOU) in February 2022, the secretariat's first MOU with an international organization, cemented the mutual commitment of ADB and BIMSTEC to expand and strengthen their partnership in pursuit of stronger cooperation and a more integrated Bay of Bengal region.

In the immediate future, ADB supports the implementation of the BIMSTEC Master Plan for Transport Connectivity. ADB's assistance covers other areas of cooperation such as public–private partnerships, digitalization, the environment, and climate change. ADB may also provide support in developing an action plan for climate change, disaster risk management, and environmental conservation, as requested by the BIMSTEC secretariat.

A recently approved technical assistance from ADB promotes knowledge sharing, capacity-building activities, and regional policy dialogue, including knowledge exchange and meetings with ASEAN, the United Nations Economic and Social Commission for Asia and the Pacific (UNESCAP), and other international organizations. ADB and the BIMSTEC secretariat are working closely to identify and implement a program aimed at enhancing the secretariat's institutional capacity in promoting RCI in the subregion.

**SAARC.** SAARC and ADB have been long-term development partners promoting RCI in South Asia. Several proposals from the SAARC secretary-general under consideration for possible future implementation will focus on regional public goods such as climate change and the environment.

Intraregional connectivity, trade facilitation, power trade, and climate change are some of the SAARC initiatives common with other subregional organizations in South Asia and Central Asia. With many members overlapping under these regional groupings, it is important to enhance intersubregional dialogue to promote synergy and complementarity. ADB, as secretariat of SASEC and CAREC and development partner of BIMSTEC and SAARC, is in a good position to collaborate with all regional organizations to bring about better results.

**SASEC.** The SASEC program plans to work on the following areas to enhance connectivity and economic resilience:

- **Transport.** This involves improving regional connectivity while reducing greenhouse gas emissions from transport and logistics by (i) transitioning from transport corridors to trade corridors; (ii) promoting multimodal transport (road, railway, inland waterway, and maritime transport) and supporting sustainable modal shifts; (iii) improving logistics efficiency and sustainability; and (iv) facilitating comprehensive transport agreements.
- **Energy.** The program seeks to accelerate the transition to clean energy, enhance power interconnections, and use digital technologies to improve energy efficiency and sustainability.
- **Trade facilitation.** The focus will be on enabling seamless and sustainable movement of goods and services across borders. Priorities include promoting sustainable food trade to support food security and implementing digital solutions to enhance trade efficiency.
- **Economic corridor development.** The program will establish strong subregional supply chains, promote intra-SASEC trade and investment, and develop sustainable tourism corridors.

## Southeast Asia

### *Key initiatives, projects, and plans under GMS, IMT-GT, and BIMP-EAGA over the past 5 years, progress so far, and ADB support and investments*

**Greater Mekong Subregion**

**GMS Strategic Framework 2030 (GMS-2030).** Approved in 2021, GMS-2030 envisions a more integrated, prosperous, sustainable, and inclusive GMS. It focuses on strengths like community, connectivity, and competitiveness while aligning regional initiatives with the UN SDGs. Key principles include environmental sustainability, resilience, integration, and inclusivity. Achieving these goals requires innovative approaches such as leveraging digital transformation, enhancing spatial perspectives, engaging in policy dialogue, increasing private sector participation, establishing a GMS open platform, and focusing on tangible results, all supported by ADB.

**Digitalization.** Digitalization offers GMS economies a chance to leverage their young and tech-savvy population. The GMS Digitalization Action Plan, 2025–2027 outlines a framework for regional cooperation to promote digitalization in agriculture, tourism, and trade. By promoting capacity building, policy dialogue, and innovative pilot programs, the digital action plan aims to help GMS governments digitize effectively.

**Innovation.** To enhance economic outcomes and address regional and global challenges, GMS economies developed the GMS Innovation Strategy for Development 2030. The strategy should accelerate progress toward GMS-2030 by helping set up a subregional innovation system that promotes cross-border collaboration. It focuses on three strategic areas: digitalization, green transition, and connectivity through infrastructure investment. Key implementation steps include creating a GMS task force on innovation, organizing innovation forums, providing training, establishing a GMS innovation fund, partnering with the private sector, and developing a monitoring framework.

**Embracing private sector solutions.** Recognizing that public funds are insufficient for achieving growth and SDG commitments, GMS economies are launching initiatives to enhance private sector participation. These include developing a GMS strategy for private sector engagement, organizing private sector roundtables, conducting training on public–private partnerships for GMS officials, and increasing the participation of the GMS Business Council in various working groups and GMS program bodies.

**Transforming the GMS into an open platform.** GMS-2030 emphasizes greater stakeholder engagement and collaboration with other RCI initiatives. Two supporting studies conducted to implement this mandate are the Strategic Approach for Strengthening Local Government Engagement in GMS, which explores how to enhance provincial and local government participation, and the Study on Deepening Development Partners' Engagement in the GMS Program, which examines challenges faced by development in support of the subregion.

**GMS Knowledge Network (GMSKN).** The GMSKN, including knowledge centers from GMS members, was established in 2022. It aims to provide expertise, stimulate discussion, and raise awareness on emerging GMS policy issues, offering relevant innovative knowledge solutions to enhance policy dialogue among GMS economies. A 3-year (2025–2027) GMSKN workplan will be prepared by the group's steering committee.

**Enhancing spatial approach to development.** Urban sector development initiatives are advancing along various border and specific areas in GMS economic corridors. Key initiatives include the People's Republic of China (PRC) Guangxi Regional Cooperation and Integration Promotion Investment Program, which promotes integrated development between Guangxi and northern Viet Nam, and the Lao People's Democratic Republic (Lao PDR) Urban Environment Improvement Investment Project in Luang Prabang, which complements the new railway link between the Lao PDR and the PRC. A study has been completed to enhance connectivity between Vientiane and Ha Noi along the GMS North–South Economic Corridor, and an ongoing study focuses on setting new strategies for GMS border economic zones.

**Dialogue on policies and regulations, underpinned by knowledge-based solutions and capacity building.** In all GMS sectors—agriculture, energy, the environment, health, tourism, trade and investment, transportation, and urban development—policy dialogue and capacity-building are underway. To revitalize the GMS Cross-Border Transport Facilitation Agreement after COVID-19 border closures, the Early Harvest Program was relaunched in December 2023 up to the end of 2026 and national authorities began issuing permits in April 2024. New sector strategies for agriculture, the environment, energy, health, and tourism are expected in 2024 while transport and urban strategies will be completed in 2025. A GMS Energy Transition Task Force was established in 2022 to help shift to cleaner energy sources and energy efficiency, while the GMS Task Force on Trade and Investment became a working group in 2024.

There are also some noteworthy projects. In energy, the 600-megawatt Monsoon Wind Power Project (2022) in the Lao PDR is the first cross-border project with private sector financing and the largest in Southeast Asia. It will provide clean renewable energy supply to Viet Nam. In agriculture, the $129 million GMS Cross-Border Livestock Health and Value Chains Improvement Project (2022) is projected to reduce transboundary animal disease, enhance food safety, strengthen livestock value chains and infrastructure investment. In health, the GMS Border Areas Health Project in Cambodia (2022) and in the Lao PDR (2024) will improve access to quality health services of people residing in select border provinces. From 2020 to 2024, 19 GMS projects were approved at a cost of $4.2 billion.

**Gender mainstreaming.** Achieving gender equality is part of the GMS-2030 principle of inclusivity. The GMS gender strategy, endorsed in 2022, takes a regional approach to gender equality and women's empowerment. In September 2024, the GMS Gender Strategy Implementation Plan 2025–2030 was endorsed to recommend activities, target outputs, and performance indicators to achieve the gender strategy objectives. Gender will be mainstreamed in the GMS Regional Investment Framework with gender indicators or elements integrated into the GMS-2030 Results Framework and other GMS strategies. On capacity building, the first GMS Gender Equality and Inclusion Forum was held in September 2024.

### Indonesia–Malaysia–Thailand Growth Triangle and Brunei Darussalam–Indonesia–Malaysia–Philippines East ASEAN Growth Area

**Strategy formulation.** ADB helped prepare the Accelerating Cooperation Together strategic document, a midterm review of BIMP-EAGA Vision 2025. ADB is also assisting in the development of the BIMP-EAGA Blue Economy Strategy 2030. It also helps to implement key actions identified in the cooperation report to fast-track the implementation for the remaining period of Vision 2025.

**Priority infrastructure projects and transport connectivity.** As of October 2024, BIMP-EAGA has a rolling pipeline of 210 priority infrastructure projects worth $65.5 billion developed with ADB assistance, located in economic corridors.

ADB supported the upgrade of 388 km of roads worth $136 million in West and North Kalimantan in Indonesia. It supported the $380 million 300 km road network improvement project in Western Mindanao, the Mindanao Road Master Plan, and Mindanao's Development Corridors Study. ADB also approved the $1 billion Davao Public Transport Modernization Project to introduce a low-carbon and climate-resilient bus system.

**Economic corridors and special economic zones (SEZs).** For BIMP-EAGA, ADB completed a study on SEZs for shared prosperity. In IMT-GT, ADB supported the Review and Assessment of the IMT-GT Economic Corridors Study, and the study on SEZs in IMT-GT Opportunities for Collaboration.

ADB now supports a study on BIMP-EAGA economic corridors for the BIMP-EAGA Summit in 2025. Findings and recommendations of the IMT-GT economic corridors study and the study on SEZs in IMT-GT Opportunities for Collaboration are being disseminated to help better operationalize IMT-GT economic corridors.

**Tourism.** ADB supported various initiatives under BIMP-EAGA and IMT-GT, including developing an IMT-GT Tourism Strategic Framework 2017–2036 and Action Plan 2017–2021, the Joint BIMP-EAGA and IMT-GT Tourism Recovery Communications Plan and Toolkit 2022–2024, and capacity building for tourism recovery, planning, and adopting digital solutions.

ADB supported capacity building for tourism officials on RCI, tourism communications and planning, smart tourism ecosystems, and public policies for alternative accommodations. It also held several training of trainers to teach micro, small, and medium-sized enterprises to adopt digital solutions.

**Green and smart cities development.** The BIMP-EAGA green cities initiative facilitated the development of green city action plans (GCAPs) for BIMP-EAGA cities. Similarly, IMT-GT helped prepare GCAPs and integrated green transport plans for IMT-GT cities, including GCAPs for IMT-GT cities in Malaysia supported by reimbursable technical assistance for Malaysia. Knowledge-sharing events include regular green cities conferences and forums also featured in both BIMP-EAGA and IMT-GT green city initiatives.

The preparation of GCAPs have been completed for BIMP-EAGA and IMT-GT cities—Melaka and Kuching (Malaysia), Songkhla and Hat Yai (Thailand), and Medan and Batam (Indonesia); along with Kendari, Indonesia; Kota Kinabalu, Malaysia; and General Santos City, Philippines. The GCAP for Labuan, Malaysia is under development. Under the reimbursable cluster technical assistance for Malaysia, the final GCAPs for Penang, Kota Bharu, and Langkawi were presented in the Green Cities Investment Forum on 26–27 November 2024 in Kuala Lumpur, Malaysia. GCAPs are being prepared for the Malaysian cities of Kangar, Kulim Hi-Tech, Manjung, Teluk Intan, and Ipoh under the same reimbursable technical assistance.

**Blue economy development.** ADB is supporting the development of a BIMP-EAGA Blue Economy Strategy while strengthening collaboration with IMT-GT and ASEAN.

ADB conducted the Fostering Coastal Resilience and the Blue Economy Workshop in November 2023 and the BIMP-EAGA and IMT-GT Stakeholders Consultation Meeting in June 2024 on how to collaborate and develop a blue economy strategy. A High-Level Investor Forum on the New Ocean Energy Economy was organized in February 2023.

**Capacity building and knowledge sharing.** Through the BIMP-EAGA, IMT-GT, and GMS Capacity Building Program (B-I-G Program), 3,103 officials from BIMP-EAGA, IMT-GT, and GMS attended training and knowledge events covering ECDs, SEZs, integrated transport, tourism, project management, value management in projects, the Fourth Industrial Revolution, green cities, and big data and artificial intelligence solutions, smart tourism ecosystems, and coastal resilience. Nineteen virtual Policy Actions for COVID-19 Economic Recovery Dialogues were organized with 22 policy briefs produced and available on ADB's knowledge platform, DevAsia. A compendium of 13 policy briefs was produced in June 2021, with the second edition delivered at the BIMP-EAGA and IMT-GT summits in May 2023.

### *ADB support and investment in these initiatives*

**ADB's role.** ADB has served as regional development advisor in BIMP-EAGA since 2001 and has been IMT-GT's regional development partner since 2006, with similar finance and leadership functions. ADB plays various roles as (i) a financier, providing or mobilizing financial resources; (ii) a development partner, collaborating and working with various stakeholders; (iii) a knowledge provider, creating, consolidating, and disseminating knowledge on RCI and other development issues; (iv) a capacity builder, helping members better manage RCI; and (v) an honest broker, serving as a catalyst and facilitator. The BIMP-Facilitation Center is secretariat. The Centre for IMT-GT Subregional Cooperation serves as IMT-GT secretariat, based in Putrajaya, Malaysia.

**Technical Assistance**

**BIMP-EAGA.** As of 2024, ADB has provided 47 technical assistance (TA) projects to or involving BIMP-EAGA amounting to $70.3 million (with cofinancing, and with ADB supplying $30.4 million), and with select TA projects concurrently supporting IMT-GT. Only five of the 47 TA projects are active and focus on enhancing BIMP-EAGA and IMT-GT cooperation, smart and livable cities, transport connectivity, clean energy, health, and food security.

**IMT-GT.** As of August 2024, ADB has provided 32 TA projects totaling $39.57 million dedicated to or involving IMT-GT (and its members), with select TA projects concurrently providing support to BIMP-EAGA. Only 16 of the 32 TA projects are still ongoing, while the rest have been completed.

### *Some next steps to strengthen cooperation in Southeast Asia*

Strengthening links with other RCI initiatives is a key element of open regionalism. An important example is the GMS energy program's enhanced cooperation with ASEAN in energy-related initiatives, particularly the discussions on the ASEAN power grid aimed at deeper coordination on multilateral and regional power trade. The GMS Tourism Sector Strategy 2016–2025 also supports the ASEAN Tourism Strategic Plan 2016–2025. The GMS program coordinates and collaborates with the Mekong–Lancang Cooperation, Ayeyawady–Chao Phraya–Mekong Economic Cooperation Strategy, and the Cambodia–Lao PDR–Myanmar–Viet Nam Cooperation.

Implementing the new GMS innovation strategy will guide GMS cooperation over the next 5 years, with a focus on digitalization, the green transition, and connectivity across all priority sectors to promote more sustainability, growth, and inclusivity in the GMS.

**BIMP-EAGA.** ADB will continue supporting BIMP-EAGA initiatives, especially strategic refinements and key actions identified in the cooperative strategy report to accelerate the implementation of the remaining period of the BIMP-EAGA Vision 2025. ADB will continue ongoing assistance to develop a BIMP-EAGA Blue Economy Strategy 2030, and analytical work on its economic corridors. The blue economy strategy and economic corridor study are major summit deliverables in May 2025.

**IMT-GT.** ADB will continue to support key IMT-GT program initiatives under the IMT-GT Vision 2036 and the Implementation Blueprint 2022–2026. ADB helped develop the IMT-GT implementation blueprints, currently amid midterm reviews. ADB has an MOU with the Center for IMT-GT—a self-funded international organization by members—and the subregional secretariat.

## The Pacific

ADB recognizes the specific needs and challenges of the Pacific subregion and seeks a variety of ways to increase support for the regional public goods that generate shared benefits for participating countries. ADB's deep involvement in the Pacific subregion helps promote and strengthen RCI, which is also an operational priority of ADB's Strategy 2030 (ADB 2018). To foster RCI and to promote regional and/or global public goods—such as climate action, protection of shared natural resources, and health and education services—ADB works closely with existing regional institutions.

Regional cooperation is vital for addressing the diverse challenges faced by Pacific developing member countries (DMCs). Through collaboration, these countries can mitigate issues stemming from geographic isolation, small economies, and vulnerability to natural hazards and climate change. ADB has several key TA projects in the Pacific that emphasize regional collaboration to enhance knowledge sharing among Pacific DMCs.

Examples include the Pacific Region Infrastructure Facility (PRIF), the Pacific Financial and Technical Assistance Center, technical assistance (TA) for Pacific Economic Management, and the Private Sector Development Initiative (PSDI). These initiatives consolidate resources, including knowledge, technical expertise, and financial support, to address common challenges and develop solutions grounded in regional cooperation and mutual benefits.

### *Progress so far*

**Pacific Region Infrastructure Facility.** The initiatives proposed in the PRIF have effectively supported regional integration and private sector development. The phase 4 midterm review concluded that the PRIF performed well during the challenging COVID-19 period, demonstrating strong management and administration. Key stakeholders recognized an ongoing necessity for high-quality donor coordination and targeted technical assistance. PRIF's practical and targeted support to its members and its central role in coordinating regional development partner efforts were central. The coordination function had a significant impact on PRIF, as it brought together diverse partners who contributed their collective experience, knowledge, and financial resources to the region. PRIF's alignment with member and development partner priorities demonstrated a high degree of coherence without duplication. PRIF also effectively integrated cross-cutting themes, including climate change, disaster risk reduction, the environment, and gender equality and social inclusion. Overall, PRIF has served as an effective mechanism for coordinating and supporting infrastructure in the Pacific. It aligns with the knowledge needs and priorities of its members, as outlined in country knowledge plans and other relevant country or regional policies, strategies, and action plans.

**Technical Assistance for Pacific Economic Management (Phase 3).** ADB also supports the Pacific DMCs through the Pacific Economic Management Program, which strengthens the capacity for public sector management and economic policy formulation, including public financial management. These initiatives are important for Pacific DMCs to better prepare, plan for, and respond to economic shocks. Through this program, ADB is helping the Pacific subregion to use approaches specifically designed to cater to the needs of small island developing states and help them cope with challenges emanating from their vulnerability to external demand shocks and limited institutional capacity. Pacific economies have derived substantial benefits from policy and institutional reform advice, as well as improved economic modeling, as part of the Pacific Economic Management Technical Assistance. ADB has offered technical support to develop straightforward fiscal management models and has conducted capacity building for technical staff in selected Pacific DMCs—including the Cook Islands, the Federated States of Micronesia, Fiji, the Marshall Islands, Solomon Islands, Tonga, and Tuvalu. This assistance has enhanced the ability of policymakers to evaluate the long-term budget implications, thereby contributing to improved expenditure efficiency, enhanced budget planning, and better public service delivery.

**Private Sector Development Initiative.** The primary objective of PSDI is to reduce unnecessary costs of doing business in the Pacific subregion and help formalize and expand the private sector. This, in turn, generates employment opportunities, increases tax revenues, and contributes to poverty reduction. To do this, PSDI concentrates on five focal areas: (i) upgrade business legislation; (ii) cultivate financial markets and services to augment financial accessibility; (iii) overhaul state-owned enterprises and advocate public–private partnerships; (iv) institute effective competition and consumer protection; and (v) promote the economic empowerment of women.

Secured transaction frameworks have been established in 10 countries to make it easier for lenders to accept movable assets as collateral for loans. PDSI has supported the transformation of government-owned banks to better manage retirement funds. Online business registries in five countries have improved the business environment and facilitated new investments. State-owned enterprise reforms have doubled the profitability of their infrastructure portfolios in five countries. PSDI has strengthened competition and consumer protection safeguards in the Pacific DMCs. And they have helped women gain technical skills, establish formal businesses, access credit and markets, and compete for senior professional roles.

### *ADB support and investment in these initiatives*

**ADB works through PRIF to promote quality, climate, and socioeconomic resilient infrastructure.** PRIF is a multi-partner coordination and technical assistance facility established in 2008 to improve the quality and coverage of infrastructure and service delivery for its 14 Pacific member countries. PRIF is managed by the Pacific Region Infrastructure Coordination Office and is aligned with ADB's 2030 priority to foster regional cooperation and integration. A TA project continues to support PRIF for the 4-year period from 1 January 2024 until 31 December 2027. During this PRIF Phase 5, the PRIF coordination office will continue to support improving infrastructure quality and coverage with a new emphasis on infrastructure quality and greater climate and socioeconomic resilience. It also mainstreams cross-cutting themes—including gender equality and social inclusion, regional integration, private sector participation, and sustainable infrastructure management across all PRIF activities.

ADB has provided $3.0 million to support Phase V from November 2023 to December 2027, with cofinancing from the EU (€13.45 million,) Australia ($4.0 million), New Zealand ($3.0 million), and the US ($1.25 million). All cofinancing is administered by ADB.

**ADB has provided $1.5 million for capacity development and policy advice to help governments make better informed policy decisions.** High-level officials from economic agencies of Pacific DMCs have requested ADB for assistance to strengthen policy-oriented economic analyses. Knowledge and support technical assistance has been instrumental in providing support for macroeconomic stability, building analytical capacity, and developing more effective planning and forecasting models.

**PSDI—an ADB TA facility in partnership with the governments of Australia and New Zealand—has worked with Pacific DMCs since 2007 to improve the business environment.** PSDI provides advisory and capacity-building assistance on a holistic and enduring basis to achieve gender-inclusive, private-sector-led growth. PSDI is supporting business legal reforms, public–private partnerships, state-owned enterprise reforms, the economic empowerment of women, stronger consumer protection and competition policies, and improved access to finance for businesses and households. PSDI works to develop low-cost, inclusive business law systems and processes that suit the economy context while providing strong incentives for formalizing businesses, facilitating regulatory compliance, and increasing opportunities for business growth. PSDI works to improve the business environment by simplifying and modernizing laws to promote business growth in line with individual economy needs.

Three PSDI phases have been implemented since 2007, which have helped Pacific DMCs carry out reforms and introduce new policies to improve conditions for private sector development and investment. PSDI disbursed $60.8 million during its first three phases, funding more than 600 subprojects. This included $6.1 million funding from ADB, alongside grant cofinancing of $54.7 million from Australia ($49.8 million) and New Zealand ($4.9 million). For Phase IV which began on 1 January, 2020, ADB has committed $5.0 million until December 2024.

Major initiatives under PSDI aim to promote private business and support inclusive growth:

- In Papua New Guinea (PNG), PSDI helped implement a new online registry to streamline business registration processes. ADB, through PSDI, is committed to providing long-term support for a comprehensive business law reform program in PNG, with the goal of fostering entrepreneurship and attracting FDI.
- Similarly, in Palau, PSDI has contributed to the establishment of an online registry to align with the Corporations Law. In the Cook Islands, PSDI is engaged in planning an upgrade to the existing International Entities Register, which is over 9 years old. This upgrade aims to ensure compliance with international anti-money laundering and combating the financing of terrorism best practices and facilitate business expansion.
- In Kiribati, PSDI has supported initiatives for implementing laws, including finalizing specifications for Kiribati's inclusion on the regional registry.
- PSDI has also closely collaborated with the Fiji Development Bank as part of a regional support program, focusing on enhancing the operations of government-owned banks and fostering a more commercial orientation. In Fiji, PSDI successfully assisted the central bank in introducing a capital projections model.

**To enhance connectivity, ADB has supported PNG, the leading economy in the Pacific subregion.**

ADB has provided $213 million, with counterpart funding of $27 million for the PNG Civil Aviation Development Investment Program. ADB has provided transaction advisory services for a public–private partnership that will enable PNG's National Airports Corporation to select a concessionaire to develop a new international passenger terminal at Jacksons International Airport in Port Moresby. The new terminal will be capable of meeting passenger demand for the next 30 years. The investment program has assisted existing infrastructure to improve airport operations.

## *Some next steps to strengthen cooperation in the Pacific*

Given the unique development challenges facing Pacific DMCs—whether large distances from global markets, high transportation costs, heavy dependence on imports, poor connectivity, vulnerability to shocks, and less diversified economic base—as described above, only limited progress has been made. Working closely with Pacific DMCs, ADB has contributed to improving infrastructure, the business environment, and provided analytical support through knowledge products. Capacity constraints in economic analysis and policymaking remain a key concern that needs to be addressed through further support, particularly in smaller DMCs where there is a shortage and high turnover of technically qualified economic staff. TA projects are also required to help with analytical work to sustain growth and enhance resilience. ADB work through policy-based operations often requires technical support (coordinated with development partners) to lay the groundwork for policy actions and to preserve reform momentum. Therefore, sustained effort is needed to build capacity and promote constructive policymaking and institutional changes in Pacific DMCs.

Special emphasis needs to be given to the development of robust data needed to provide indicators in strategic areas such as digital connectivity, climate change, and private sector development. ADB will continue to provide advice and technical assistance to support business-friendly policies and legal reforms as well as transaction advisory services to help Pacific DMCs mobilize private sector investment and public–private partnerships.

Given the unique development challenges facing Pacific DMCs, measuring the impact and progress of RCI development in the Pacific should consider these development constraints, using more flexible and tailored approaches to better understand the relevance and scope of RCI across the subregion.

## ADB Investments in Regional Cooperation and Integration

ADB has long supported the RCI approach to development, growth, and recovery. That is because RCI leads to shared economic benefits such as closer trade, more efficient intraregional supply chains, stronger financial interconnectedness, and more coordinated responses to challenges. Through RCI, economies in the region can collectively and more effectively address cross-border challenges such as climate change, pandemics like COVID-19, and financial shocks. RCI also helps economies wield more influence as they participate in regional and global policy discussions. Reaching agreement on common challenges also means Asian economies can speak with a unified voice, making a greater global impact, commensurate with the region's growing economic strength.

Since 2000, ADB has committed to 2,430 RCI projects amounting to $87.155 billion. Prior to the COVID-19 pandemic, ADB's RCI projects traditionally focused on transport (24%) and public sector management (23%) in terms of number of projects, and on transport (60%) and energy (17%) sectors in the amount of committed investment (Figure 1.10).

During the pandemic years of 2020–2021, while transport projects were still large in number, RCI investments in public sector management surged as economies availed of ADB's COVID-19 Active Response and Expenditure Support Program, and health investments soared as ADB provided funds to support expanded vaccination programs. Transport and public sector management projects continued to dominate RCI commitments from 2022 onward as economies pursued recovery programs to rise above the challenges left by the pandemic. Though RCI investments seem to have moderated in 2024, settling at about $2.1 billion, it may not be like that for long. RCI projects will pick up steam as Asian economies recognize the public good nature of RCI initiatives in trade, connectivity, digital transformation, and other areas, particularly to achieve sustainable and resilient outcomes.

**Figure 1.10: ADB Commitments in Regional Cooperation and Integration, by Sector**

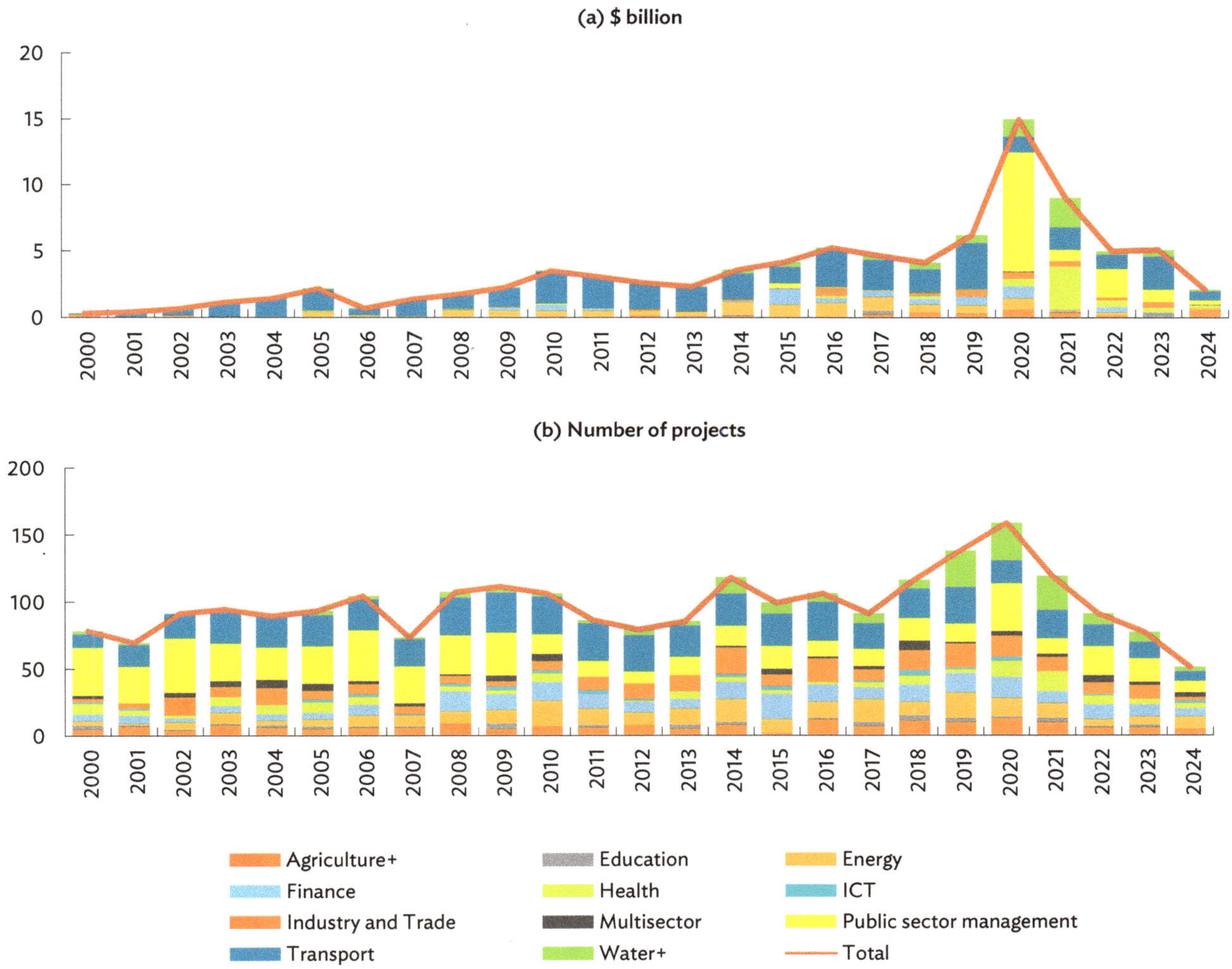


ADB = Asian Development Bank; Agriculture+ = Agriculture, natural resources and rural development; ICT = information and communication technology; Water+ = Water and other urban infrastructure and services.

Source: ADB Regional Cooperation and Integration dashboard.

## References

Albis, M., M. C. Tayag, and J. W. Kang. 2023. Estimating Regional Integration Using the Bayesian State-Space Approach. *ADB Economics Working Paper Series.* No. 712. Asian Development Bank.

Asian Development Bank (ADB). 2018. *ADB Strategy 2030: Achieving a Prosperous, Inclusive, Resilient, and Sustainable Asia and the Pacific.*

———. 2023. *Measuring Globalization: Framework, Analysis, and Implications.*

Brunei Darussalam–Indonesia–Malaysia–Philippines East ASEAN Growth Area (BIMP-EAGA). 2023. *Accelerating Cooperation Together (ACT) BIMP-EAGA Vision 2025 Midterm Review: Progress and Prospects.*

Central Asia Regional Economic Cooperation (CAREC) Program. CAREC Project Portfolio. https://www.carecprogram.org/projects/portfolio (accessed January 2025).

Chan, J., G. Koop, D. J. Poirier, and J. L. Tobias. 2019. *Bayesian Econometric Methods.* Cambridge University Press.

Clarivate. 2024. *Web of Science Platform.* https://clarivate.com/academia-government/scientific-and-academic-research/research-discovery-and-referencing/web-of-science/ (accessed July 2024).

Huh, H. S. and C. Y. Park. 2021. A New Index of Globalization: Measuring Impacts of Integration on Economic Growth and Income Inequality. *The World Economy.* 44 (2). pp. 409–443.

International Telecommunication Union. Statistics. https://www.itu.int/en/ITU-D/Statistics/Pages/stat (accessed July 2024).

Koop, G. 2003. *Bayesian Econometrics.* Wiley.

Rayp, G. and S. Standaert. 2017. Measuring Actual Economic Integration: A Bayesian State-Space Approach. In P. Lombarde and E. S. Acosta, eds. *Indicator-Based Monitoring of Regional Economic Integration.* pp. 341–360. Springer.

United Nations. UN Comtrade Database. https://comtrade.un.org (accessed September 2024).

# Annex 1a: ADB's Bilateral Economic Integration Index—Economy and Regional Coverage

| Regions/Subregions | Individual Economy (retained) | "All Others" (aggregated) |
|---|---|---|
| Central Asia (7) | Azerbaijan<br>Kazakhstan<br>Kyrgyz Republic<br>Uzbekistan | Armenia<br>Georgia<br>Tajikistan |
| East Asia (6) | Hong Kong, China<br>Japan<br>Mongolia<br>People's Republic of China<br>Republic of Korea<br>Taipei,China | |
| South Asia (6) | Bangladesh<br>India<br>Pakistan<br>Sri Lanka | Maldives<br>Nepal |
| Southeast Asia (10) | Indonesia<br>Malaysia<br>Philippines<br>Singapore<br>Thailand<br>Viet Nam | Brunei Darussalam<br>Cambodia<br>Lao People's Democratic Republic<br>Timor-Leste |
| Pacific (4) | Fiji<br>Papua New Guinea | Samoa<br>Vanuatu |
| Oceania (2) | Australia<br>New Zealand | |
| EU+UK (28) | Austria<br>Belgium<br>Czechia<br>Denmark<br>Finland<br>France<br>Germany<br>Greece<br>Ireland<br>Italy<br>Netherlands<br>Poland<br>Portugal<br>Romania<br>Spain<br>Sweden<br>United Kingdom | Bulgaria<br>Croatia<br>Cyprus<br>Estonia<br>Hungary<br>Latvia<br>Lithuania<br>Luxembourg<br>Malta<br>Slovakia<br>Slovenia |
| North America (2) | Canada<br>United States | |

*continued on next page*

*Annex 1a continued*

| Regions/Subregions | Individual Economy (retained) | "All Others" (aggregated) |
|---|---|---|
| Caribbean (13) | Cuba<br>Puerto Rico | Antigua and Barbuda<br>Aruba<br>Bahamas<br>Barbados<br>Belize<br>Cayman Islands<br>Dominican Republic<br>Guyana<br>Jamaica<br>Saint Kitts and Nevis<br>Trinidad and Tobago |
| Central America (7) | Costa Rica<br>Guatemala<br>Mexico | El Salvador<br>Honduras<br>Nicaragua<br>Panama |
| South America (10) | Argentina<br>Brazil<br>Colombia | Bolivia<br>Chile<br>Ecuador<br>Paraguay<br>Peru<br>Uruguay<br>Venezuela |
| Central and West Africa (17) | Ghana<br>Nigeria | Benin<br>Burkina Faso<br>Cabo Verde<br>Cameroon<br>Congo<br>Cote d'Ivoire<br>Gabon<br>Gambia<br>Guinea<br>Liberia<br>Mali<br>Niger<br>Senegal<br>Sierra Leone<br>Togo |
| Eastern Africa (9) | Ethiopia<br>Kenya | Djibouti<br>Madagascar<br>Mauritius<br>Rwanda<br>Seychelles<br>Sudan<br>Uganda |
| Northern Africa (5) | Algeria<br>Egypt | Libya<br>Morocco<br>Tunisia |
| Southern Africa (10) | Angola<br>South Africa | Botswana<br>Eswatini<br>Lesotho<br>Malawi<br>Mozambique<br>Namibia<br>Zambia<br>Zimbabwe |

*continued on next page*

*Annex 1a continued*

| Regions/Subregions | Individual Economy (retained) | "All Others" (aggregated) |
|---|---|---|
| Rest of the World (27) | Russian Federation | Albania<br>Bahrain<br>Belarus<br>Bermuda<br>Bosnia and Herzegovina<br>Iceland<br>Iran<br>Iraq<br>Israel<br>Jordan<br>Kuwait<br>Lebanon<br>Macau, China<br>Moldova<br>Montenegro<br>Norway<br>Oman<br>Qatar<br>Saudi Arabia<br>Serbia<br>Switzerland<br>Syrian Arab Republic<br>Türkiye<br>Ukraine<br>United Arab Emirates<br>Yemen |

Source: ADB compilation based on Albis, Tayag, and Kang (2023).

# 2 Trade and Global Value Chains

## Introduction

**While the deepening of regional integration is due in part to the region's multiplying trade agreements, the proliferation of overlapping trade agreements has introduced challenges for implementation and created complexity for businesses.**

Economies in Asia and the Pacific have engaged in extensive regional cooperation and integration over the past few decades.[12] These efforts have included broad economic cooperation programs, the largest being the Association of Southeast Asian Nations (ASEAN), Central Asia Regional Economic Cooperation (CAREC), the Greater Mekong Subregion (GMS), and the South Asian Association for Regional Cooperation (SAARC). Such programs have improved cooperation in several areas, including in private sector development, environmental sustainability and protection, and disaster planning and management. They have helped build the infrastructure, institutions, and capabilities to facilitate increased cross-border trade.

Despite these efforts, the major form of trade liberalization in the region over the past 3 decades has been the rise of bilateral and regional preferential trade agreements (PTAs). According to the World Bank's Deep Trade Agreements database, there were just four intra-Asian PTAs in 1990, with Asian economies engaged in a further three trade agreements with non-Asian economies. These tended to be partial scope plurilateral agreements, with the main intra-Asian agreements being the Asia-Pacific Trade Agreement and the South Pacific Regional Trade and Economic Cooperation Agreement. Extra-Asian agreements included agreements among a larger number of developing economies, including the Protocol on Trade Negotiations and the Global System of Trade Preferences among a larger number of developing economies. By 2023, intra-Asian agreements had risen to 77 in number. Agreements with non-Asian economies (extra-Asian agreements, hereafter) increased to 104, reflecting efforts to establish links with global export markets. Agreements involving Asian economies thus accounted for 45% of the 399 agreements in the Deep Trade Agreements database.

While the set of drivers of this increase in PTAs is broad, including aspects related to the perceived and observed benefits of trade for economic development and the rise of global value chains (GVCs) that often require a higher degree of policy coordination and certainty, the slow progress in multilateral negotiations to liberalize trade has been important in the rising trend of PTAs both in Asia and globally. The presence of an increasing set of overlapping trade agreements with different provisions creates confusion and a risk of uncertainty for firms in identifying the most appropriate ways of serving markets and sourcing inputs, which in the extreme can limit the trade-creation benefits of agreements. For policymakers, it also creates challenges in implementing overlapping agreements and negotiating new agreements.

12 Asia refers to the 49 members of ADB in Asia and the Pacific, which include Australia, Japan, and New Zealand in addition to 46 developing economies.

This chapter takes stock of Asia's activity in developing trade agreements over the past 3 decades. The chapter takes a comparative perspective in considering the number, size, and provisions within Asian trade agreements relative to trade agreements between non-Asian economies. It also examines the drivers of Asian trade agreements and estimates their impact on trade within the region.

## The Evolving Nature of Preferential Trade Agreements

### The rise in PTAs is largely driven by free trade agreements, reflecting a shift toward bilateral and regional liberalization.

The number of PTAs has increased rapidly since the 1990s. While trade liberalization proceeded either unilaterally or multilaterally under the auspices of the General Agreement on Tariffs and Trade prior to the 1990s, the focus shifted toward bilateral, plurilateral, and regional trade agreements in the 1990s. This reflected concerns over the impact of unilateral liberalization on inclusive development, a lack of progress in multilateral trade negotiations, and the rise of GVCs that called for increased coordination of activity across GVC partner economies. According to World Bank data, over 1990–2023 the number of PTAs increased from 21 to 399 (Figure 2.1).[13] Over this period the share of agreements that are intra-Asian have risen from around 15% to 19%, with the share of extra-Asian PTAs increasing from 12% to 26%.[14]

A simple count of the number of PTAs can be misleading. Trade agreements differ in their ambition to reduce trade barriers, with partial scope agreements (PSAs) reducing tariffs on a specific group of products and free trade agreements (FTAs) eliminating tariffs in most sectors. In each case, members retain independent trade policies, with a deeper form of agreement being a customs union that harmonizes trade policy and imposes a common external tariff. Economic integration agreements (EIAs) introduce additional forms of liberalization, including of services.

**Figure 2.1: Developments in the Number of Preferential Trade Agreements**

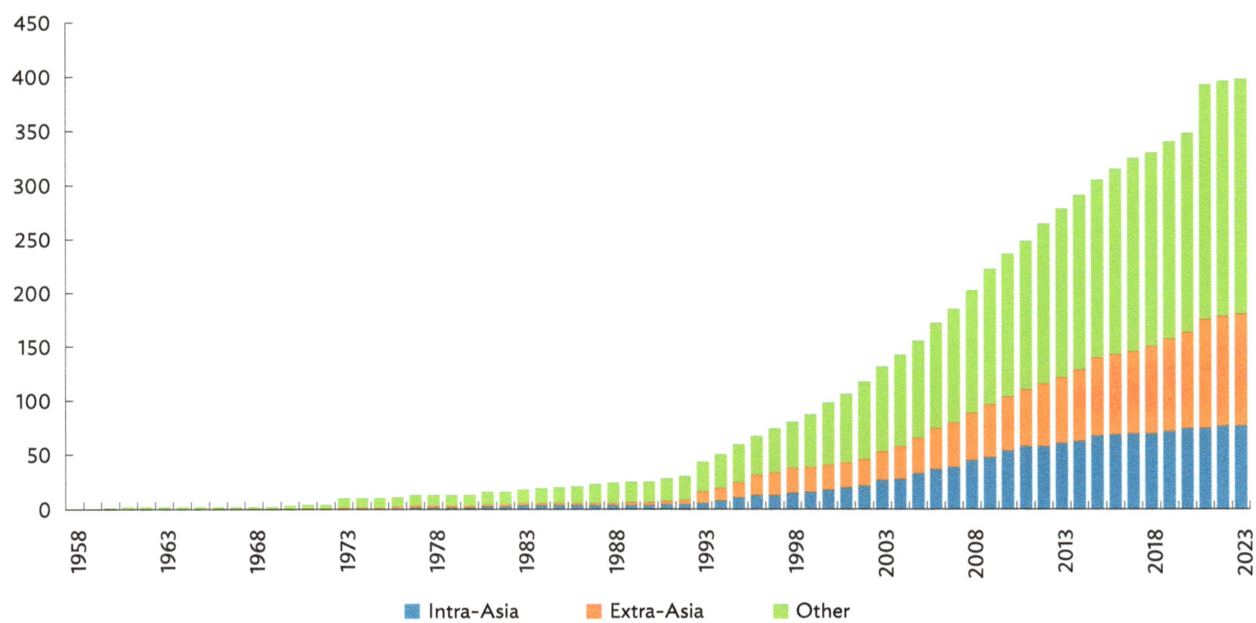


Source: ADB calculations using World Bank. Deep Trade Agreements Database. https://datatopics.worldbank.org/dta/table.html (accessed August 2024).

---

13 The World Bank's Deep Trade Agreements database lists 400 trade agreements, but 399 are in force.

14 Intra-Asian agreements are defined as agreements that involve only ADB regional member economies, while extra-Asian agreements include at least one ADB regional member and at least one economy that is not an ADB regional member.

Most trade agreements (84%) in force at the end of 2023 were either FTAs (36%) or combined FTAs and EIAs (48%). Customs unions (with or without EIAs) accounted for about 8% of agreements, with PSAs accounting for about 7% and pure EIAs less than 1%. Agreements signed between Asian economies tend to involve FTAs (22%) or combined FTAs and EIAs (64%), with PSAs accounting for about 13% of agreements (Figure 2.2). Compared with agreements signed between Asian and non-Asian economies or between economies outside of Asia, intra-Asian agreements show a higher share of PSAs and of combined FTAs and EIAs, with lower shares of customs unions and EIAs. Although the depth of commitments can also vary substantially within a given type of agreement, such figures provide an initial suggestion that PTAs in Asia are different to those elsewhere, with a higher share of agreements that are less ambitious in the degree of liberalization and coordination.

**Figure 2.2: Depth of Intra-Asian, Extra-Asian, and Other Trade Agreements**

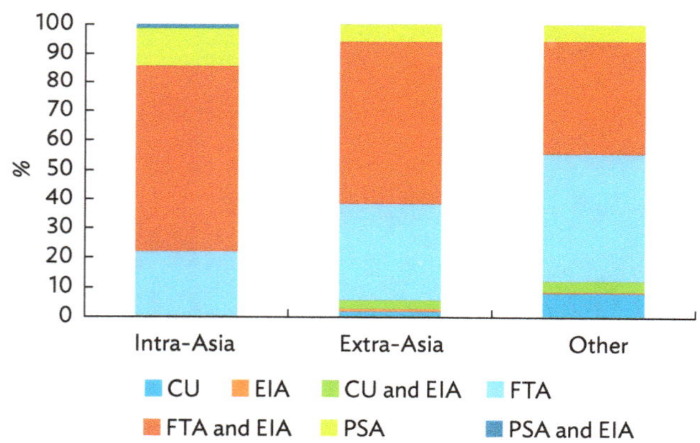


CU = customs union, EIA = economic integration agreement, FTA = free trade agreement, PSA = partial scope agreement.

Source: ADB calculations using World Bank. Deep Trade Agreements Database. https://datatopics.worldbank.org/dta/table.html (accessed August 2024).

Beyond different ambitions on the extent of liberalization, PTAs also differ in the provisions included. Whereas early agreements tended to focus on the liberalization of tariff and nontariff barriers, particularly in industry and, to a lesser extent, agriculture over the past decades the number of provisions included in agreements has increased. Many of these provisions are targeted at reducing trade costs, either at or behind the border, while others have more ambiguous effects on trade costs. Provisions introduced into trade agreements include those related to intellectual property, technology transfer, the environment, energy, labor markets, and investment, among others. Considering the range of provisions to capture the breadth of PTAs, the evidence suggests that PTAs have become broader since the 1990s. Using both a broad and a narrower measure of provisions in trade agreements it can be observed that since the 1990s the average number of provisions included in new trade agreements has increased (Figure 2.3).[15]

## PTAs in Asia tend to include fewer provisions and less ambitious commitments than agreements involving non-Asian economies.

In 2022, and using the broad definition of trade agreement provisions, intra-Asian agreements included around 28% of the 52 provisions while extra-Asian agreements included around 35% (Figure 2.4). In contrast, this share was around 39% for agreements signed between non-Asian economies. This gap has decreased over time, however. In 1990, intra-Asian and extra-Asian agreements included 19% and 20% of the 52 provisions, with agreements between non-Asian economies including 31% of provisions.

Differences in the breadth of intra-Asian and extra-Asian agreements and others remain even after controlling for the income of trade partners and the geographic distance between them. Estimating the association between the number of provisions in PTAs and explanatory factors, including average income per capita, distance between trade partners, and geographic scope, suggests that trade agreements involving Asian economies are significantly narrower than other trade agreements (Figure 2.5). Specifically, the analysis suggests that holding the (average) level of GDP per capita and distance between trade partners constant, an intra-Asian agreement would be expected to include 17% fewer of the 52 provisions and 10% fewer of the

[15] The broad measure includes the 52 provisions identified by Hofmann, Osnago, and Ruta (2017). The narrow measure includes 18 provisions that define a set of market rules for the smooth functioning of global value chains (Hofmann, Osnago, and Ruta 2017).

**Figure 2.3: Average Number of Preferential Trade Agreement Provisions in New Trade Agreements**

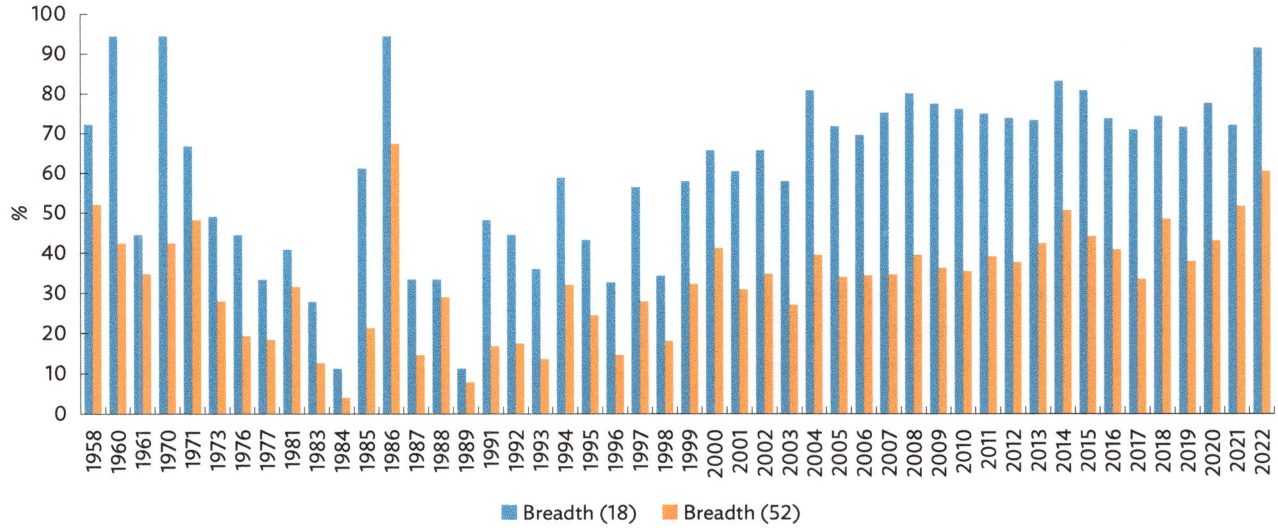


Notes: The left-hand axis refers to the share to the maximum number of provisions. The orange bars refer to the broad measure which includes the 52 provisions. The blue bars refer to a more streamlined 18 provisions that define a set of market rules for the smooth functioning of global value chains.

Source: ADB calculations using World Bank. Deep Trade Agreements Database. https://datatopics.worldbank.org/dta/table.html (accessed August 2024).

**Figure 2.4: Average Share of 52 Provisions in Cumulative Trade Agreements for Asian and Non-Asian Trade Agreements**

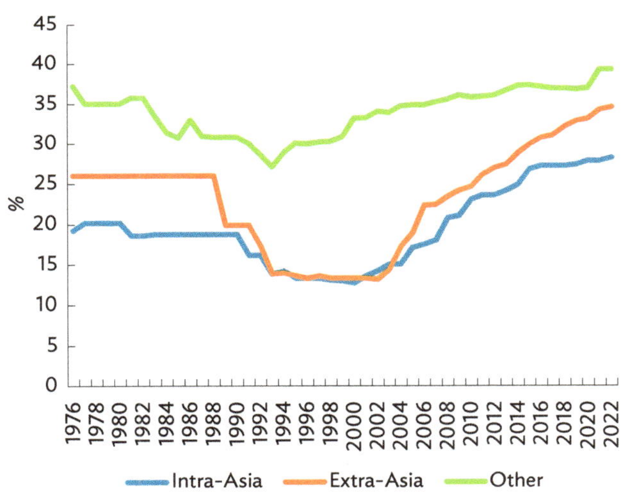


Source: ADB calculations using data from World Bank. Deep Trade Agreements Database. https://datatopics.worldbank.org/dta/table.html (accessed August 2024).

**Figure 2.5: Estimated Association Between the Breadth of Trade Agreements and Potential Determinants**

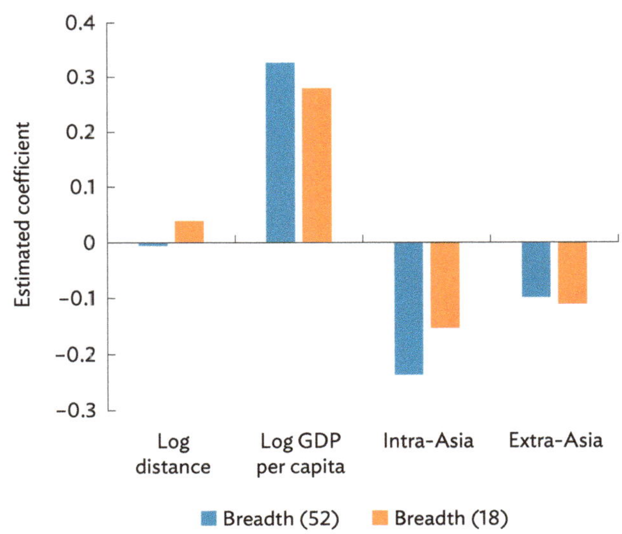


GDP = gross domestic product, log = logarithm.

Notes: The figure reports the estimated coefficients from a regression with the number of provisions in preferential trade agreements as the dependent variable and the log of distance and GDP per capita, a variable capturing whether the agreement is an intra-Asian agreement and a variable capturing whether the agreement is extra-Asian as explanatory variables.

Source: ADB calculations using data from World Bank. Deep Trade Agreements Database. https://datatopics.worldbank.org/dta/table.html (accessed August 2024).

18 provisions in PTAs relative to agreements signed between non-Asian economies. For extra-Asian agreements results suggest that they have 10% fewer of the 52 provisions and 11% fewer of the 18 provisions relative to agreements signed between nonmembers. The analysis further indicates that a higher average per

capita GDP of PTA partners is associated with a broader trade agreement, while the average distance between trade partners has no significant association.

Despite intra-Asian agreements being narrower than agreements signed elsewhere, some provisions are more likely to appear in intra-Asian agreements. Using a similar set of explanatory variables and estimating the likelihood of a particular provision appearing in a PTA, it can be observed that some provisions are more likely to appear in intra-Asian agreements than in agreements signed between non-Asian economies (Figure 2.6). These differences are statistically significant for trade-related investment measures, visa and asylum, investment, education and training, and consumer protection.[16]

For 37 (out of 52) provisions, there is a lower probability of these provisions appearing in intra-Asian agreements than those between non-Asian economies.[17] The pattern for extra-Asian agreements shows some similarities to intra-Asian agreements, but also notable differences. Provisions on regional cooperation, anticorruption, and energy are substantially less likely to be included in extra-Asian agreements when compared with intra-Asian agreements. Conversely, extra-Asian agreements are more likely to include provisions on industrial cooperation, health, trade-related aspects of intellectual property rights, research and technology, the movement of capital, innovation policies, cultural cooperation, public administration, environmental laws, and labor market regulations.

**Figure 2.6: Estimated Association Between the Presence of Preferential Trade Agreement Provisions and the Geographic Scope of the Agreement**

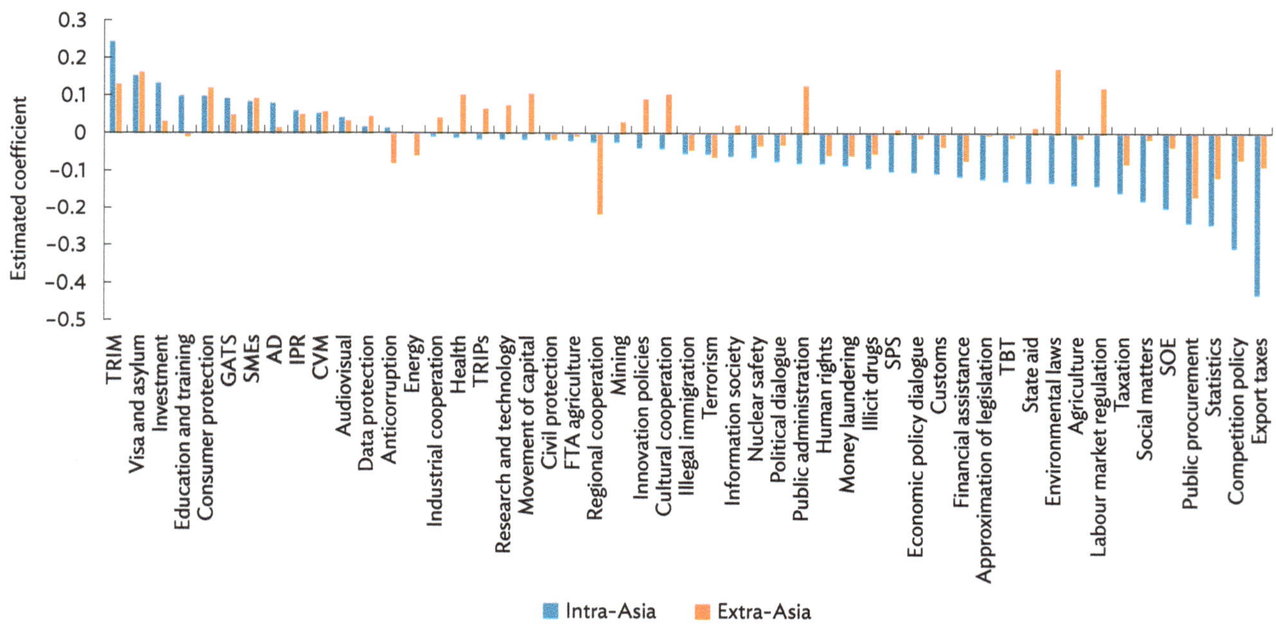


AD = antidumping measures, CVM = countervailing measure, FTA = free trade agreement, GATS = General Agreement on Trade in Services, IPR = intellectual property rights, SMEs = small and medium-sized enterprises, SOE = state-owned enterprise, SPS = sanitary and phytosanitary standards, TBT = technical barrier to trade, TRIM = trade-related investment measure, TRIP = trade-related aspect of intellectual property rights.

Notes: The figure reports the estimated coefficients from a regression with the dependent variable capturing the presence of a particular provision in a trade and the log of distance and gross domestic product per capita, a variable capturing whether the agreement is an intra-Asian agreement and a variable capturing whether the agreement is extra-Asian as explanatory variables.

Source: ADB calculations using World Bank. Deep Trade Agreements Database. https://datatopics.worldbank.org/dta/table.html (accessed August 2024).

[16] Results suggest that provisions on the General Agreement on Trade in Services, small and medium-sized enterprises (SMEs), antidumping duties, intellectual property rights, countervailing measures, audiovisual, data protection, and anticorruption and energy provisions are also more likely to appear in intra-Asian agreements than in those signed by non-Asian economies, but these differences are not statistically significant.

[17] Of these, 24 of the estimated coefficients are statistically significant at the 10% level or better.

## Intra-Asian agreements have fewer preferential and nondiscriminatory provisions and tend to include fewer members than agreements among non-Asian economies.

Distinguishing between provisions in trade agreements that are preferential to agreement partners and those that are nondiscriminatory suggests that both intra-Asian and extra-Asian agreements have fewer of both sets of provisions relative to agreements between non-Asian economies. In general, agreements tend to include a higher share of the available preferential provisions, with this being as high as 85% in 2022 for non-Asian agreements (Figure 2.7a). For intra-Asian agreements this share was 70%, while for extra-Asian agreements the share was 78%. For nondiscriminatory provisions, the shares were similar for extra-Asian (67%) and other (69%) agreements, but somewhat lower for intra-Asian agreements (57%). Such results provide initial evidence suggesting that the construction of trade agreements within Asia does not necessarily facilitate open regionalism through the inclusion of provisions that can have a more general liberalizing effect.

The average number of trade partners in PTAs increased steadily for intra-Asian agreements, rising from 3.6 in 1990–2004 to 4.4 in the 2015–2023 period (Figure 2.7b). In contrast, the number of partners in extra-Asian agreements increased from 2.4 members in 1990–2004 to 7.5 in 2015–2023. For agreements between non-Asian economies, the average number dropped from 8.2 in 1990–2004 to 7.6 in 2015–2023. While this difference between intra-Asian agreements and the rest is expected since there are fewer potential partners within Asia than with the rest of the world, these figures highlight a further difference between intra-Asian agreements and those signed elsewhere. One reason for this is the large number of bilateral agreements that have been signed within Asia. In 2022, 75% of all intra-Asian agreements were pure bilateral agreements, a share that rose from 60% in 1991 (Figure 2.8). This compares with a share of 57% for all agreements in the database.

**Figure 2.7: Share of Preferential and Nondiscriminatory Provisions in Trade Agreements, 2022**

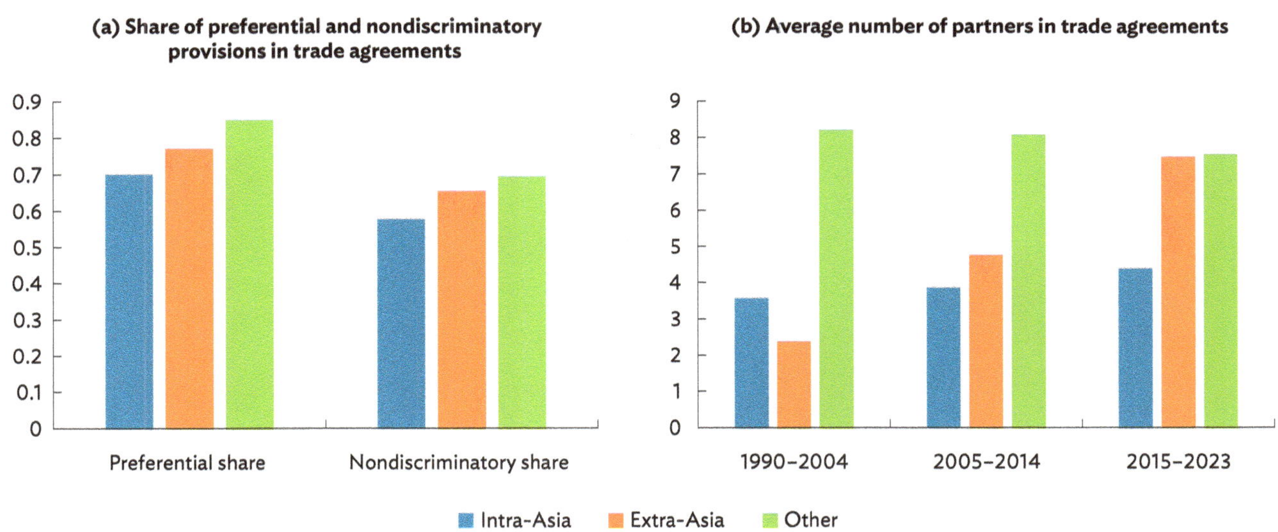


Notes: Preferential provisions include free trade arrangements for agriculture, free trade arrangements for industry, export taxes, anti-dumping, countervailing measures, and public procurement, while nondiscriminatory provisions are customs, sanitary and phytosanitary standards, technical barriers to trade, state aid, trade-related investment measures, general agreement on trade in services, trade-related aspects of intellectual property rights, competition policy, investment, and the movement of capital (see Falvey and Foster-McGregor 2022).

Source: ADB calculations using data from World Bank. Deep Trade Agreements Database. https://datatopics.worldbank.org/dta/table.html (accessed August 2024).

**Figure 2.8: Bilateral Versus Plurilateral Trade Agreements in Asia and the Pacific**

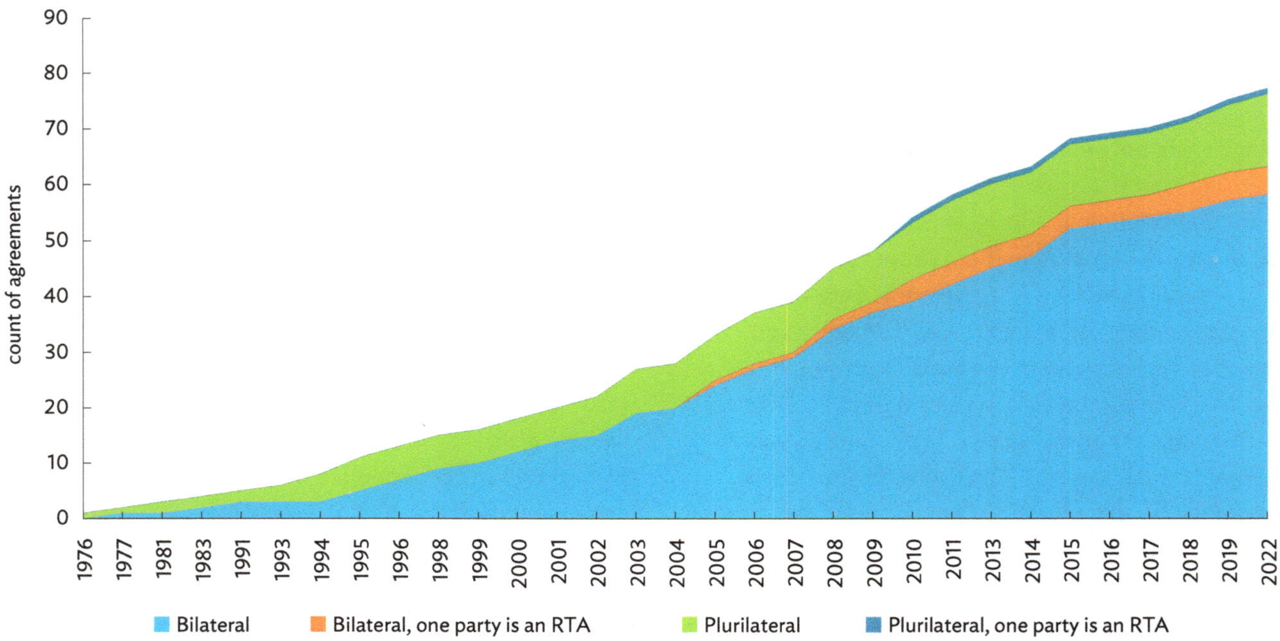


RTA = regional trade agreement.

Source: ADB calculations using data from World Bank. Deep Trade Agreements Database. https://datatopics.worldbank.org/dta/table.html (accessed August 2024).

**The increasing inclusion of services, investment, and other policy areas in intra-Asian PTAs highlights a shift toward broader economic integration, though limited commitments in goods-related provisions may constrain their impact on trade flows and regional value chains.**

Figure 2.9 reports information on the share of trade agreements that cover services, further considering this share over time and by regional focus. Across time and agreements, around 65% of agreements cover services, though this hides variation across time and regions. Prior to 2000, few agreements included services. This changed in the new millennium, with 59% of agreements signed in the 2000s covering services, and 65% of agreements since 2010. Since 2000, the share of new intra-Asian and extra-Asian agreements including services has been higher than the share in agreements signed elsewhere. For intra-Asian agreements, the shares were 71% for 2000–2010 and 91% for 2011–2024, while for extra-Asian the corresponding shares were 74% and 78%. This contrasts with shares of 49% and 51% for agreements signed outside Asia.

**Figure 2.9: Share of Agreements with Services** (%)

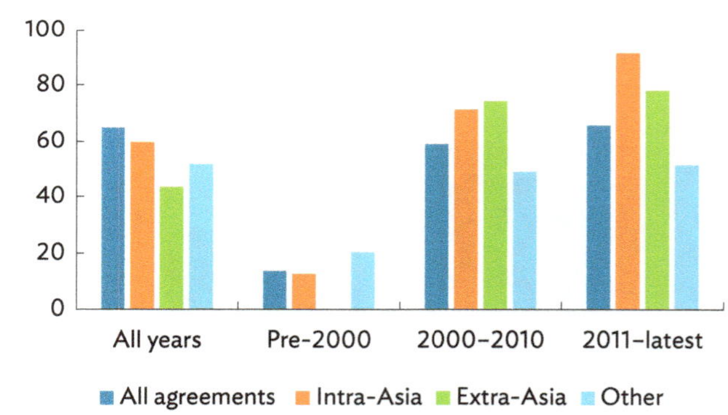


Source: ADB calculations using data from World Bank. Deep Trade Agreements Database. https://datatopics.worldbank.org/dta/table.html (accessed August 2024).

Figure 2.10 details the depth of PTAs throughout various policy areas. In comparison to agreements between non-Asian economies, intra-Asian agreements (blue bars) are likely to be deeper in the areas of investment, movement of capital, services, and visa and asylum. Comparing between PTAs that involve at least one regional economy (that is, intra- versus extra-Asian agreements), labor market regulations, public procurement, competition policy, export restrictions, and intellectual property are, on average, deeper in extra-Asian agreements (orange bars).

**Figure 2.10: Estimated Association Between the Depth of Preferential Trade Agreement Provisions and the Geographic Scope of the Agreement**

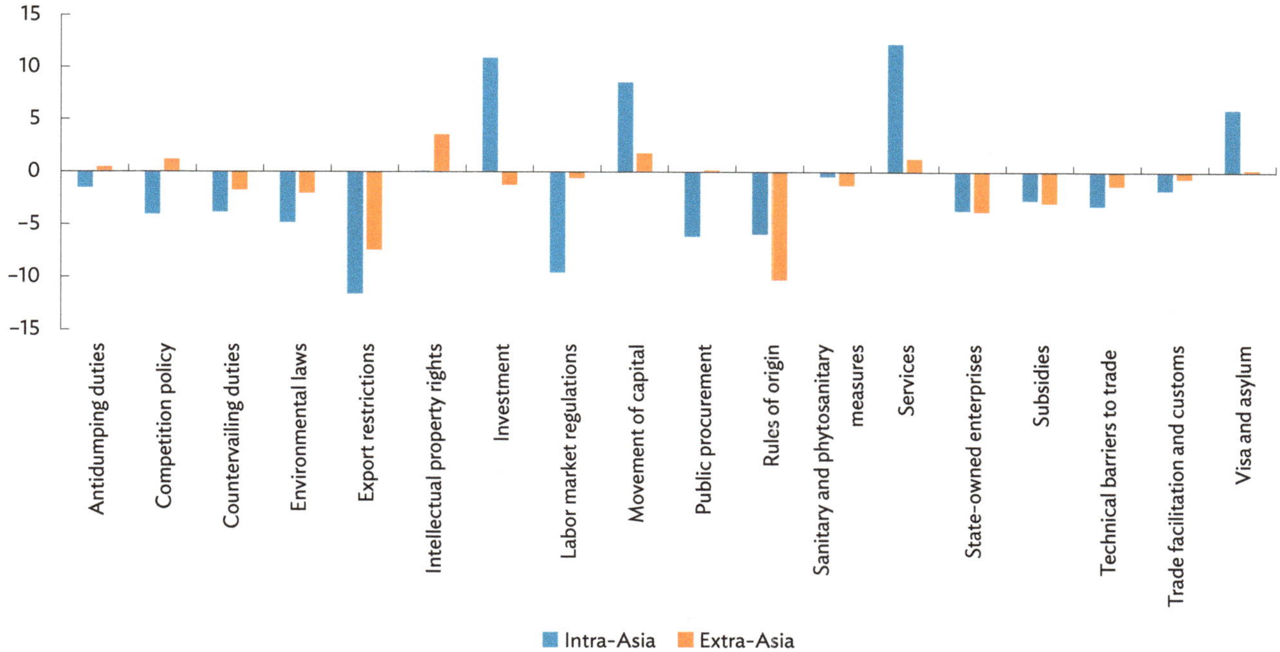


Source: ADB calculations using data from World Bank. Deep Trade Agreements Database. https://datatopics.worldbank.org/dta/table.html (accessed August 2024).

While the emphasis on services and investment liberalization signals an interest in expanding trade beyond goods, it may also require regulatory reforms and the application of higher standards that could be challenging for some member economies to meet, potentially affecting trade flows.

Both intra- and extra-Asian agreements show relatively shallower commitments in areas directly tied to market access for trade in goods, such as rules of origin and export restrictions, technical barriers to trade, and trade facilitation. These provisions are essential to foster regional value chains, ensuring that goods, whether final products or intermediates, can move across borders efficiently, with reduced costs and minimal regulatory hurdles. These linkages illustrate the strategic importance of PTAs, not only as tools for market access but also as frameworks that support regional sourcing networks essential for Asia's participation in global value chains (Box 2.1). However, the lower commitments in goods-related areas may limit the positive impact of PTAs on trade flows.

## Recent Drivers of Preferential Trade Agreements

### Trade relations both within Asia and beyond the region continue to expand and flourish through the creation of new preferential trade agreements.

Six trade agreements that include at least one Asian economy entered into force in 2024 (Figure 2.11 and Table 2.1). The Philippines–Republic of Korea FTA entered into force on 31 December. Under the agreement, tariffs on approximately 95% of items traded between the economies shall be removed. The FTA also includes a comprehensive chapter on economic and technical cooperation.

Three PTAs for the People's Republic of China (PRC) also entered into force throughout 2024, with Serbia, Nicaragua, and Ecuador. The agreement with Serbia aims to exempt about 90% of products traded between the PRC, where 60% of products will immediately benefit from

## Box 2.1: Developments in Regional Value Chain Integration

Regional value chains (RVCs) refer to production sharing activities that take place within a specific geographical region rather than globally. RVCs offer opportunities for economies to climb up value chains by using the region to boost competitiveness and move to higher value-added activities. The increased prosperity within Asia means that RVCs have a strong potential to contribute to this upgrading and competitiveness. RVCs also offer other potential benefits, including the possibility of creating more resilient value chains by shortening and reducing the complexity of value chains. To examine the relative importance of regional versus global value chain (GVC) integration, box figure 1 reports information on the share of overall GVC activity that takes place within RVCs in Asia. The approach adopts a definition of an RVC as production that takes place wholly among ADB regional members.

Many economies are heavily reliant on RVCs for their backward integration in GVCs, with Bhutan, Cambodia, the Lao People's Democratic Republic (Lao PDR), Malaysia, Nepal, the Philippines, and Viet Nam all having RVC shares above 70% (box figure 1). In contrast the People's Republic of China (PRC), India, and Kazakhstan have RVC shares below 40%. A similar range of values is reported for forward GVC linkages, with Bhutan, Brunei Darussalam, Indonesia, the Lao PDR, Malaysia, and Mongolia reporting RVC shares above 70% and Bangladesh, India, Kazakhstan, the Kyrgyz Republic, Maldives, Pakistan, and Sri Lanka reporting shares below 40%. Such patterns suggest that economies with a high RVC share in backward linkages also tend to have a high share in forward linkages, with this confirmed by a positive Spearman rank correlation of 0.47. Despite this, there are also examples of economies that show large differences in the RVC share for forward and backward linkages. Backward RVC shares tend to be substantially larger than forward RVC shares in the Kyrgyz Republic, Maldives, Sri Lanka, and Viet Nam with the reverse being the case in Australia, Brunei Darussalam, Japan, and Mongolia.

The values of RVC integration in 2023 present a snapshot of the extent of RVC integration, but changes over time have been substantial in many cases. Box figure 2 reports on changes in the RVC shares of forward and backward linkages between 2000 and 2023. It is notable that in most cases RVC integration in both forward and backward linkages increased. The average change in the RVC indicator was somewhat higher for forward linkages (0.15) than backward linkages (0.12), suggesting that the regionalization of value chains in Asia has been faster for forward linkages. There are a couple of exceptions, with Viet Nam seeing a decline in its forward RVC integration and Fiji in both backward and forward linkages. The PRC also represents an interesting example, seeing an increase in forward RVC share and a decline in backward RVC share. Such an outcome is consistent with the idea that the PRC has become a more important supplier of intermediate goods for regional partners but less reliant on regional partners for its imported intermediate inputs. This is also true for Bangladesh and Brunei Darussalam. Notably, the forward RVC share for the PRC has increased substantially since 2016 (from 0.31 to 0.47 in 2023), suggesting a reorientation of forward linkages in response to rising geopolitical tensions.

Source: ADB staff.

### 1: Regional Value Chain Integration by Economy in 2023

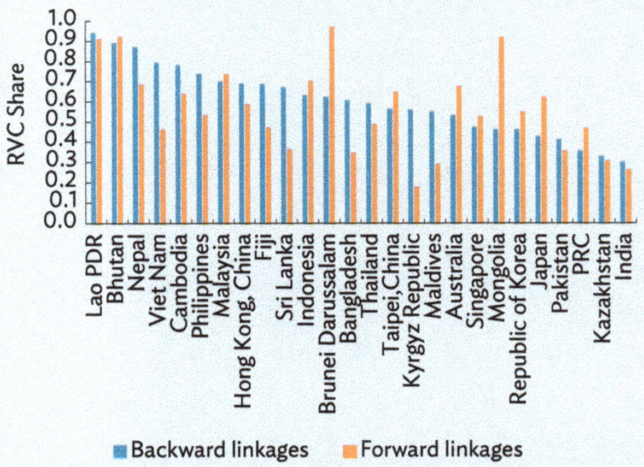


PRC = People's Republic of China, Lao PDR = Lao People's Democratic Republic, RVC = regional value chain.

Notes: The regional value chain indicators are calculated using hypothetical extraction, wherein trade in value-added with no trade in intermediates between Asian economies is compared with the scenario allowing trade in intermediates between Asian economies. Participation rates are calculated as the share of forward global value chain (GVC) activity in total value-added in the case of forward linkages and as the share of backward GVC activity in final production in the case of backward linkages.

Sources: ADB calculations using data from ADB. Multiregional Input Output Tables; and methodology by Los and Timmer (2018).

### 2: Change in Forward and Backward Regional Value Chain Integration by Economy, 2000–2023

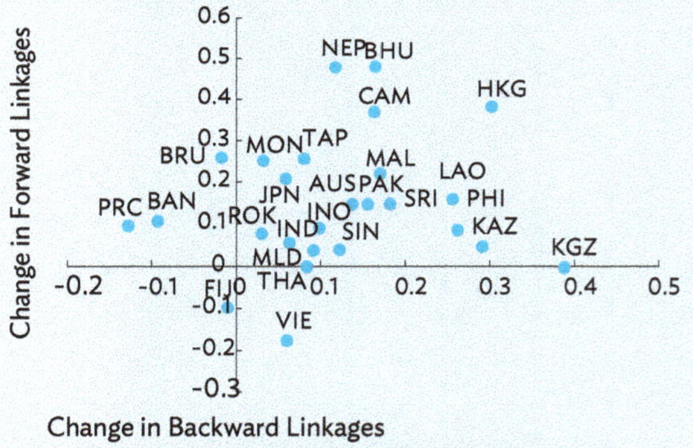


AUS = Australia; BAN = Bangladesh; BHU = Bhutan; BRU = Brunei Darussalam; CAM = Cambodia; PRC = People's Republic of China; FIJ = Fiji; HKG = Hong Kong, China; IND = India; INO = Indonesia; JPN = Japan; KAZ = Kazakhstan; KGZ = Kyrgyz Republic; ROK = Republic of Korea; LAO = Lao People's Democratic Republic; MAL = Malaysia; MLD = Maldives; MON = Mongolia; NEP = Nepal; PAK = Pakistan; PHI = Philippines; SIN = Singapore; SRI = Sri Lanka; TAP = Taipei,China; THA = Thailand; and VIE = Viet Nam.

Notes: The regional value chain indicators are calculated using hypothetical extraction, wherein trade in value-added with no trade in intermediates between Asian economies is compared with the scenario allowing trade in intermediates between Asian economies. Participation rates are calculated as the share of forward global value chain (GVC) activity in total value-added in the case of forward linkages and as the share of backward GVC activity in final production in the case of backward linkages.

Sources: ADB calculations using data from ADB. Multi Region Input Output Tables; and methodology by Los and Timmer (2018).

zero tariffs upon entering into force. This is also the case for the agreement with Ecuador, where tariffs on major exports from both economies such as fruits, seafood, coffee, plastics, machines, and electrical equipment, among others, shall gradually be reduced to zero. Nicaragua also stands to benefit from tariff-free exports of key products such as meat, seafood, sugar, and rum.

Another key agreement that entered into force in 2024 is the PTA between New Zealand and the European Union (EU). The agreement is estimated to cut €140 million worth of annual duties for EU companies in the first year of application. Bilateral trade is expected to grow by 30%, while the EU's investment in New Zealand may potentially grow by 80%. The agreement also contains sustainability commitments, such as adherence to the Paris Climate Agreement and labor rights.

This year also marked the entry into force of the United Arab Emirates–Georgia Comprehensive Economic Partnership Agreement (CEPA), which covers about 92% of tariff lines between the two economies. This agreement is seen as an opportunity for market expansion, as well as to enhance investment, empower small and medium-sized enterprises (SMEs), and streamline trade procedures.

Within the region, three PTAs were signed: the Republic of Korea–Georgia CEPA, the Viet Nam–Lao People's Democratic Republic (Lao PDR) trade agreement, and the Thailand–Sri Lanka FTA. Asian economies have also signed eight agreements with partners beyond the region, including the Indonesia–Canada CEPA, Hong Kong, China–Peru FTA, Australia–United Arab Emirates FTA, Maldives–Türkiye, Viet Nam–United Arab Emirates CEPA, Malaysia–United Arab Emirates CEPA, India-European Free Trade Association FTA, and the Republic of Korea–Gulf Cooperation Council FTA.

### Total trade turnover, most-favored nation tariff rates, and bilateral trade interventions have been significant drivers in the formation of PTAs in the past 2 decades.

The analysis of trade dynamics between economy pairs highlights several key trade factors influencing PTA

**Figure 2.11: Newly Effective Free Trade Agreements—Asia and the Pacific**

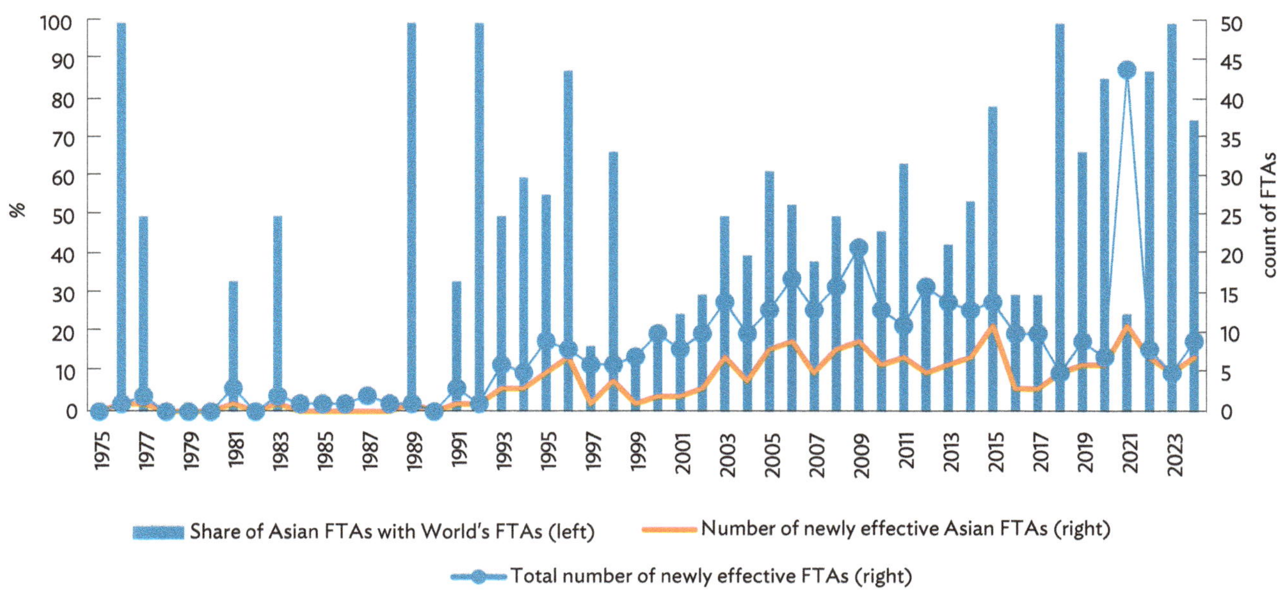


FTA = free trade agreement.

Notes: Trends for 1975–2022 derived using the World Trade Organization's Regional Trade Agreement Information System. The number of FTAs in 2023 is derived using the Asia Regional Integration Center FTA Database and various sources. The share of Asian FTAs is the ratio between the number of newly effective FTAs including at least one Asian economy and the total number of newly effective FTAs.

Sources: ADB calculations using data from ADB. Asia Regional Integration Center FTA Database. https://aric.adb.org/database/fta; and World Trade Organization. Regional Trade Agreement Information System. http://rtais.wto.org (both accessed December 2024).

**Table 2.1: New Regional Trade Agreements in Asia and the Pacific, 2024**

| Name | Type | Status (Date) |
|---|---|---|
| **Intraregional** | | |
| Philippines–Republic of Korea FTA | FTA | In force (31 December) |
| Republic of Korea–Georgia Economic Partnership Agreement | EPA | Signed (27 November) |
| Viet Nam–Lao PDR Trade Agreement | PTA | Signed (9 April) |
| Thailand–Sri Lanka FTA | FTA | Signed (3 February) |
| **Extraregional** | | |
| Indonesia–Canada CEPA | CEPA | Signed (2 December) |
| Hong Kong, China–Peru FTA | FTA | Signed (15 November) |
| Australia–United Arab Emirates FTA | FTA | Signed (6 November) |
| Maldives–Türkiye PTA | PTA | Signed (4 November) |
| Viet Nam–United Arab Emirates CEPA | CEPA | Signed (29 October) |
| Malaysia–United Arab Emirates CEPA | CEPA | Signed (11 October) |
| People's Republic of China–Serbia FTA | FTA | In force (1 July) |
| Georgia–United Arab Emirates CEPA | CEPA | In force (27 June) |
| People's Republic of China–Ecuador FTA | FTA | In force (1 May) |
| EU–New Zealand FTA | FTA | In force (1 May) |
| India–EFTA FTA | FTA | Signed (11 March) |
| Republic of Korea–Gulf Cooperation Council FTA | FTA | Signed (2 January) |
| People's Republic of China–Nicaragua FTA | FTA | In force (1 January) |

CEPA = comprehensive economic partnership agreement, EFTA = European Free Trade Association, EPA = economic partnership agreement, EU = European Union (27 members), FTA = free trade agreement, Lao PDR = Lao People's Democratic Republic, PTA = preferential trade agreement.

Note: All agreements cover both goods and services. Cover information available as of 31 December 2024.

Source: ADB compilation based on national sources.

formation. Table 2.2 shows that a higher average most-favored nation (MFN) tariff rate of an economy-pair is associated with a lower likelihood of PTA formation. This suggests that the higher the degree of multilateral liberalization, the more likely economies are to sign a PTA to further reduce trade barriers and enhance market access. As shown in column (3), the deterrent effect of MFN on PTA formation is insignificant in the absence of trade.

Further, the total trade volume between two economies positively correlates with PTA formation. This suggests that as economies become more interconnected through trade, they may seek PTAs to secure predictable and favorable terms for market access.

Similarly, the total number of trade interventions, including both restrictive and liberalizing measures imposed by the reporter and partner economy, are positively associated with PTA formation. This is consistent with the role of PTAs as structured frameworks to manage trade relations. By creating formalized agreements, economies can establish clear and predictable rules and guidelines for trade in sensitive or strategic sectors where interventions are implemented.

Interaction terms are incorporated to better understand how these relationships change under different conditions. Results indicate that the association between trade volumes and PTA formation is U-shaped with respect to MFN rates (Figure 2.12). Starting from a zero MFN rate, results show that the positive impact of total trade on PTA formation decreases as average MFN rates between two economies increase, but the relationship then reverses as MFN rates reach an 11.8 threshold. This suggests that economies with substantial trade volumes may seek PTAs either when (i) MFN tariffs are relatively low, as in developed economies where

PTAs could represent quick wins with high duty saving given the significant amount of trade, and moderated negotiating complexity given the degree of openness already achieved; or (ii) when MFN rates are high, as an attempt to reduce trade barriers. Conversely, interaction between trade interventions and MFN rates is positively correlated with PTA formation, while the squared term remains insignificant. This suggests that economies with complex trade relationships and high tariffs are more likely to negotiate PTAs to manage these complexities. In such cases, high tariffs combined with frequent trade interventions may create a need for more structured trade agreements to simplify and stabilize economic relations, even more so in a highly protectionist environment.

**Table 2.2: Panel Logistic Regression on Preferential Trade Agreement Formation Drivers, Economy-Pair, and Year Fixed Effects**

| | (1) | (2) | (3) |
|---|---|---|---|
| Average MFN rates | −0.90***<br>(−8.32) | −0.67***<br>(−3.93) | −0.59<br>(−0.71) |
| Average MFN^2 | | | −0.03<br>(−0.81) |
| Total Trade | 0.08**<br>−2.21 | 0.29***<br>−2.77 | 1.63***<br>−5.83 |
| Total Trade # MFN | | −0.02**<br>(−2.09) | −0.30***<br>(−5.61) |
| Total Trade # MFN^2 | | | 0.01***<br>−5.44 |
| Trade Interventions | 2.76***<br>−23.24 | 1.29***<br>−4.38 | 0.85**<br>−2.09 |
| Trade Interventions # MFN | | 0.22***<br>−5.06 | 0.29***<br>−2.83 |
| Trade Interventions # MFN^2 | | | 0<br>−0.21 |
| Observations | 64,200 | 64,200 | 64,200 |

MFN = most-favored nation.

Notes: T statistics in parentheses. * $p < 0.10$, ** $p < 0.05$, *** $p < 0.01$.
An analysis of the reporter and partner components of dependent variables is presented in Annex 2.a.

Sources: ADB calculations using World Bank. Deep Trade Agreements Database. https://datatopics.worldbank.org/dta/table.html; International Monetary Fund. Direction of Trade Statistics. https://data.imf.org/dots; and Global Trade Alert Database. https://www.globaltradealert.org (accessed August 2024).

**Figure 2.12: Contribution of Trade Flows and Trade Restrictions to the Log-Odds of Preferential Trade Agreement Formation**

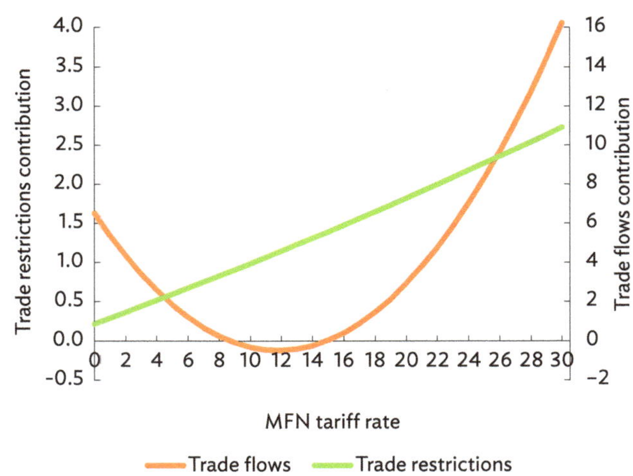


MFN = most-favored nation.

Note: The figure reports the results of the panel logistic regression on preferential trade agreement formation drivers, reporter-partner and year-fixed effects reported in Table 2.2, as follows:

*Trade flow contribution* = 1.626181-0.2967379 MFN+0.0125873 MFN^2

*Trade restriction contribution* = 0.8476344+0.2929988 MFN-0.0014124 MFN^2

Sources: ADB calculations using World Bank. Deep Trade Agreements Database. https://datatopics.worldbank.org/dta/table.html; International Monetary Fund. Direction of Trade Statistics. https://data.imf.org/dots; and Global Trade Alert Database. https://www.globaltradealert.org (accessed August 2024).

## Trade Within Preferential Trade Agreements

Trade shares under intra-Asian PTAs have been significantly rising over the past decade. However, the broader context of global trade challenges—such as the recent contraction in goods trade and slowing services growth—has impacted the region's overall trade performance. While Asia remains resilient in some sectors, regional PTAs must navigate these pressures effectively. Box 2.2 offers further insights into how external factors influence Asia's trade flows and underscores the importance of adaptive strategies within PTAs. These dynamics highlight the need for PTAs that not only support existing trade flows but also bolster Asia's response to global trade disruptions.

### Merchandise exports within trade agreements rose steadily in Asia, led by Southeast Asia and Oceania.

Using data from the United Nations Commodity Trade (UN Comtrade) database, Figures 2.13a and 2.13b present the share of merchandise exports in Asia that takes place under trade agreements covering goods trade. The data include all economies in the region as well as individual ADB subregions. For the region, the share of merchandise trade occurring within trade agreements rose from less than 20% in 2000 to over

**Box 2.2 Recent Developments in Trade in Goods and Services**

The global trade environment in 2023 was marked by a slowdown in global gross domestic product (GDP) growth, tight financial conditions, geoeconomic fragmentation, and increasing trade-distorting measures. World trade in goods contracted by 1%, while global services trade growth slowed to 4%, down from 14% in 2022 (box figure 1). Despite these headwinds and a shift in global demand from goods to services, the Asian region remained a key driver of global growth.

The Asian overall real GDP grew by 4.4% in 2023, outpacing global economic growth of 3.2%. Trade in the region also marginally outperformed global trade, owing to a 2.9% recovery in merchandise trade in the People's Republic of China (PRC) and a robust 9.8% growth in the rest of Asia's services trade. However, excluding the PRC, merchandise trade in the region contracted by 2.3%, driven by declines in goods trade in Hong Kong, China; Taipei,China; and the Association of Southeast Asian Nations (ASEAN). On the other hand, the recovery of tourism and rising demand for information and communication technology and financial services fueled strong services trade growth in economies like India and ASEAN.

Asia's trade volume posted positive year-on-year growth in the first quarter of 2024, boosted by a strong recovery in PRC trade (box figure 2). However, the faster growth in trade volume relative to its value points to deflationary pressures in the PRC, as exporters cut prices to stimulate demand.[a] This deflation, potentially linked to weak domestic demand and excess industrial capacity, could spill over into global disinflation and put downward pressure on global industrial prices, prompting trade restrictions from economies like the United States (US), the European Union (EU), and Canada to counter the surge of low-cost PRC exports. Despite positive trends early in 2024, the potential for geopolitical tensions and emerging industrial policy impacts tempered the outlook for the rest of the year (UNCTAD 2024).

The share of Asia's merchandise trade with itself, the US, and the EU and the United Kingdom (UK) (EU+UK) has been falling since 2020, coinciding with the coronavirus disease pandemic and rising geoeconomic tensions (box figure 3). The downturn in Asia's intraregional trade has been primarily driven by reduced trade with and among East Asian economies, particularly the PRC. Similarly, the diminishing role of the US and the EU+UK in Asia's trade since 2020 is due largely to reduced trade with the PRC. Nevertheless, these recent trends have opened new opportunities. Economies like the Republic of Korea and Taipei,China have seen rising trade shares with these partners, potentially benefiting from the US and the EU+UK's gradual decoupling from the PRC, while Asia's trade with the rest of the world has grown in importance, positioning the region for new trade dynamics.

**1: Merchandise and Services Trade Volume and Real Output Growth—Asia and the Pacific, and the World**

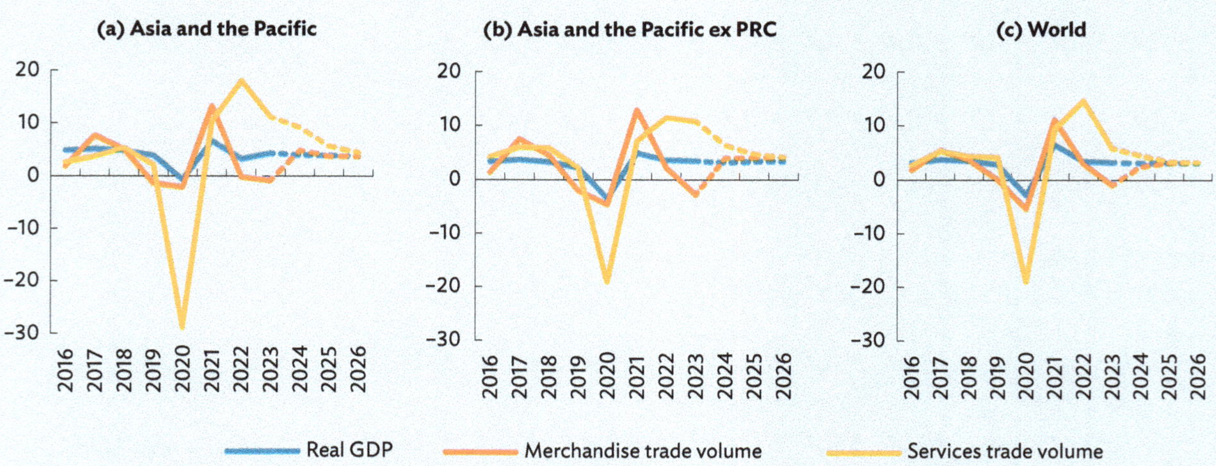


PRC = People's Republic of China, GDP = gross domestic product.

Sources: ADB calculations using data from International Monetary Fund (IMF). World Economic Outlook April 2024 Database. https://www.imf.org/en/Publications/WEO/weo-database/2024/April; IMF. Direction of Trade Statistics. https://data.imf.org/dot; and Organisation for Economic Co-operation and Development (OECD). OECD–World Trade Organization Balanced Trade in Services—BPM6. https://www.wto.org/english/res_e/statis_e/trade_datasets_e.htm (all accessed December 2024).

*continued on next page*

*Box 2.2: continued*

**2: Monthly Trade by Value and Volume—Asia and the Pacific**

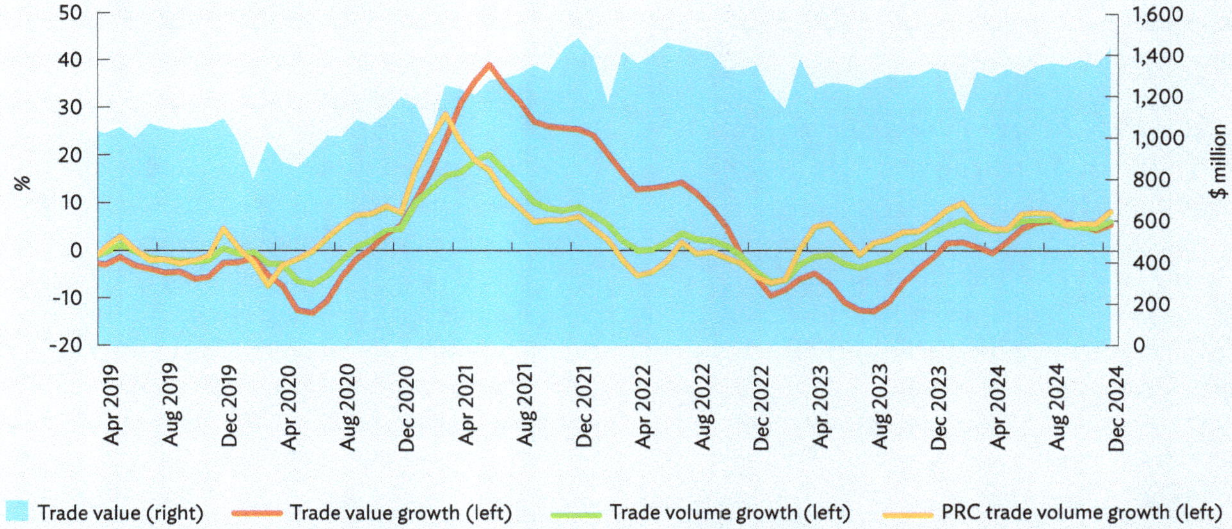


PRC = People's Republic of China.

Notes: Trade volume growth rates were computed as the 3-month moving average year-on-year growth using volume indexes. For each period and trade flow type (i.e., imports and exports), available data include indexes for the PRC and Japan, and aggregate indexes for selected economies in Asia and the Pacific: (i) advanced economies excluding Japan (Hong Kong, China; the Republic of Korea; Singapore; and Taipei,China); and (ii) emerging market economies excluding the PRC (India, Indonesia, Malaysia, Pakistan, the Philippines, Thailand, and Viet Nam). The aggregate index for Asia and the Pacific was computed using trade values as weights.

Sources: ADB calculations using data from CEIC Data Company; and CPB Netherlands Bureau for Economic Policy Analysis. World Trade Monitor. https://www.cpb.nl/en/world-trade-monitor-december-2024 (both accessed March 2025).

**3: Merchandise and Services Trade of Asia and the Pacific, by Partner** (%)

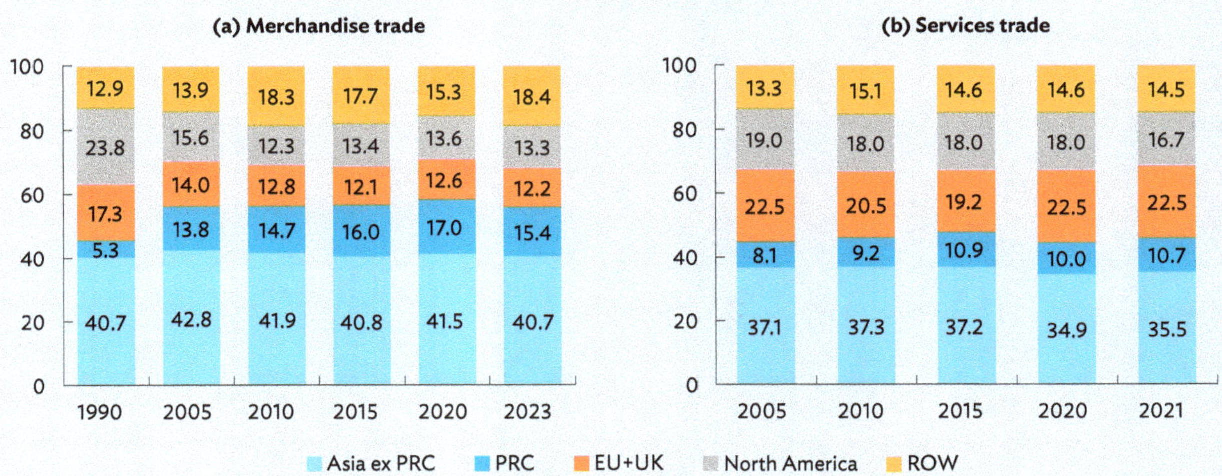


PRC = People's Republic of China, EU = European Union (27 members), ROW = rest of the world, UK = United Kingdom.

Notes: Values expressed as percentage of the region's total trade value (sum of exports and imports). North America covers Canada, Mexico, and the United States.

Sources: ADB calculations using data from International Monetary Fund. Direction of Trade Statistics. https://data.imf.org/dot; and Organisation for Economic Co-operation and Development (OECD). OECD–World Trade Organization Balanced Trade in Services—BPM6. https://www.wto.org/english/res_e/statis_e/trade_datasets_e.htm (both accessed December 2024).

[a] Currency depreciation across Asian economies and a shift toward lower-value goods may also be contributing factors.

Source: United Nations Trade and Development. Global Trade Update (July 2024). https://unctad.org/publication/global-trade-update-july-2024 (accessed August 2024).

50% by 2023. Of this trade, 21% occurred within intra-Asian agreements alone, 13% exclusively within extra-Asian agreements, and 18% between partners involved in both (and the same) intra- and extra-Asian agreements. However, there were notable variations across subregions.

### The share of services exports under trade agreements has risen across Asia, reaching the global average.

Using data from the Organisation for Economic Co-operation and Development–World Trade Organization Balanced Trade in Services database, Figures 2.14a and 2.14b report information on the share of services exports that takes place between partners with trade agreements covering services. Data are reported for all Asia and Pacific economies, as well as for ADB subregions. Considering all Asia, the figure indicates a rising share of services trade taking place with economies with which they share a trade agreement.

Between 2005 and 2021, the share of services trade taking place in trade agreements increased from below 25% to above 50%, reaching the same level as the rest of the world (Figure 2.14a). Of this trade, 31% occurs exclusively within intra-Asian agreements, 14% within extra-Asian agreements alone, and 6% within both intra- and extra-Asian agreements. Notably, services trade under the intra- and extra-Asian agreements categories saw a significant rise after 2018, spurred by the signing and enforcement of the Comprehensive and Progressive Agreement for Trans-Pacific Partnership.

This rising trend, however, hides substantial variation within subregions (Figure 2.14b). Southeast Asia reports high shares of services within trade agreements, with a notable jump from 55% to 80% between 2018 and 2021. Oceania and Central Asia witnessed a similar jump between 2014 and 2015, with the share of services exports within trade agreements also rising rapidly in East Asia over 2005–2021. In contrast, shares have been stagnant in South Asia and the Pacific.

**Figure 2.13: Share of Merchandise Trade Within Trade Agreements in Asia and the Pacific** (%, 5-year moving average)

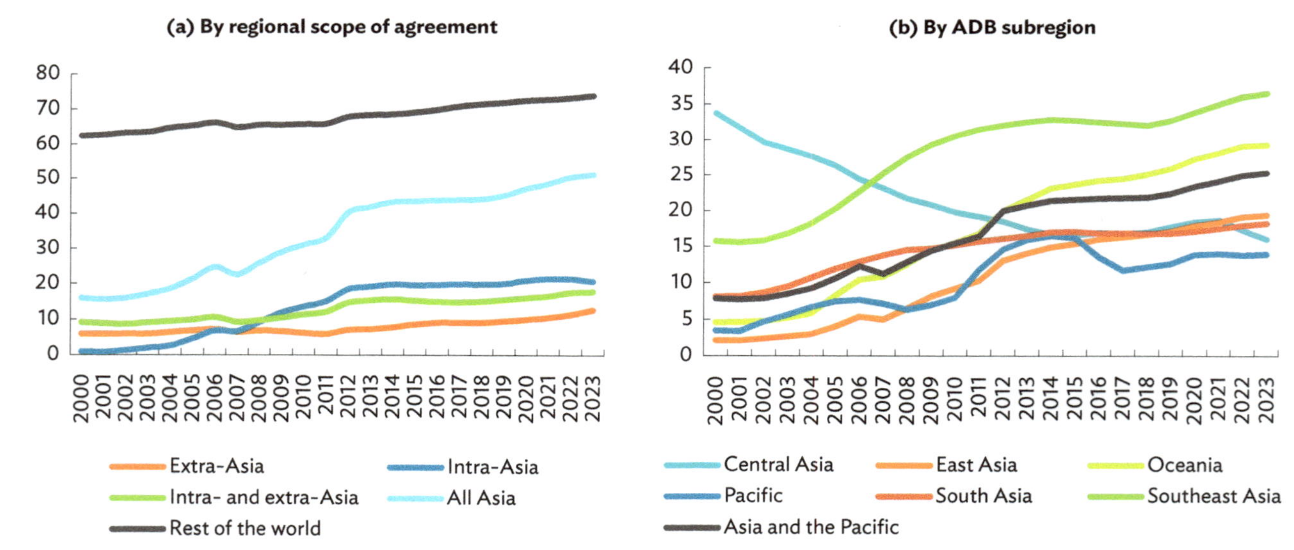


Notes: To reduce the volatility of the data, the figure reports data on five-year averages of the shares of exports that take place within trade agreements. Extra-Asia refers to trade covered by agreements that include both Asian and non-Asian economies, while intra-Asia refers to trade covered by agreements signed exclusively by Asian economies. "Intra- and extra-Asia" indicates trade between economy pairs covered by both intra- and extra-Asian agreements. All Asia encompasses trade under all intra-Asian and extra-Asian agreements, and rest of the world includes trade solely between non-Asian economies.

Source: ADB calculations using data from United Nations. UN Comtrade Database. https://comtrade.un.org/ (accessed September 2024).

**Figure 2.14: Share of Services Trade Within Trade Agreements in Asia and the Pacific** (%)

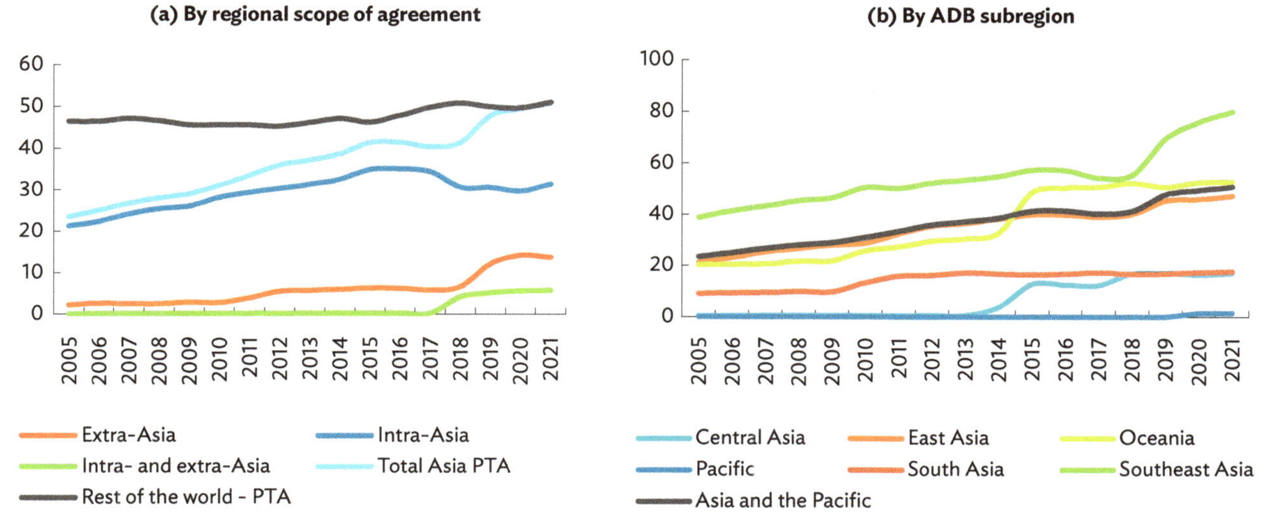


PTA = preferential trade agreement.

Notes: Extra-Asia refers to trade covered by agreements that include both Asian and non-Asian economies, while intra-Asia refers to trade covered by agreements signed exclusively by Asian economies. "Intra- and extra-Asia" indicates trade between economy pairs covered by both intra- and extra-Asian agreements. All Asia encompasses trade under all intra-Asian and extra-Asian agreements, and rest of the world includes trade solely between non-Asian economies.

Sources: ADB calculations using data from Organisation for Economic Co-operation and Development (OECD). OECD–World Trade Organization Balanced Trade in Services. https://www.oecd-ilibrary.org/trade/data/oecd-statistics-on-international-trade-in-services/oecd-wto-balanced-international-trade-in-services-ebops-2010_08dba674-en (accessed August 2024); and World Bank. Deep Trade Agreements Database. https://datatopics.worldbank.org/dta/table.html (accessed September 2024).

## Trade Effects of Preferential Trade Agreements

**The increasing breadth of trade agreements over time reflects an evolving role in fostering trade, though Asian PTAs show smaller increases in export flows compared to agreements outside the region.**

The increase in the breadth of trade agreements over time highlights that the role and purpose of trade agreements has evolved. Yet, the main rationale for trade agreements remains to increase the level of trade among partners. With PTAs signed by Asian economies—both intra- and extra-Asian agreements—shown to be different to those in other regions in various ways, the question arises as to whether trade agreements in Asia impact trade flows, and to the same extent as elsewhere. This can be evaluated using the gravity model of trade, which models bilateral trade flows between economies.[18]

Figure 2.15 indicates that the presence of a trade agreement is associated with 10% more exports between partners relative to when no trade agreement exists. Considering the breadth of agreements, the figure also shows that the broadest trade agreement—including all 52 provisions in the Deep Trade Agreements database—is associated with increased export flows between members of about 20% relative to the case of no trade agreement. Differences in effects are found between Asian agreements and those elsewhere. While the presence of an agreement outside of Asia is associated with about 20% more exports relative to no agreement, for both intra-Asian and extra-Asian agreements the effect is estimated at about 3%. Considering the breadth of agreements, the results suggest that the broadest agreement is associated with 30% more exports for non-Asian agreements relative to no agreement, with effects of about 12% for intra- and extra-Asian agreements. While the differing effects of agreements involving Asian economies relative to others cannot

[18] In the analysis, the structural gravity model is adopted (see, for example, Yotov 2024). Specifically, the analysis uses data from Feenstra et al. (2005) and UN Comtrade for 1962–2022 and the Poisson Pseudo-Maximum Likelihood approach of Santos Silva and Tenreyro (2006) with importer-time, exporter-time, and economy-pair fixed effects.

be easily determined, differences in the extent of liberalization and the membership of agreements may help explain these results.

**Figure 2.15: Estimated Impact of Preferential Trade Agreements on Merchandise Trade**

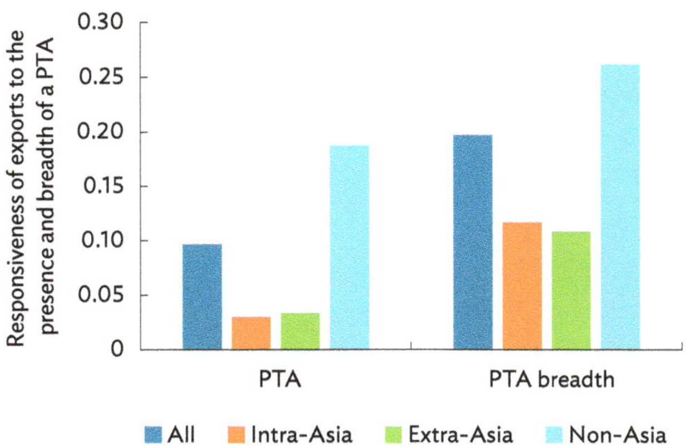


PTA = preferential trade agreement.

Notes: The figure reports the estimated impact of the presence of a trade agreement and the breadth of that trade agreement on exports between agreement partners. The results come from a structural gravity model using data over 1962–2022 and the Poisson Pseudo-Maximum Likelihood approach of Santos Silva and Tenreyro (2006).

Sources: ADB calculations using data from Feenstra et al. (2005); United Nations. UN Comtrade Database. https://comtrade.un.org/; and World Bank. Deep Trade Agreements Database. https://datatopics.worldbank.org/dta/table.html (accessed September 2024).

## Trade agreements involving Asian economies primarily increase the intensity of existing exports (the intensive margin) but tend to reduce the variety of goods traded (the extensive margin).

Beyond the value of exports, it is instructive to distinguish between the intensive and extensive margin of exports. The approach follows Hummels and Klenow (2005), with the extensive margin capturing the variety of goods traded and the intensive margin capturing the intensity with which existing varieties are traded. Figure 2.16 reports estimates of the effect of the presence of a trade agreement on these two margins of exports, again distinguishing between agreements signed by Asian economies and those signed by non-Asian economies.[19] Results indicate that while the presence of a trade agreement promotes exports along the intensive margin, it reduces exports along the extensive margin, consistent with the results of Falvey and Foster-McGregor (2022).[20] Similar patterns also hold for intra-Asian agreements and non-Asian agreements, while for extra-Asian agreements the effects work in the opposite direction and tend to be small (though statistically significant). The results thus suggest that intra-Asian agreements do have a substantial impact on the intensity of exports in goods (the intensive margin), but that this effect is offset by a reduction in the variety of goods traded with a trade agreement. While this pattern is consistent with results for agreements signed by non-Asian economies, the extent of the negative effect on the extensive margin is much larger for intra-Asian agreements. In contrast, agreements between Asian and non-Asian economies results in a larger variety of goods exported, but with lower intensity.

## Trade agreements outside Asia boost exports across sectors, whereas intra-Asian agreements show limited impacts, especially in manufacturing, with Asian economies minor in services trade.

Considering the impact of trade agreements on sector exports also helps underline the differences in the impact of trade agreements across regions. Figure 2.17 reports the estimated impact of the presence of a trade agreement on sector exports for intra-Asian, extra-Asian, and non-Asian agreements. While variations in the size of the estimated effects are relatively large, the estimated impact of trade agreements in non-Asia is statistically significant in six of the eight sectors, with no significant effect observed in the sectors' crude materials and miscellaneous manufacturing. Effects are estimated to be large in many of the primary sectors, notably food and live animals, beverages and tobacco, and animal and vegetable oils. In contrast, effects are estimated to be smaller in manufacturing sectors. In the case of extra-Asian agreements, a significant impact of

19 Trade data are converted to Standard International Trade Classification (SITC) Revision 1 for all years, with the margins constructed at the four-digit SITC product level.

20 When using a linear estimator, such as ordinary least squares estimation, it is possible to decompose the overall effect of a trade agreement into an effect working along the intensive and extensive margins. The use of the nonlinear Poisson Pseudo-Maximum Likelihood approach, however, does not allow for an exact decomposition.

**Figure 2.16: Estimated Impact of Preferential Trade Agreements on the Intensive and Extensive Margins of Merchandise Trade**

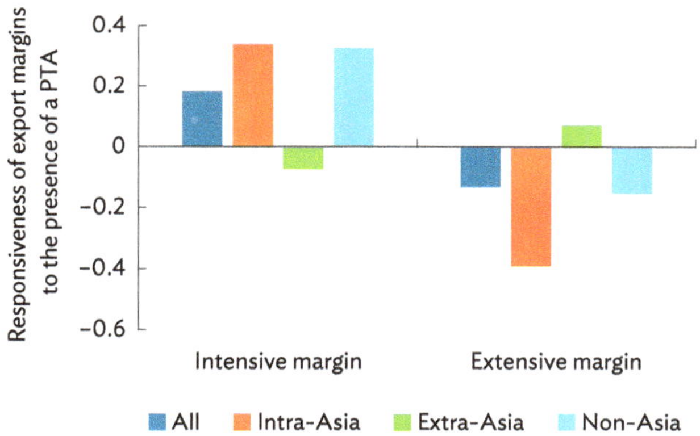


PTA = preferential trade agreement.

Notes: The figure reports the estimated impact of the presence of a trade agreement on the intensive and extensive margins of exports constructed according to Hummels and Klenow (2005). The results come from a structural gravity model using data over 1962–2022 and the Poisson Pseudo-Maximum Likelihood approach of Santos Silva and Tenreyro (2006).

Sources: ADB calculations using data from Feenstra et al. (2005); United Nations. UN Comtrade Database. https://comtrade.un.org/; and World Bank. Deep Trade Agreements Database. https://datatopics.worldbank.org/dta/table.html (accessed September 2024).

a trade agreement is again found in the case of food and live animals and animal and vegetable oils, but so too for chemicals and manufactured goods. Results therefore suggest that agreements signed between Asian and non-Asian economies have succeeded in increasing manufactured exports between partners. In contrast, the effects for intra-Asian agreements are only found to be significant in one classification: beverages and tobacco. Such results confirm that intra-Asian agreements have had a limited effect on exports, with this especially so in manufactured sectors.

Considering services trade, it is notable that Asian economies account for a relatively small share of total services exports, especially when considering services trade between Asian economies (Figure 2.18).

**Figure 2.17: Estimated Impact of Preferential Trade Agreements on Merchandise Trade by Sector**

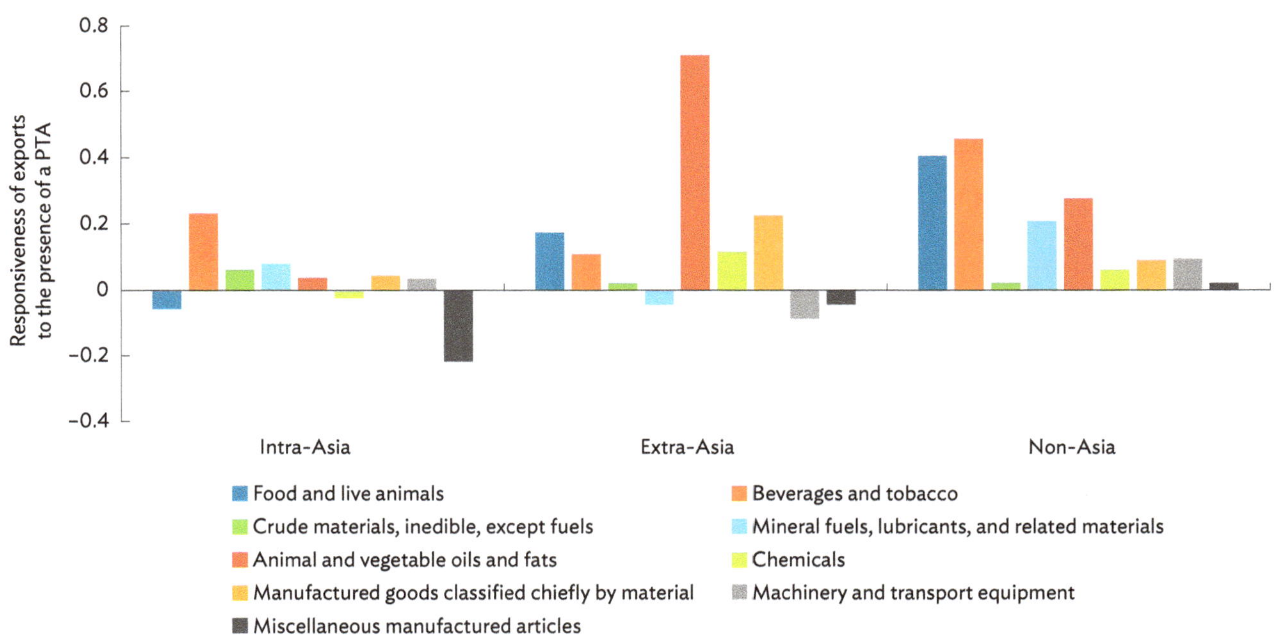


PTA = preferential trade agreement.

Notes: The figure reports the estimated impact of the presence of a trade agreement on sector exports. The results come from a structural gravity model using data over 1962–2022 and the Poisson Pseudo-Maximum Likelihood approach of Santos Silva and Tenreyro (2006).

Sources: ADB calculations using data from Feenstra et al. (2005); United Nations. UN Comtrade Database. https://comtrade.un.org/; and World Bank. Deep Trade Agreements Database. https://datatopics.worldbank.org/dta/table.html (accessed September 2024).

**Figure 2.18: Services Trade and Components Associated with Asian Economies** ($ million)

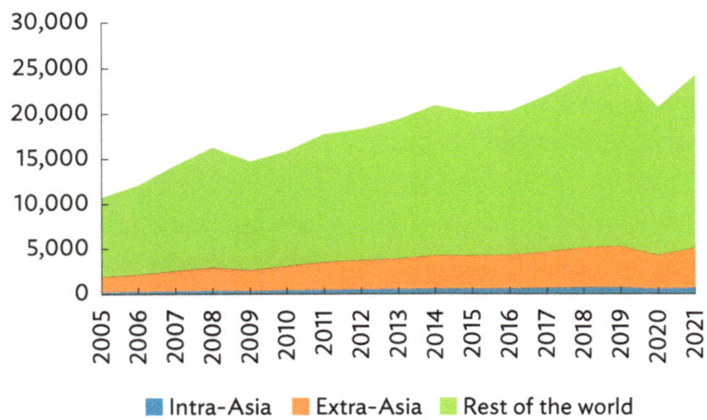


Source: ADB calculations using data from Organisation for Economic Co-operation and Development (OECD). OECD–World Trade Organization Balanced Trade in Services Database. https://www.oecd.org/en/data/datasets/oecd-balanced-trade-statistics.html (accessed August 2024).

## Services trade agreements positively impact services exports for non-Asian economies but show no significant effect for Asian economies.

Estimating the effects of the presence of a trade agreement that covers services on services trade using the gravity model suggests no statistically significant impact for agreements involving Asian economies, despite evidence of a positive effect for agreements involving non-Asian economies (Figure 2.19). For non-Asian agreements, the estimated effect of the presence of a (services) trade agreement on bilateral services exports is about 6%, while for agreements involving Asian economies the effects are statistically no different from zero.

Adopting the definition of ADB (2022a) to distinguish between digital and non-digital services trade, differences are found in the effect of services trade agreements (Figure 2.19). In the case of non-digital services, the presence of a services trade agreement is estimated to increase non-digital services exports by about 2.5%. The effect is estimated to be 4.5% for non-Asian agreements, whereas there is no significant impact on non-digital services exports for either intra-Asian or extra-Asian agreements. In the case of digital services, services trade agreements have no significant impact on digital services exports. This reflects two offsetting forces, however. For non-Asian agreements, there is a strong positive association between the presence of a services trade agreement and digital services exports, with such an agreement estimated to increase services exports by just over 7.5%. For intra-Asian agreements, however, the effect is estimated to be negative, with the presence of a services agreement reducing digital services trade by nearly 9%. This could result from an additional regulatory burden imposed by PTA commitments, which may make it more difficult for businesses to deliver services in general. It is also important to keep in mind the relative nature of this figure, as services exports remain limited in Asia. For extra-Asian agreements, no significant relationship between the presence of a services trade agreement and digital exports is found.

**Figure 2.19: Structural Gravity Estimates of Effects of Trade Agreement Presence on Services Trade**

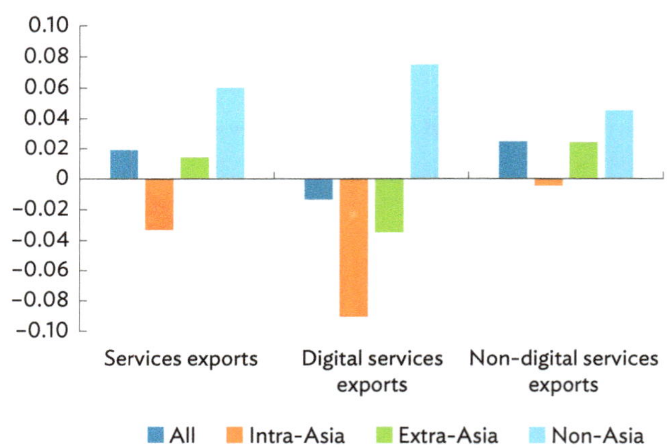


Note: The figure reports estimated coefficients from a structural gravity estimation of bilateral services exports using data for 2005–2021.

Source: ADB calculations using data from Organisation for Economic Co-operation and Development (OECD). OECD–World Trade Organization Balanced Trade in Services. https://www.oecd.org/en/data/datasets/oecd-balanced-trade-statistics.html (accessed August 2024).

## Asian PTAs show signs of "open regionalism" but the deeper PTAs are associated with stricter MFN tariffs.

Open regionalism, a key feature of economic integration in Asia, emphasizes inclusivity and nondiscrimination toward economies outside the region. This approach seeks to maximize the benefits of regional cooperation without creating exclusive trade blocs that disadvantage nonmembers. It aligns with the "building block" theory of regional integration, where PTAs support multilateral trade liberalization, particularly in developing economies (Estevadeordal, Freund, and Ornelas 2008; Calvo-Pardo et al. 2014; Crivelli 2016).

Figure 2.20 highlights a positive relationship between preferential tariff rates negotiated under PTAs and MFN tariff rates. This association is stronger for both intra-Asian and extra-Asian PTAs compared to non-regional PTAs, reflecting the region's commitment to open regionalism. Preferential tariff reductions under PTAs appear to foster more open trade regimes. However, the broader range of provisions negotiated in these agreements may introduce complexities in implementation and policy alignment, potentially leading economies to adjust MFN tariffs upward (or reduce them more slowly) as a compensatory measure.

**Figure 2.20: Estimated Impact of Preferential Tariffs and PTA Breadth on MFN Tariffs (The Open Regionalism Hypothesis)**

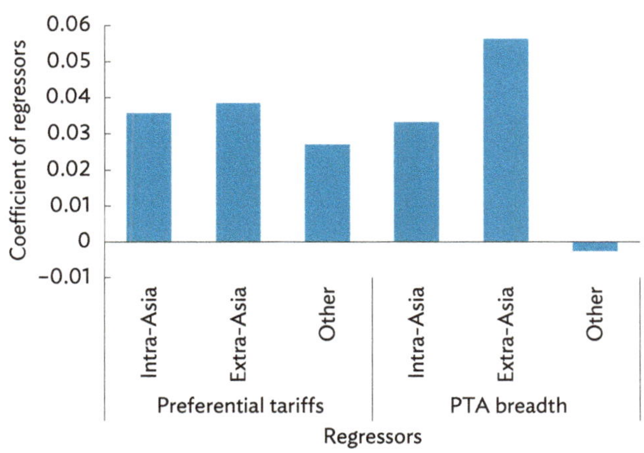


MFN = most-favored nation, PTA = preferential trade agreement.

Notes: The figure reports estimated coefficients from a Poisson Pseudo-Maximum Likelihood regression model with the MFN tariff rates as the dependent variable, and preferential tariff rates, and PTA breadth as regressors, using data from 1996–2023. The regression includes reporter-partner-sector fixed effects, and year fixed effects.

Source: ADB calculations using data from United Nations. UN Comtrade Database. https://comtrade.un.org/; World Trade Organization. Integrated Data Base. https://tao.wto.org/site/glossary/en/IDB_-_INTEGRATED_DATA_BASE.htm; and World Bank. Deep Trade Agreements Database. https://datatopics.worldbank.org/dta/table.html (accessed November 2024).

In contrast, broader non-regional PTAs are associated with lower MFN tariffs, suggesting that the inclusion of a wide range of provisions in these agreements complements, rather than contradicts, efforts to promote open regionalism in the rest of the world.

## Rising Complexity and Compliance Costs of Trade Agreements

Preferential trade agreements in Asia look different to those in other regions. They tend to be narrower and tend to involve fewer partners than agreements signed elsewhere. They also tend to have more limited impacts on trade flows than agreements elsewhere, potentially because of the differences in the scope of the agreements. These limitations of intra-Asian trade agreements coincide with emerging trade issues that present challenges and opportunities for the future of regional integration in the region.

A key factor shaping the evolution of PTAs in Asia is the economic diversity among member economies and the growing scope of the agreements. As PTAs have grown more complex, involving broader sets of provisions such as labor standards, intellectual property, and environmental safeguards, the challenges of negotiating and ratifying these agreements have intensified. Higher-income economies in Asia are more prepared to implement comprehensive agreements, equipped with proper infrastructure and regulatory frameworks. In contrast, lower-income economies may face constraints that make adherence and enforcement of stringent provisions difficult.

This divergence can slow negotiations, as economies must balance ambitious trade liberalization goals with domestic capacity considerations. Both the Regional Comprehensive Economic Partnership (RCEP) and the Comprehensive and Progressive Agreement for Trans-Pacific Partnership encountered these challenges, as lower-income members voiced concerns over their ability to comply with the higher standards.

**Box 2.3: The Overlapping Trade Agreements Challenge in Asia: The Noodle Bowl Effect**

The rise of free trade agreements (FTAs) has provided an alternative to global economic integration, as multilateral efforts under the World Trade Organization (WTO) have stalled since the Doha Round in 2001. Unlike the consensus required for WTO-led liberalization, bilateral and plurilateral FTAs allow for faster implementation among a few like-minded nations. However, this shift has led to a complex web of overlapping agreements—coined the "spaghetti bowl effect" by Bhagwati (1995)—with varied tariffs and rules that result in trade diversion, increased compliance costs, and administrative burdens that harm trade. Small firms, in particular, face challenges managing multiple FTAs, often limiting their access to preferential tariffs.

Asia has seen exponential growth in FTAs since the early 2000s, driven by economic integration and the absence of a shared economic institution. By 2023, Asian economies' engagement in overlapping FTAs was more than twice the global average, with 22% of Asian economy pairs involved in multiple agreements with the same partner (box figure 1a). Within Asia, 13% of economy pairs with a trade agreement are parties in a bilateral agreement in addition to at least one plurilateral agreement, while 59% are engaged in multiple plurilateral agreements if not engaged bilaterally (box figure 1b).

However, the surge in Asian FTAs has created a complex trade environment, posing challenges for businesses and raising concerns about the potential counterproductive effects of these agreements—dubbed the Asian "noodle bowl effect." Empirical studies highlight the costs of this trend, especially for small and medium-sized enterprises (SMEs), which often struggle to comply with complex requirements and underutilize FTA preferences. Kawai and Wignaraja (2010) found that only 28% of surveyed Asian exporting firms use FTA preferences, compared to 54% of Canadian exporters under the North American Free Trade Agreement. Larger firms in Japan and the People's Republic of China exhibit higher utilization rates, suggesting that a classic firm size effect underlies Asian FTA usage: the high fixed costs like learning FTA provisions and obtaining certificates of origin present significant barriers for Asian SMEs.

More recently, the region has witnessed the development of broader plurilateral agreement such as the Regional Comprehensive Economic Partnership (RCEP) or the Comprehensive and Progressive Agreement for Trans-Pacific Partnership. These mega-regional agreements were expected to simplify the "noodle bowl" of trade agreements by providing a common set of trade rules across multiple

**1: Frequency of Overlapping Trade Agreements**

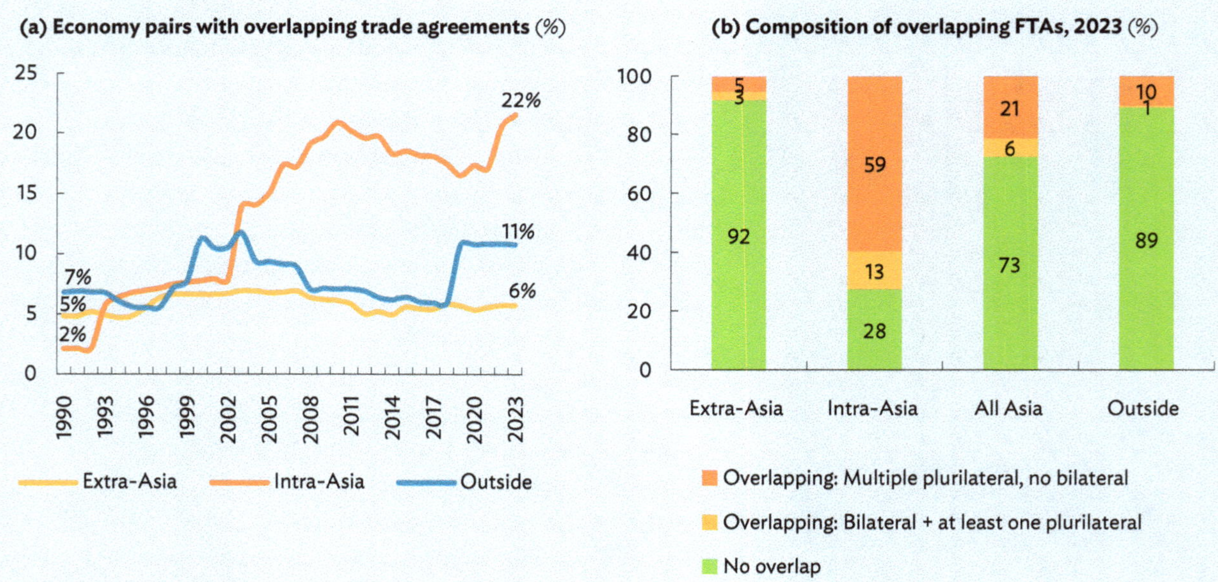


FTA = free trade agreement.

Notes: Extra-Asia covers economy pairs that include one Asian and one non-Asian partner, while intra-Asia involves exclusively Asian economy pairs. All Asia combines both extra-Asia and intra-Asia economy pairs. Outside refers to non-Asian economy pairs involved in at least one trade agreement. Economy pairs are classified as having overlapping agreements if both partners participate in multiple, identical trade agreements within the same year. Bilateral agreements involve only two economies, while plurilateral agreements include more than two economies and encompass agreements where at least one participant is a regional trade agreement.

Source: ADB calculations using data from World Bank. Deep Trade Agreements database (accessed September 2024).

*continued on next page*

*Box 2.3: continued*

partners. However, these agreements do not supersede the existing ones (ADB 2022b). In addition, the RCEP agreement has not been found to provide greater market access in terms of tariff commitments and rules of origin criteria and administration.

For policymakers, the challenge lies in minimizing the costs and maximizing the benefits of this network of FTAs. Key strategies to enhance Asian FTAs utilization and impact include support systems for FTA users, performance monitoring through the collection and analysis of utilization rates, and technical assistance for the renegotiations of critical provisions in view of expanding the depth of commitments and streamlining rules of origin criteria and operational certification procedures (ADB 2022b, 2022c; Crivelli and Inama 2022; Crivelli, Inama, and Pearson 2022, 2023, forthcoming).

Source: ADB calculations using data from World Bank. Deep Trade Agreements Database. https://datatopics.worldbank.org/dta/table.html (accessed September 2024).

Economic diversity and unbalanced negotiating capacities among RCEP members can result in shallower agreements, implementation challenges, and low utilization rates of trade preferences. ASEAN utilization rates have been low (Inama, Crivelli, and Ha 2022). In the context of overlapping agreements (Box 2.3), the private sector may lack incentives to use RCEP preferences.

### RCEP's complex rules and lengthy tariff schedules contribute to low utilization rates among ASEAN firms, which tend to prefer existing agreements with simpler compliance requirements.

Analyses by ADB (2022b), Crivelli and Inama (2022), and Crivelli, Inama, and Pearson (2022, 2023) indicate that RCEP's value for the private sector in ASEAN could be limited, particularly due to the lengthy and complex tariff phase-down schedules and rules of origin that do not bring additional benefits over existing agreements in the region. The complexity of operational certification procedures also poses significant compliance costs to firms which may prefer to continue using the ASEAN Trade in Goods Agreement rather than trying to comply with cumbersome and unpredictable proof of origin requirements under the RCEP (Crivelli, Inama, and Pearson 2024).

This trend is reflected in the most recent Japanese RCEP utilization data. Although RCEP is progressively graining shares over other agreements applied in Japan (Figure 2.21), most trade under RCEP is benefiting economies that were not part of a preexisting agreement with Japan. The PRC and the Republic of Korea are the main users of RCEP in Japan, representing together more than 90% of the Japanese imports entering under the RCEP (Figure 2.22), and amounting to $4.5 billion in 2023 (Figure 2.23). Other RCEP members continue to trade with Japan under other more favorable schemes of preferences. As an illustration, only 0.67% of exports from Viet Nam to RCEP member economies were covered by an RCEP certificate of origin in 2022, against 39% for the ASEAN Trade in Goods Agreement, 50.9% under either the Republic of Korea–Viet Nam or ASEAN–Republic of Korea FTA, and 29.3% under the ASEAN–PRC FTA (Crivelli, Inama, and Pearson forthcoming).

These limitations may stem from the compromises needed among many economies with varying capacities to negotiate effectively, leading to shallow commitments, stringent rules, and unpredictable practices in implementing procedures. Along the same lines, Crivelli, Inama, and Pearson (2023) highlight that developing RCEP members (excluding the PRC) are disadvantaged by stringent rules of origin on products where they hold a comparative advantage. These findings call for additional assistance in negotiating and implementing trade agreements in Asia (ADB 2022b).

**Figure 2.21: Trade Values and Trade Shares Using Regional Comprehensive Economic Partnership in Japan**

**(a) Total value of imports from RCEP economies entering through EPAs, by type** ($ billion)

**(b) Share of imports from RCEP economies entering through EPAs, by type** (%)

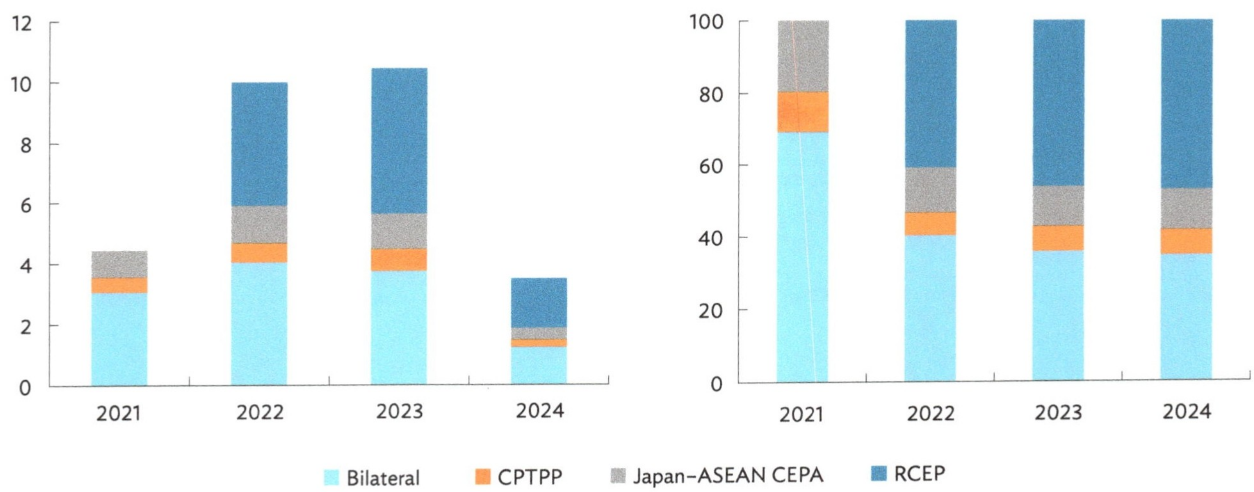


ASEAN = Association of Southeast Asian Nations, CEPA = Comprehensive Economic Partnership Agreement, CPTPP = Comprehensive and Progressive Agreement for Trans-Pacific Partnership, EPA = Economic Partnership Agreement, RCEP = Regional Comprehensive Economic Partnership.

Note: Data for 2024 cover the months of January to July only.

Source: ADB calculations using data from the Japan Customs. EPA Time Series Database. https://www.customs.go.jp/kyotsu/kokusai/toukei/index_e.htm (accessed September 2024).

**Figure 2.22: Shares of Japanese Imports Entering Through Regional Comprehensive Economic Partnership, by Economy of Origin**

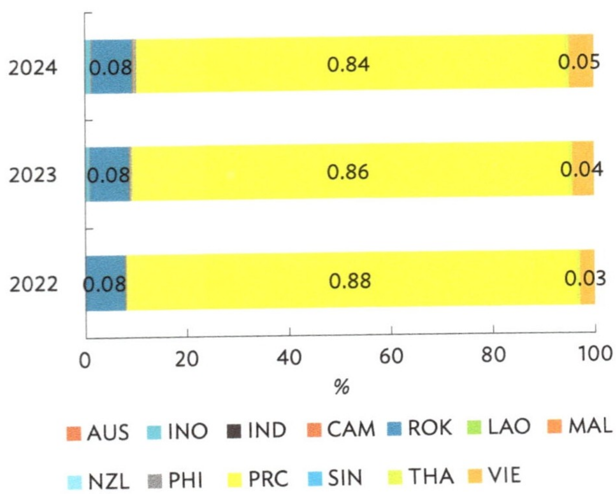


AUS = Australia, CAM = Cambodia, PRC = People's Republic of China, IND = India, INO = Indonesia, ROK = Republic of Korea, LAO = Lao People's Democratic Republic, MAL = Malaysia, NZL = New Zealand, PHI = Philippines, SIN = Singapore, THA = Thailand, VIE = Viet Nam.

Note: Data for 2024 cover the months of January to July only.

Source: ADB calculations using data from the Japan Customs. EPA Time Series Database. https://www.customs.go.jp/kyotsu/kokusai/toukei/index_e.htm (accessed September 2024).

## Challenges and Opportunities for Regional Cooperation and Integration

The findings of this chapter underscore the transformative role of PTAs in shaping trade dynamics within Asia. In recent decades, the number of PTAs has increased significantly, with the objective among Asian economies to improve market access and drive economic cooperation, particularly considering the limited progress in multilateral trade liberalization. However, the effectiveness of these agreements is constrained by shallow commitments, especially in critical market access provisions. PTAs in Asia tend to reduce tariffs but often fall short of dealing with deeper structural barriers to trade, which restricts their potential impact on trade flows and economic growth across the region. Furthermore, the overlapping network of PTAs—commonly known as the "noodle bowl" effect—creates compliance challenges and administrative costs, particularly for SMEs. These complexities discourage the use of PTAs and, in turn, lower their overall impact.

**Figure 2.23: Trade Values Using Regional Comprehensive Economic Partnership in Japan, by Economy of Origin** ($)

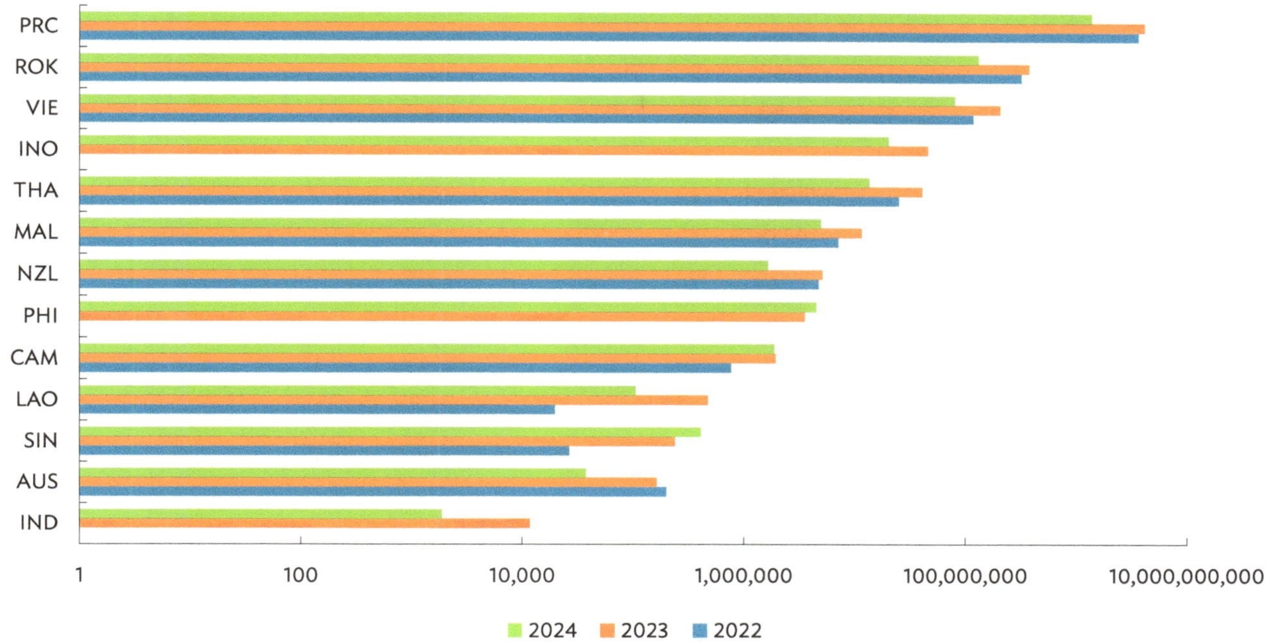


AUS = Australia, CAM = Cambodia, PRC = People's Republic of China, IND = India, INO = Indonesia, ROK = Republic of Korea, LAO = Lao People's Democratic Republic, MAL = Malaysia, NZL = New Zealand, PHI = Philippines, RCEP = Regional Comprehensive Economic Partnership, SIN = Singapore, THA = Thailand, VIE = Viet Nam.

Notes: Data are expressed in logarithmic scale, with 2024 estimates covering January to July only.

Source: ADB calculations using data from the Japan Customs. EPA Time Series Database. https://www.customs.go.jp/kyotsu/kokusai/toukei/index_e.htm (accessed September 2024).

This complexity extends beyond overlapping agreements to the scope of provisions negotiated within PTAs. While the chapter highlights signs of open regionalism—characterized by a positive association between preferential tariffs and MFN tariffs—broader PTAs are associated with higher MFN tariffs. This suggests that as the breadth of PTAs increases, the associated challenges may prompt economies to adopt more protective tariff policies, further limiting their potential to drive inclusive and open trade.

The chapter's sector analysis reveals that the benefits of PTAs are concentrated in specific industries, notably primary sectors such as food and animal products, while results in manufacturing sectors are limited. This pattern suggests that PTAs, as currently structured, may reinforce sector specialization without broadening trade across diverse industries. This concentration effect is also evident in the intensive margin of trade, where PTAs increase the quantity of goods traded but not necessarily the variety. This limited product diversity suggests that PTAs in Asia tend to promote trade within established sectors rather than foster a broader array of traded goods. This outcome aligns with the observed determinants of PTA formation: economies with high existing trade volumes are more likely to enter PTAs, reinforcing current trade patterns. To unlock the full potential of PTAs, future agreements could emphasize new sectors and prospective markets, supporting export diversification rather than merely amplifying established trade flows.

In services trade, PTAs have similarly limited impact in Asia, pointing to underlying constraints such as insufficient digital infrastructure and the need for substantial domestic reforms. Service provisions in PTAs often require regulatory standards that some members, particularly lower-income economies, may find challenging to meet. Until investments in digital infrastructure and regulatory frameworks are made, the region's PTAs are unlikely to drive robust growth in services trade, limiting Asia's competitive position in the global services market.

Administrative burdens and the complexity of rules of origin also contribute to the limited impact of PTAs in Asia. Stringent and sometimes inconsistent requirements for rules of origin across PTAs increase compliance costs for firms, hampering their ability to access preferential tariffs. This issue is especially pronounced in RCEP, where complex tariff schedules and rules of origin discourage firms from fully utilizing available trade preferences. Streamlining rules and simplifying compliance procedures across PTAs could alleviate these burdens, enhancing the agreements' effectiveness and improving trade preference utilization.

In conclusion, while PTAs have increased intraregional trade shares in Asia, their effectiveness is hampered by shallow commitments, complex administrative requirements, and limitations in promoting export diversification and services trade. Addressing these challenges requires policy reforms aimed at simplifying trade rules, deepening commitments, and aligning rules of origin criteria with regional production patterns. In addition, fostering diversification by negotiating agreements with prospective markets rather than solely reinforcing existing trade relationships could expand the economic impact of PTAs. Providing technical support to developing economies for PTA implementation would also help ensure that all members benefit more equitably, building a cohesive and competitive trade environment across Asia.

## References

Asian Development Bank (ADB). 2022a. *Asian Economic Integration Report 2022: Advancing Digital Services Trade in Asia and the Pacific.*

———. 2022b. *The Regional Comprehensive Economic Partnership Agreement: A New Paradigm in Asian Regional Cooperation?*

———. 2022c. *Aid for Trade in Asia and the Pacific: Leveraging Trade and Digital Agreements for Sustainable Development.*

Bhagwati, J. N. 1995. *US Trade Policy: The Infatuation with FTAs.* Columbia University, Department of Economics.

Calvo-Pardo, H., C. Freund, E. Ornelas. 2014. The ASEAN Free Trade Agreement: Impact on Trade Flows and External Trade Barriers. *World Bank Policy Research Working Paper Series.* No. 4960.

Crivelli, P. 2016. Regionalism and Falling External Protection in High and Low Tariff Members. *Journal of International Economics.* 102. pp. 70–84.

Crivelli, P. and S. Inama. 2022. *A Preliminary Assessment of the Regional Comprehensive Economic Partnership.* Asian Development Bank.

Crivelli, P., S. Inama, and M. Pearson. 2022. *An Analysis of the Product-Specific Rules of Origin of the Regional Comprehensive Economic Partnership.* Asian Development Bank.

———. 2023. *An Assessment of Rules of Origin in RCEP and ASEAN+1 Free Trade Agreements.* Asian Development Bank.

———. 2024. *Operational Certification Procedures of Free Trade Agreements in Asia: An In-Depth Analysis for Implementing Trade Facilitation Reforms*. Asian Development Bank.

Estevadeordal, A., C. Freund, and E. Ornelas. 2008. Does Regionalism Affect Trade Liberalization Toward Nonmembers? *Quarterly Journal of Economics*. 123 (4). p. 1531.

Falvey, R. E. and N. Foster-McGregor. 2022. The Breadth of Preferential Trade Agreements and the Margins of Exports. *Review of World Economics*. 158 (1). pp. 181–251.

Feenstra, R. C., R. E. Lipsey, H. Deng, A. C. Ma, and H. Mo. 2005. World Trade Flows: 1962–2000. *NBER Working Paper*. No. 11040. National Bureau of Economic Research.

Hofmann, C., A. Osnago, and M. Ruta. 2017. *Horizontal Depth: A New Database on the Content of Preferential Trade Agreements*. World Bank.

Hummels, D. and P. J. Klenow. 2005. The Variety and Quality of a Nation's Exports. *American Economic Review*. 95 (3). pp. 704–723.

Inama, S., P. Crivelli, and P. M. Ha. 2022. The Low Use by Firms of ASEAN Trade Preferences: Will RCEP Follow the Same Destiny? An Agenda for Rescue to Reform Rules of Origin in the Asian and Pacific Region. *Global Trade and Customs Journal*. 17 (6). pp. 248–251.

Kawai M. and G. Wignaraja. 2010. Asian FTAs: Trends, Prospects, and Challenges. *ADB Economics Working Paper Series*. No. 226. Asian Development Bank.

Los, B. and M. P. Timmer. 2018. Measuring Bilateral Exports of Value Added: A Unified Framework. *NBER Working Paper*. No. 24896. National Bureau of Economic Research.

Santos Silva, J. M. C. and S. Tenreyro. 2006. The Log of Gravity. *Review of Economics and Statistics*. 88 (4). pp. 641–658.

Yotov, Y. V. 2024. The Evolution of Structural Gravity: The Workhorse Model of Trade. *Contemporary Economic Policy*. 42 (4). pp. 578–603.

# Annex 2a: Directional Analysis of Drivers of Preferential Trade Agreements in Asia and the Pacific

The main text reports the results of a "nondirectional" analysis where dependent variables of the reporter and the partner have been combined (ex. average most-favored nation [MFN], total trade). The analysis is further disaggregated in this annex, distinguishing between the reporter and partner components of all variables to investigate deeper nuances in drivers for preferential trade agreement (PTA) formation. This bilateral model reveals additional layers of complexity in PTA drivers, highlighting how differing policy choices between reporting and partner economies influence PTA negotiations (see table).

In terms of trade, export value remains a robust positive determinant of PTA formation, as economies with significant export flows to a partner tend to pursue PTAs to secure or expand market access. However, this effect is diminished by higher MFN rates on the reporter's side, suggesting that protectionist economies may be less inclined to rely on PTAs as a vehicle for export growth. On the other hand, partners to MFN rates exhibit no significant interaction with export values, indicating that the exporting economy's motives in forming a PTA are driven more by its own trade policies than the partner's protectionist stance.

Restrictive trade measures display a notable role in shaping PTA formation. A higher number of restrictive measures implemented by the reporter positively correlates with PTA formation, reflecting that economies with more protectionist tendencies may see PTAs as a strategic tool to balance market access commitments with domestic trade priorities. However, this positive effect is tempered by higher most-favored nation rates on the reporter's side, indicating that protectionist economies may rely more on unilateral measures than on PTAs to manage trade policies. Moreover, partner-implemented restrictive measures also show a strong association with PTA formation with a decreasing impact as the partner's MFN status is increasing.

Liberalizing measures, implemented either by the reporter or partner, remain critical in driving PTA formation, even more so when the MFN rate in other economies is increasing. This is consistent with strategies to leverage PTAs as a means to enhance trade openness and deepen integration with key partners. However, higher domestic MFN rates dampen this effect, indicating that protectionist reporting economies are less inclined to pursue further liberalization through PTAs.

MFN rates of both the reporter and partner economy negatively impact the probability of PTA formation. The relationship is however nonlinear for the MFN of the partner economy where the relationship reverses as MFN rates increase.

**Panel Logistic Regression on Preferential Trade Agreement Formation Drivers, Economy-Pairs, and Year Fixed Effects**

| | (1) | (2) |
|---|---|---|
| Exports | 0.22** | 0.40* |
| | (2.17) | (1.91) |
| Imports | 0.17 | 0.21 |
| | (1.56) | (0.98) |
| Restrictive trade interventions (by reporter) | 2.38*** | 12.57*** |
| | (4.28) | (4.41) |
| Restrictive trade interventions (to partner) | 1.76*** | 14.88*** |
| | (3.06) | (4.03) |
| Liberalizing trade interventions (by reporter) | 1.24* | 15.02*** |
| | (1.70) | (4.34) |
| Liberalizing trade interventions (to partner) | 2.17*** | 14.95*** |
| | (2.95) | (4.22) |
| Partner MFN | -0.76*** | -1.24** |
| | (-4.56) | (-2.25) |
| Reporter MFN | -0.08 | -1.26*** |
| | (-0.57) | (-2.59) |
| Exports # Reporter MFN | -0.01 | -0.06** |
| | (-1.10) | (-2.03) |
| Exports # Partner MFN | -0.01 | -0.01 |
| | (-1.16) | (-0.26) |
| Imports # Reporter MFN | -0.01 | 0.01 |
| | (-0.96) | (0.46) |
| Imports # Partner MFN | -0.01 | -0.05** |
| | (-0.72) | (-1.98) |
| Restrictive trade interventions (by reporter) # Reporter MFN | -0.14** | -1.57*** |
| | (-2.39) | (-2.84) |
| Restrictive trade interventions (by reporter) # Partner MFN | 0.36*** | 0.30 |
| | (6.25) | (1.39) |
| Liberalizing trade interventions (by reporter) # Reporter MFN | -0.09 | -2.83*** |
| | (-1.42) | (-4.37) |
| Liberalizing trade interventions (by reporter) # Partner MFN | 0.55*** | 0.79*** |
| | (7.11) | (3.88) |
| Restrictive trade interventions (to partner) # Reporter MFN | 0.43*** | 0.20 |
| | (7.46) | (0.96) |
| Restrictive trade interventions (to partner) # Partner MFN | -0.11* | -2.00*** |
| | (-1.69) | (-2.95) |
| Liberalizing trade interventions (to partner) # Reporter MFN | 0.42*** | 0.85*** |
| | (6.98) | (4.59) |
| Liberalizing trade interventions (to partner) # Partner MFN | -0.14** | -2.84*** |
| | (-2.22) | (-4.29) |
| Reporter MFN^2 | | 0.02 |
| | | (0.86) |

*continued on next page*

*Table: continued*

| | (1) | (2) |
|---|---|---|
| Partner MFN^2 | | 0.03** |
| | | (1.99) |
| Exports # Reporter MFN^2 | | 0.00* |
| | | (1.92) |
| Exports # Partner MFN^2 | | 0.00 |
| | | (0.18) |
| Imports # Reporter MFN^2 | | −0.00 |
| | | (−0.44) |
| Imports # Partner MFN^2 | | 0.00* |
| | | (1.81) |
| Restrictive trade interventions (by reporter) # Reporter MFN^2 | | 0.06** |
| | | (2.18) |
| Restrictive trade interventions (by reporter) # Partner MFN^2 | | −0.01 |
| | | (−1.09) |
| Liberalizing trade interventions (by reporter) # Reporter MFN^2 | | 0.11*** |
| | | (3.61) |
| Liberalizing trade interventions (by reporter) # Partner MFN^2 | | −0.02** |
| | | (−2.14) |
| Restrictive trade interventions (to partner) # Reporter MFN^2 | | −0.01 |
| | | (−1.21) |
| Restrictive trade interventions (to partner) # Partner MFN^2 | | 0.08** |
| | | (2.57) |
| Liberalizing trade interventions (to partner) # Reporter MFN^2 | | −0.02*** |
| | | (−3.36) |
| Liberalizing trade interventions (to partner) # Partner MFN^2 | | 0.11*** |
| | | (3.52) |
| Observations | 57,124 | 57,124 |

MFN = most-favored nation.

Notes: T statistics in parentheses. * $p < 0.10$, ** $p < 0.05$, *** $p < 0.01$.

Source: ADB calculations using World Bank. Deep Trade Agreements Database. https://datatopics.worldbank.org/dta/table.html; International Monetary Fund. Direction of Trade Statistics. https://data.imf.org/dots; and Global Trade Alert Database. https://www.globaltradealert.org (accessed 8 August 2024).

# 3 Cross-Border Investment

## Updates on Foreign Investment in Asia and the Pacific

### Foreign direct investment inflows slumped globally and in Asia in 2023.[21]

Global foreign investment inflows dipped mildly in 2023, as the global economic landscape remained challenging.[22] Increased geoeconomic fragmentation, as well as tight financial conditions, drove foreign direct investment (FDI) inflows down by 2% globally to $1.3 trillion based on balance of payments data from the United Nations Trade and Development (UNCTAD).[23] While FDI flows in the rest of the world grew by 13%, investment flows to Asian economies declined by 15%. The People's Republic of China (PRC) remained the largest regional recipient of FDI, with receipts amounting to $163 billion. Other financial powerhouses such as Singapore ($160 billion) and Hong Kong, China ($113 billion) were also among top destinations of investment in Asia.

### Multinational enterprise investment in Asia reached a new high in 2023, surpassing inflows prior to the COVID-19 pandemic.

Based on firm-level data, which may be a leading indicator for possible trends, investments from multinational enterprises (MNEs) accelerated in Asia in 2023. Much of the reported 58% growth is due to large gains in mergers and acquisitions (M&As) in the region, as these doubled in 2023 after dipping in 2022. Deal receipts amounted to $329 billion compared with 2022's $156 billion. Growth in greenfield capital expenditure further boosted MNE investments in the region, as project values reached $441 billion, 33% higher than the year before.

Tertiary sectors constituted the largest share of MNE investment, accounting for 48% of total receipts in Asia. Manufacturing sectors followed with 44%, while primary sectors accounted for only 8%. While MNE investment expanded in all three major industries, growth in primary industry was a notable result of large M&A deals in some economies, particularly in Australia, where the United States (US)-based Newmont Corporation acquired Newcrest Mining for nearly $18 billion in 2023.

## A Decade of Foreign Investment in Asia

### Notwithstanding external challenges, Asia remained a major recipient of global foreign direct investment flows.

While FDI into Asia has fluctuated over the past 10 years, the region remained a major recipient of global FDI flows, accounting for an average of 40% of global inflows annually (Figure 3.1). Despite shocks, including

---

21 Asia refers to the 49 members of ADB in Asia and the Pacific, which include Australia, Japan, and New Zealand in addition to 46 developing economies.

22 For discussions on recent FDI trends, this chapter analyzes standard balance of payments data along with firm-level data by mode of entry (greenfield investment and mergers and acquisitions).

23 Data from the World Investment Report of United Nations Trade and Development. The report excludes the Caribbean financial centers from its total estimate.

the pandemic and geopolitical tensions, investment in the region remained resilient at times outpacing growth trends globally and in non-Asian economies.

Inflows to the main FDI recipients in Asia remained stable over the decade. The PRC was the most important FDI recipient in the region, consistently accounting for about one-fourth of total inflows in 2013–2023. Despite this, noticeable changes in shares have been apparent. While the PRC remained at the top, its share in total regional inflows has declined slightly in the past decade, reflecting both a structural slowdown in global investment and a possible investment diversion to alternative destinations (Figure 3.2). The PRC's share in total regional inflows contracted mildly from 28% to just above 26%, while Singapore's share increased from 13% to almost 26%.

**Figure 3.1: Global Foreign Direct Investment Inflows, Balance of Payments**

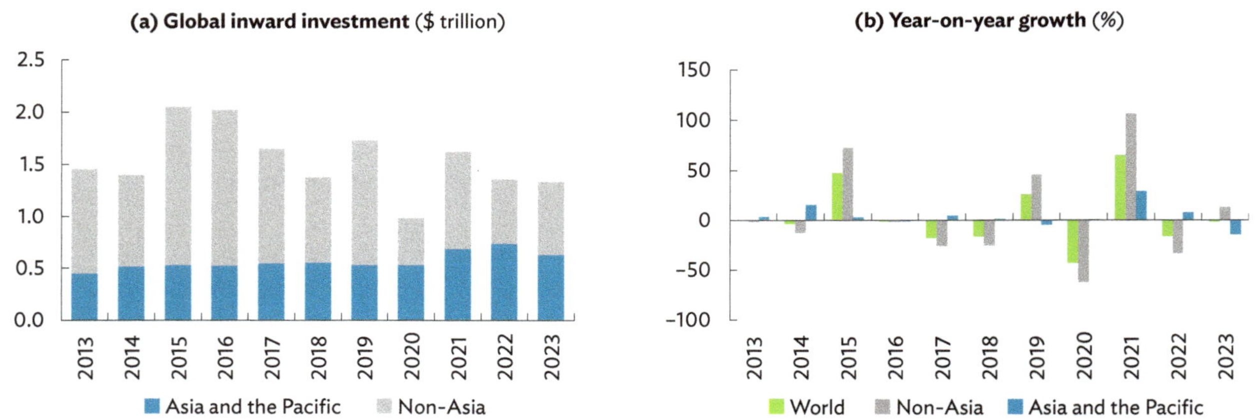


Source: ADB calculations using data from UN Trade and Development. World Investment Report 2024 Statistical Annex Tables. https://unctad.org/topic/investment/world-investment-report (accessed July 2024).

**Figure 3.2: Top Destinations of Foreign Investment, Asia and the Pacific**

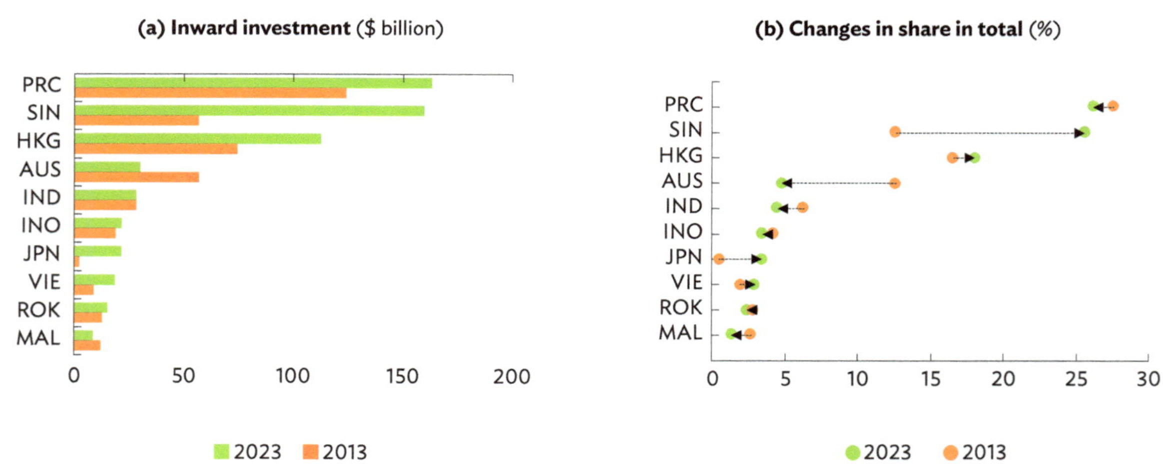


AUS = Australia; PRC = People's Republic of China; HKG = Hong Kong, China; IND = India; INO = Indonesia; JPN = Japan; ROK = Republic of Korea; MAL = Malaysia; SIN = Singapore; VIE = Viet Nam.

Source: ADB calculations using data from UN Trade and Development. World Investment Report 2024 Statistical Annex Tables. https://unctad.org/topic/investment/world-investment-report (accessed July 2024).

Based on balance of payments data, Asia also strengthened intraregional linkages through foreign investment during the past decade, and even more so in the past 5 years. In 2013, intraregional investment accounted for about 47% of regional flows, peaking at 60% during the height of the pandemic and easing to 55% in 2023.

## MNEs remained heavily invested in Asia, cementing the region's importance in supply chains.

Over the past decade, different shocks have affected MNE investments in the region, from macroeconomic and structural adjustments to pandemic-related and geopolitical tensions. In 2017, for example, repatriation of earnings from MNEs based in the US resulted in a dip in global FDI flows. Earnings repatriation also explains to some extent the decline in the PRC's inward flows in recent years. Meanwhile, between 2019 and 2020, multiple shocks such as continued trade tensions and the pandemic drove FDI down globally and in Asia. However, because the region is a hub for manufacturing and a significant source of labor, investments recovered relatively quickly, as seen in 2018 and in 2021, with noticeable effects on the composition of investment (Figure 3.3a). Since 2022, the effects of geopolitical fragmentation and efforts to ensure supply-chain resilience have become more visible, both in trade and in foreign investment. While the long-term effects are still to be realized, shifts in investment patterns in Asia are expected in the coming years.

Services-based sectors have been dominant in attracting foreign affiliates (Figure 3.3b). On average, over the past 10 years, tertiary sectors have accounted for over half of MNE investment into Asia. The region's increasing emphasis on services-related FDI is consistent with the global trend toward asset-light investment (UNCTAD 2024a). Meanwhile, manufacturing sectors generally accounted for about one-third of total inflows and primary sectors typically accounted for less than 10%.

Intraregional investment also factored in significantly in MNE investment flows into Asia. Between 2013 and 2023, about 40% of the region's receipts were from Asian investors, with greenfield inflows comprised of 45% intraregional investments and merger and acquisition (M&A) receipts, 26%.

MNE investment in Asia shows some geographic reallocation, especially in greenfield investments, as destination markets changed amid the recent slowdown of inflows to the PRC (Figure 3.4). Sentiment favoring alternative investment destinations, in conjunction with trade tensions, is seen in recent FDI shifts (UNCTAD 2024a).

**Figure 3.3: Investment in Asia and the Pacific—Firm-Level Activity, Total Greenfield and Mergers and Acquisitions**

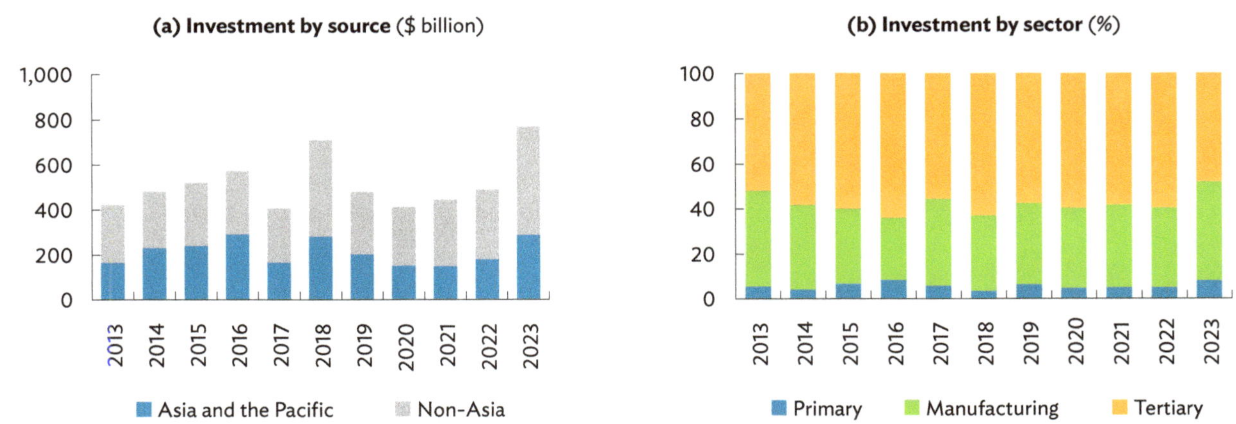


Sources: ADB calculations using data from Financial Times. fDi Markets; and Moody's Analytics. Orbis M&A (formerly Zephyr M&A Database) (both accessed May 2024).

Growth in greenfield investment in Southeast Asian economies, apart from Singapore, its largest investment hub, is also notable. Inflows to economies such as Indonesia, Malaysia, the Philippines, Thailand, and Viet Nam have grown significantly over the past 10 years, with most of these inflows gained in the manufacturing and utilities sectors (Aiyar, Malacrino, and Presbitero 2023; ASEAN Secretariat and UNCTAD 2024). Indeed, Southeast Asian economies have been regarded as alternative FDI destinations to the PRC. Greenfield investment in manufacturing shows that the Association of Southeast Asian Nations (ASEAN) as a bloc has overtaken the PRC in greenfield project values in the past 5 years (Irwin-Hunt 2024).

In contrast, key destinations for M&A deals in Asia appear relatively unchanged in the past decade (Figure 3.5). Australia, Japan, the PRC, and Singapore remained the largest recipients of M&A deals in the region, with Singapore playing a more prominent role. Manufacturing and some service sectors (e.g., finance and insurance, utilities, education) continue to account for a large share of acquisitions across economies. While M&A deals have traditionally been more common in industrialized economies, they are increasingly used as a mode of entry by investors in Asia. Several factors may have contributed to this trend. First, more favorable financial conditions since early 2023 in certain economies (e.g., Indonesia, the Philippines, Viet Nam) have lowered deal valuations and made M&A more attractive. This, together with capital account restrictions favoring outright purchases over portfolio flows, could have increased appetite for M&A deals. Second, more transparent and flexible screening and approval procedures for mergers in developing economies in Asia have contributed to more stable investment flows (ADBI and ADB 2024). Third, increasing market concentration in some industries, such as banking and financial services, have favored cross-border M&A transactions in the region in recent years.

Trends in foreign investment by business activity indicate that manufacturing continued to carve a large portion of Asia's greenfield investments (Figure 3.6).[24] Investments geared toward manufacturing doubled from $103 billion in 2013 to $227 billion in 2023. Semiconductors, specifically, gained substantial investments, with receipts in the sector quintupling between 2013 and 2023.

**Figure 3.4: Greenfield Investment in Asia and the Pacific, by Destination and Sector**

PRC = People's Republic of China.

Sources: ADB calculations using data from Financial Times. fDi Markets; and Moody's Analytics. Orbis M&A (formerly Zephyr M&A Database) (both accessed May 2024).

24 Business activity is defined as the actual function of the operation in greenfield projects. In this case, the project, not the company, is classified. This facilitates the identification of upstream and downstream activities where multinationals are more actively investing.

**Figure 3.5: Merger and Acquisition Deals in Asia and the Pacific, by Destination and Sector**

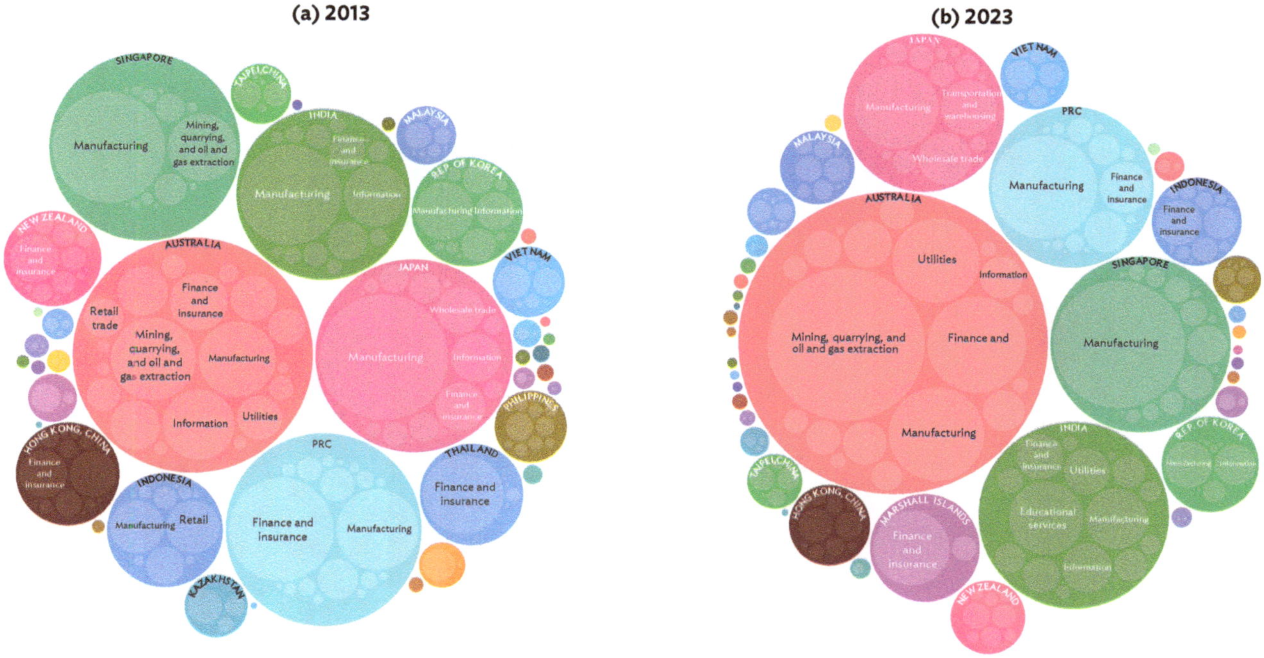


PRC = People's Republic of China.

Sources: ADB calculations using data from Financial Times. fDi Markets; and Moody's Analytics. Orbis M&A (formerly Zephyr M&A Database) (both accessed May 2024).

**Figure 3.6: Greenfield Investment in Asia and the Pacific, by Business Activity**

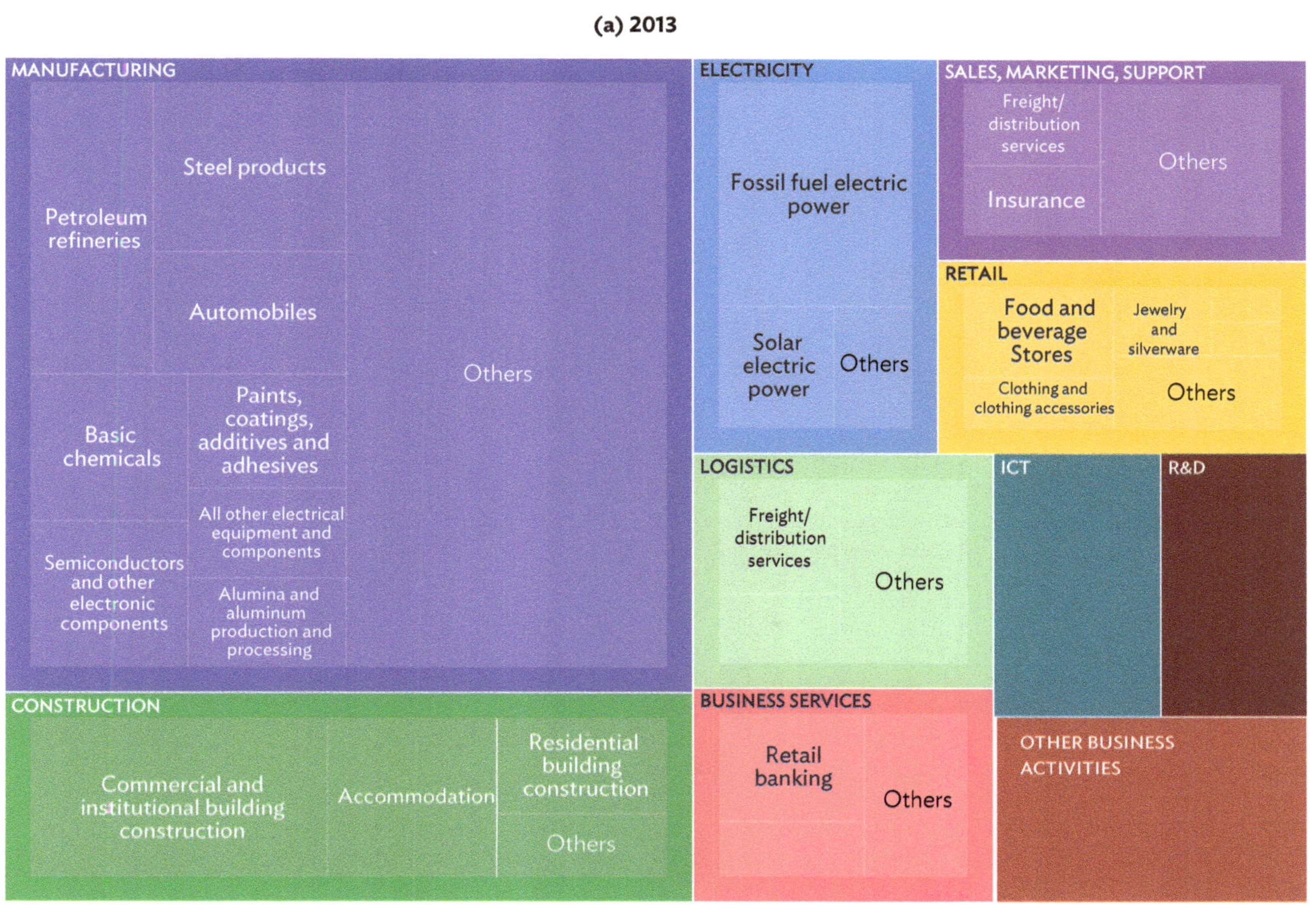


*continued on next page*

*Figure 3.6: continued*

**(b) 2023**

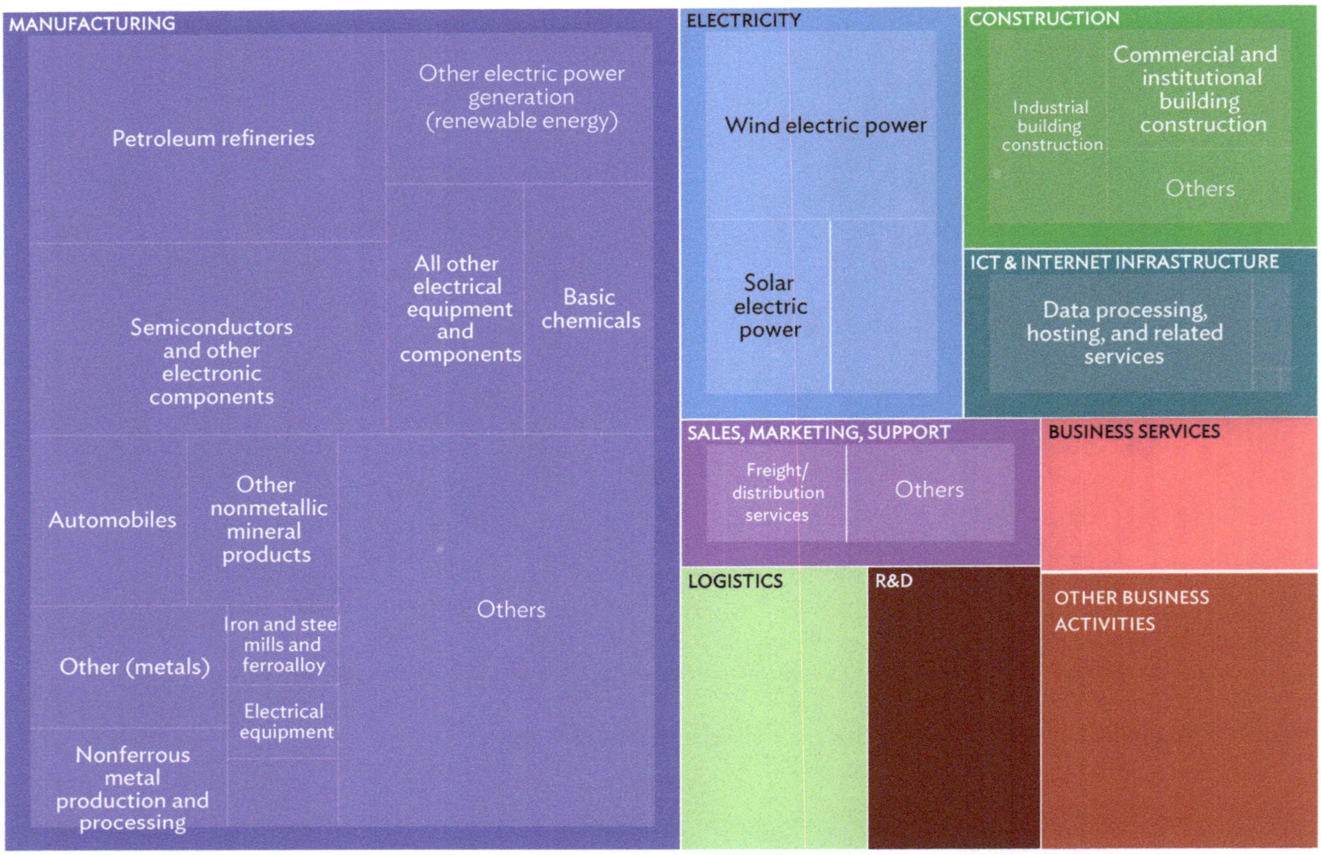


ICT = information and communication technology, R&D = research and development.

Sources: ADB calculations using data from Financial Times. fDi Markets; and Moody's Analytics. Orbis M&A (formerly Zephyr M&A Database) (both accessed May 2024).

There were also some noticeable changes in subsector composition in electricity projects (Figure 3.6b). Greenfield investment used to be more concentrated in fossil fuel electric power in 2013 ($15 billion); however, by 2023, renewable energy prevailed, with wind electric power amassing $24 billion and solar electric power $12 billion in investment. In the past 10 years, increased efforts to address climate change and the preference for renewables have doubled greenfield investments in electricity projects from $23 billion in 2013 to $46 billion in 2023.

Despite this positive shift, capital investments in the oil and gas sectors resurged in 2023 globally. Fossil fuels and coal brought in significant investments and is still the third-largest sector for greenfield projects globally (Financial Times 2024). Even in Asia, petroleum refineries had the largest receipts in terms of greenfield investments, with the sector amassing $34 billion in capital expenditures in 2023. As such, supportive policies for green investments remain key in ensuring that the shift toward greener industries and production does not unravel.

## Strategic sectors gained importance, accounting for over one-third of MNE investment in Asia in the past 10 years.

Strategic sectors have become increasingly important in driving MNE investment to Asia over the past decade. From one-fifth of MNE investments into Asia in 2013, receipts in the region's strategic sectors peaked at 46% in 2022 and settled at 44% in 2023.[25] MNE investment in

[25] Strategic sectors are termed such as they have the potential for spillovers in innovation and in infrastructure. Strategic sectors are based on reference lists from Atlantic Council (2022) and from the International Monetary Fund's April 2023 World Economic Outlook (IMF 2023).

strategic sectors also quadrupled, from $79 billion in 2013 to $335 billion in 2023. Much of this trend is explained by growing investment in equipment for the green energy transition, critical minerals, and semiconductors. Between 2013 and 2023, investment in green transition equipment saw average annual growth of 26%; semiconductors, 55%; and critical minerals, 74%. Investments in critical minerals have quickened in the past 4 years (Box 3.1). On average, inflows toward strategic sectors also sped up in the second half of the decade (Figure 3.7). Average annual growth between 2018 and 2023 reached 29%, compared with 11% between 2013 and 2017.

By recipient, inflows in strategic sectors appear to have concentrated more on equipment for green energy transition by 2018–2023, particularly in Southeast Asia (Figure 3.7). This is in contrast with trends in 2013–2017, when investments in strategic sectors were mostly in East Asia. This trend aligns with more recent investor strategies toward diversification of supply and investment bases, as well as intensified efforts in green technologies and energy.

Growing MNE concerns to ensure supply chain resilience and reduce geopolitical risks also explains the reconfiguration of FDI in strategic sectors. The most palpable case is for semiconductors, with regional investments toward East Asia decreasing and a diversion of investment toward neighboring economies or other regions (as covered as a special theme in this chapter). In contrast, investments in other industries, such as pharmaceuticals and motor vehicles, have been stickier.

## Outbound FDI from Asia grew but remains volatile.

While global outward FDI grew overall in the past decade, some key developments, such as the US tax reform in 2018, heightened trade tensions and the COVID-19 pandemic in 2020, subjected flows to much fluctuation (Figure 3.8a). These events resulted in sharp downturns, particularly in 2020 when outflows dipped below $1 trillion, the lowest since 2005. Foreign investment outflows have since rebounded.

Asia saw similar trends between 2013 and 2023, with outflows from the region amounting to $610 billion in 2023, about a third higher than outflows in 2013 (Figure 3.8b). Similar fluctuations had been observed throughout the past decade, with outflows from Asia dipping in 2018 because of uncertainties arising from trade tensions and again in 2020 due to the pandemic. Despite these shocks, outflows from the region have recovered and have surpassed prepandemic levels.

**Figure 3.7: Investment in Strategic Sectors—Asia and the Pacific, Firm-Level Activity, Total Greenfield and Mergers and Acquisitions** (% share to total investment inflows)

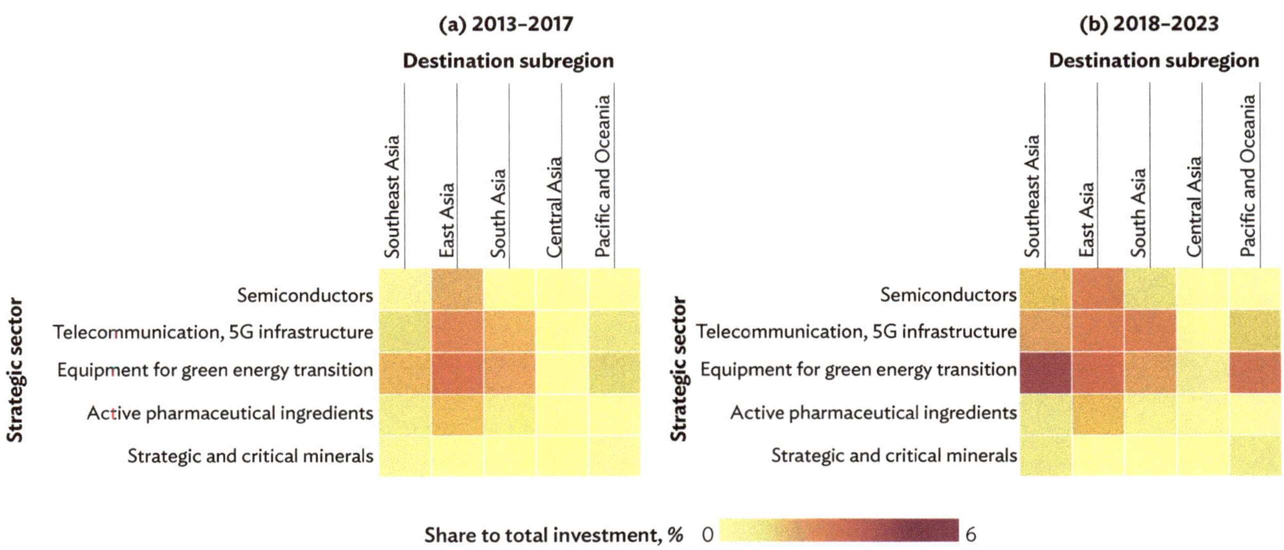


Note: Total investment refers to the sum of capital expenditures for greenfield projects and deal values for mergers and acquisitions for the given period.

Sources: ADB calculations using data from Financial Times. fDi Markets; and Moody's Analytics. Orbis M&A (formerly Zephyr M&A Database) (both accessed May 2024); and methodology from Atlantic Council (2022) and International Monetary Fund (2023).

Japan remains the primary Asian source of global investment in the past decade, typically accounting for 30% of regional outflows and 10% of global outflows (Figure 3.8b and Figure 3.9). FDI from Japan also saw significant growth between 2013 and 2023, averaging 11% annually, above the 5% growth observed in the region. The PRC was the second-largest Asian source, with the economy accounting for one-fourth of regional outflows between 2013 and 2023. Where top destinations seem to have changed in terms of inflows in Asia, top Asian

**Box 3.1: Critical Mineral Production and Foreign Direct Investment for Electric Vehicle Batteries in Asia and the Pacific**

The transition to clean energy is driving unprecedented demand for critical minerals integral to clean energy technologies, such as electric vehicles. Compared to conventional vehicles, electric vehicles require significantly more critical minerals, particularly graphite, nickel, lithium, cobalt, copper, and rare earth elements driven by battery and motor needs.

Asia and the Pacific is a major producer of critical minerals essential for electric vehicle battery production, with a few key players dominating the markets. Australia and the People's Republic of China (PRC) produce most of the world's rare earths, graphite, and lithium, while Indonesia is a major source of nickel, copper, and cobalt (box figure 1). Southeast Asia contributes to rare earths, manganese, copper, and cobalt production.

Asia and the Pacific is also a leading destination and source of cross-border critical mineral investments. From 2015 to 2024, the region attracted 54% of North America's merger and acquisition (M&A) deals, with the United States leading the acquisitions, particularly in Australia (box figure 2a). Intraregional M&A is strong, with Japan acquiring assets in the Pacific, while Central Asia and South Asia see limited activity. Greenfield investments are active, especially in Indonesia's metals processing, driven by PRC investments (box figure 2b). Beyond the region, the PRC invested in Argentina's lithium, Australia in Chile's copper, and the United Kingdom in Mongolia's mining sector.

**1: Mining Production in Asia and the Pacific, 2022** (% of global production)

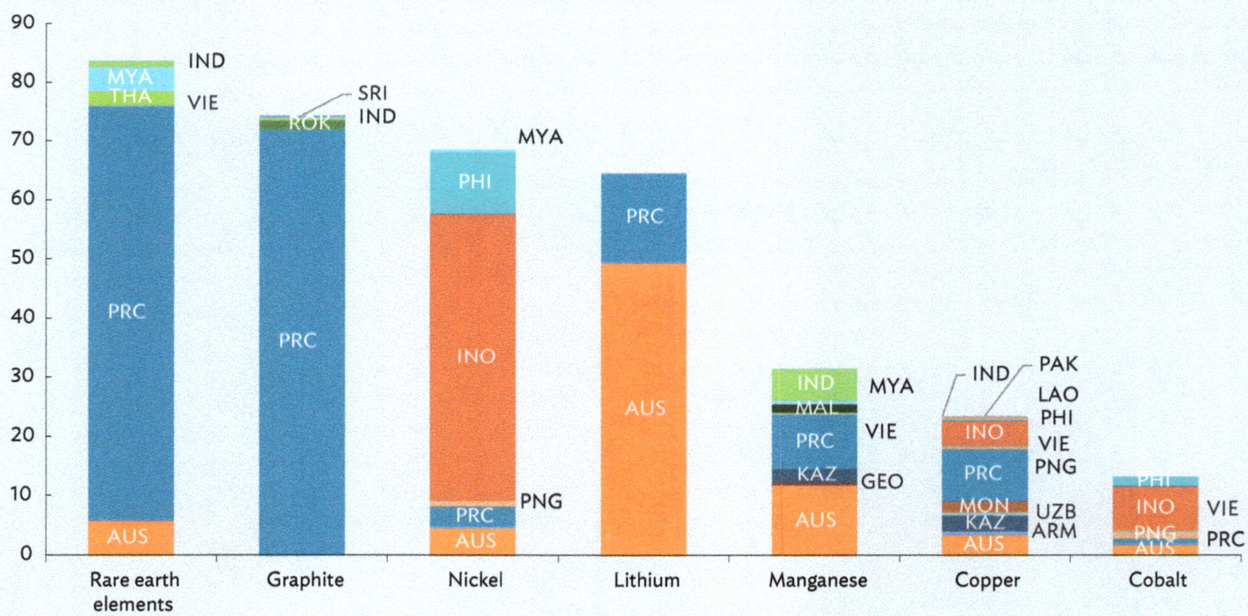


ARM = Armenia, AUS = Australia, AZE = Azerbaijan, PRC = People's Republic of China, GEO = Georgia, IND = India, INO = Indonesia, JPN = Japan, KAZ = Kazakhstan, KGZ = Kyrgyz Republic, LAO = Lao People's Democratic Republic, MAL = Malaysia, MON = Mongolia, MYA = Myanmar, PAK = Pakistan, PHI = Philippines, PNG = Papua New Guinea, ROK = Republic of Korea, SRI = Sri Lanka, TAJ = Tajikistan, THA = Thailand, UZB = Uzbekistan, VIE = Viet Nam.

Sources: British Geological Survey. World Mineral Statistics Data. https://www.bgs.ac.uk/mineralsuk/statistics/world-mineral-statistics/; and US Geological Survey. Mineral Commodity Summaries 2023: US Geological Survey. https://doi.org/10.3133/mcs2023 (both accessed December 2024).

*continued on next page*

*Box 3.1 continued*

**2: Flows of Mergers and Acquisitions and Greenfield Investment Deal Values in Critical Minerals Industries, 2015–2024** ($ million)

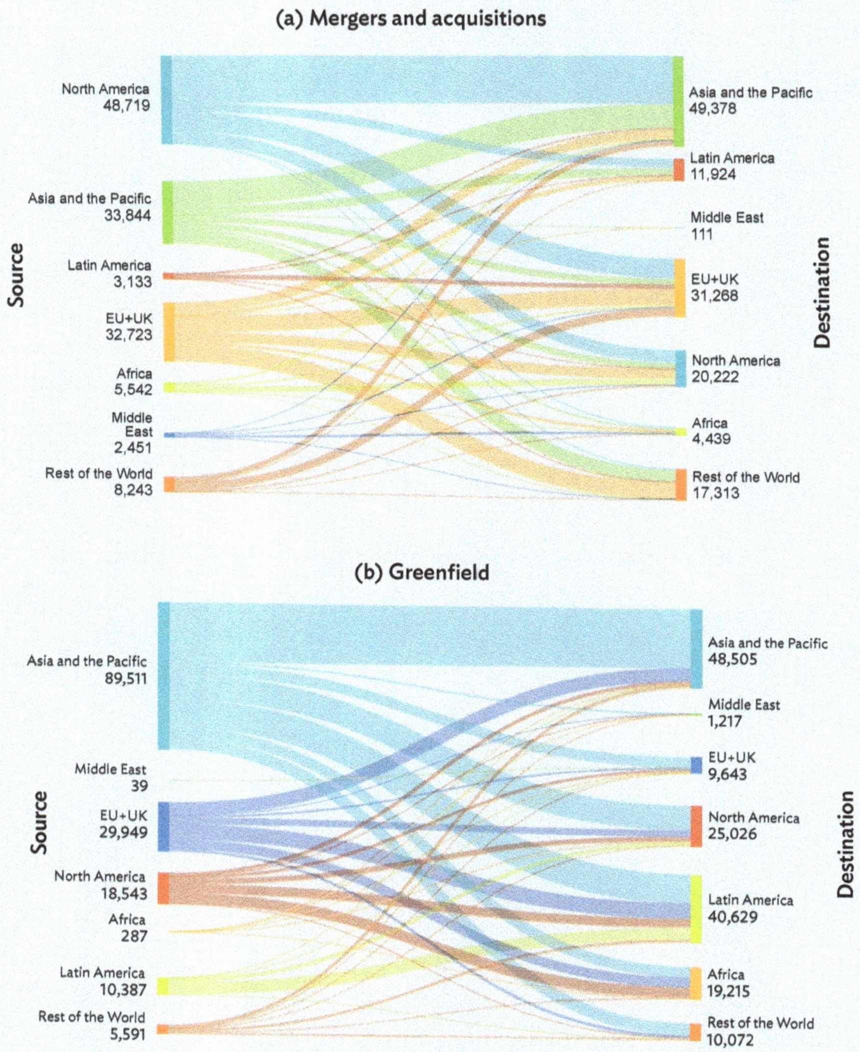


EU = European Union (27 members), UK = United Kingdom.

Notes:

(i) Figure (a) is based on the following subsectors, classified under the North American Industry Classification System 2017: 212399–All Other Nonmetallic Mineral Mining involves graphite, considered a critical mineral, used for anodes in Lithium-ion batteries (LIBs); 213115–Support Activities for Nonmetallic Minerals (except Fuels) Mining includes support activity for phosphate rock mining, with phosphate being used for lithium iron phosphate batteries, as well as graphite mining, with graphite being used for anodes in LIBs; 212299–All Other Metal Ore Mining involves cobalt, manganese, and rare earths mining; 212230 - Copper, Nickel, Lead, and Zinc Mining which involves critical minerals (i.e., copper and nickel); 213114–Support Activities for Metal Mining involves support for mining of cobalt, copper, nickel, and rare earths; 331410–Nonferrous Metal (except Aluminum) Smelting and Refining involves refining of cobalt, copper, and nickel.

(ii) Figure (b) is based on the following fDi Markets subsectors: Copper, Nickel, Lead, & Zinc Mining, which involves critical minerals (i.e., copper and nickel); Nonferrous Metal Production & Processing, which includes copper smelting and refining, as well as nickel refining, and recovery from scrap; Nonmetallic Mineral Mining & Quarrying, which involves graphite mining and phosphate rock mining; Other (Minerals) and Other Non-Metallic Mineral Products, both involving natural graphite manufacturing; and Support Activities for Mining, which includes support activities for mining metals such as copper and nickel.

Source: Kim et al. (forthcoming) based on data from Financial Times. fDi Markets; and Moody's Analytics. Orbis M&A (formerly Zephyr M&A Database) (both accessed December 2024).

Source: Kim et al. (forthcoming).

**Figure 3.8: Foreign Direct Investment Outflows—Balance of Payments**

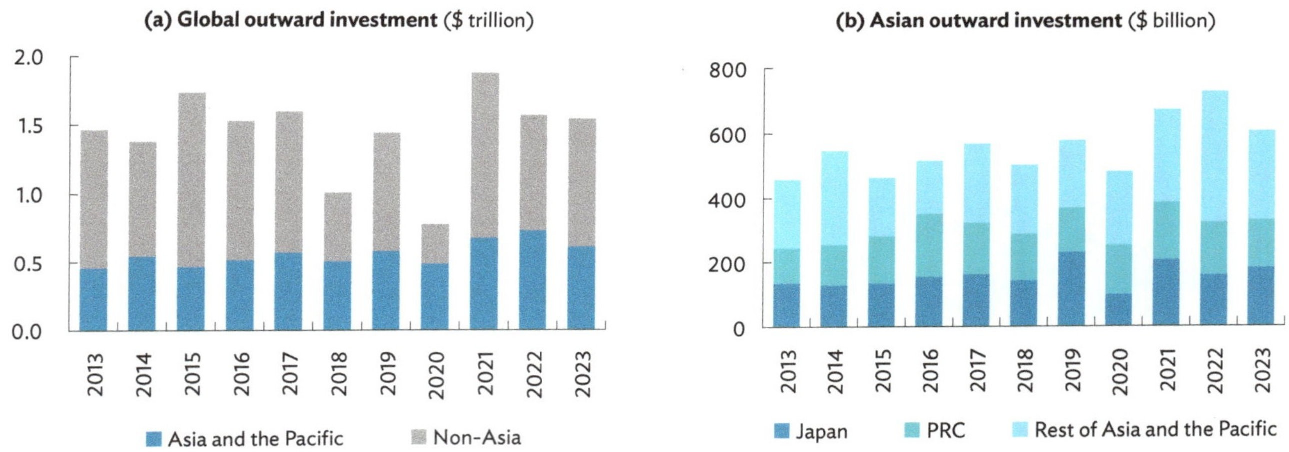


PRC = People's Republic of China.

Source: ADB calculations using data from UN Trade and Development. World Investment Report 2024 Statistical Annex Tables. https://unctad.org/topic/investment/world-investment-report (accessed July 2024).

**Figure 3.9: Top Sources of Foreign Investment—Balance of Payments, Asia and the Pacific**

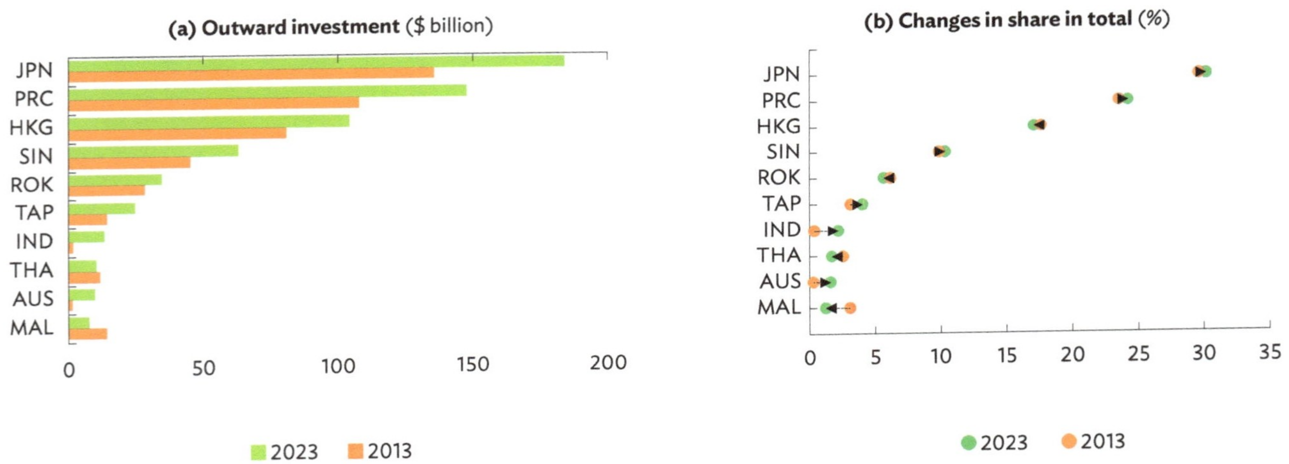


AUS = Australia; PRC = People's Republic of China; HKG = Hong Kong, China; IND = India; JPN = Japan; ROK = Republic of Korea; MAL = Malaysia; SIN = Singapore; TAP = Taipei,China; THA = Thailand.

Source: ADB calculations using data from UN Trade and Development. World Investment Report 2024 Statistical Annex Tables. https://unctad.org/topic/investment/world-investment-report (accessed July 2024).

investors have remained broadly stable. Financial hubs dominate foreign investment outflows, with Japan; the PRC; Hong Kong, China; and Singapore as primary sources, accounting for about 80% of Asian outward FDI between 2013 and 2023.

## Despite new and ongoing challenges, 2024 may see an uptick in global investment activity.

While foreign investment dipped by 2% globally, global FDI may still see some growth in 2024 as financing conditions have improved. Easing interest rates, along with continued MNE profitability and stable reinvestment of earnings, have induced a more positive investment climate. The strong showing from greenfield investment in 2023, as well as the possible recovery of M&As in 2024, may help propel foreign investment (UNCTAD 2024b).

Despite the FDI slowdown in Asia in 2023, leading indicators such as investment in greenfield projects and M&A deal values hint at stability in 2024 as both grew in 2023. Continued growth in strategic sectors such as telecommunications and equipment for green energy transition may help maintain the region's status as a prime destination of FDI. Asia's outlook for inbound FDI is expected to see strong interest from MNEs looking to expand supply chain networks in emerging sectors such as electric vehicles, coupled with the PRC's growth in outbound FDI given its expansion of renewables, rising production costs in some sectors, and less optimistic economic outlook.

Downside risks for FDI include rising geopolitical and trade tensions, which loom over the global economic landscape. As MNEs seek to diversify production and investment bases, FDI flows may be contingent on near-shoring strategies. Along with the relatively tempered outlook for global economic growth, foreign investors may have become more risk-averse in 2024. Moreover, potential US tax reforms similar to those implemented in 2017 and additional FDI restrictions on the PRC may exacerbate downside risks. As such, proactive and supportive investment policies, both regional and domestic, are imperative in ensuring that economies can leverage current robust trends.

## Structural Trends in Foreign Investment in Asia

### Service-related, digital, and green sectors have consolidated their importance in driving foreign investments into Asia.

While FDI still plays a central role in Asia's economic model, its contribution to growth and industrial development has changed over the past decade. This shift is confirmed by the overall stable trend, at best, in Asia's inward investment. Indeed, the region's average economic growth of 3.7% from 2013 to 2023 was matched by a similar pace in regional FDI growth (3.9%). However, aggregate trends may hide changes in the composition and role of FDI in the region.

Three main trends encapsulate the re-composition of FDI in Asia in the past decade:

First, services-related sectors have consolidated as recipients of foreign investment in the region. This growth is not startling, given the importance of service industries in the growth of manufacturing and increasing internal demand. From 2013 to 2023, trade in services in Asia increased from $2.5 billion to $3.9 billion. And with it, the contribution of cross-border investment to the internationalization of services. FDI trends follow the shift from export-oriented manufacturing-led growth strategies toward domestic consumption, including services, that Asian economies continue to undergo as a result of servicification (Mercer-Blackman and Ablaza 2018), consumption (Chen et al. 2023), and structural transformation (Gibson 2024).

In the wake of regulatory reforms and more flexible, proactive investment frameworks, a growing share of MNEs have pursued internationalization strategies in services. Regionally, service-related sectors increased their investment share relative to manufacturing, in both domestic and foreign investment. Between 2003 and 2007, half of Asia's greenfield investment would typically be in manufacturing; in 2018–2023, services accounted for half of greenfield projects in the region (Figure 3.10). In contrast, M&As have consistently been focused on services, with the sector accounting for nearly two-thirds of total deal receipts in the region.

Second, the past decade has seen the growing importance of digital-related sectors for foreign investment. Investment in digital infrastructure, e-commerce, and financial technologies have driven the digital sector and continue to rise. Overall investments in digital service sectors, for example, increased from $92 billion in 2013 to $141 billion in 2023, accelerating significantly during the COVID-19 pandemic (ADB 2022). While a large share of FDI into the region is still directed at traditional manufacturing and services, industry 4.0 and automation-related sectors such as AI, cloud computing, and other investments have also seen an increase. Planned investments by large digital conglomerates, including digital platforms, e-commerce and digital solutions, indicate a surge in digital FDI in coming years. Also, governments in the region have eased investment restrictions in the digital sectors, including Malaysia's measures to improve labor mobility and Viet Nam's opening of digital industries to foreign ownership.

Third, growth of green FDI continues to be a major factor in explaining the investment dynamics. FDI in green transition equipment signals an inflection point for the region (Figure 3.10). Investment in renewable energy, electric vehicles, and other clean technologies has surged globally, with the sector accounting for more than one quarter of global FDI between 2020 and 2023. Together with decarbonization objectives, the diversification of the energy matrix and affordability have made investments in solar, wind, green hydrogen, and battery storage increasingly attractive (IEA 2024). Governments in the region have also introduced policies to entice foreign investors to invest in green sectors. In fact, economies introducing climate policies, from regulatory policies to green incentives, have seen a substantial increase in renewable energy FDI (Jaumotte et al. 2024). Such progress has also called for more suitable mechanisms to manage the associated regulatory risks involved in foreign participation in the energy sector.

## While vertical investment growth propelled growth in Asia, horizontal investment is increasingly important.

Another structural development in Asia's FDI can be attributed to changes in the investment motive. As a hub for manufacturing production, efficiency-seeking investments have helped Asia consolidate its position in export markets and participation in value chains. Comparing FDI trends and export capacity in the region's top three efficiency-seeking sectors is illustrative.[26] Foreign investment in sectors such as chemicals and chemical products, computer and electronics, and motor vehicles is associated with larger exports in the sectors from the host economy (Figures 3.11a–c). In market-seeking service sectors, this association is not necessarily clear, provided that the foreign presence is primarily aimed at meeting domestic demand, as in the case of

**Figure 3.10: Average Annual Share in Total Investment by Sector—Firm-Level** (% share in total)

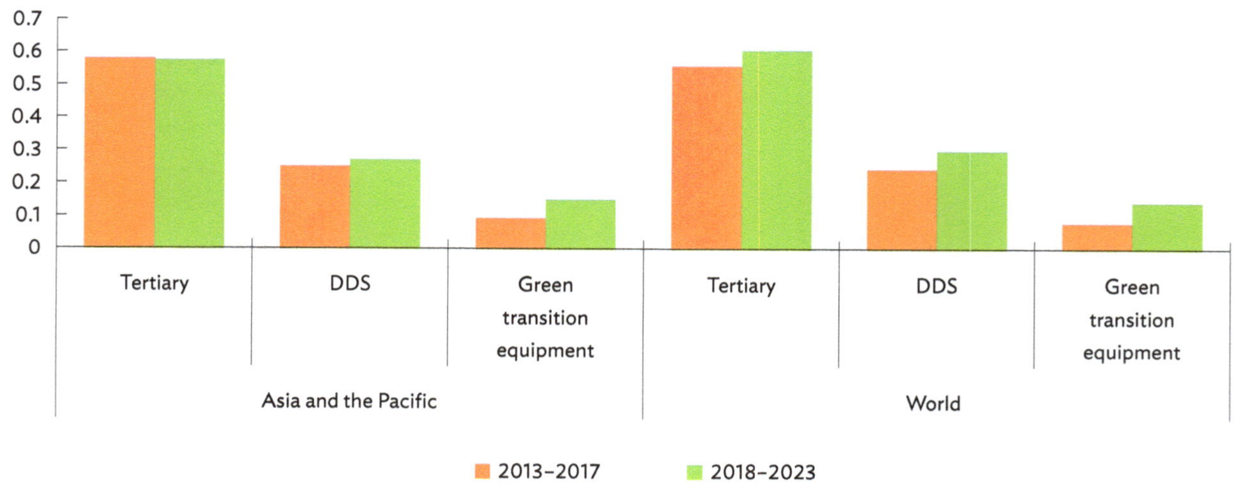


DDS = digitally deliverable services.

Sources: ADB calculations using data from Financial Times. fDi Markets; and Moody's Analytics. Orbis M&A (formerly Zephyr M&A Database) (both accessed May 2024).

26 Efficiency-seeking sectors are defined as those with a higher proportion of exports from foreign firms (relative to gross output), while market-seeking sectors are defined as those with a higher proportion of household final consumption expenditure from foreign firms (relative to gross output). For details, see Box 3.3 in ADB (2024).

**Figure 3.11: Investment Versus Exports in Selected Sectors—Firm-Level, Asia and the Pacific** ($ billion, 5-year moving average)

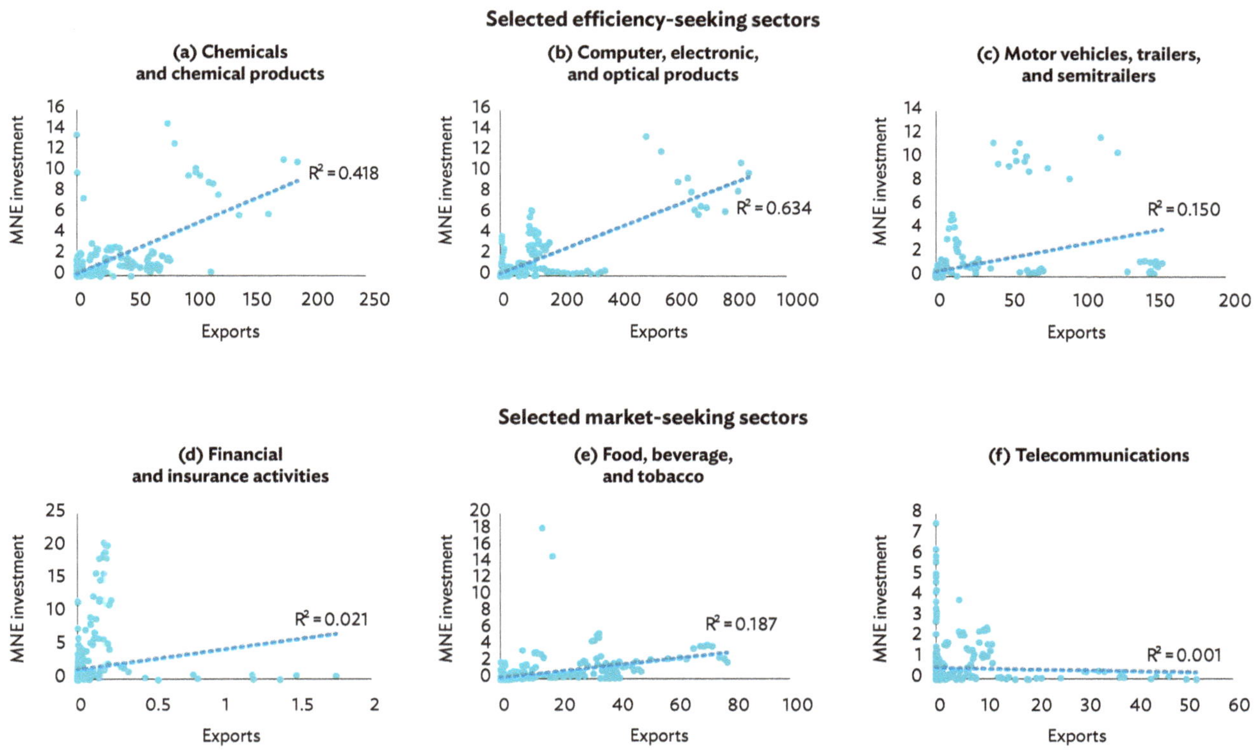


MNE = multinational enterprise.

Sources: ADB calculations using data from Financial Times. fDi Markets; and Moody's Analytics. Orbis M&A (formerly Zephyr M&A Database).

financial activities and telecommunications (Figure 3.11d and Figure 3.11f). Production-based sectors, such as food, beverage, and tobacco, may exhibit a positive association with exports despite being market-seeking (Figure 3.11e).

Where efficiency-seeking (or vertical) FDI has allowed Asia to scale up global value chain participation and production, market-seeking (or horizontal or platform) investments have enabled regional economies to service domestic demand (ADB 2024). The share of the top five efficiency-seeking and market-seeking sectors in Asia has remained generally stable and increased in 2023 (Figure 3.12a). Overall, efficiency-seeking sectors still constitute nearly half of total investment flows into Asia; they are also more concentrated in fewer sectors. The top market-seeking sectors had larger shares in the past decade (about 20% of total inflows) compared with the top efficiency-seeking sectors (about 15% of total inflows).

In addition, the contribution from the top efficiency-seeking sectors to total FDI growth has been positive on average over the past decade, while the contribution of market-seeking is more volatile (Figure 3.12b).

## Industrial developments also explain shifts of foreign investment in the region.

Together with major trends in servicification, digitalization, and the green transition, some industries have experienced significant shifts which translate into an expansion or reallocation of foreign investment.

The automotive sector has experienced important industry shifts in the past decade. Large economies such as the PRC and Indonesia remain important FDI hosts for motor industries, with Singapore a major hub for investment in the sector (Figure 3.13a and Annex

3a for the earlier period). However, investment in electric vehicles, a major trend in Southeast Asia, has grown substantially and is motivating new investments. The annual average greenfield projects in automotive production during 2015–2025 in ASEAN members rose to $3 billion, from $1.9 billion 10 years earlier, with the supply chain for electric vehicles accounting for most of this growth (ASEAN Secretariat and UNCTAD 2024). Indonesia, Malaysia, and Thailand dominate as investment recipients, focused not only on production (i.e., original equipment manufacturers) but also on other parts of the supply chain (i.e., batteries, distribution).

In the computer, electronics, and optical products sector, Japan, the PRC, Singapore, and Viet Nam attracted the most investment. ASEAN members remain major recipients of FDI in semiconductors, with some of the largest investments taking place in the region. Economies such as Malaysia and Taipei,China also gained ground as hubs for investment (Figure 3.13b). Equally important has been the strengthened bilateral investment linkages, as observed between Japan and Taipei,China.

In chemicals and chemical products, investment remained concentrated in a relatively small group of economies (the PRC, Indonesia, and Kazakhstan), while the PRC continued to attract higher investments than other Asian economies (Figure 3.13c).

In telecommunications, South Asian economies continued to receive the largest investments in the past 5 years, mainly from extraregional companies from the US and the European Union (EU). Investments in the sector remain relatively small for large economies, such as the PRC (Figure 3.13d).

As diversification and geopolitical considerations become important factors in investment reallocation, their effects by investment motive and across industries are yet to be quantified. This may be more apparent in market-seeking sectors such as finance or telecommunications, where investment in the PRC seems to have been eclipsed by other economies such as Hong Kong, China.

**Figure 3.12: Foreign Investment by Motive—Firm-Level, Asia and the Pacific**

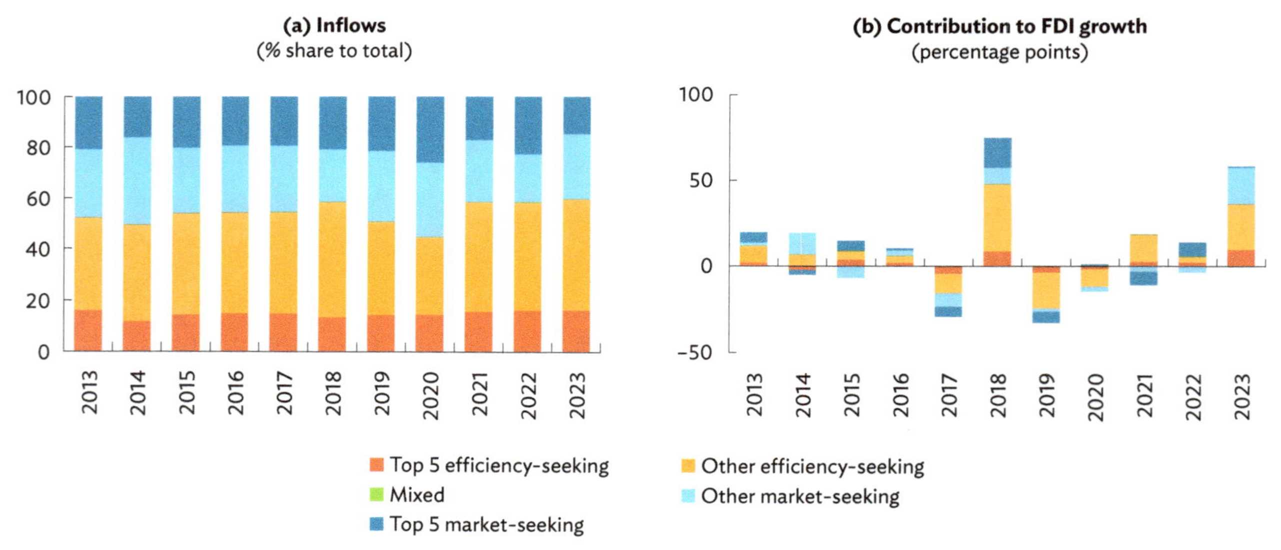


FDI = foreign direct investment.

Notes: Efficiency-seeking and market-seeking sectors are identified as in ADB (2024). Sectors identified as both efficiency-seeking and market-seeking are labeled "mixed" in these charts.

Sources: ADB calculations using data from Financial Times. fDi Markets; and Moody's Analytics. Orbis M&A (formerly Zephyr M&A Database) (both accessed May 2024).

**Figure 3.13: Foreign Investment Linkages in Selected Sectors—Firm-Level, Asia and the Pacific, 2018–2023**
($ million, average annual investment)

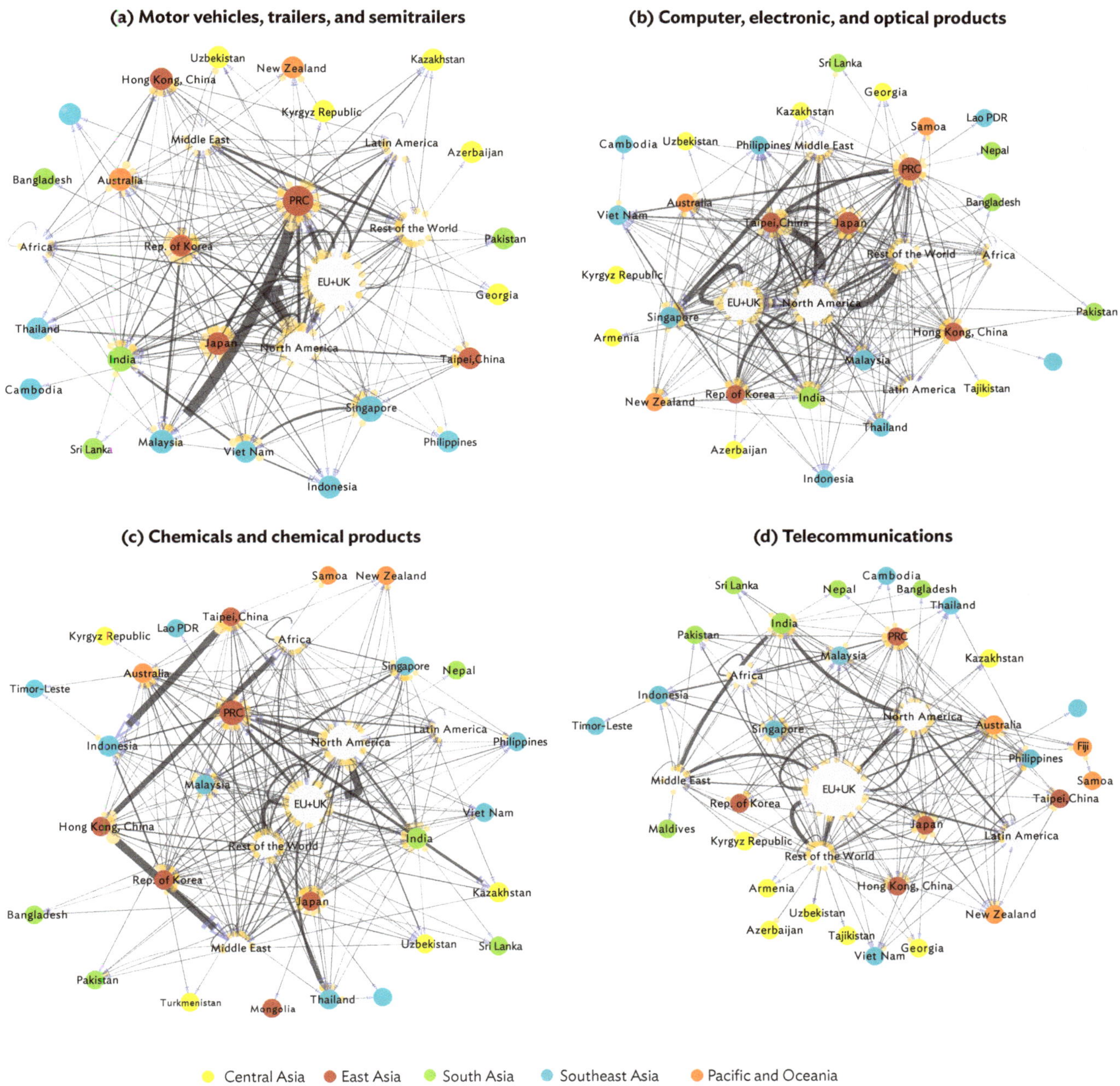


PRC = People's Republic of China, EU = European Union (27 members), Lao PDR = Lao People's Democratic Republic, UK = United Kingdom.

Notes: Nodes are sized according to each economy's or region's share in the total inward investment for the indicated period. Each link represents average investment from a source node (round end) to a target node (arrow end). Sectors are harmonized based on the classification used in the Analytical Activity of Multinational Enterprises from the Organisation for Economic Co-operation and Development (OECD).

Sources: ADB calculations using data from Financial Times. fDi Markets; and Moody's Analytics. Orbis M&A (formerly Zephyr M&A Database); and OECD. Activity of Multinational Enterprises. https://www.oecd.org/en/data/datasets/activity-of-multinational-enterprises.html (all accessed May 2024).

## Leveraging FDI Through Regional Cooperation

Foreign investment has enabled Asian economies not just to scale up production and participate in global value chains, but also to create jobs, transfer skills, and fulfill other domestic needs. Over the past decade, governments in the region have recognized the importance of FDI and the role that regional cooperation can play in leveraging the presence and contribution of foreign entities to attain development objectives. Today, a myriad of international investment agreements and platforms, whether bilateral, regional, or multilateral, coexist. Thus far, there are over 1,000 bilateral investment treaties in force in the Asian region and more than 90 regional agreements including investment provisions.

Regional cooperation and integration (RCI) can be a cornerstone for FDI development through several channels. To begin, RCI provides benefits from agglomeration and geographic proximity, enabling the creation of larger production networks, in the case of vertical FDI, and offering larger markets for regional MNEs in the case of horizontal FDI. Moreover, RCI can also provide the institutional foundations of a single market, contributing to harmonizing investment frameworks and regulations (De Lombaerde 2024). Finally, RCI can leverage economies of scale when implementing industrial development agendas, such as the energy transition or developing new ecosystems in areas such as electric vehicles (ASEAN and UNCTAD 2024). The section below explores the opportunities that RCI offers to leveraging foreign investment to attain these objectives.

### Policies for strengthening investment facilitation in Asia are needed.

Investment facilitation is one area of FDI policy receiving increasing attention in the region and G20 economies (Santos-Paulino et al. 2024). Broadly, investment facilitation refers to the actions designed to attract FDI and maximize the effectiveness of government support through all stages of the investment cycle. As in the case of investment liberalization, domestic policies have been most commonly relied upon when implementing investment promotion and facilitation. While regional cooperation could, in principle, contribute to the implementation of investment facilitation arrangements, such as single digital platforms (ASEAN Secretariat and UNCTAD 2024),[27] taxation (Chaisse 2023), or aftercare services (Ahn 2024), it has not always been utilized. Indeed, not many international investment agreements include these areas. By 2018, only 35 investment treaties explicitly included provisions for facilitation out of several thousand concluded at the time (Lazo 2018). In response to this gap, support for investment facilitation initiatives has increased.

The World Trade Organization (WTO) Investment Facilitation for Development (IFD) Agreement aims to create a transparent, predictable, and streamlined environment for FDI. Endorsed by more than 120 WTO members, including 26 from Asia, the IFD has gathered momentum among members. Its key objectives are to improve the transparency of investment-related measures, streamline administrative procedures to make investment processes more efficient, facilitate sustainable investments, and provide special treatment and capacity-building support for developing economies. Rather than emphasizing liberalization of investment policies, the IFD emphasizes the importance of simplifying, speeding up, and coordinating investment processes.

To improve transparency and predictability, the agreement emphasizes the publication of investment measures, including laws, regulations, and procedures, to reduce uncertainty for investors. To streamline administrative procedures, the IFD aims to simplify investment-related processes, including the use of digital platforms such as single windows and e-portals. One important feature is the special and differential treatment for developing members, which will be given longer implementation periods and support to ensure they can fully benefit from the agreement. Areas excluded from the IFD are market access, investment protection, and investor–state dispute settlement. Importantly, the agreement also includes a "firewall provision" aimed at insulating the IFD from international investment agreements to prevent spillover

[27] Single digital platforms aim to minimize the requirement of foreign investors for the submission of all documents required by agencies or regulatory bodies involved in the admission, establishment, acquisition, and expansion of investments.

effects between them. While these topics continue to be critical for states and foreign investors, they will continue to be negotiated under the umbrella of investment treaties.

As the importance of investment facilitation grows, so does tracking the adoption of related policies. The Investment Facilitation Index (IFI), developed by the German Institute of Development and Sustainability and WTO, measures the degree of adoption of investment facilitation policies among 142 WTO member economies.[28] Latest estimates indicate large heterogeneity among economies on the adoption of investment facilitation measures, with higher-income economies having higher degrees of adoption. Overall, Asian economies have good adoption of investment facilitation measures, with large regional variation (Figure 3.14). The degree of adoption is highest in the Republic of Korea, followed by Japan, Australia, New Zealand, and Kazakhstan. Asian economies with relatively low adoption of investment facilitation measures include the Lao People's Democratic Republic, Papua New Guinea, Samoa, Tajikistan, and Maldives. While investment facilitation measures may primarily be in manufacturing sectors, foreign investments, especially market-seeking ones, have the potential to benefit infrastructure and service-based industries in services-oriented economies.

More than other areas of investment policy, investment facilitation has been a common element among RCI initiatives in Asia to attract foreign investment. Several Asian subregional initiatives include provisions on investment facilitation. While some exclusively target foreign investment, others are enshrined in broader cooperation agreements or linked to trade facilitation measures (Table 3.1, see Annex 3b for details). Other initiatives such as the ASEAN Comprehensive Investment Agreement include more ambitious provisions in other areas such as negative lists and dispute settlement mechanisms. These developments underline the potential of RCI initiatives to support the implementation of investment facilitation measures more effectively.

**Figure 3.14: Investment Facilitation Index**

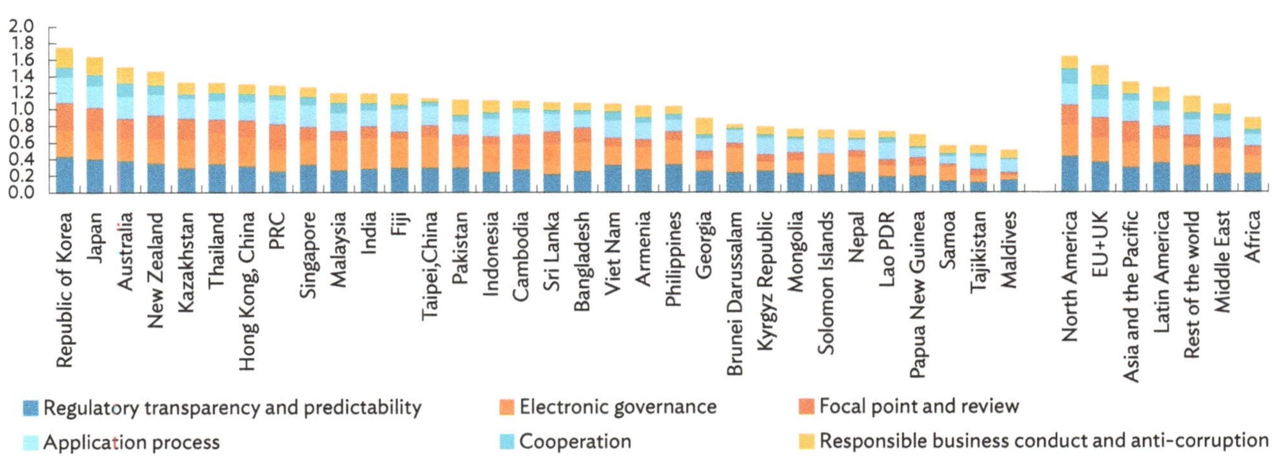


PRC = People's Republic of China, EU = European Union (27 members), Lao PDR = Lao People's Democratic Republic, UK = United Kingdom.

Notes: The Investment Facilitation Index measures the degree by which economies have adopted investment facilitation policies. The composite index—developed by the German Institute of Development and Sustainability (IDOS) and the World Trade Organization (WTO) based on work by Berger, Dadkhah, and Olekseyuk in 2021—uses a scoring scheme on 101 measures categorized across 6 regulatory dimensions for 142 WTO member economies. Values range from 0 to 2, with values close to 2 indicating a higher degree of adoption. Regional estimates are obtained using a weighted average of scores, with 2023 real gross domestic product used as weights.

Source: ADB calculations using data from IDOS and WTO. WTO Investment Related Databases. Investment Facilitation Index Database. https://www.wto.org/spanish/res_s/reser_s/invest_related_db_s.htm (accessed 24 October 2024).

28 The current version of the IFI is based on an earlier version developed by Berger, Dadkhah, and Olekseyuk in 2021. The updated IFI tracks 101 measures across six regulatory dimensions (regulatory transparency and predictability, electronic governance, focal point and review, application process, cooperation and responsible business conduct, and anticorruption), with values ranging from 0 to 2. Values close to 2 indicate a higher degree of adoption of facilitation measures.

**Table 3.1: Support of Asia's Subregional Initiatives to Foreign Direct Investment Policy**

| In Asia and the Pacific | With Non-Regional Participants |
|---|---|
| **ASEAN Investment Facilitation Framework.** The ASEAN Investment Facilitation Framework was adopted in 2021 as the region's response to the postpandemic environment. It outlines 10 principles and actions to leverage investment for sustainable recovery. | **APEC Investment Facilitation Action Plan.** This action plan for investment facilitation was developed in 2007 in Sydney, Australia to further promote investment cooperation among APEC member economies. |
| **ASEAN+3 Cooperation Framework.** The ASEAN+3 cooperation was formed in 1997 to help promote East Asian cooperation with ASEAN as one of the drivers. The cooperation has since evolved to encompass trade, investment, and various other areas. The latest iteration of the ASEAN Plus Three Cooperation Work Plan outlines goals for 2023–2027 in trade, investment facilitation, tourism, and finance, among others. | **Comprehensive and Progressive Agreement for Trans-Pacific Partnership (CPTPP).** The CPTPP is a free trade agreement involving several economies in Asia and the Pacific. The United Kingdom is the latest economy to join the CPTPP, acceding on 15 December 2024. |
| **BIMP-EAGA Trade and Investment Facilitation.** The landmark Memorandum of Cooperation was signed on 20 August 2024 to "enhance trade and investments in the BIMP-EAGA subregion." One of the key goals is to promote and facilitate investment among members. | **US–ASEAN Trade and Investment Facilitation Agreement.** The framework signed in 2006 sets forth broad goals and principles toward facilitating trade and investment between the United States and ASEAN. This outlines their economic engagement and builds upon existing agreements to promote and facilitate trade and investment. |
| **CAREC Trade and Investment Facilitation (CARTIF).** The CARTIF is a prospective framework that aims to facilitate trade and investment in the region. The framework will be formulated as an open plurilateral partnership agreement and will be flexible and modular. | **WTO Investment Facilitation for Development.** The WTO Investment Facilitation for Development Agreement is made among 126 WTO member economies. Apart from addressing investment facilitation, it also "strengthens the WTO and the rules-based multilateral trading system." This will be added to Annex 4 of the WTO Agreement. |
| **Regional Comprehensive Economic Partnership Agreement (RCEP).** The RCEP is a free trade agreement involving ASEAN member economies, Australia, the People's Republic of China, Japan, New Zealand, and the Republic of Korea. The FTA builds upon ASEAN's plus one agreements and adjusts for the changing economic landscape. The agreement includes a chapter covering the four pillars of investment: protection, liberalization, promotion, and facilitation. | |
| **South Asia Subregional Economic Cooperation (SASEC).** The SASEC program was implemented as a project-based partnership to boost intraregional trade and cooperation among member economies, and to connect South Asian economies with Southeast Asia. | |

APEC = Asia-Pacific Economic Cooperation; ASEAN = Association of Southeast Asian Nations; ASEAN+3 = ASEAN plus the People's Republic of China, Japan, and the Republic of Korea; BIMP-EAGA = Brunei Darussalam–Indonesia–Malaysia–Philippines East ASEAN Growth Area; CAREC = Central Asia Regional Economic Cooperation; FDI = foreign direct investment; FTA = free trade agreement; WTO = World Trade Organization.

Source: ADB compilation.

Subregional cooperation initiatives can play a more prominent role in fostering more and better quality FDI, by enabling technological upgrading, strengthening global value chain (GVC) participation, and incentivizing sustainable investment. With the exception of ASEAN, a substantial portion of investment for Asian economic blocs come from Asian sources (Figure 3.15). For subregional blocs such as the Brunei Darussalam–Indonesia–Malaysia–Philippines East ASEAN Growth Area (BIMP-EAGA), Central Asia Regional Economic Cooperation (CAREC), and South Asia Subregional Economic Cooperation (SASEC), intra-bloc investments typically constitute less than 5% of inward flows; they appeared to rely heavily on investment from other Asian economies. While they may have been effective in fostering investment from external partners, regional cooperation programs offer platforms to tackle regional investors through investment facilitation and more tailored approaches.

**Figure 3.15: FDI Composition in Selected Regional Economic Blocs by Source—Balance of Payments** (%)

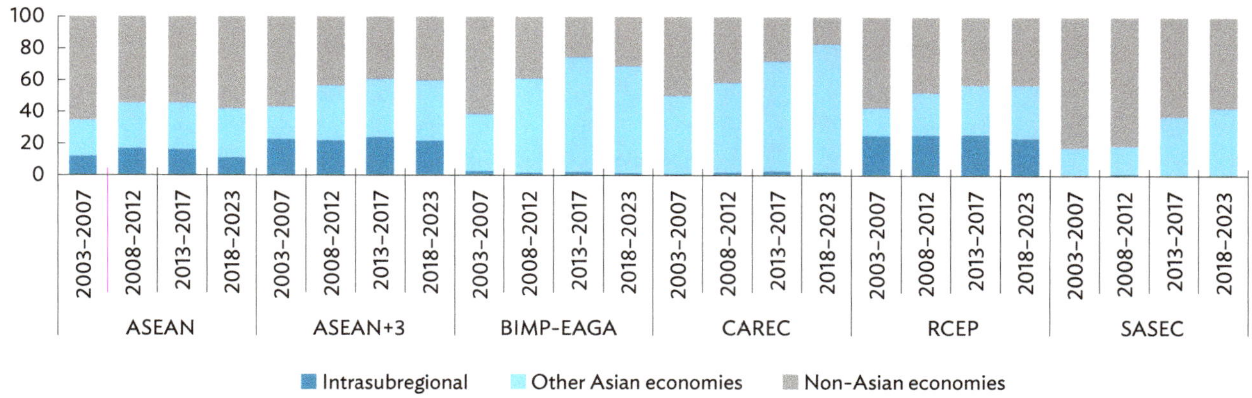


ASEAN = Association of Southeast Asian Nations; ASEAN+3 = ASEAN plus the People's Republic of China, Japan, and the Republic of Korea; BIMP-EAGA = Brunei Darussalam–Indonesia–Malaysia–Philippines East ASEAN Growth Area; CAREC = Central Asia Regional Economic Cooperation; RCEP = Regional Comprehensive Economic Partnership; SASEC = South Asia Subregional Economic Cooperation.

Sources: ADB calculations using data from the ASEAN Secretariat. ASEANstats Data Portal. https://data.aseanstats.org (accessed July 2024); CEIC Data Company; Eurostat. Balance of Payments. https://ec.europa.eu/eurostat (accessed July 2024); International Monetary Fund. World Economic Outlook Database, April 2024. https://www.imf.org/en/Publications/WEO/weo-database/2024/April (accessed April 2024); and UN Trade and Development. World Investment Report 2024 Statistical Annex Tables. https://unctad.org/topic/investment/world-investment-report (accessed July 2024).

## Enhancing coherence between international, regional, and domestic FDI policies.

Policy coherence in investment policy is a growing area of interest for companies and policymakers alike. International investment frameworks and progress in regional cooperation for investment are welcome developments, but they need to align with domestic investment policies. Over the past decade, the region has seen a gradual modernization of its investment treaty network, expanding in investment partners and in the depth of investment commitments. Together with treaty reform, some economies have opted to terminate old investment treaties and include more robust investment chapters in trade agreements (Figure 3.16a). Apart from the quantity of agreements, the quality has also improved in recent years, with newer agreements including stronger provisions for safeguarding the rights of states to regulate. Important reforms have been implemented, for example, for upgrading international investment agreements in the definition of investment, public interest obligations, and arbitration, among others (Figure 3.16b).

Much like international investment regimes, domestic investment laws have also been pivotal for promoting and attracting investment. They contain provisions on key policy instruments, such as tax incentives and other facilitating measures by sector or geography.[29] In recent years, implemented FDI-related policies are not only investment-specific but part of broader industrial policy plans. Some economies have enacted industrial policies including provisions on investment tax incentives and foreign ownership (Figure 3.17a). While some FDI-related industrial policies aimed to safeguard national security interests, more policies are still geared toward facilitating foreign investments in key sectors. This is a global trend, with over half of new investment measures in the last 10 years being facilitative rather than restrictive (Figure 3.17b).

Progress in upgrading international and regional investment frameworks is important, yet domestic policy measures are still the backbone of investment policy for many economies in the region (Figure 3.18). The rise of investment tax incentives and increasing use of industrial and sector policies, together with coexisting legal frameworks oriented

29 See ADB (2023) for a review of domestic investment laws in Asia and the Pacific.

**Figure 3.16: Overview of International Investment Agreements**

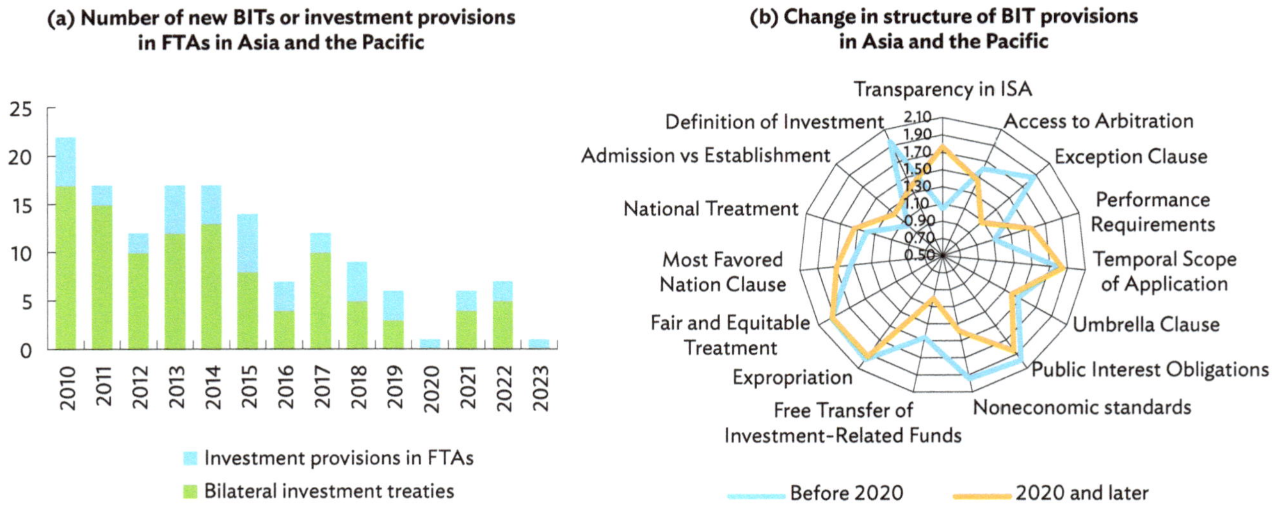


BIT = bilateral investment treaty, FTA = free trade agreement, ISA = investor–state arbitration.

Notes: (a) By date entered into force; (b) Provisions are scored depending on whether they grant circumscribed rights (score = 1) or extensive rights (score = 2) to the investor.

Sources: ADB calculations based on ADB. ADB International Investment Agreement Tool Kit. https://aric.adb.org/database/iias; and United Nations Trade and Development (UNCTAD). UNCTAD International Investment Agreements Navigator. https://investmentpolicy.unctad.org/international-investment-agreements (both accessed June 2024).

**Figure 3.17: Overview of Domestic Policies on Foreign Investment**

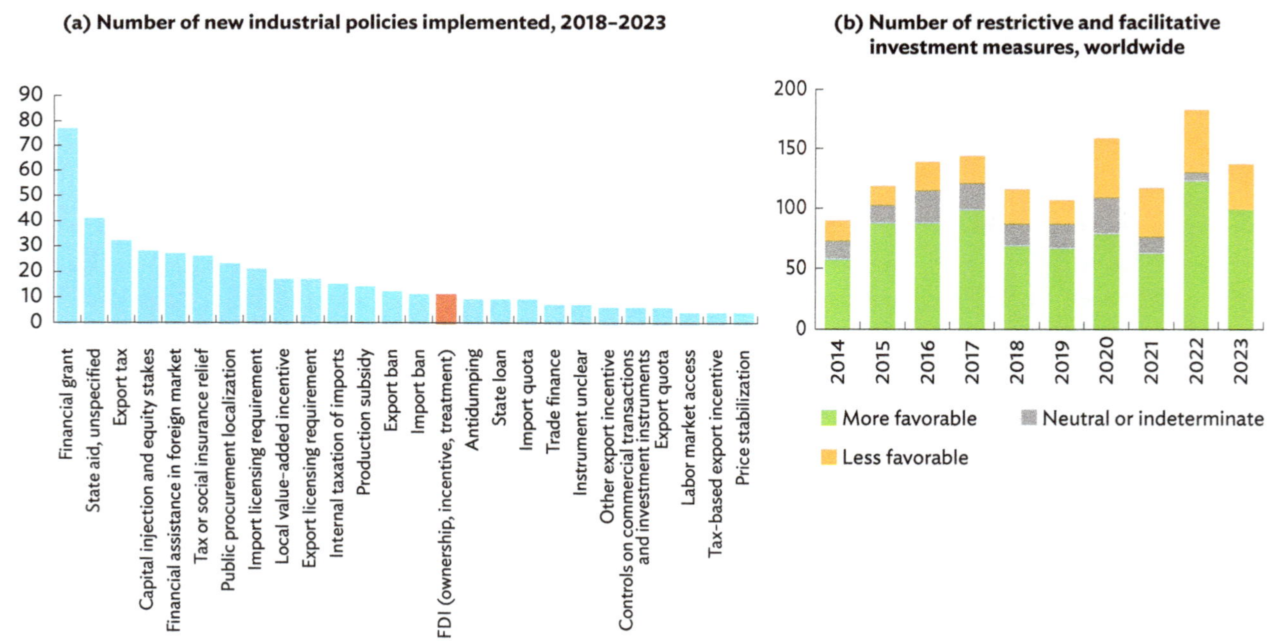


FDI = foreign direct investment.

Note: Excludes import tariffs. FDI measures include measures on FDI ownership, FDI incentives, and FDI treatment.

Source: ADB calculations using data from Evenett et al. (2024); and UNCTAD (2024).

**Figure 3.18: Global, Regional, and Domestic Foreign Direct Investment Policies in Asia and the Pacific**

**Global: Modernize IIAs**

- Align investment provisions and national objectives
- Ensure coherence with international commitments
- Modernize dispute resolution mechanisms
- Adopt new provisions on key areas: climate change, public interest, digital assets

**Regional: Investment Facilitation**

- Increase transparency for investment rules and regulations
- Simplify procedures on investment projects
- Adopt sector and supply-chain focus
- Modernize investment promotion agencies

**Domestic: Industrial Policies**

- Balance investment tax incentives
- Ensure compatible instruments (investment, SEZs, PPP laws)
- Track adoption and impact of FDI-related industrial policies

FDI = foreign direct investment, IIA = international investment agreement, PPP = public–private partnership, SEZ = special economic zone.

Source: ADB compilation.

at attracting FDI underscore the importance of better aligning and ensuring compatibility between investment policy goals and instruments. This is particularly relevant in the context of the climate transition, as investment regimes are being revisited and linked to climate negotiations (IISD 2024; UNCTAD 2024c).

## Geopolitical Fragmentation and Foreign Direct Investment

### Introduction

Geopolitical tensions are reshaping firms' decisions to undertake new greenfield investment. As global tensions intensify, the costs and risks for companies have increased, through rising trade barriers, greater scrutiny in investment screening and possible reputational costs. The shifting dynamics of FDI in recent years also reflect the complex interplay of trade conflicts and industrial policies, which affect traditional determinants of investment and impact developing economies' prospects for attracting FDI.

Geopolitical alignment is also prompting firms to adopt friend-shoring strategies to align investments with politically stable or allied economies. This trend is more evident in sensitive sectors such as telecommunications and renewable energy, where MNEs prioritize geopolitical stability over efficiency (Aiyar et al. 2023; UNCTAD 2024b). Some economies also tend to form smaller, regional alliances rather than multilateral frameworks, as these present opportunities to create stable FDI platforms for MNEs seeking reliable access to regional markets.

Trade conflicts are a central factor in this investment reorientation amid geopolitical tensions. Evidence from the US–PRC trade tensions before the pandemic highlighted how rising tariffs and trade restrictions could prompt firms to adjust global investment strategies to mitigate risks (Bekkers and Schroeter 2020; Blanchard et al. 2021). More recent work (Alfaro and Chor 2023; Freund et al. 2024) highlights the role of geopolitical fragmentation in accelerating trends in reshoring, nearshoring, and friend-shoring. Beyond trade conflicts, recent literature highlights the role of national industrial policies in influencing FDI flows. Industrial policies, traditionally aimed at domestic sector enhancement are now deployed to protect critical industries through subsidies and trade restrictions (Evenett et al. 2024). In principle, they can hinder FDI flows into certain sectors while motivating MNEs to seek alternative destinations with more favorable conditions for foreign entities.

Geopolitical tensions continue to impact FDI decisions outside of trade. They can deter FDI flows in sectors more sensitive to institutional factors, such as manufacturing and infrastructure, although critical sectors like energy exhibit resilience (Soussane, Fakhouri, and Mansouri 2023). Economies with stable political and economic climates are better positioned to attract firms seeking alternatives to conflict-prone regions. The role of "connector economies"—those that do not align exclusively with one bloc but serve as intermediaries—further emphasizes how strategic neutrality and balanced alliances can enhance FDI appeal in an increasingly fragmented landscape (Gopinath et al. 2024). Finally, recent FDI trends reflect a broader reexamination of global economic dependencies (Arslanalp, Eichengreen, and Simpson-Bell 2022).

The existing literature highlights the far-reaching effects of geopolitical tensions, trade policies, and industrial strategies on FDI flows. Traditional FDI determinants have broadened, with geopolitical alignment, regional alliances, and proactive policy adjustments as central for economies seeking to attract foreign investment. This section presents structural trends on greenfield investment and examines whether and how geopolitical tensions are reshaping firms' decisions, with a special focus on Asia.

## A recomposition of greenfield investment

Global trends in greenfield investment projects point out the possible role of geopolitical shifts on investment patterns. Notwithstanding cyclical downturns, especially during the pandemic, the global number of new greenfield FDI projects remained relatively flat in recent years, with some important shifts in the composition of FDI. Whereas FDI between high-income economies has remained robust, investment flows from high- to low- and middle-income economies have decreased since 2005. A decline in projects to the PRC accounts for the overall fall in greenfield investments (Figure 3.19).

## Assessing the impact of geopolitical tensions on FDI flows

While global trends are informative, an assessment of how foreign investments are changing in response to geopolitical fragmentation poses some empirical challenges.[30] However, the identification of geopolitical inflection points may be useful in examining shifts in FDI patterns. This allows to examine how geopolitical tensions may affect FDI differently across sectors and business activities, how best to capture broader investment trends, and the potential for investment diversion to alternative markets.

Importantly, effects from geoeconomic fragmentation may differ depending on the investment motive of MNEs (efficiency- or market-seeking) and the final business activity of the investment. Geopolitical tensions often translate into measures which are likely to affect efficiency-seeking and market-seeking investments differently. Efficiency-seeking FDI, undertaken to minimize production costs within cross-border value chains, is particularly vulnerable to such barriers. In contrast, market-seeking FDI, focused on accessing local consumers rather than cross-border production, is less dependent on open trade flows and may respond less acutely to geopolitical tensions. In the case of tariff jumping FDI (Brecher and Bhagwati 1981), market-seeking investments may even increase when bilateral trade barriers rise. The business activity of a project, such as manufacturing, logistics, extraction or services, likewise influences sensitivity to geopolitical tensions. Thus, activities linked to logistics operations that depend on or support trade are more vulnerable to trade disruptions.

[30] For example, FDI is typically a "sticky" and effectively sunk cost, which makes it challenging to detect incremental changes in investment behavior. Second, the concept of geopolitical tension is complex and multifaceted, with no single definition alone capturing it (Caldara and Iacoviello 2022). Third, a challenge lies on the empirical identification, specifically on how to distinguish the effects of geopolitical tensions from broader "push" and "pull" factors driving FDI.

**Figure 3.19: Greenfield Foreign Direct Investment Projects From High Income Economies to Low and Middle Income Economies** (number of projects)

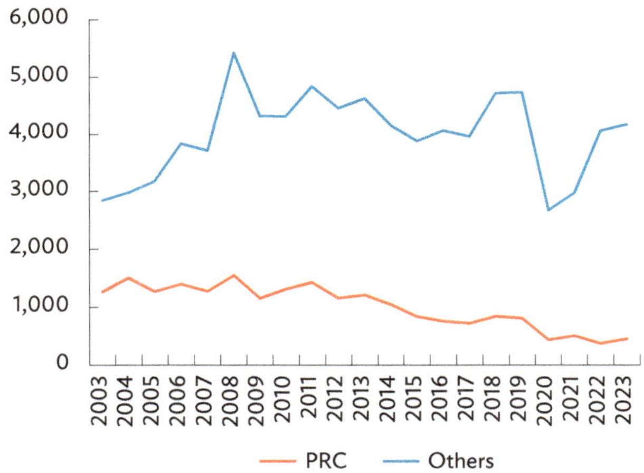


PRC = People's Republic of China.

Source: Blanchard et al. (2025) using data from Financial Times. fDi Markets (accessed September 2024).

ADB's analysis on FDI flows suggest that geopolitical tensions are fundamentally affecting the geography and sectoral composition of global investment (Blanchard et al. 2025). The findings also reveal that trade-exposed efficiency-seeking sectors experience stronger reductions in new investment projects and underscore the double burden faced by these sectors in a context of geoeconomic fragmentation. As FDI often relies on established global sourcing networks, GVC interdependence may explain why these investments exhibit sharper constraints. Not only are they more likely to face geopolitical disruptions, but their reliance on GVCs makes adaptation more challenging when trade relationships deteriorate. Examining potential investment diversion, the analysis also finds evidence of increasing FDI from the PRC to alternative markets, in particular ASEAN economies. Robustness tests using broader geopolitical tensions corroborate these results, where heightened tensions correspond to reductions in FDI flows, particularly among trade-exposed investment projects in efficiency-seeking sectors. Overall, geopolitical factors have become increasingly important to explain investment patterns, but not all investments respond uniformly to geopolitical tensions. This calls for further consideration on the policy responses that economies in the region lay out looking forward.

## Policy Recommendations

Despite a slowdown in 2023, inward FDI in Asia has shown to be resilient overall. Growth in strategic sectors has helped the region maintain its position as a prime destination for investment. Indeed, over the past decade, services, digital, and green industries have emerged as major areas of inward FDI in Asia, hinting at the shift from manufacturing-based investment to other areas. Intraregional investment linkages have also remained strong, with nearly half of investments coming from the region. While regional economies have made important progress in introducing FDI-inducing reforms, several areas for improvement can be considered:

**Strengthen investment facilitation.** Economies may consider adopting more ambitious investment facilitation policies in the future to reduce administrative barriers, provide aftercare services to investors and utilize investment promotion for their own development goals. Reducing administrative barriers through digitalization, ensuring coherence among regulatory agencies, and leveraging investment promotion agencies to enhance FDI quality and diversify investing partners is a first step. Equally important is the development of other aftercare services, including mediation mechanisms and adequate data systems (such as taking censuses in special economic zones) to track progress and measure the impact of investment. Building on the experience of trade facilitation, Asia can adopt a proactive strategy to strengthen investment facilitation policies. Many of these measures are already being deployed through regional cooperation initiatives in the region, and efforts should continue.

**Take strategic account of geopolitical risk.** Economies should also rethink FDI strategies in the context of current geopolitical risks. As stressed in the chapter, FDI determinants have broadened beyond traditional economic fundamentals and are no longer solely dependent on macroeconomic, institutional, or efficiency considerations. Trade tensions, national industrial policies, and geopolitical alignment increasingly shape firms' investment choices, pushing economies to rethink their strategies for attracting FDI. Economies in the region should realign their investment strategies accordingly to better respond to this trend. Ensuring institutional stability, seeking strategic alignment, and aiming to diversify activity will be important factors for Asian economies to remain attractive investment destinations. This also involves assessing how tariff structures, geographic proximity, and export potential determine their position in this reconfigured FDI landscape.

**Strengthen policy compatibility.** Ensuring coherence among investment policies—international, regional, and domestic—remains critical for economies to benefit from FDI spillovers and safeguard broader development objectives. Investment policies are being implemented across all levels of government. At the international level, Asia's progress in modernizing its investment treaty network and including more robust investment provisions in new trade and investment agreements is laudable. Regional initiatives are also supporting key pillars for FDI enhancement in the region, including investment facilitation. A major challenge, however, remains in ensuring compatibility between domestic measures, often implemented in national investment laws or other policy instruments, with international commitments. Governments should identify international commitments, establish linkages with investment governance tools, and assess areas of convergence to ensure policy coherence.

## References


Ahn, C. Y. 2024. *South Korea and Foreign Direct Investment: Policy Dynamics and the Aftercare Ombudsman.* Routledge.

Aiyar, S., J. Chen, C. Ebeke, R. Garcia-Saltos, R. Gudmundsson, A. Ilyina, A. Kangur, T. Kunaratskul, S. Rodriguez, M. Ruta, T. Schulze, G. Soderberg, and J. P. Trevino. 2023. Geoeconomic Fragmentation and the Future of Multilateralism. *IMF Staff Discussion Notes* 2023/001. International Monetary Fund.

Aiyar, S., D. Malacrino, and A. F. Presbitero. 2023. *Investing in Friends: The Role of Geopolitical Alignment in FDI Flows.* International Monetary Fund.

Alfaro, L. and D. Chor. 2023. Global Supply Chains: The Looming "Great Reallocation". *NBER Working Paper Series.* 31661. National Bureau of Economic Research.

Arslanalp, S., B. Eichengreen, and C. Simpson-Bell. 2022. The Stealth Erosion of Dollar Dominance: Active Diversifiers and the Rise of Nontraditional Reserve Currencies. *IMF Working Paper Series.* WP/22/58. International Monetary Fund.

Asian Development Bank (ADB). 2022. *Asian Economic Integration Report 2022: Advancing Digital Services Trade in Asia and the Pacific.*

———. 2023. *Asian Economic Integration Report 2023: Trade, Investment, and Climate Change in Asia and the Pacific.*

———. 2024. *Asian Economic Integration Report 2024: Decarbonizing Global Value Chains.*

Asian Development Bank Institute (ADBI) and ADB. 2024. *Designing Competition Policy for Economic Development in Asia and the Pacific.*

Association of Southeast Asian Nations (ASEAN) Secretariat. ASEANstats Data Portal. https://data.aseanstats.org (accessed July 2024).

ASEAN Secretariat and UN Trade and Development (UNCTAD). 2024. *ASEAN Investment Report 2024: ASEAN Economic Community 2025 and Foreign Direct Investment.*

Atlantic Council. 2022. Our Guide to Friend-Shoring: Sectors to Watch. https://www.atlanticcouncil.org/in-depth-research-reports/issue-brief/our-guide-to-friend-shoring-sectors-to-watch/

Berger, A., A. Dadkhah, and Z. Olekseyuk. 2021. Quantifying Investment Facilitation at Country Level: Introducing a New Index. *Deutsches Institut für Entwicklungspolitik Discussion Paper.* 23/2021. Deutsches Institut für Entwicklungspolitik.

Bekkers, E. and S. Schroeter. 2020. An Economic Analysis of the US-China Trade Conflict. *WTO Staff Working Papers.* ERSD-2020-04. World Trade Organization.

Blanchard, E., W. Olney, R. Avendano, A. Santos-Paulino, and C. Trentini. 2024. The Great Reallocation Revisited: How FDI Is (and Is Not) Evolving Amid Heightened Geopolitical Tensions. Background Paper for the *Asian Economic Integration Report 2025* Cross-Border Investment Chapter.

Blanchard, E., A. Santos-Paulino, C. Trentini, and E. Milet. 2021. Implications of Rising Trade Tensions for FDI Projects. *Transnational Corporations.* 28 (2). pp. 161–93.

Brecher, R. A. and J. N. Bhagwati. 1981. Foreign Ownership and the Theory of Trade and Welfare. *Journal of Political Economy*. 89 (3). pp. 497–511.

Caldara, D. and M. Iacoviello. 2022. Measuring Geopolitical Risk. *American Economic Review.* 112 (4). pp. 1194–1225.

Chaisse, J. 2023. Tax, Trade and Investment Conundrum in Asia-Pacific Regionalism. *Asia Pacific Law Review.* 31 (2). pp. 535–55.

Chen, X., G. Pen, Z. Song, and F. Zilibotti. 2023. Tertiarization like China. *Annual Review of Economics.* 15. pp. 485–512.

De Lombaerde, P., ed. 2024. *Handbook of Regional Cooperation and Integration.* Edward Elgar Publishing.

Eurostat. Balance of Payments. https://ec.europa.eu/eurostat (accessed July 2024).

Evenett, S., A. Jakubik, F. Martín, and M. Ruta. 2024. The Return of Industrial Policy in Data. *IMF Working Paper Series.* WP/24/1. International Monetary Fund.

Financial Times. 2024. *The fDi Report 2024: Global Greenfield Investment Trends.*

Freund, C., A. Mattoo, A. Mulabdic, and M. Ruta. 2024. Is US Trade Policy Reshaping Global Supply Chains? *Journal of International Economics.* 152.

Fugazza, M. and A. Nicita. 2013. The Direct and Relative Effects of Preferential Market Access. *Journal of International Economics.* 89. pp. 357–368.

German Institute of Development and Sustainability (IDOS) and World Trade Organization (WTO). WTO Investment-Related Databases. Investment Facilitation Index Database. https://www.wto.org/spanish/res_s/reser_s/invest_related_db_s.htm (accessed October 2024).

Gibson, J. 2024. Structural Transformation in Asia and the Pacific. *Asian Development Review.* 41 (2). pp. 1–5.

Gopinath, G., P. O. Gourinchas, A. F. Presbitero, and P. Topalova. 2024. Changing Global Linkages: A New Cold War? *IMF Working Paper Series.* WP/24/76. International Monetary Fund.

International Energy Agency (IEA). 2024. *World Energy Outlook 2024.*

International Institute for Sustainable Development (IISD). 2024. *A Practical Tool to Enhance Horizontal Coherence Across Policy Areas.*

International Monetary Fund (IMF). 2023. Geoeconomic Fragmentation and Foreign Direct Investment. In *World Economic Outlook: A Rocky Recovery*, April.

———. World Economic Outlook April 2023 Database. https://www.imf.org/en/Publications/WEO/weo-database/2024/April (accessed April 2024).

Irwin-Hunt, A. 2024. ASEAN Overtakes China for Manufacturing FDI. *fDi Intelligence.* 24 April. https://www.fdiintelligence.com/content/news/asean-overtakes-china-for-manufacturing-fdi-83610.

Jaumotte, F., J. Kim, S. Pienknagura, and G. Schwerhoff. 2024. Policies to Foster Green FDI: Best Practices for Emerging Market and Developing Economies. *IMF Staff Climate Note.* No. 2024/004. International Monetary Fund.

Kim, K., K. J. Jeong, A. Gaduena, and M. Capistrano. Forthcoming. Advancing Resilient and Sustainable Development of Critical Minerals in Asia and the Pacific. *ADB Briefs*. Asian Development Bank.

Lazo, R. 2018. Facilitation 2.0: Investment and Trade in the Digital Age. *RTA Exchange.* International Centre for Trade and Sustainable Development and Inter-American Development Bank.

Mercer-Blackman, V. and C. Ablaza. 2018. The Servicification of Manufacturing in Asia: Redefining the sources of Labor Productivity. *ADBI Working Paper Series.* No. 902. Asian Development Bank Institute.

Organisation for Economic Co-operation and Development (OECD). Activity of Multinational Enterprises. https://www.oecd.org/en/data/datasets/activity-of-multinational-enterprises.html (accessed May 2024).

Santos-Paulino, A., Z. Olekseyuk, U. Panizza, J. Poole, C. Trentini, and C. V. Martincus. 2024. Investment Facilitation for Sustainable Development. *T20 Policy Brief.* TF04. https://www.t20brasil.org/media/documentos/arquivos/TF04_ST_04_Investment_Facilita67532f96eeae8.pdf.

Soussane, J., M. Y. Fakhouri, and Z. Mansouri. 2023. The Effect of Geopolitical Risks on TNC Location Decisions from Antagonizing Countries in the Russian Federation in Light of the Ukrainian Crisis. *Transnational Corporations Review.* https://doi.org/10.1016/j.tncr.2023.01.002.

Syropoulos, C., G. Felbermayr, A. Kirilakha, E. Yalcin, and Y. V. Yotov. 2024. The Global Sanctions Data Base–Release 3: COVID-19, Russia, and Multilateral Sanctions. *Review of International Economics.* 32 (1). pp. 12–48.

United Nations Trade and Development (UNCTAD). 2024a. *Global Economic Fracturing and Shifting Investment Patterns: A Diagnostic of 10 FDI Trends and their Development Implications.*

———. 2024b. *World Investment Report 2024: Investment Facilitation and Digital Government.*

———. 2024c. *Mapping Sustainable Development and Investment Facilitation Provisions in IIAs Concluded by G20 Members and Invited Countries.* G20 Brazil 2024 Trade and Investment Working Group.

———. World Investment Report 2024 Statistical Annex Tables. https://unctad.org/topic/investment/world-investment-report (accessed July 2024).

Voeten, E., A. Strezhnev, and M. Bailey. 2009. United Nations General Assembly Voting Data. Harvard Dataverse, V11.

# Annex 3a: Foreign Investment Linkages in Selected Sectors—Firm-Level, Asia and the Pacific, 2013–2017 ($ million, average annual investment)

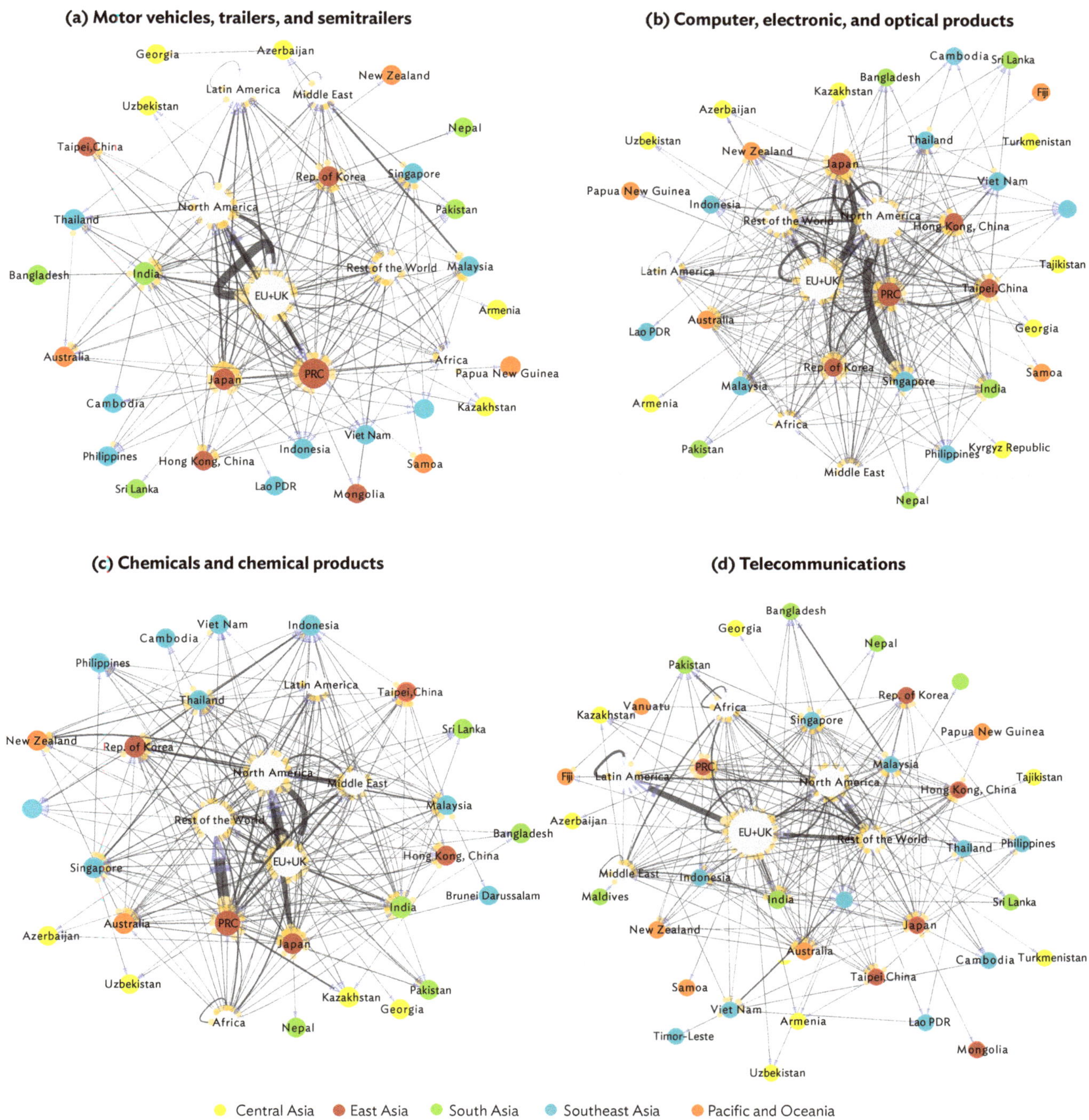


PRC = People's Republic of China, EU = European Union (27 members), Lao PDR = Lao People's Democratic Republic, UK = United Kingdom.

Notes: Nodes are sized according to each economy's or region's share in the total inward investment for the indicated period. Each link represents average investment from a source node (round end) to a target node (arrow end). Sectors are harmonized with the classification used in the Analytical Activity of Multinational Enterprises from the Organisation for Economic Co-operation and Development (OECD).

ADB calculations using data from Financial Times. fDi Markets; Moody's Analytics. Orbis M&A (formerly Zephyr M&A Database); and OECD. Activity of Multinational Enterprises. https://www.oecd.org/en/data/datasets/activity-of-multinational-enterprises.html (all accessed May 2024).

# Annex 3b: Subregional Cooperation Initiatives and Foreign Direct Investment Policy in Asia and the Pacific

| Name | Summary | Goals |
|---|---|---|
| APEC Investment Facilitation Action Plan (IFAP) | The IFAP was developed in 2007 to further promote investment cooperation among APEC member economies. APEC's past efforts in investment facilitation include<br>(1) APEC Non-Binding Investment Principles (1994);<br>(2) Options for Investment Liberalization and Business Facilitation to Strengthen APEC Economies (1997);<br>(3) Guide to the Investment Regimes of APEC Member Economies (6th edition, 2007); and<br>(4) Study on Enhancing Investment Liberalization and Facilitation in Economic Development in the Asia-Pacific Region, which examined ways to reduce "behind-the-border" barriers to domestic investment. | IFAP mainly aims to<br>(1) strengthen regional economic integration;<br>(2) strengthen the competitiveness and sustainability of economic growth of APEC member economies;<br>(3) expand prosperity and employment opportunities in the APEC region; and<br>(4) make further progress toward achievement of the "Bogor Goals." |
| ASEAN Investment Facilitation Framework | The framework was adopted in 2021 as the regional response to the post-pandemic environment. It outlines 10 principles and actions to leverage investment for sustainable recovery post-pandemic. | (1) Transparency of Measures and Information;<br>(2) Streamlining and Speeding Up Administrative Procedures and Requirements; (3) Use of Digital and Internet Technologies; (4) Single Digital Platform;<br>(5) Assistance and Advisory Services to Investors;<br>(6) Independence of Competent Authorities;<br>(7) Temporary Entry and Stay of Business Persons for Investment Purposes; (8) Facilitation of Investment Supporting Factors; (9) Consultative Mechanism for Investment Policies; and (10) Cooperation |
| ASEAN+3 Cooperation | ASEAN+3 Cooperation was formed in 1997 to promote East Asian cooperation with ASEAN as one of the drivers of economic growth. It has since evolved to enhance collaboration in trade, investment, tourism, and finance, as stated in the latest ASEAN Plus Three (APT) Cooperation Work Plan. | Building on the achievements of the previous work plan, this will help ASEAN realize the goals of both its Community Vision 2025 and successor document. It is also aimed to further strengthen the APT partnership in accordance with the principles of the ASEAN Charter and the Treaty of Amity and Cooperation in Southeast Asia, as well as the ASEAN Outlook on the Indo-Pacific. |
| US–ASEAN Trade and Investment Facilitation Agreement (TIFA) | The framework was signed in 2006 and sets forth broad goals and principles toward facilitating trade and investment between the US and ASEAN. This outlines the economic engagement between the US and ASEAN and builds upon existing agreements to promote trade and investment. | - Strengthens trade and investment relations<br>- Includes a provision to establish a joint council to review trade and investment relations, implement work plans, and resolve any issues regarding TIFA interpretation and implementation. |
| BIMP-EAGA Trade and Investment Facilitation | The landmark Memorandum of Cooperation was signed on 20 August 2024 to "enhance trade and investments in the BIMP-EAGA subregion." | The BIMP-EAGA trade and investment facilitation strategy aims to lower barriers to trade and investment within the region. Boosting trade and fostering a good investment environment will likely drive economic growth in the region, and so allow agribusiness, manufacturing, and tourism to also flourish. |
| CAREC Trade and Investment Facilitation (CARTIF) | CARTIF is a prospective framework to facilitate trade and investment in the region. The framework will be formulated as an open plurilateral partnership agreement and will be flexible and modular. | CARTIF aims to move the region's "trade agenda to another level" while supporting "economic diversification in the region through increased market access (Fugazza and Nicita 2013), and provisions to facilitate green cross-border trade and investment." |
| Comprehensive and Progressive Agreement for Trans-Pacific Partnership (CPTPP) | CPTPP is a free trade agreement involving several economies in Asia and the Pacific. The United Kingdom is the latest economy to join the CPTPP, acceding on 15 December 2024. | CPTPP facilitates trade flow among signatory economies and cooperates on corresponding regulations and standards. It also has an investment chapter that aims to facilitate investment flow by protecting against discriminatory treatment, compensate for expropriated investment, and liberalize investment-related capital transfers, among others. |

*continued on next page*

*Annex 3b continued*

| Name | Summary | Goals |
|---|---|---|
| Regional Comprehensive Economic Partnership Agreement (RCEP) | RCEP is a free trade agreement involving ASEAN member economies, Australia, PRC, Japan, New Zealand, and the Republic of Korea. It builds upon ASEAN's plus one agreements and adjusts for the changing economic landscape. | Besides facilitating trade relations among member economies, RCEP includes an investment chapter which covers the four pillars of investment: protection, liberalization, promotion, and facilitation. |
| Investment Facilitation for Development | The WTO Investment Facilitation for Development Agreement is made among 126 WTO member economies. Besides addressing investment facilitation, it "strengthens the WTO and the rules-based multilateral trading system." This will be added to Annex 4 of the WTO Agreement. | The IFDA aims to "improve the international business climate and make it easier for investors in all sectors to conduct business." It also intends "to increase the participation of developing and least-developed WTO members in global investment flows to promote sustainable economic development." |
| South Asia Subregional Economic Cooperation (SASEC) | The SASEC program is a project-based partnership bringing together economies in South Asia to "promote regional prosperity, improve economic opportunities, and build a better quality of life for the people of the subregion." | The SASEC program aims to boost intraregional trade and cooperation within the subregion and foster linkages with Southeast Asia with the PRC, and with the global market. |

APEC = Asia-Pacific Economic Cooperation; ASEAN = Association of Southeast Asian Nations; ASEAN+3 = ASEAN plus the People's Republic of China, Japan, and the Republic of Korea; CAREC = Central Asia Regional Economic Cooperation; PRC = People's Republic of China; FTA = free trade agreement; US = United States; WTO = World Trade Organization.

Notes: The Bogor goals aimed to achieve free and open investment by 2010 for industrialized APEC economies and by 2020 for the group's developing economies. Member economies of APEC, ASEAN, CAREC, and SASEC are outlined in ADB. Asia Regional Integration Center. Economy Groupings. https://aric.adb.org/integrationindicators/groupings.

Sources: ADB compilation.

# 4 Financial Integration

## Financial Integration Fosters Prosperity

### New Policy Challenges Require Active Regional Cooperation to Sustain Economic Growth

Financial integration in Asia and the Pacific increased steadily over the last 3 decades. Cross-border assets increased from 55% to 83% of regional gross domestic product (GDP) in 2010–2020 before settling at 75% in 2023. Cross-border liabilities exhibit a similar path. The region's share as a recipient of global portfolio flows increased from 6.5% in the first half of the 1990s to 22.5% before the coronavirus disease (COVID-19) pandemic. This progress in integration benefited growth and prosperity in Asia through lower cost of capital, expanded resource pools for investment, and enhanced international risk sharing. Efficiency gains followed from increased financial openness. Improved finance sector competitiveness and knowledge transfers fostered the development of regional capital markets.

Advances in building more integrated capital markets were grounded in regional cooperation initiatives. Regional cooperation remains essential to balance the benefits and costs of financial openness. However, new policy challenges such as geopolitical fragmentation, technological innovations, public health emergencies, climate change and biodiversity loss require more effective collaboration for continued integration to serve as the region's growth engine. This chapter discusses the challenges, highlights opportunities for improved cooperation, and draws attention to nature conservation as a new frontier for regional cooperation.

### Financial Integration Has Prevailed amid Volatile Global Financial Conditions

Global monetary easing since mid-2024 has improved the financial conditions in Asia. Regional financial integration is set to benefit from the global easing of monetary policy that began in the second half of 2024 (Figure 4.1). As a prologue to this easing cycle, central banks in advanced economies aggressively tightened monetary policy in 2022 to tame excessively high inflation after the pandemic (Figure 4.2). While the United States (US) Federal Reserve embarked on the steepest rate hike since the 1980s, raising the policy rate from 0.25% in February 2022 to 5.5% in July 2023, central banks in developing Asia preemptively mirrored the tightening to guard against capital outflows and currency depreciations (Figure 4.1). On signs of ebbing inflation and in a nod to the effectiveness of the tight monetary policy stance, the European Central Bank, Bank of Canada, Bank of England, and Reserve Bank of New Zealand started to cut policy rates in mid-2024, followed by the US Federal Reserve in September 2024. In anticipation of the US Federal Reserve's moves, central banks in developing Asia started to lower policy rates, allowing financial conditions to improve.

**Figure 4.1: Monetary Policy Rates** (%, as of 31 December 2024)

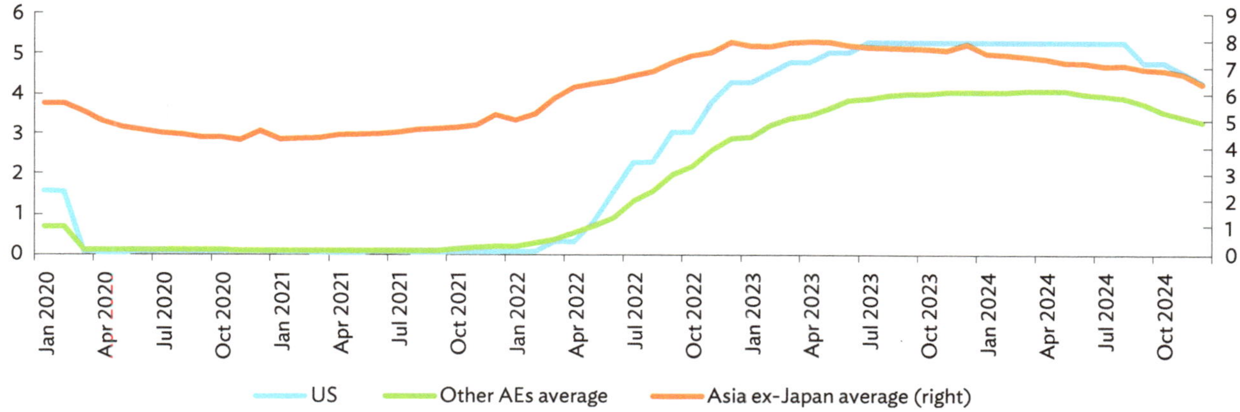


AE = advanced economy, US = United States.

Note: Advanced economies include Australia, Canada, eurozone, Japan, New Zealand, and the United Kingdom. Asian economies include Armenia; Azerbaijan; Bangladesh; Georgia; Hong Kong, China; India; Indonesia; Kazakhstan; the Republic of Korea; the Kyrgyz Republic; the Lao People's Democratic Republic; Malaysia; Mongolia; Pakistan; the Philippines; Sri Lanka; Taipei,China; Tajikistan; Thailand; Uzbekistan; and Viet Nam.

Source: ADB calculations using data from CEIC Data Company (accessed January 2025).

**Figure 4.2: Inflation—Selected Advanced Economies** (%, as of 31 December 2024)

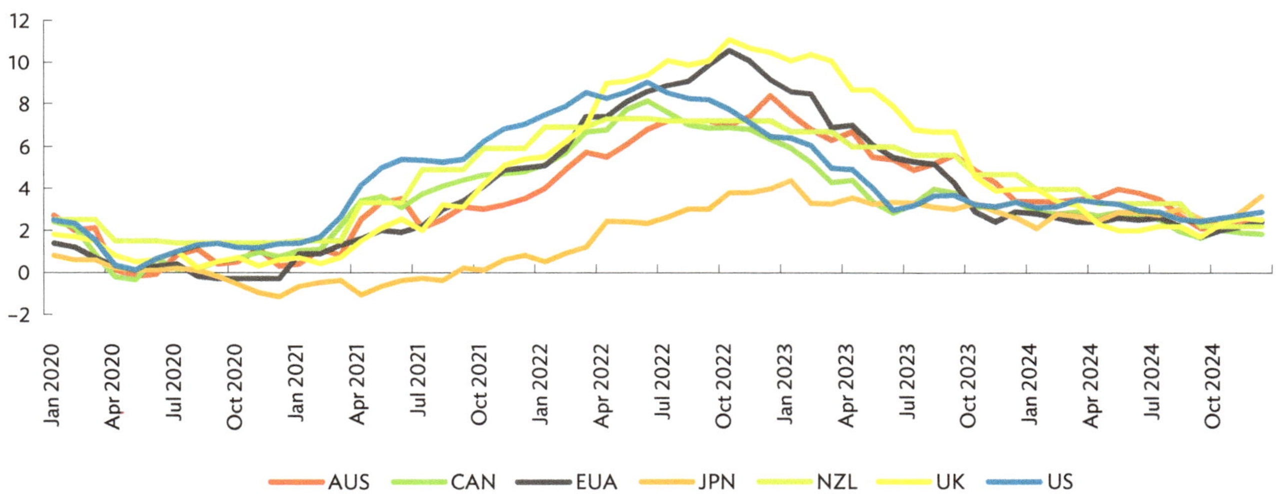


AUS = Australia, CAN = Canada, EUA = Euro area, JPN = Japan, NZL = New Zealand, UK = United Kingdom, US = United States.

Note: Inflation refers to the year-on-year change of the consumer price index.

Source: CEIC Data Company (accessed January 2025).

## Capital Flows into Asia Have Rebounded, Continuing the 2023 Recovery

Higher policy rate differentials between the US and Asian economies following the easing in the US along with a rise in global investors' risk appetite are likely to increase capital inflows in continuation of the 2023 recovery, as shown in Figure 4.3 (IIF 2024).[31] The region experienced capital outflows in the third quarter of 2022 as carry trades unwound in the wake of the US monetary policy hike in early 2022, leading to narrower policy rate differentials (Figure 4.4a), and due to the growth slowdown in the People's Republic of China (PRC) in the

[31] The Asian Economic Integration Report (ADB 2024c) includes an in-depth discussion of the role of the US dollar as a key driver of capital flow volatility in Asia. Given its proxy for the risk-taking propensity of global investors, the role of the US dollar has strengthened over the past decade amid an increase in the region's foreign borrowing in local currency (Gelos, Patelli, and Shim 2024).

**Figure 4.3: Policy Rate Differential with the US Policy Rate—Selected Asian Economies** (percentage points, as of 31 December 2024)

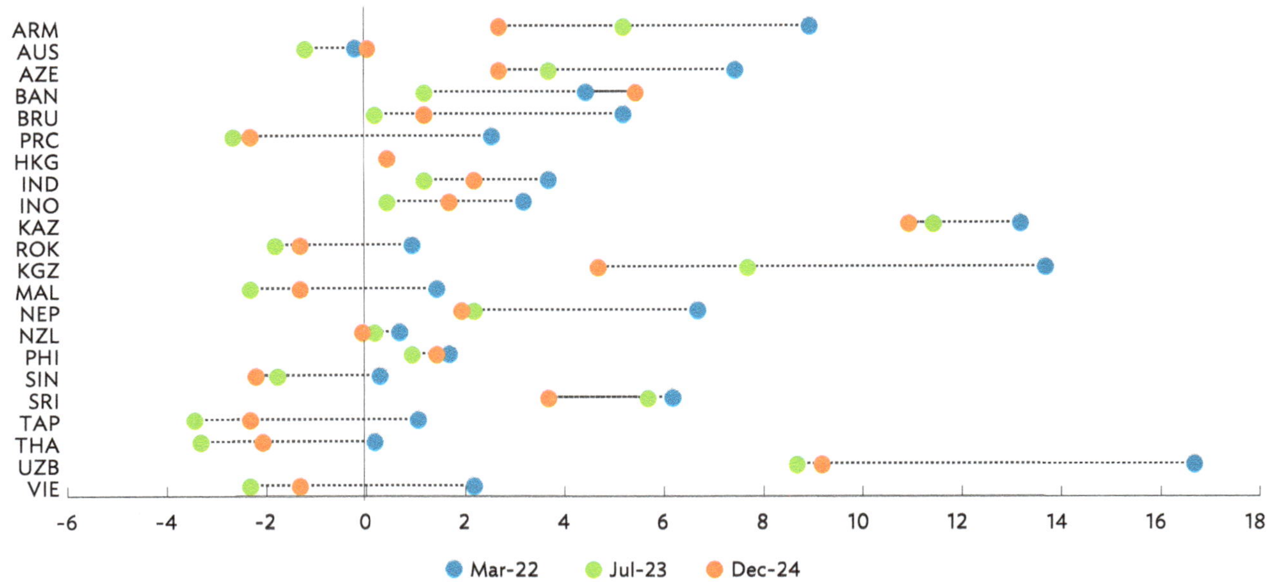


ARM = Armenia; AUS = Australia; AZE = Azerbaijan; BAN = Bangladesh; BRU = Brunei Darussalam; PRC = People's Republic of China; HKG = Hong Kong, China; IND = India; INO = Indonesia; KAZ = Kazakhstan; ROK = Republic of Korea; KGZ = Kyrgyz Republic; MAL = Malaysia; NEP = Nepal; NZL = New Zealand; PHI = Philippines; SIN = Singapore; SRI = Sri Lanka; TAP = Taipei,China; THA = Thailand; US = United States; UZB = Uzbekistan; VIE = Viet Nam.

Note: The Hong Kong dollar is pegged to the US dollar. The peg results in a negligibly small policy differential over the period March 2022 to December 2024.

Source: ADB calculations using data from CEIC Data Company (accessed January 2025).

wake of its zero-COVID-19 policy. With US monetary policy turning less hawkish in 2023, robust growth in the region, and markets' expectation for a soft landing of the PRC's property market, capital inflows gained momentum throughout 2023. This momentum was carried into the first half of 2024, with inflows exceeding the prepandemic average on the back of solid growth in the region and US monetary easing. Developing Asia recorded cumulative net portfolio inflows for the remainder of 2024, with the PRC; Hong Kong, China; and India posting the highest inflows (Figure 4.4b). Overall, capital inflows also benefit from a decline of US dollar-denominated refinancing costs, in turn encouraging investors in Asia to borrow in the globally dominant vehicle currency for trade and investment (Avdjiev et al. 2017, 2018; ADB 2024a; Boz et al. 2020; Gopinath et al. 2020).

## Capital Inflows Are Set to Boost Asset Markets in Asia

Except for the Brunei dollar, Singapore dollar, and Hong Kong dollar, as of the end of 2024, regional local currencies have not yet recovered from the broad-based depreciation against the US dollar following the 2022 US monetary tightening (Figure 4.5a). Economy-specific circumstances dominated some currency movements. Since the US Federal Reserve hinted at policy easing in July 2024, most regional currencies have begun to appreciate (ADB 2024a). The inflows observed throughout 2024 broadly lifted asset valuations across the region, with stock prices gaining 12% and bond prices gaining 4.3% on average since the start of the year (Figure 4.5b). Stock price gains were concentrated in Sri Lanka; Kazakhstan; Taipei,China; Japan; Hong Kong, China; and Singapore. In 2024, developing Asia's market-weighted return increased by 11.2% to September (ADB 2024b).

**Figure 4.4: Nonresident Capital Flows—Selected Asian Economies** ($ billion)

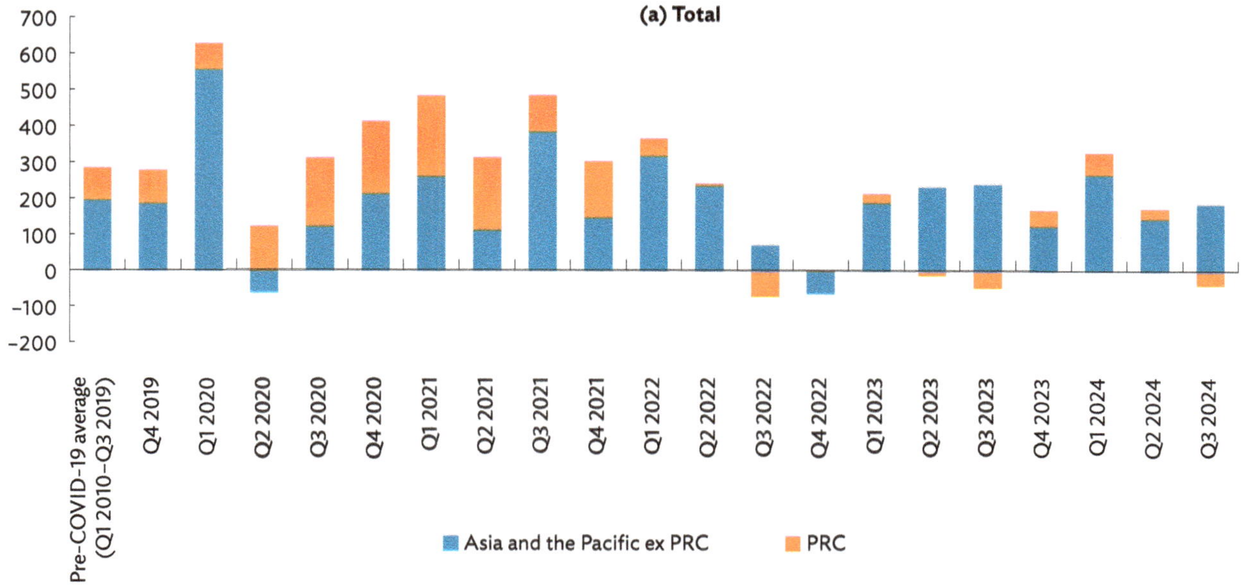


PRC = People's Republic of China, COVID-19 = coronavirus disease, Q = quarter.

Notes:

1. Nonresident capital flows are composed of foreign direct investment, portfolio equity and debt flows, and other investment flows. Other investment flows include currency and deposits; insurance, pension, and standardized guaranteed schemes; loans; other accounts payable; other equity; special drawing rights; and trade credit and advances.
2. Positive values denote net inflows, negative values denote net outflows.
3. Selected Asian economies refer to Armenia; Azerbaijan; Bangladesh; Cambodia; the People's Republic of China; Fiji; Georgia; Hong Kong, China; India; Indonesia; Japan; Kazakhstan; the Republic of Korea; Malaysia; Pakistan; the Philippines; Samoa; Tajikistan; Taipei,China; Thailand; and Uzbekistan.

Source: ADB calculations using data from the International Monetary Fund. Balance of Payments and International Investment Position Statistics. Accessed from CEIC Data Company (accessed January 2025).

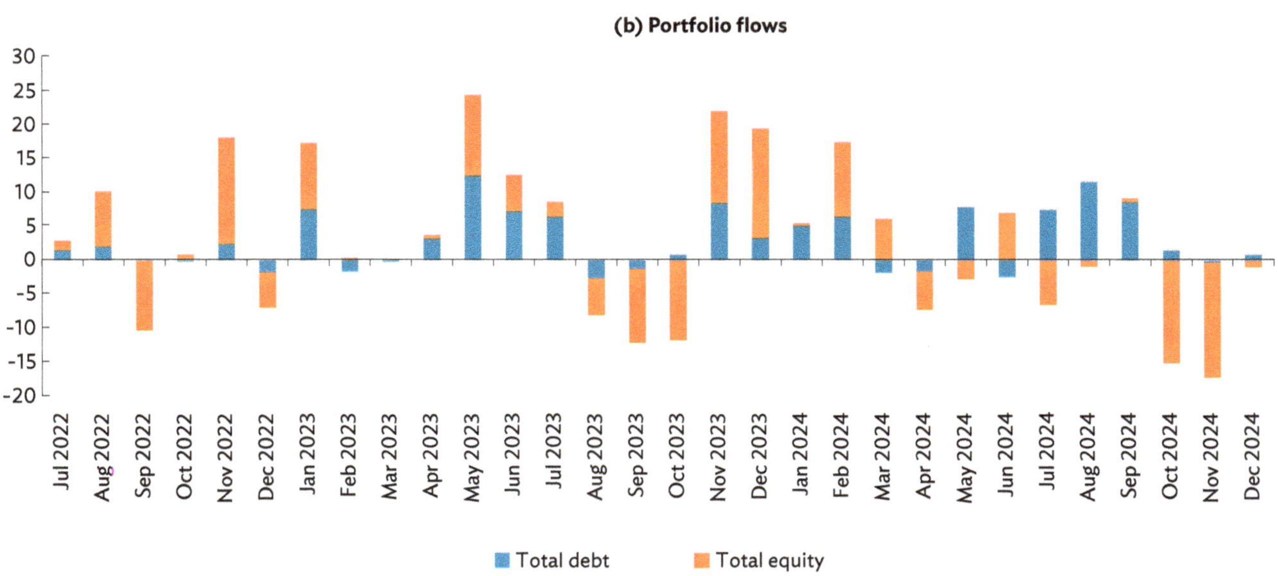


Notes: Positive values denote net inflows, negative values denote net outflows. Selected Asian economies include India; Indonesia; the Republic of Korea; Malaysia; Mongolia; Pakistan; the Philippines; Sri Lanka (equity only); Taipei,China; Thailand; and Viet Nam (equity only).

Source: ADB calculations using data from the Institute of International Finance. Capital Flows Tracker. https://www.iif.com (accessed February 2025).

**Figure 4.5: Year-to-Date Change—Selected Asian Economies** (%, as of 31 December 2024)

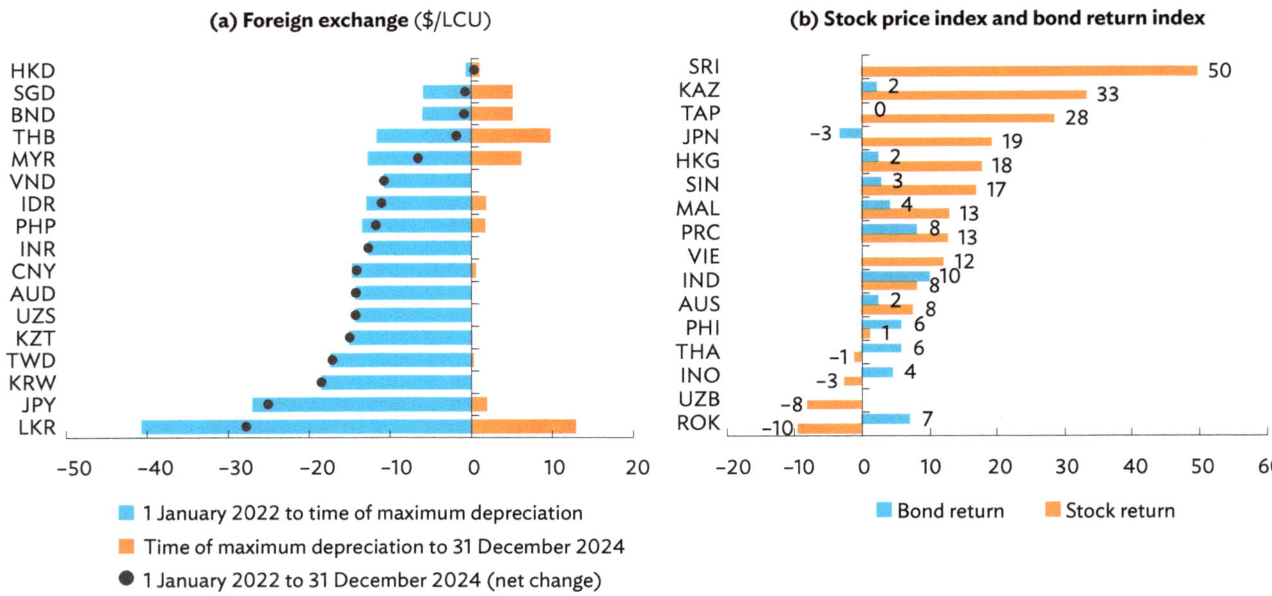


AUD = Australian dollar; AUS = Australia; BND = Brunei dollar; PRC = People's Republic of China; CNY = yuan; HKD = Hong Kong dollar; HKG = Hong Kong, China; IDR = rupiah; IND = India; INO = Indonesia; INR = Indian rupee; JPN = Japan; JPY = yen; KAZ = Kazakhstan; ROK = Republic of Korea; KRW = won; KZT = tenge; LCU = local currency unit; LKR = Sri Lanka rupee; MAL = Malaysia; MYR = ringgit; PHI = Philippines; PHP = peso; SGD = Singapore dollar; SIN = Singapore; SRI = Sri Lanka; TAP = Taipei,China; THA = Thailand; THB = baht; TWD = NT dollar; UZB = Uzbekistan; UZS = sum; VIE = Viet Nam; VND = dong.

Source: ADB calculations using Bloomberg; CEIC Data Company; and Haver Analytics (all accessed January 2025).

While capital inflows rebounded, Asia remains exposed to volatile capital flows. Foreign direct investment (FDI) proved the most stable source of foreign capital for the region, contributing one-third of the rebound over 2023 and 2024. In contrast, portfolio investment and other investment flows remain most sensitive to changing global financial conditions, and they contributed relatively more to the recovery of total capital flows in 2023 and 2024 (Eichengreen, Gupta, and Masetti 2018).

Potential global financial stress calls for vigilance of sudden capital flow reversals. Given these flows' volatility, policymakers must remain vigilant of sudden capital flow reversals if global financial stress were to increase suddenly. A brief episode of financial turmoil in global markets in early August 2024 served as important reminder. During that period, portfolio equity flows experienced outflows exceeding 130% of the region's average inflows in the preceding 2 years.

This episode of extreme volatility was triggered by an unwinding of leveraged trades in equity and currency markets in response to a perceived hawkish rate hike by the Bank of Japan amplified by US recession fears, and thus the expectation of a more cautious pace of US policy rate cuts (Aquilina et al. 2024). A long period of low borrowing costs in Japan with contained volatility exacerbated the outsized market reaction, worsened by a correction of what seemed overvalued global technology company stocks amid thin markets in August 2024 (Scheid 2024). At least $250 billion of carry trades unwound, leading to rapid asset sales globally, and thus a reversal of portfolio equity flows from the region (Figure 4.4b). Besides sudden bursts of market volatility, policymakers need to monitor the health of the US economy and associated changes to the pace of monetary easing (ADB 2024b). For instance, the region experienced portfolio outflows in April 2024 as investors anticipated delays in US monetary easing.

## Regional Financial Integration Remains Robust to Volatility

### Asset and Liability Exposures Remained Broadly Unchanged

Despite significant movement in the global financial cycle, Asia's intraregional cross-border asset and liability exposures remained broadly unchanged over 2022–2023 (Figures 4.6 and 4.7). As for cross-border asset exposures, the intraregional share of portfolio equity fell by 1 percentage point to 21%, while portfolio debt fell by 2 percentage points to 21%, and FDI assets rose by 1 percentage point to 51%. Cross-border intraregional liabilities exhibited similarly small changes, with portfolio debt up 1 percentage point to 30%, and portfolio equity and bank liabilities down by 2 and 1 percentage points to 20% and 44%, respectively. The intraregional shares for bank assets and FDI liabilities remained unchanged. Asia's total cross-border assets and liabilities also remained largely unchanged, with both assets and liabilities increasing by 4 percentage points, to 75% and 74% of regional GDP. Both were down from their pandemic era peaks of 83% and 80% of regional GDP, but still on par with the 10-year average.

**Figure 4.6: Cross-Border Assets—Asia and the Pacific, by Type**

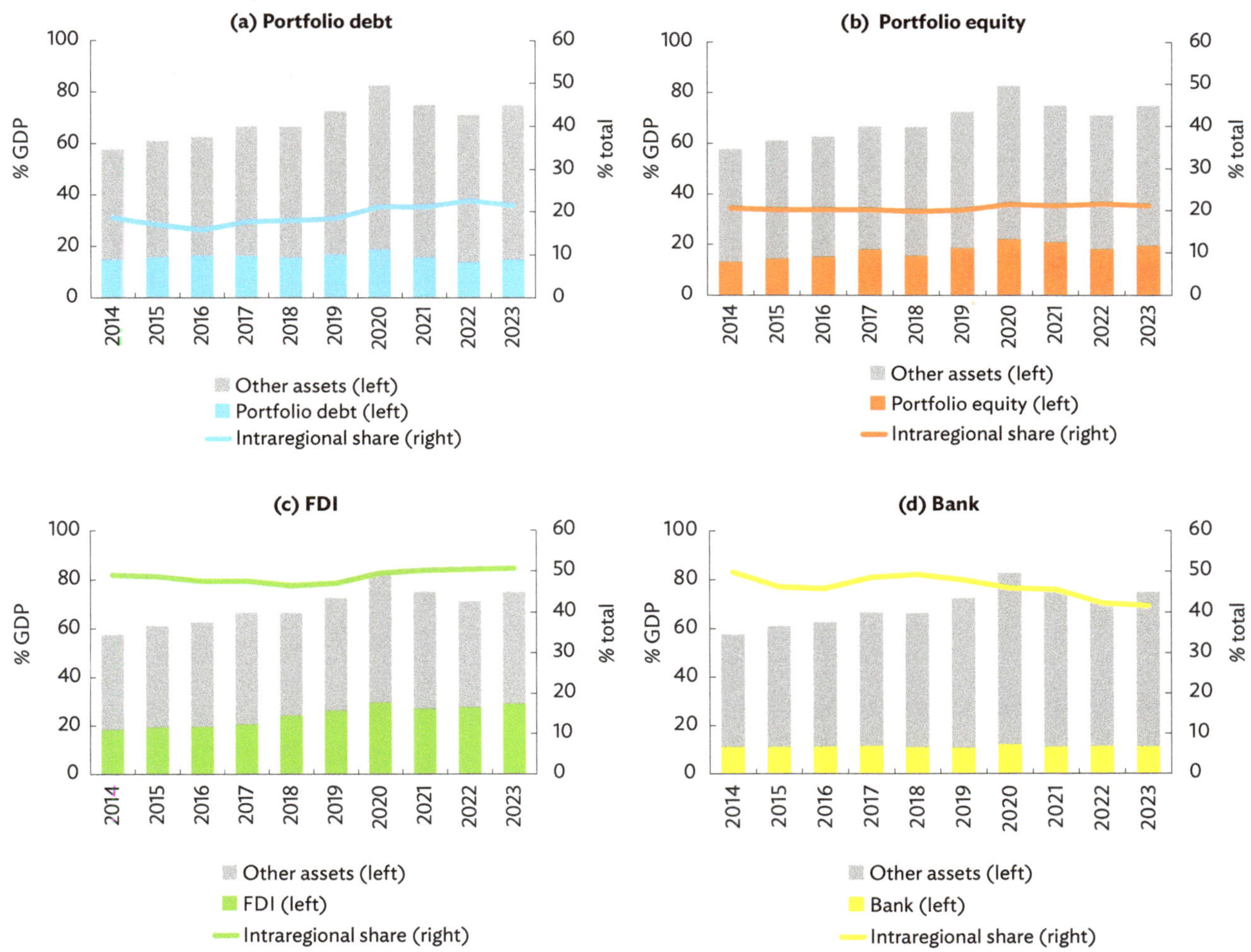


FDI = foreign direct investment, GDP = gross domestic product.

Notes: Estimates are as of the end of 2023. FDI assets refer to outward FDI holdings. Bank assets (claims) are limited to bank loans and deposits. Asia and the Pacific includes ADB regional members for which data are available.

Sources: ADB calculations using data from Bank for International Settlements. Locational Banking Statistics. https://www.bis.org/statistics/bankstats.htm; International Monetary Fund (IMF). Coordinated Direct Investment Survey. https://data.imf.org/cdis; and IMF. Coordinated Portfolio Investment Survey. https://data.imf.org/cpis (all accessed January 2025).

**Figure 4.7: Cross-Border Liabilities—Asia and the Pacific, by Type**

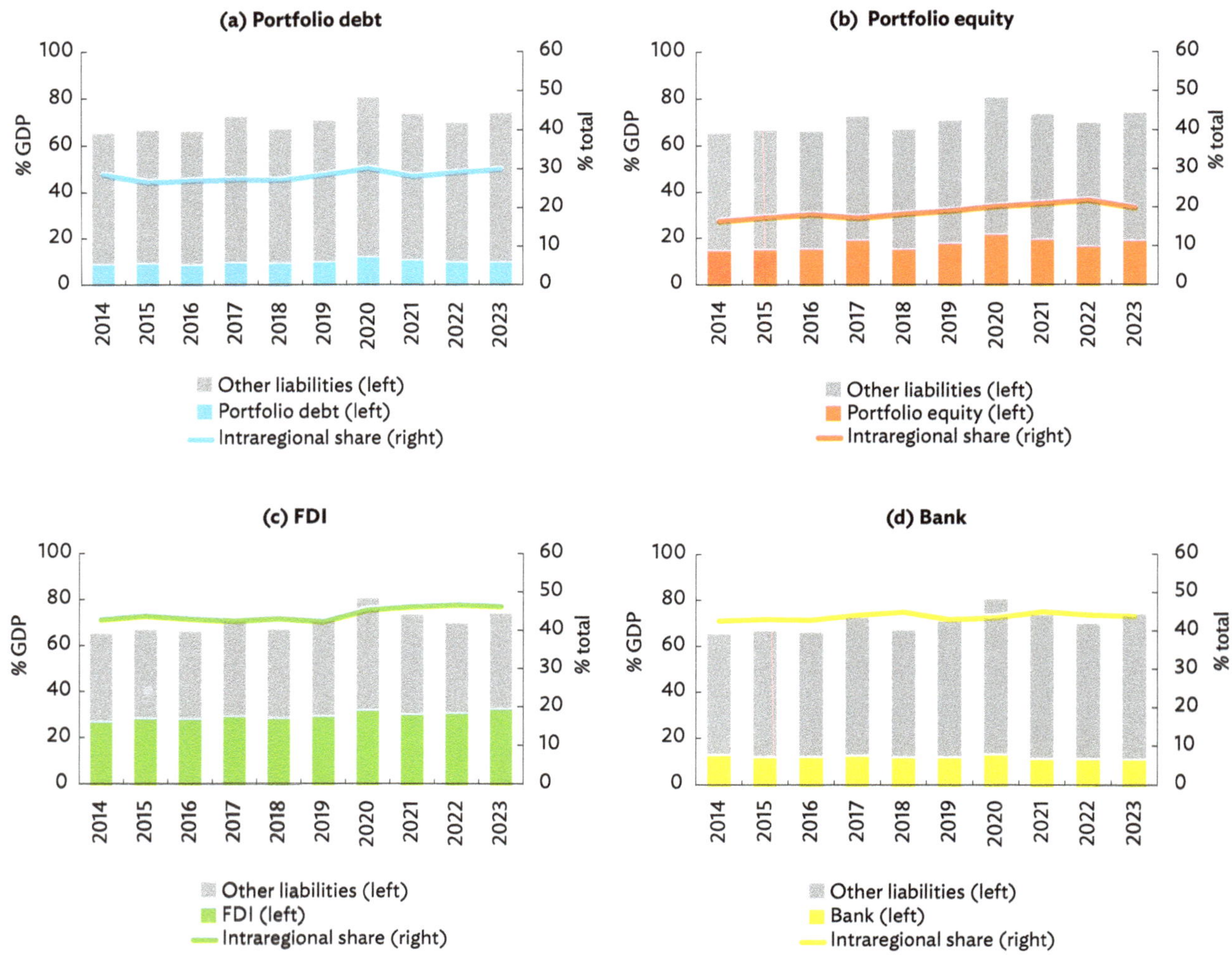


FDI = foreign direct investment, GDP = gross domestic product.

Notes: Estimates are as of the end of 2023. FDI liabilities refer to inward FDI holdings. Bank liabilities are limited to loans and deposits. Asia and the Pacific includes ADB regional members for which data are available.

Sources: ADB calculations using data from Bank for International Settlements. Locational Banking Statistics. https://www.bis.org/statistics/bankstats.htm; International Monetary Fund (IMF). Coordinated Direct Investment Survey. https://data.imf.org/cdis; and IMF. Coordinated Portfolio Investment Survey. https://data.imf.org/cpis (all accessed January 2025).

## Easing Global Financial Conditions Bode Well for Financial Integration

The easing of global conditions is likely to help extraregional investors search for yield and sets the scene for increased investments in the region. In addition, Asian investors seek to diversify portfolios by investing regionally. The steady increase in the share of FDI in cross-border assets and liabilities over recent years is welcome as it helps reduce the region's exposure to asset repricing risks in foreign markets. Asian investors have raised their FDI allocation from one-third to two-fifths over the past decade (Figure 4.8a). Over the same period, foreign investors' FDI allocation has remained largely unchanged at 45% as a share of Asia's cross-border liabilities. However, portfolio liabilities and bank liabilities still represent more than half of external investments in the region, making it susceptible to capital flow reversals in response to global financial shocks (Figure 4.8b).[32]

[32] See ADB (2024c) for a detailed discussion on Asia's vulnerability to capital flow reversals.

**Figure 4.8: Cross-Border Investment—Asia and the Pacific, by Type** (% of total)

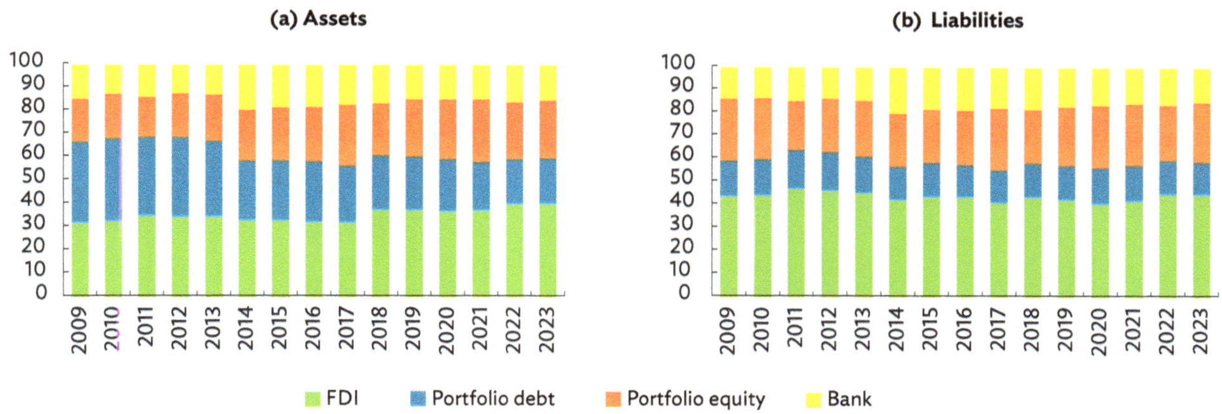


FDI = foreign direct investment.

Notes: Estimates are as of the end of 2023. FDI assets refer to outward FDI holdings, while FDI liabilities refer to inward FDI holdings. Bank claims and liabilities are limited to bank loans and deposits. Asia and the Pacific includes ADB regional members for which data are available.

Sources: ADB calculations using data from Bank for International Settlements. Locational Banking Statistics. https://www.bis.org/statistics/bankstats.htm; International Monetary Fund (IMF). Coordinated Direct Investment Survey. https://data.imf.org/cdis (accessed January 2025); and IMF. Coordinated Portfolio Investment Survey. https://data.imf.org/cpis (accessed January 2025).

# Regional Financial Cooperation as a Key Pillar of Macrofinancial Stability

## Reinvigorating Regional Cooperation Can Reignite the Growth Potential of Financial Integration

The previous section provided evidence for largely stable regional financial integration in 2022–2023. This stability follows a slowdown in the integration momentum over the past decade. The slowdown contrasts with regional cooperation as a backbone to macroeconomic stability in Asia over the past 3 decades, as presented in this section. Thus, it is vital to strengthen regional cooperation as an engine of growth and prosperity. To this end, policymakers need to improve the cost-benefit balance of integration, as further discussed below. New policy challenges including geopolitical fragmentation, technological innovations, public health emergencies, climate change and biodiversity loss add urgency to strengthening regional cooperation.

Over the past 30 years, financial integration in Asia has advanced in the slipstream of globalization. Financial deregulation and capital account liberalizations from the 1990s led to a surge in capital flows to Asia. The pattern of capital flows mirrored the broader trends in globalization for trade and migration. While various restrictions on cross-border capital flows remain, capital flows to and between Asian economies rose in tandem with the improvement in de jure measures of capital account openness over 2000–2021, as captured by the Chinn–Ito Index on capital account openness (Figure 4.9).

**Figure 4.9: Average Chinn-Ito Index—Asia and the Pacific**

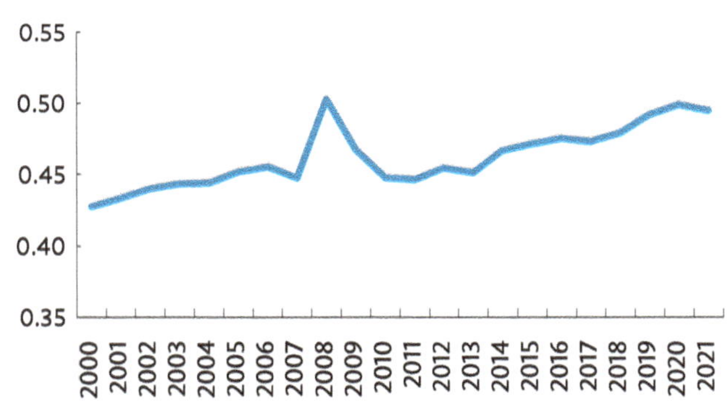


Note: The data show the average Chinn–Ito index (KAOPEN) for Asian economies. A higher index means the economy is more open to cross-border capital transactions.

Source: ADB calculations using data from Chinn and Ito (2006, 2008).

Asia attracted an increasing share of global FDI inflows, from an annual average of 18.6% in 1990–1994 to 24.3% in 2015–2017, rising to 94.3% in 2018–2019 before settling to 65.9% during the COVID-19 pandemic (Figure 4.10a). Portfolio investment flows to the region as a share of the global total rose from 6.5% to 16.4%, further to 22.5%, and settled at 9% in the same four intervals (Figure 4.10b).

Similarly, cross-border asset and liability exposures expanded significantly in the late 1990s until the global financial crisis. Cross-border asset holdings in Asia increased from 55.1% of regional GDP in 2009 to 82.6% in 2020 before dipping to 74.8% in 2023 in the aftermath of the pandemic (Figure 4.6). The share of intraregional assets held within Asia also rose significantly, from 25.7% in 2009 to 36.2% in 2023. Intraregional shares for all asset classes, except portfolio equity, increased, with intraregional FDI recording the highest—51% in 2023. Total cross-border liabilities also grew from 54.2% of GDP in 2009 to 80.4% in 2020 before declining to 73.8% in 2023 (Figure 4.7). The share of liabilities from within the region ranged from 30% in 2009 to 37% in 2023. Intraregional shares for all categories of liabilities increased during the period shown, with intraregional FDI also recording the highest level at 46.6% in 2023.[33]

However, regional financial integration has lost steam over the past decade. The path of cross-border exposures of Asian economies diverged from emerging market and developing economies after the 1997 Asian financial crisis, and grew significantly slower after the global financial crisis, also compared to global average cross-border exposures (Figure 4.11). As a result, both equity and bond markets are more sensitive to global than regional factors (Figure 4.12). The relatively low intraregional financial integration contradicts the trend in trade (Montanes and Schmukler 2018; Park and Rajan 2021). Figure 4.13 shows that the shares of intraregional trade in goods (41%) and services (36%) exceed the intraregional share of cross-border asset and liabilities exposures discussed above. Moreover, a comparison between the Association of Southeast Asian Nations Plus Three (ASEAN+3) economies and the euro area suggests nearly identical intraregional trade shares, but significantly lower portfolio and bank holdings within ASEAN+3 (Figure 4.14). Asia's relatively slow progress on financial integration may help explain a persistently low degree of integration in the "money and finance" dimension of the Asia-Pacific Regional Cooperation and Integration Index discussed in Chapter 1.

**Figure 4.10: Nonresident Financial Flows to Asia—By Type** (% of total global inflows, period average)

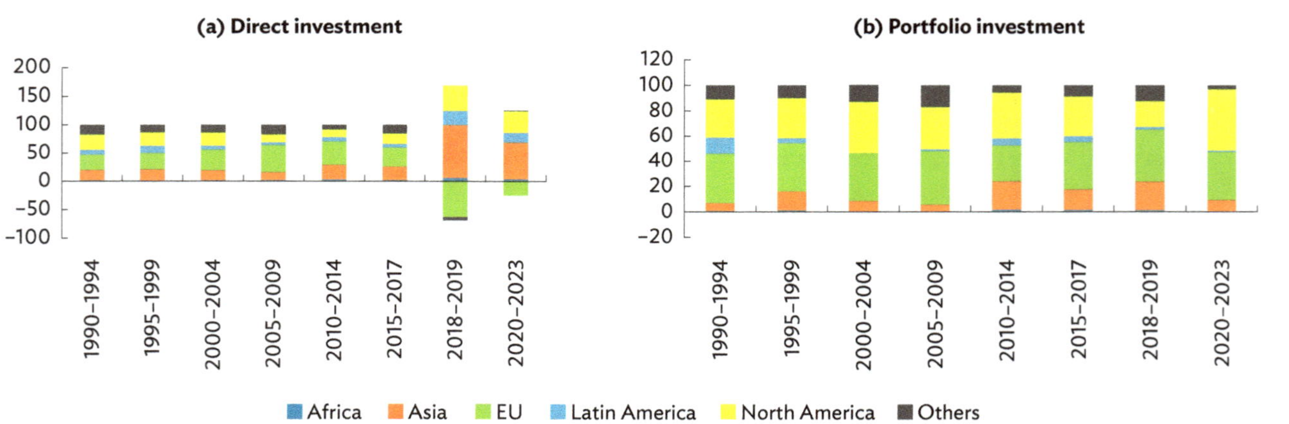


EU = European Union (27 members).

Source: ADB calculations using data from the International Monetary Fund. Balance of Payment and International Investment Position Statistics. http://data.imf.org/BOP (accessed December 2024).

[33] For both assets and liabilities, intraregional bank lending in Asia increased sharply after 2013 when data for the PRC became available.

**Figure 4.11: External Financial Assets and Liabilities** (% of GDP)

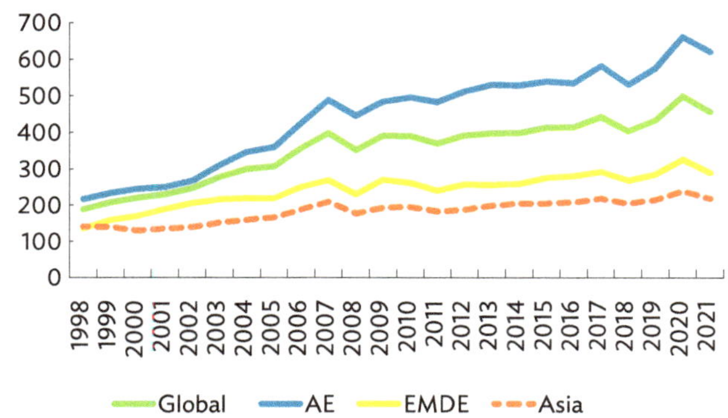


AE = advanced economy, EMDE = emerging market and developing economies, GDP = gross domestic product.

Notes: Asia includes Armenia; Australia; Azerbaijan; Bangladesh; Bhutan; Brunei Darussalam; Cambodia; the People's Republic of China; Fiji; Georgia; Hong Kong, China; India; Indonesia; Japan; Kazakhstan; Kiribati; the Republic of Korea; the Kyrgyz Republic; the Lao People's Democratic Republic; Malaysia; Maldives; the Marshall Islands; the Federated States of Micronesia; Mongolia; Nauru; Nepal; New Zealand; Pakistan; Palau; Papua New Guinea; the Philippines; Samoa; Singapore; Solomon Islands; Sri Lanka; Taipei,China; Tajikistan; Thailand; Timor-Leste; Tonga; Turkmenistan; Tuvalu; Uzbekistan; Vanuatu; and Viet Nam.

Source: ADB calculations using IMF (2023) and Milesi-Ferretti (2024).

**Figure 4.13: Trade in Merchandise and Services and Cross-Border Assets and Liabilities of Asia and the Pacific, by Partner** (%)

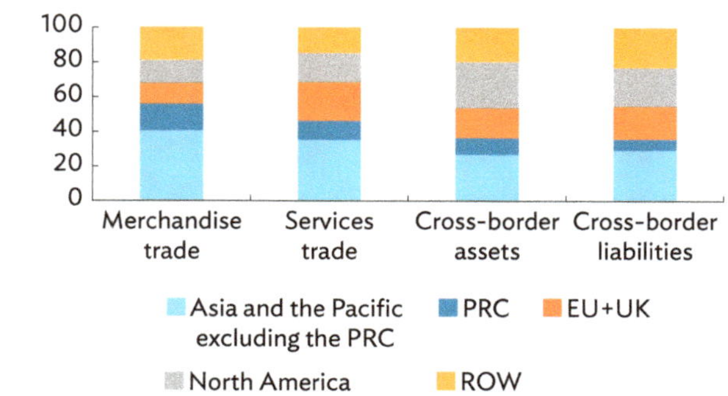


PRC = People's Republic of China, EU = European Union (27 members), ROW = rest of the world, UK = United Kingdom.

Note: Estimates are as of 2021 for services trade and as of the end of 2023 for merchandise trade and cross-border assets and liabilities.

Sources: ADB calculations using data from Bank for International Settlements. Locational Banking Statistics. https://stats.bis.org/statx/toc/LBS.html; International Monetary Fund (IMF). Coordinated Direct Investment Survey. https://data.imf.org/cdis; IMF. Coordinated Portfolio Investment Survey. https://data.imf.org/cpis (all accessed January 2025); IMF. Direction of Trade Statistics. https://data.imf.org/dot; IMF. World Economic Outlook October 2023 Database. https://www.imf.org/en/Publications/WEO/weo-database/2023/October; and WTO-Organisation for Economic Cooperation and Development (OECD). Balanced Trade in Services Dataset (BaTIS)—BPM6. https://www.wto.org/english/res_e/statis_e/trade_datasets_e.htm (all accessed November 2024).

**Figure 4.12: Variance Decomposition of Equity and Bond Returns** (%)

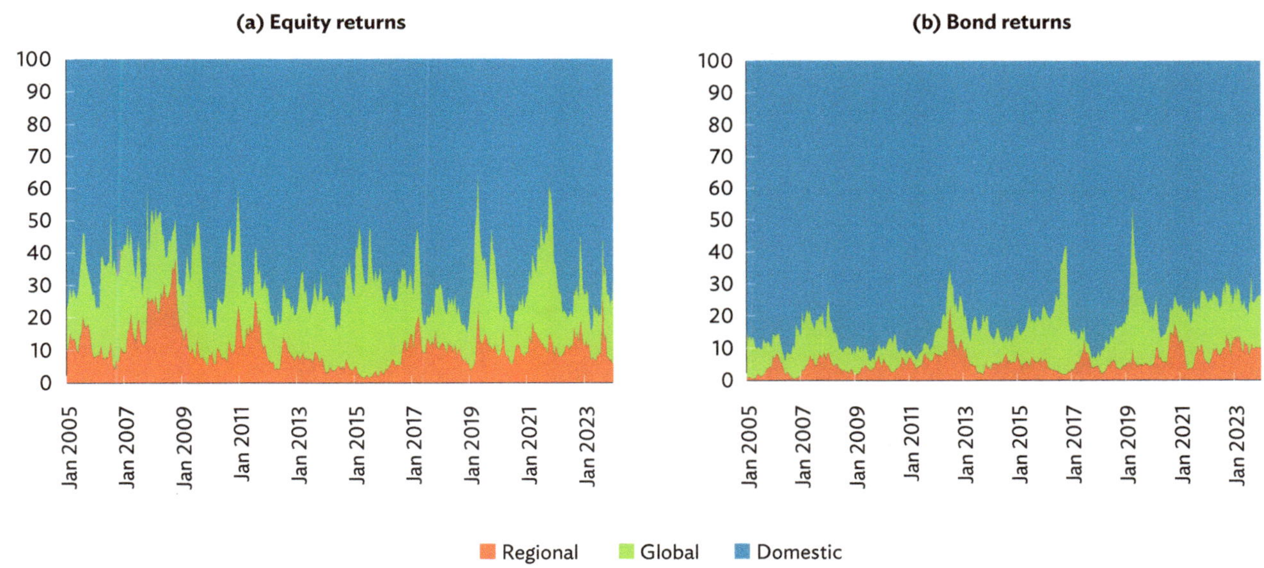


Notes: Asia includes Australia; Bangladesh (equities only); Cambodia (equities only); the People's Republic of China; Georgia (equities only); Hong Kong, China; India; Indonesia; Japan; Kazakhstan; the Republic of Korea; the Kyrgyz Republic (equities only); the Lao People's Democratic Republic (equities only); Malaysia; Mongolia (equities only); Nepal (equities only); New Zealand (equities only); Pakistan (equities only); the Philippines; Singapore; Sri Lanka (equities only); Taipei,China; Thailand; Uzbekistan (equities only); and Viet Nam.

Sources: ADB calculations using data from Bloomberg; CEIC Data Company (both accessed January 2025); and methodology by Lee and Park (2011) using 1-year rolling window estimations.

**Figure 4.14: Intraregional Shares, 2023—ASEAN+3 Versus Euro Area** (%)

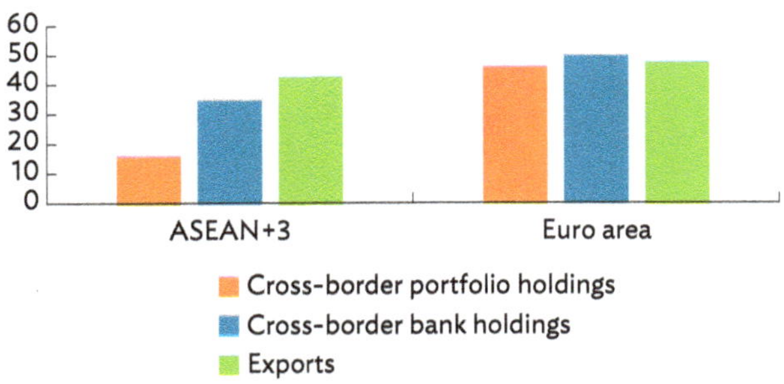


ASEAN = Association of Southeast Asian Nations; ASEAN+3 = ASEAN plus the People's Republic of China, Japan, and the Republic of Korea.

Note: ASEAN+3 includes Hong Kong, China.

Sources: ADB calculations using data from Bank for International Settlements. Locational Banking Statistics. https://www.bis.org/statistics/bankstats.htm; International Monetary Fund (IMF). Coordinated Portfolio Investment Survey. http://data.imf.org/cpis (both accessed January 2025); and IMF. Direction of Trade Database. https://www.imf.org/en/Data (accessed November 2024).

Accelerating financial integration requires developing domestic financial markets. Park, Rosenkranz, and Tayag (2020) attribute the less than complete financial integration in Asia to lower financial development in the form of high transaction costs and information asymmetries. A comparison of the higher financial development of European Union (EU)—known to be more financially integrated—with the lower development in Asia confirms the importance of domestic financial market development for integration (Figure 4.15). Lower transaction costs in the EU enabling deeper integration is in part due to regional governance structures such as the European Commission and European Securities Markets Authority issuing regulations for the EU-wide capital market, underpinned by the single currency. Figure 4.15 also highlights the lack of regional convergence as Malaysia and Thailand developed faster than Indonesia, the Philippines, and Viet Nam.

## Benefits Outweigh the Costs of Well-Managed Financial Integration

### Gains Stem from Macrofinancial Stability and Openness That Boost Investment and Growth

Financial integration bestows several benefits. Financial integration is recognized for reducing the cost of capital, expanding investment opportunities, and enhancing economic resilience through international risk sharing. Efficiency gains derive from integration thanks to foreign competition. This competition deepens and broadens the domestic finance sector, lowering the costs associated with information collection, contract enforcement, and transactions. Consequently, allocative efficiency improves, promoting economic growth.

**Figure 4.15: Financial Development Index—Selected Asian Economies**

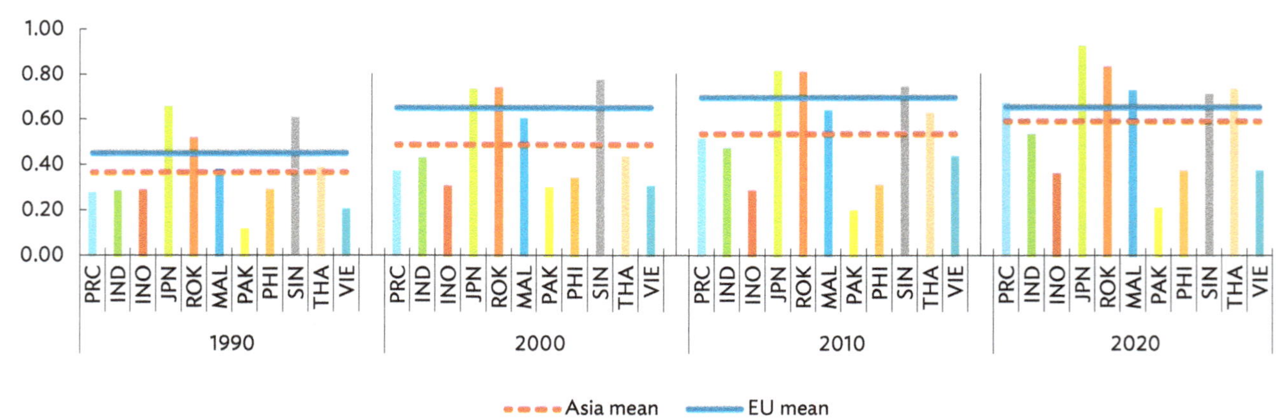


PRC = People's Republic of China, EU = European Union, IND = India, INO = Indonesia, JPN = Japan, ROK = Republic of Korea, MAL = Malaysia, PAK = Pakistan, PHI = Philippines, SIN = Singapore, THA = Thailand, VIE = Viet Nam.

Notes: An index closer to 1 indicates high financial development. EU refers to Austria, Belgium, Finland, France, Germany, Greece, Hungary, Ireland, Italy, Luxembourg, Netherlands, Poland, Portugal, and Spain.

Source: ADB calculations using International Monetary Fund. Financial Development Index Database. https://www.imf.org/en/Data (accessed September 2024).

Moreover, financial openness attracts foreign investment to capital-scarce developing economies, thereby boosting investment and growth. Several studies confirm the growth-enhancing effect of financial integration. Bong and Premaratne (2019) find evidence for a positive relationship between growth and integration through FDI for Southeast Asia. The positive relationship stands confirmed for East Asia (Fry-McKibbin, Hsiao, and Martin 2018). Besides pro-growth effects, Yadav, Goyari, and Mishra (2019) point at reduced income and consumption volatility for financially more integrated economies. Financial integration may also relieve exchange market pressure (Phylaktis and Aftab 2024).[34]

Institutions, financial development, and sequencing of reforms are decisive to harness the benefits of financial integration. Research indicates that the advantages of financial integration for growth are contingent on income levels, trade openness, and institutional quality (Caporale, Sova, and Sova 2023; Chen and Kim 2023; Taghizadeh-Hesary et al. 2019). In addition, the capital account openness is more beneficial at advanced stages of financial development, whereas the associated costs and risks are more pronounced at lower stages. For instance, Selvarajan and Ab-Rahim (2020) find that the positive relationship between growth and financial integration in Asia declined after the Asian financial crisis because financial development was constrained by concerns about shareholder protection schemes, creditor rights, and the limited capacity of regulators. In addition, the sequencing of capital account liberalizations is essential to unleash growth accelerations. This involves developing the domestic financial market and regulatory frameworks before embracing financial openness and prioritizing long-term capital inflows over short-term ones.

Besides numerous advantages, financial integration raises the vulnerability to external shocks such as from volatile capital flows. Large capital inflows and their abrupt reversals can entail large swings in the exchange rate, exacerbating financial imbalances. During the Asian financial crisis, these swings inflicted significant damage on Asian economies, further amplified by currency mismatches and foreign currency denominated liabilities accumulated prior to the crisis. As a result, within 1 year GDP fell by a combined 30% in the most-affected economies—Indonesia, Malaysia, the Philippines, the Republic of Korea, and Thailand (ADB 2020). Banks succumbed to high nonperforming loans, leading to a collapse of investment.

Currency mismatches remain widespread almost 3 decades after the Asian financial crisis. Advances in local currency debt markets only partially remedy capital flow reversal risk from the transfer of currency mismatches to international investors (ADB 2024c; Hofmann, Shim, and Shin 2020). Given most of the region's foreign debt is denominated in US dollars, it remains prone to spillovers from the US financial system and shocks to the global financial cycle. High US dollar dependence across all dimensions of currency use amplifies the risk of sudden capital flow reversals (ADB 2024c).[35]

High interconnectedness between national financial markets can amplify vulnerabilities from financial integration. Network analysis using equity prices revealed relatively high interconnectedness among Asia's financial markets (ADB 2017). Pericoli and Yilmaz (2024) emphasize that stock markets account for most of the spillovers to other asset markets—notably bonds, foreign exchange, and commodities—with commodities receiving most of the volatility spillovers. This highlights the need for coordinated action to raise the resilience of the region's financial systems to shocks from interconnected markets.

34 Exchange market pressure is defined as the change in the exchange rate combined with an estimated counterfactual of the change associated with the central bank's intervention in the foreign exchange market.

35 About four-fifths of Asia's exports and imports are denominated in US dollars; over half of bank assets and liabilities, half of debt issued, and two-thirds of foreign exchange reserves are denominated in US dollars, which also serve as exchange rate anchor for 18 economies in the region (ADB 2024c).

## Vulnerabilities Must Be Well Managed for the Region to Benefit from Integration

The discussion has highlighted both the benefits and costs of financial integration. The costs can be mitigated by a combination of domestic policies strengthening resilience, regional cooperation for policy coordination, and joint regional stabilization initiatives.

Policy responses to dampen vulnerabilities should address macrofinancial linkages (ADB 2020). These linkages are at the nexus between macroeconomic outcomes and financial variables. On the demand side, macroeconomic fluctuations can become more volatile in response to changes in balance sheets of borrowers. On the other side, shocks to supply affect bank lending, bank capital, the leverage cycle, and liquidity conditions. Domestically, macroprudential policies can be effective in minimizing the procyclicality of the financial system, notably in emerging markets (Bergant et al. 2023). These comprise countercyclical provisions, capital and liquidity buffers, and balance sheet instruments such as leverage ratios and limits on debt-to-income and loan-to-value ratios.

Cross-border policy spillovers warrant close coordination of policies addressing macrofinancial risks. Cross-economy differences in the design and implementation of macroprudential policies can become a source of contagion (Agénor 2024). For instance, a tightening of capital requirements at home may induce banks to increase foreign lending, in turn magnifying the international transmission of financial shocks. An internationally coordinated minimum standard on capital requirements can guard against such regulatory arbitrage. Coordination can ease the adoption of international standards, lowering the learning costs for regulatory authorities in each economy.

# Regional Cooperation Is the Engine of Financial Integration

## Regional Cooperation on Financial Policies Was Born from Crises

The Asian and global financial crises exposed major challenges, notably highly bank-dependent financing, inadequate regulatory frameworks, and shallow financial markets (Park 2011). At the same time, regional policymakers sought to overcome the stigma attached to the conditionality associated with requests for emergency liquidity from the International Monetary Fund (IMF) by establishing their own regional crisis management framework (Han 2022). Several new regional cooperation forums and initiatives were created. While the full potential of integration in Asia may yet to be achieved, as outlined in the discussion so far, the new institutional structures proved instrumental to create effective communication channels for coordination in times of crisis.

The Asian financial crisis unleashed a wave of forums and initiatives for regional cooperation. Several regional forums have been created to exchange information, conduct economic monitoring, as well as research and training, and engage in policy dialogue to develop expertise and build capacity for better policymaking (Lee and Kring 2024). Immediately following the Asian financial crisis, in 1998, the Association of Southeast Asian Nations (ASEAN) Surveillance Process was established, followed by the ASEAN+3 Economic Review and Policy Dialogue in 1999, later to be integrated in the Chiang Mai Initiative Multilateralisation (CMIM). These early cooperation bodies emphasized consensus and noninterference in the peer review, at the expense of forthright and comprehensive policy discussions (Menon 2012). These issues persisted until the creation of the ASEAN+3 Macroeconomic Research Office (AMRO) in 2011 and its formal mandate for regional surveillance in 2016. The setup of AMRO eventually dominated proposals for largely similar regional cooperation forums, notably the Asian Financial Stability Dialogue and Asian Systemic Risk Council (Kawai and Morgan 2014; Buckley, Avgouleas, and Arner 2020).

CMIM and AMRO constitute the backbone of Asia's financial safety net. Financial cooperation post-Asian financial crisis centered on establishing a regional financial safety net, economic and financial surveillance mechanisms accompanied by initiatives for financial market development. These functions are primarily served by the liquidity pool created with the CMIM and AMRO's macrofinancial surveillance. Created as bilateral swap lines among ASEAN+3 members under the Chiang Mai Initiative in 2000, these were consolidated into the CMIM as one multilateralized arrangement in 2007, and became effective in 2010. Initially consisting only of the crisis resolution facility, called the CMIM Stability Facility (CMIM-SF) of $120 billion for temporary balance of payment shocks, a precautionary credit line (CMIM-PL) was added for members with sound macroeconomic fundamentals. In 2014, the CMIM-SF was upgraded to $240 billion, and in 2021 the IMF delinked portion was raised to 40%, denoting the quota amount that can be drawn from member economies without simultaneous IMF program. Thus, the CMIM disposes of both a crisis resolution and a crisis prevention tool (Khor et al. 2022). A significantly smaller emergency liquidity pool of $2 billion is provided by the Reserve Bank of India for members of the South Asian Association for Regional Cooperation to cover short-term foreign exchange liquidity needs (Lee and Kring 2024).[36]

The Asian Bond Markets Initiative (ABMI) and Asian Bond Fund (ABF) exemplify effective regional cooperation mechanisms put in place after the Asian financial crisis. First, in August 2003, ASEAN+3 finance ministers launched the ABMI to mitigate currency and maturity mismatches which lay at the heart of the crisis. The ABMI established local currency bond markets by strengthening the demand for and supply of local currency bonds through information sharing and credit guarantees. To this end, the Asian Bonds Online website was launched in 2004, the Credit Guarantee and Investment Facility created in May 2010, and the ASEAN+3 Bond Market Forum (ABMF) established in 2010. The ABMF provides a common platform to foster standardization of market practices and harmonization of regulations relating to cross-border bond transactions in the region and produces stock-taking reports on regional bond markets. Second, the ABF, launched in 2003, further strengthened the demand for local currency bonds. ABF-1 equipped as a $1 billion bond fund invested in sovereign and quasi-sovereign bonds issued by eight of the Executives' Meeting of East Asia Pacific Central Banks members. The investment volume was raised to $2 billion under ABF-2.

### ASEAN Serves as an Anchor of Financial Cooperation in Asia

ASEAN is seen as the "most ambitious organization of regional cooperation and integration in the developing world" (Chia and Plummer 2015). Member economies pursued close financial integration since the launch of the Roadmap for ASEAN Integration in Finance in 2003, with its main elements carried over into the ASEAN Economic Community launched in 2015. In addition to facilitating policy dialogue and capacity building for capital account and financial services liberalization, the community started several integration initiatives such as the ASEAN Banking Integration Framework, and ASEAN Payments Policy Framework for Cross-Border Real Time Retail Payment, further pursued under the Strategic Action Plan for Financial Integration 2016–2025. Box 4.1 provides details about these initiatives.

## Strengthening the Regional Financial Safety Net Is Key for Deeper Integration

### Limited Liquidity and Lending Instruments Could Hamstring the CMIM

The CMIM-SF has not been used despite several crises ranging from the 2013 taper tantrum to the COVID-19 pandemic and subsequent cost of living pressures (Khor et al. 2022; Lee and Kring 2024). While the mere existence of the CMIM may have calmed financial

[36] The South Asian Association for Regional Cooperation comprises Afghanistan, Bangladesh, Bhutan, India, Maldives, Nepal, Pakistan, and Sri Lanka. ADB placed on hold its regular assistance to Afghanistan effective 15 August 2021.

**Box 4.1: ASEAN Regional Financial Cooperation Initiatives**

**Banking integration.** Under the Association of Southeast Asian Nations (ASEAN) Banking Integration Framework established in 2014, ASEAN agreed on bilateral reciprocal arrangements to create qualified ASEAN banks (QABs). QABs are granted greater market access and operational flexibility similar to indigenous banks in the host economy.

**Payment and settlement systems integration.** The ASEAN Committee on Payment and Settlement Systems is tasked to implement interconnected and safe, innovative, competitive, efficient payment systems. Adoption of the international standard ISO20022 is the main avenue of implementation, supported by bilateral and multilateral payment system linkages for the development of settlement infrastructure for cross-border transactions. The ASEAN Payment Policy Framework sets guidelines for cross-border real-time retail payments.

**Capital market integration.** Three pillars define the ASEAN road map for capital market integration. First, the ASEAN working committee on capital account liberalization facilitates a freer flow of capital by gradually removing restrictions on current accounts. Second, the ASEAN working committee on capital market development focuses on capacity building and infrastructure to advance the regional integration of bond markets. Third, the ASEAN Capital Markets Forum (ACMF) aims at a regionally integrated, liquid equity capital market. Under the ACMF, several initiatives have been completed such as the ASEAN Collective Investment Scheme framework among Malaysia, Singapore, and Thailand (established in 2014), the 2017 launch of ASEAN green bond standards, the 2018 ASEAN social and sustainability bond standards, and 2021 ASEAN sustainability-linked bond standards. Over $50 billion worth of bonds have been issued under these standards.

**Regional financial stability.** ASEAN established the ASEAN Integration Monitoring Office in 2011, later restructured to the ASEAN Integration Monitoring Directorate (AIMD) in 2016. AIMD spearheads the implementation of regional surveillance and economic integration monitoring in ASEAN, provides technical advice on economic integration initiatives, shapes research and policy analysis programs, and ensures effective information dissemination.

Source: Ariyasajjakorn, Sirivunnabood, and Molineris (2020); ACMF (2024).

markets and thus mitigated the loss of financing access for the region's sovereigns, several factors account for its underutilization. First, the liquidity pool of $240 billion combined with fixed borrowing quotas for each member could be viewed as too restrictive if several large members were hit by shocks. Flexible multiples of swap quotas for small economies could represent a solution for financing needs below the IMF-delinked portion (Han 2022). Second, its set of lending instruments are geared for short-term balance of payment crises requiring rapid liquidity injections. In contrast, other regional financing arrangements like the European Stability Mechanism also provide for bank recapitalization and sovereign bond purchase programs (Park and Rajan 2021). The IMF also offers loan programs such as the Resilience and Sustainability Trust to tackle longer-term structural challenges like climate change.

The CMIM's arrangement as a contract among central banks and finance ministries without pre-committed funds may slow down decisions on disbursements in crises. In contrast, pooling the reserves that back the CMIM into a single account—as a quota contribution or paid-in capital, such as in the European Stability Mechanism—would allow for acting more swiftly and autonomously. The institutional setup is further complicated by the contractual nature of the CMIM. Recently announced plans to introduce a paid-in capital structure against which the CMIM would issue debt to finance emergency lending would help improve the CMIM's governance (ASEAN 2024).[37] A clear guideline for operational coordination with the IMF would also help remove uncertainty about how to resolve divergent views on surveillance and program conditionality (Han 2022). For the combined institution to stand alone, it would need to craft its own institutional views on key policy issues such as capital flow management (Khor et al. 2022).

[37] Details on the modalities of this paid-in capital structure are expected to be released in 2025.

Strengthening the regional financial safety net can mitigate the trade-offs of the financial trilemma (Figure 4.16), which states that financial stability, financial integration, and national financial policies are incompatible (Schoenmaker 2011). A larger and more institutionalized regional financial safety net as outlined in this chapter can lower these trade-offs. A stronger financial safety net implies that financial autonomy can be reoriented toward promoting greater financial openness without engendering financial stability, because the regional safety net creates more flexibility for domestic financial policy. For instance, it allows member states to accumulate fewer reserves for self-insurance and relax current account restrictions.

**Figure 4.16: The Financial Trilemma**

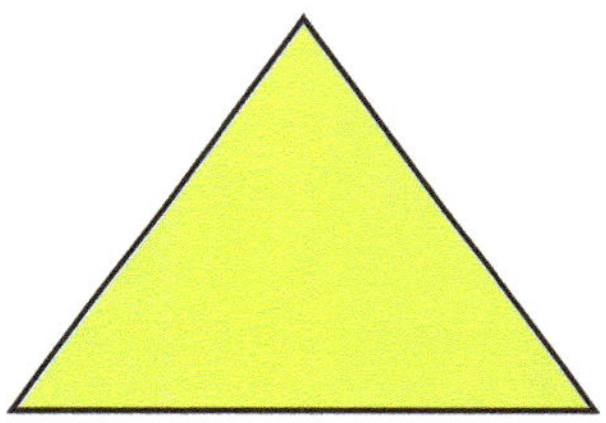


Source: Schoenmaker (2011).

## New Policy Challenges Define the Frontiers of Regional Financial Cooperation

Climate change, biodiversity loss, geopolitical fragmentation, health crises, and technological disruptions define the new frontiers of regional financial cooperation. This section discusses potential repercussions for regional integration, notably for capital flows, balance sheet vulnerabilities, and the effectiveness of financial supervision. Next, the section outlines how regional cooperation can address potential adverse effects for financial integration.

### *Health emergencies*

Regional cooperation can help with rebuilding more resilient post-pandemic economies. Asian economies entered the COVID-19 pandemic with sound macroeconomic and financial fundamentals, allowing for a swift response with substantial fiscal and monetary stimulus, including cash transfers, job retention schemes, debt relief and moratoria on debt repayments, as well as relaxing macroprudential policies (Khor et al. 2022). Prudent macroeconomic policy management and finance sector reforms since the Asian financial crisis created ample policy space. Banking systems were equipped with robust capital and liquidity buffers, and thus well positioned to absorb pandemic-related losses. The post-pandemic priorities for Asian economies comprise managing new balance sheet vulnerabilities from record high public and private debt and pursuing structural changes in preparation for similar primarily noneconomic shocks. In this context, regional cooperation is key to (i) assist economies with more severely impaired balance sheets, (ii) strengthen the financial safety net, and (iii) provide financing for structural reforms and related infrastructure, such as for health care facilities.

The pandemic underscored the need to adapt the regional financial safety net to structural shifts. While Asian economies entered the last pandemic with sufficient policy space, this may not hold for larger shocks in the future. The extraordinarily large financing needs raised by the pandemic combined with permanent shifts in productive capacities highlights that the current mandate of the CMIM geared toward short-term balance of payments crises may be too narrow to cover longer-term financing needs such as for pandemic-resilient health care systems. During the pandemic, ample financing was made available by other layers of the global financial safety net, notably the IMF and bilateral swap lines, the nonactivation of regional financing arrangements like CMIM suggests that its limited toolkit, complex deployment as multilateral agreement and the link to IMF conditionality may suppress demand for its liquidity (Mühlich, Fritz, and Kring 2022).

A range of measures can serve to upgrade the regional financial safety net. Greater flexibility in the use of the CMIM-SF is warranted to manage primarily noneconomic shocks and associated structural shifts, e.g., by extending the maturity of liquidity support (Khor et al. 2022). The 2024 launch of AMRO's Rapid Financing Facility is an important innovation in this respect, although financial support remains limited to 1 year. Additional ways to support medium- to long-term financing needs in the post-pandemic era are also important to explore. Mühlich, Fritz, and Kring (2022) suggest that enhanced coordination among regional financing arrangements and the IMF could lower transaction costs for borrowers and multilateral lenders. Moreover, the pandemic showed that multilateral development banks can complement the safety net through advisory services, knowledge, capacity development and financing for regional cooperation projects and emergency budget support (ADB 2022a).

## *Geopolitical fragmentation*

Geopolitical fragmentation is a danger to macrofinancial stability in Asia. The breakup of the postwar geopolitical order increased amid deteriorating trading links between the US and the PRC. As tensions are likely to impair global trade as Asia's decade-long engine of growth, emerging market and low-income economies are most at risk (Aiyar et al. 2023). Harm to financial integration in Asia arises through financial and real channels (Figure 4.17). First, restrictions on capital flows and cross-border payments from capital controls and sanctions, or because investors have heightened risk aversion to future restrictions, could distort capital allocations. In turn, asset prices may fall as investors adjust international portfolios and cut cross-border credit lines. Second, restrictions on international trade, commodity markets, and technology transfers can reduce growth and raise inflation because of their negative knock-on effects to supply chains. These factors could, in turn, imperil the liquidity of nonfinancial corporations, generating credit risks for banks and undermining financial stability.

Regional financial cooperation can help mitigate adverse impacts from geopolitical tensions. First, geopolitical risks need to be consistently introduced and applied in regional macroeconomic surveillance. Second, cooperation mechanisms should strengthen the resilience of cross-border payment systems and develop frameworks for improved interoperability. Third, the CMIM should be relied on as primary regional safety net instead of bilateral swap lines, as these may reinforce

**Figure 4.17: Transmission Channels of Geopolitical Fragmentation to Macrofinancial Stability**

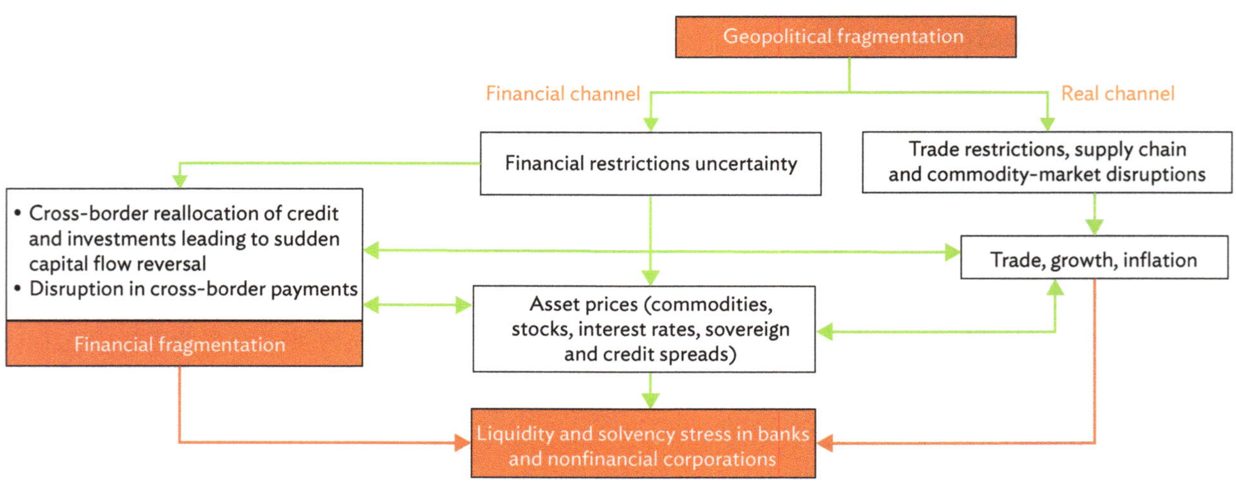


Notes: The figure shows the two key channels of transmission, financial and real, through which geopolitical fragmentation could contribute to financial fragmentation and exacerbate macrofinancial stability risks. In addition to these channels, macrofinancial stability could also be affected if geopolitical fragmentation increases cybersecurity risks, compliance, legal and reputational risks for entities, risks associated with money laundering and financing of terrorism, or climate-related risks because of lack of international coordination to mitigate climate change.

Source: International Monetary Fund (2023).

fragmentation. Fourth, CMIM's lending instruments require a broader scope. For instance, the CMIM-PL could explicitly account for an escalation of geopolitical tensions as trigger event.

### *Technological disruptions*

Disruptive innovations in financial services bestow efficiency gains on financial systems in Asia. The digitalization of financial services drawing on financial technology has become ubiquitous as a function of the spread of smartphones and big data availability in combination with artificial intelligence. Digitalization, including of currencies, offers several benefits: faster transactions at lower cost, increased competition and thus higher service quality thanks to higher transparency, and improved financial inclusion by widening access to underbanked populations.

However, the digitalization of financial services and currencies can challenge Asia's financial stability. The innovations also carry microfinancial and macrofinancial risks. Microfinancial risks refer to governance and process control, cybersecurity, and legal risks. A prominent example is the rise of cyber threats, intensified during the COVID-19 pandemic because new online applications were rolled out quickly (Ong et al. 2023). The efficiency of financial services may suffer as the digitalization of financial services can lead to more fragmented processes and—absent mechanisms ensuring interoperability—outright monopolies (Beau 2021). Macrofinancial risks include unsustainable credit growth, contagion, procyclicality, excess volatility, and the rise of systemically important financial institutions (Morgan and Huang 2021). Cross-border transactions in digital currencies handled in private payment platforms could raise the volatility of capital flows, which regulators are currently not equipped to monitor because balance of payment methodologies do not account for them. This may entail blind spots for surveillance and risk mitigation (Ong et al. 2023). Privately issued digital currencies by globally dominant technology firms bear the risk of substituting domestic currencies as legal tender, and thus undermine the domestic monetary policy transmission mechanism.

Regional cooperation is fundamental to maximize the benefits of digitalized financial services and financial technology while maintaining financial stability. Key regional institutions and forums to address risks from financial service innovations are the ASEAN+3 finance ministers' and central bank governors' meetings, ABMF, the ASEAN+3 Cross-Border Settlement Infrastructure Forum (CSIF), the ASEAN Bankers Association, and the ASEAN Financial Innovation Network, supported by AMRO's financial stability assessments (Morgan and Huang 2021). Ong et al. (2023) suggest for AMRO to expand the surveillance coverage, provide training, and conduct research on the implications of digitalization for financial stability. The ABMF and the CSIF have been discussing the role of standardization to ensure cross-border interoperability. Asian economies are already represented in some international initiatives like the Global Cybersecurity Agenda under the auspices of the United Nations International Telecommunications Union. In others, few Asian economies are active such as in pilot projects like mBridge for the use of central bank digital currencies to settle cross-border payments (BIS 2024). Notably the rise of private digital currencies requires more regional supervisory coordination and information-sharing about best practices to effectively harmonize standards, and thus safeguard the transmission of domestic monetary policy.

### *Climate change*

Substantial economic damage and financial risks from Asia's high vulnerability to climate change endangers regional financial integration. Asia is hit hard by the rising frequency and severity of storms, floods, heat waves, and droughts. The threat to livelihoods from rising sea levels is especially pronounced in the region, where 70% of the global population vulnerable to sea level rise resides. Immediately climate-dependent sectors like agriculture account for one-third of employment. Economic losses from climate change are expected to reach on average 40% by 2100 (ADB 2024f). Volz et al. (2020) enumerate several macroeconomic risks, including revenue losses from the disruption of economic activity after disasters, higher spending from subsidies to cope with rising energy prices, and adjustments in inflation and exchange rates resulting from climate change-related supply and demand shocks. Physical damages and disaster relief spending may raise contingent liabilities. Similarly, financial assets supporting carbon-intensive activities may become stranded. In turn, these macroeconomic ramifications may abet balance-of-payment and financial crises.

Regional cooperation is essential to monitor and mitigate macrofinancial risks from climate change. The regional financial safety net requires an upgrading of its policy frameworks to manage climate-related crises. Volz (2022) suggests to systematically mainstream climate-related risks into AMRO's macroeconomic and financial assessments, to align all policy recommendations with the Paris Agreement, for cooperation to harmonize disclosure standards for climate-related financial risks, and to help regional economies integrate climate risks into fiscal policy management. Moreover, adapting lending instruments available to regional economies is an important avenue to provide climate emergency funding. Thus, the recent addition of AMRO's Rapid Financing Facility to the CMIM is an important step as the facility explicitly accounts for physical hazard-driven disaster as a disbursement trigger, although access remains conditional on having an IMF program in place (ASEAN 2024).

Regional cooperation is critical to mobilize climate finance, notably from the private sector. Asia requires an estimated $1.1 trillion a year to address climate change (Lim et al. 2024). With only $300 billion currently made available in the region, the financing needs remain large. Regional cooperation has already proven effective in developing sustainable financial markets to raise the required financing. For instance, ADB introduced the Green, Social, Sustainability and Other Labeled (GSS+) Bonds Initiative in 2022 to accelerate the development of sustainable capital markets and to support the issuance of GSS+ bonds by sovereigns, municipalities, and state-owned enterprises in Southeast Asia (ADB 2022b). The initiative is implemented jointly with the ADB technical assistance program to support GSS+ bond issuances by the private sector and to develop a sustainable finance ecosystem in ASEAN+3 (ADB 2022c). The program has catalyzed highly innovative transactions such as Asia's first sovereign sustainability-linked bond issued by the Government of Thailand (ADB 2024e). Dedicated information about sustainable bonds on the Asian Bonds Online web portal and in the companion publication "Asia Bond Market Monitor" helps to build supply and attract demand. The ABMI's activities to promote local currency bond markets can be extended to create sustainable bond markets, as noted in the ABMI Road Map for 2023–2026. Scaling up similar initiatives beyond ASEAN to the entire region would lower the learning cost for other economies. Given the catalytic role of sovereign green bond issuances for the number and size of corporate bond issuances, regional cooperation initiatives could center on sovereign issuances to grow the regional sustainable bond market (Cheng et al. 2024; WEF 2024).

## Biodiversity-Proofing Regional Financial Cooperation

### Unprecedented Losses of Ecosystems and Species Impose Costly Adjustments on Asian Economies

The previous section highlighted climate change as an opportunity for regional cooperation to advance integration. With climate change as an important issue in itself, complex interactions with the environment make climate change a key driver of an acute loss of biodiversity (Brondizio et al. 2019).[38] This section sheds light on its repercussions for regional integration and designates cooperation as an important avenue to mitigate the macrofinancial repercussions of biodiversity losses and mobilize capital for biodiversity action.

Globally, biodiversity declined by 73% in 1970–2020 (Figure 4.18). Losses in Asia reached 60% over the same period.[39] As a result, about 1 million animal and plant species are threatened by extinction globally (Brondizio

[38] The Convention on Biological Diversity defines biodiversity as "the variability among living organisms from all sources including terrestrial, marine, and other aquatic ecosystems and the ecological complexes of which they are part; this includes diversity within species, between species, and of ecosystems" (Brondizio et al. 2019).

[39] Updated losses may exceed this 2019 estimate based on Sanchez-Bayo and Wyckhuys (2019).

et al. 2019). The rate of extinction exceeds its natural rate by a factor of 1,000 (Deutz et al. 2020). Without policy action, up to half of all species are expected to be lost by 2050 (Deutz et al. 2020). These losses are bound to impose large economic adjustment costs as about half of global value-added directly depends on the ecosystem services nature provides. Both the losses and mitigating policies are expected to lower growth and imperil financial stability (Gardes-Landolfini et al. 2024). For instance, three quarters of crop types require pollination by insects (Ritchie 2021). Among economically important anchor species, honeybee populations fell by almost half globally, with their decline threatening agriculture output and food supplies (Figure 4.19). The increasing use of mechanical or manual pollination suggests that a combination of labor and investment must compensate for the species lost.

Reversing biodiversity losses requires leveraging regional cooperation to mobilize significant nature-positive investments. To halt and reverse the decline in biodiversity by 2030, about $700 billion investments in nature are required annually (Deutz et al. 2020), equivalent to 0.7% of global GDP, and up from $140 billion in 2017. The biodiversity financing gap adds to the financing needs to address climate change. The public sector provides about three-fifths of currently deployed biodiversity finance (Deutz et al. 2020). Given record-high public debt and high financing costs post-pandemic, private capital needs to be mobilized to close the financing gap. Closing the gap by mobilizing and aligning financial flows with biodiversity needs defines an important new policy challenge for regional cooperation. Reducing subsidies harmful to nature—estimated at $800 billion globally—and harmonizing nature-related disclosure standards, and developing innovative nature-related financing instruments all require regional knowledge exchanges and capacity building (Deutz et al. 2020). Common reporting standards and scenario analyses coupled with mandatory disclosures for financial institutions are critical for developing regional risk-pooling initiatives (AMRO 2023).

**Figure 4.19: Decline in Selected Global Insect Populations, 2009–2019** (% change)

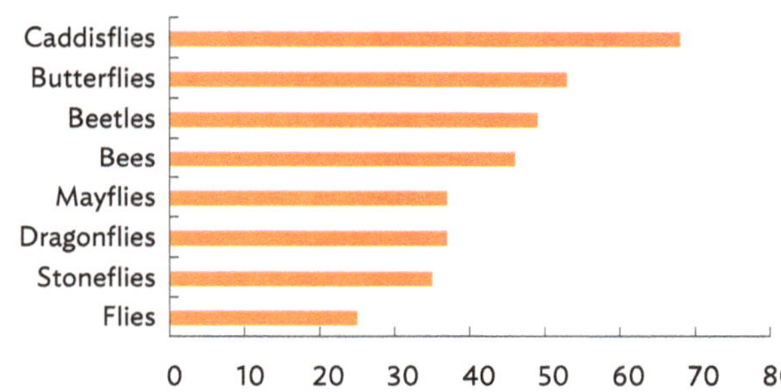


Source: Statista. https://www.statista.com/chart/16960/percentage-decline-in-selected-global-insect-populations/ (accessed December 2024).

**Figure 4.18: Living Planet Index by Region**

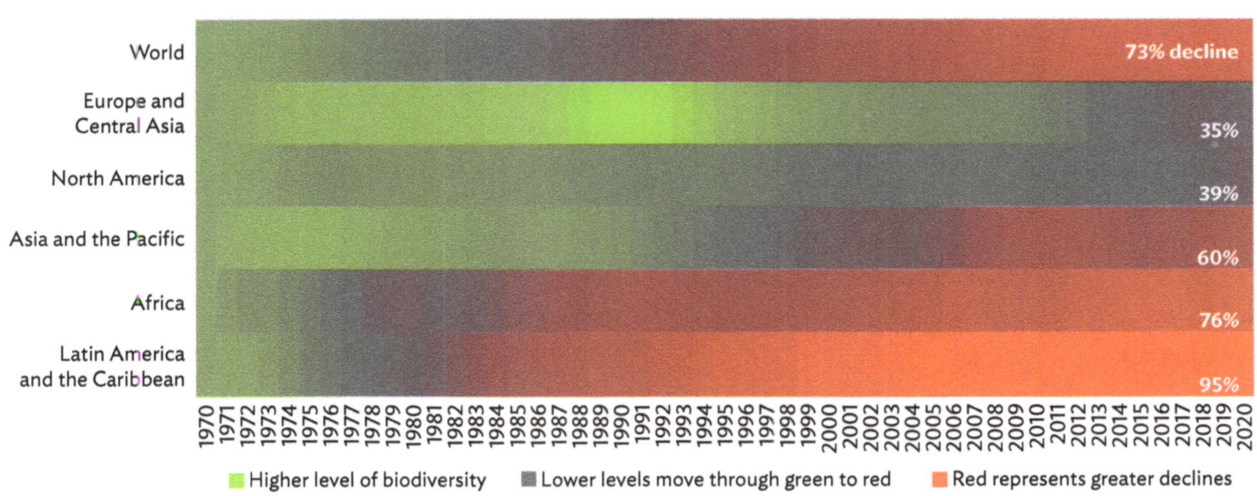


Source: World Wide Fund for Nature (2024).

## The Mispricing of Harm to Biodiversity Imperils Regional Macrofinancial Stability

Despite a strong moral and economic case to attend to biodiversity losses, financial markets do not fully price related economic risks (Xin et al. 2023; Huang et al. 2024). Markets only started to require a premium on firms' biodiversity footprint's after the 2021 Kunming Declaration marked the adoption of the Kunming–Montreal Global Biodiversity Framework at the 15th Conference of the Parties (COP 15) of the United Nations Convention on Biological Diversity (Garel et al. 2024). Coqueret, Giroux, and Zerbib (2024) confirm that this event increased the cost of capital for companies with a high biodiversity footprint. Investors increasingly care about biodiversity footprints as the harm done by economic activity on nature risks undermining future cash flows in two ways. First, given the dependence of most economic output on nature, any deterioration of biodiversity may result in lost productivity. Second, with nature-related financial regulations likely to become more stringent, investors expect higher costs due to compliance and litigation aimed at preserving biodiversity (Hoepner et al. 2023). Thus, failure to properly account for the impact of economic activity on biodiversity can give rise to transition risk.[40]

Transition risk from mispricing biodiversity losses can unleash sudden capital flow shifts. This calls for regional cooperation to mitigate negative repercussions for macrofinancial stability. A sudden materialization of transition risk because of mispriced exposure to biodiversity losses can trigger large portfolio reallocations among investors, tightening financial conditions of sectors with large biodiversity footprints, and so imperil macrofinancial stability. For instance, half to three-quarters of banks' corporate loan portfolios strongly depend on nature (Boldrini et al. 2023; Calice et al. 2023). Thus, a sudden pricing of biodiversity risk can jeopardize economy-wide credit allocation if borrowers' creditworthiness declines because their biodiversity footprint deepens, or due to the increased cost of ecosystem services when biodiversity falls (Becker, Di Girolamo, and Rho 2023). Similarly, the world's largest banks are subject to transition risk as two-fifths of loans are extended to sectors reliant on subsidies harmful to nature, and to geographic areas targeted for environmental protection under the Global Biodiversity Framework (Gardes-Landolfini et al. 2024). At the regional level, portfolio reallocations resulting from the sudden pricing of biodiversity risks can increase the volatility of cross-border capital flows to the detriment of regional financial stability and jeopardize access to foreign biodiversity finance. Regional cooperation provides an important platform to mitigate these repercussions, as has been discussed in this chapter.

The Kunming Declaration provides a recent example of global markets pricing on biodiversity risk. Similarly important as the Paris Agreement for tackling climate change, the international treaty, which was adopted by 190 governments to address biodiversity losses, sets clear objectives and quantitative targets along a global road map for conserving, protecting, restoring, and sustainably managing biodiversity. New evidence from portfolio investment funds suggests that up until the Kunming Declaration, investment funds did not pay attention to biodiversity risks, making global financial markets susceptible to transition risk shocks. This is in line with the declaration marking the start of biodiversity-risk pricing in financial markets (Garel et al. 2024; Coqueret, Giroux, and Zerbib 2024). Prior to that, investment funds increased their exposure to economies with high biodiversity risk, both in absolute terms and as share of total investments (Figure 4.20). News of the Kunming Declaration changed this instantly. The declaration raised fund managers' awareness of the risk of negative future cash flows resulting from biodiversity losses.

40 Transition biodiversity risk refers to the policy, legal, technology, reputational, and market risks arising from creating positive or reducing negative impacts on natural capital (GARP 2024).

**Figure 4.20: Investment Fund Inflows into Economies with High Versus Low Biodiversity Risk** (%)

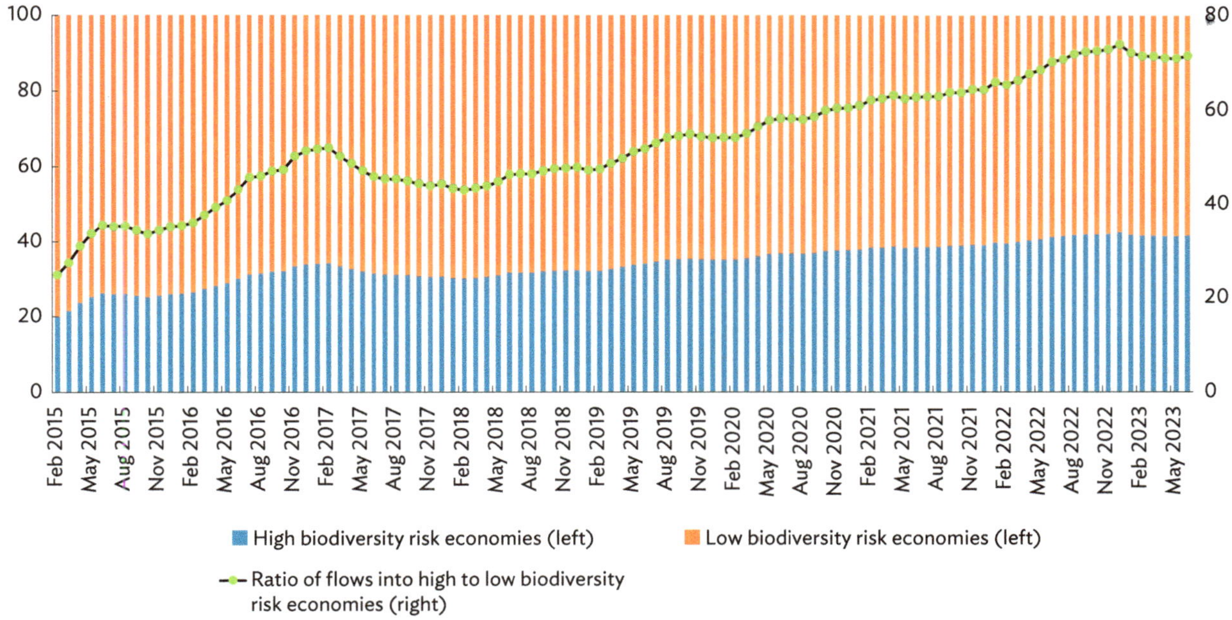


Source: te Kaat and Raabe (forthcoming).

Portfolio capital flows in Asia exhibit strong sensitivity to a sudden repricing of biodiversity risks. An empirical analysis using detailed data on global investment funds documents reallocations of fund portfolios in response to the Kunming Declaration, akin to a flight to biodiversity safety. Upon announcement of the declaration on 11 October 2021, funds reallocated investments away from economies with high biodiversity risk in favor of less risky economies. Given no change in funds' total assets under management, this portfolio rebalancing implies additional inflows for lower-biodiversity risk economies of $830 million (0.14% of GDP) for the average global economy up to 4 months after the declaration, covering about three-fifths of annual average biodiversity financing needs (Figure 4.21). For Asian economies, the inflows cover the financing needs almost half, and fully for Asia excluding the PRC. These flows result mainly from portfolio reallocations within the same geographic region a fund is specialized in, and to the benefit of economies in the same region but not yet in a fund's portfolio. That is, investment funds facilitate regional contagion after biodiversity risk materializes. Sustainable-labeled investment funds reacted most strongly to biodiversity risk revealed by the declaration. Similar capital flow shifts cannot be identified for other global biodiversity-related events other than the declaration, or for climate-change related events like the Paris Agreement.[41]

**Figure 4.21: Biodiversity Financing from Global Investment Funds After the Kunming Declaration**

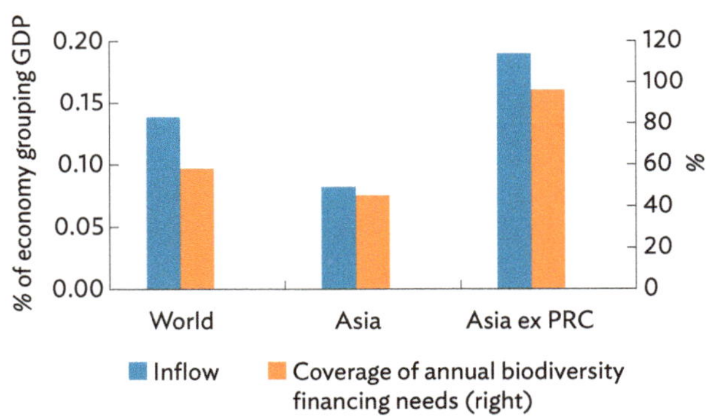


PRC = People's Republic of China, GDP = gross domestic product.

Notes: The chart shows the cumulative investment fund inflows in percentage of GDP into the average economy in the respective region over 4 months after the Kunming Declaration, and as share of annual biodiversity financing needs as computed by the United Nations Development Programme's Biodiversity Finance Initiative. Asia refers to Cambodia, Georgia, India, Indonesia, Kazakhstan, the Kyrgyz Republic, Malaysia, Nepal, the Philippines, Sri Lanka, Thailand, Viet Nam. World refers to Asia plus Belize, Botswana, Colombia, Costa Rica, Cuba, Guatemala, Madagascar, Malawi, Mexico, Niger, Peru, Rwanda, Seychelles, and Tanzania.

Source: te Kaat and Raabe (forthcoming).

41 Box 4.2 discusses the methodology.

Ambitious climate policies allow low biodiversity risk economies to attract more portfolio fund inflows. As climate change abets biodiversity losses, economies with more effective climate policies are better positioned to minimize economic damage from the functional decline of ecosystems. Moreover, stringent climate policies signal a more productive use of capital for nature-related investments. An extension of the above analysis shows that economies with simultaneously low biodiversity risk and more effective climate policies received more capital inflows resulting from portfolio reallocations and thus cross-economy spillovers induced by the announcement of the Kunming Declaration. Prudent macroeconomic management as measured by sovereign ratings also helps attract inflows. Inversely, high biodiversity risk economies with less ambitious climate policies, and lower sovereign ratings tend to experience larger outflows after the declaration.

## Options for Cooperation on Financial Integration to Rise to New Challenges

### Reinvigorating Regional Cooperation Initiatives Is Key to Maximizing the Benefits of Integration While Minimizing Its Costs

Financial integration remains an important source of growth and prosperity for the region. Progress has advanced steadily over the past few decades, but recently has slowed. The cooperation initiatives recommended here are imperatives for deepening integration by improving the cost–benefit balance.

**Box 4.2: Methodological Note on Portfolio Capital Flows and Biodiversity Risk**

The chapter discusses cross-border portfolio capital flow shifts due to investment funds' portfolio rebalancing in response to biodiversity risk revealed by the Kunming Declaration. The evidence emerges from a difference-in-difference (DiD) regression analysis symmetrically centered on the 4 months around the announcement of the declaration in October 2021, and applied to detailed data on global investment funds' portfolio allocations across economies. The regression framework is specified as follows:

First, the chapter shows that funds reallocate portfolios toward economies with lower biodiversity risk after the Kunming Declaration. For this, the DiD analysis takes as dependent variable the month-on-month change in a fund portfolio's geographic allocation, computed as the growth rate in the inverse-hyperbolic sine (IHS) transformed portfolio share of allocations to economies. The IHS transformation allows to approximate the natural logarithm, while keeping zero values (Bellemare and Wichman 2020; Burbidge, Magee, and Robb 1988). The main regressor is the interaction between a post-declaration dummy equal to one after 2021: M9, zero else, and an economy's biodiversity risk. The risk is defined as the share of endangered species, with data provided by Giglio et al. (2023). To capture nonlinearities in the distribution, biodiversity risk enters the analysis in the form of a dummy equal to one if an economy's biodiversity risk exceeds the 75th percentile of the variable's distribution. The analysis controls for various fund characteristics such as equity versus bond funds, active versus passively managed funds, funds' sustainability labeling and over or underweight of economy-specific positions, as well as a fund's assets under management and performance. The analysis further employs fund-time and fund-economy fixed effects to control for time-varying characteristics common to all funds, and time-invariant features of the relationship between funds and the economies they invest in.

Second, the chapter shows that, in response to revealed biodiversity risks, investment funds reallocate from high-biodiversity risk economies, and toward other less risky economies in the same region, notably economies where the respective fund does not yet invest. The DiD analysis is modified for this in two ways. First, a fund's economy portfolio shares in levels instead of changes is employed to allow for changes in the dependent variable to sum to zero at the fund level. Second, the set of regressors is augmented with an interaction between the post-declaration dummy and (i) the average biodiversity risk of all other economies in a fund's portfolio, (ii) the average biodiversity risk in the same region, and (iii) the average biodiversity risk of all other world regions referring to Europe, Africa, the Middle East, Asia and the Pacific, and North and South America.

Third, the chapter highlights that low biodiversity risk economies with more effective climate policies and fiscally sustainable macroeconomic management tend to benefit more from the capital flow shifts. For this, the DiD analysis additionally includes interactions with dummies equal to one when an economy's Bloomberg climate policy score and sovereign credit rating exceeds the in-sample median.

Source: te Kaat and Raabe (forthcoming).

**Maintain financial stability.** First, policymakers should pursue reducing vulnerabilities to negative external shocks and coordinate to guard against cross-border policy spillovers. Prudent domestic macroeconomic and financial policies rank first to maintain stability amid negative cross-border spillovers. In addition, adhering to internationally agreed minimum capital requirements lowers risks from regulatory arbitrage. Expanding the depth and breadth of local currency bond markets remains a priority to reduce currency and maturity mismatches that typically amplify spillovers from global financial market turmoil. At the same time, more sophisticated regional financial markets would allow the domestic investor base to grow. This is important since issuing local currency bonds is not a panacea to address mismatches transferred to the balance sheet of international investors (Hofmann, Shim, and Shin 2020; ADB 2024c).

More importantly, the region needs to be equipped with stronger safety nets. Key steps comprise

- increasing the pool of emergency funding available from CMIM;
- broadening the scope of its lending instruments spearheaded by the new rapid financing facility;
- improving the governance structure with regard to the separation between CMIM and AMRO; and
- continuously improving AMRO's analytical capacity to support more comprehensive macroeconomic surveillance.

**Rise to new challenges.** Second, regional cooperation must act on a range of new policy issues. The chapter highlights the need to mainstream new policy challenges into regional cooperation mechanisms, comprising climate change, biodiversity loss, geopolitical fragmentation, health crises, and technological disruptions:

- The COVID-19 pandemic highlighted the need to expand the lending instruments available from CMIM to unlock funding more flexibly beyond short-term balance of payments needs. The lending toolkit should explicitly account for primarily noneconomic risks like pandemics and escalating geopolitical fragmentation. These risks should also be systematically assessed in regional macroeconomic surveillance and in the resilience of cross-border payment systems.
- Regional cooperation will be essential to maintain financial stability, maximize the benefits of disruptive innovations in financial services, and manage risks from the spread of digital currencies. This may entail expanding the coverage of macroeconomic surveillance, supervisory coordination, and the harmonization of standards, training, and dedicated research.
- Stronger regional cooperation is also needed to monitor and mitigate economic risks from climate change, as well as to mobilize private climate finance to fill an $800 billion funding gap in Asia. This centers on covering climate-related risks in surveillance activities, adapting the CMIM's lending toolkit, harmonizing disclosure standards for climate-related financial risks, and expanding regional sustainable capital markets.

**Tackle biodiversity loss.** Third, the macrofinancial fallout from acute biodiversity loss requires the urgent attention of regional policymakers. Among new policy challenges, this chapter highlights unprecedented loss of biodiversity as a threat to regional financial integration. This warrants coverage of biodiversity loss and nature protection needs in regular macrofinancial stability assessments. New research suggests that reversing biodiversity loss helps attract foreign capital, including to finance biodiversity and climate action (te Kaat and Raabe 2024). Reversing losses requires both nature-positive investments and phasing out subsidies that are harming biodiversity. Production subsidies in agriculture, fisheries, and forestry are estimated to exceed financing for biodiversity conservation by a factor of four. Regional cooperation can help align private financial flows with nature-positive investment needs by

- adopting harmonized disclosure standards such as those developed by the Taskforce on Nature-Related Financial Disclosures;
- promoting natural capital accounting to mainstream the value of nature into all economic decisions;

- catalyzing private sector investments through derisking instruments like public guarantees; and
- supporting innovative financial instruments targeting biodiversity action.

In Asia, ADB is leading the way to mobilize private sector capital through the sale of biodiversity and nature-themed bonds (ADB 2024d). An extension of ABMI to cover this market can further catalyze private sector engagement.

## References

Agénor, P. 2024. Cross-Border Banking, Spillovers, and International Macroprudential Policy Coordination. In G. M. Caporale, ed. *Handbook of Financial Integration.* Edward Elgar Publishing, Inc.

Aiyar, S., J. Chen, C. H. Ebeke, R. Garcia-Saltos, T. Gudmundsson, A. Ilyina, A. Kangur, T. Kunaratskul, S. L. Rodriguez, M. Ruta, T. Schulze, G. Soderberg, and J. P. Trevino. 2023. Geoeconomic Fragmentation and the Future of Multilateralism. *IMF Staff Discussion Note.* 2023/001. International Monetary Fund.

Aquilina, M., M. Lombardi, A. Schrimpf, and V. Sushko. 2024. The Market Turbulence and Carry Trade Unwind of August 2024. *BIS Bulletin.* 90. Bank for International Settlements.

Ariyasajjakorn, D., P. Sirivunnabood, and M. Molineris. 2020. Evolution of ASEAN Financial Integration in the Comparative Perspective. *ADBI Working Paper Series.* No. 1123. Asian Development Bank Institute.

ASEAN+3 Macroeconomic Research Office (AMRO). 2023. Adapting to Climate Change in ASEAN+3. Policy Perspectives Paper.

ASEAN Capital Market Forum (ACMF). 2024. Statistics. https://www.theacmf.org/sustainable-finance/statistics (accessed January 2025).

Asian Bond Markets Initiative (ABMI). *ABMI Medium-term Road Map for 2023 to 2026.* https://asianbondsonline.adb.org/documents/abmi-medium-term-road-map-2023-2026.pdf.

Asian Development Bank (ADB). 2017. *Asian Economic Integration Report 2017: The Era of Financial Interconnectedness, How Can Asia Strengthen Financial Resilience?*

———. 2020. *Financial Integration and Macrofinancial Linkages in Asia: Crises, Responses, and Policy Considerations.*

———. 2022a. *Regional Cooperation and Integration in Asia and the Pacific: Responding to the COVID-19 Pandemic and "Building Back Better".*

———. 2022b. The Green, Social, Sustainable and Other Labeled (GSS+) Bonds Initiative for Southeast Asia. Brochures and Flyers.

———. 2022c. *Survey on Green Bonds and Sustainable Finance in ASEAN: Insights on the Perspectives of Institutional Investors and Underwriters.*

———. 2024a. *Asia Bond Monitor – September 2024.*

———. 2024b. *Asian Development Outlook (ADO) September 2024.*

———. 2024c. *Asian Economic Integration Report 2024: Decarbonizing Global Value Chains.*

———. 2024d. ADB Issues Its First Biodiversity and Nature Bond. Press Release.

———. 2024e. Mobilizing Capital Markets for a Climate-Responsive and Inclusive Southeast Asia/ Flyer. https://www.adb.org/sites/default/files/publication/958556/gss-flyer-2024.pdf (accessed January 2025).

———. 2024f. Scaling Up Private Climate Capital for Mitigation and Adaptation. In *Asia-Pacific Climate Report 2024: Catalyzing Finance and Policy Solutions.*

Association of Southeast Asian Nations (ASEAN). 2024. *Joint Statement of the 27th ASEAN+3 Finance Ministers' and Central Bank Governors' Meeting.* https://asean.org/wp-content/uploads/2024/05/Joint-Statement-of-the-27th-ASEAN3-FInance-Ministers-and-Central-Bank-Governors-Meeting-FINAL_20240503.pdf.

Avdjiev, S., V. Bruno, C. Koch, and H. S. Shin. 2018. The Dollar Exchange Rate as a Global Risk Factor: Evidence from Investment. *BIS Working Papers*. 695. Bank for International Settlements.

Avdjiev, S., W. Du, C. Koch, and H. S. Shin. 2017. The Dollar, Bank Leverage and the Deviation from Covered Interest Parity. *BIS Working Papers*. 592. Bank for International Settlements.

Bank for International Settlements (BIS). 2024. *Project mBridge Reaches Minimum Viable Product Stage and Invites Further International Participation.* https://www.bis.org/about/bisih/topics/cbdc/mcbdc_bridge.htm.

Beau, D. 2021. The Digitalisation of the Financial Sector—New Challenges, New Levers. *Closing Speech at the 4th Assises des Technologies Financières, 30 September 2021.* https://www.bis.org/review/r211012g.htm.

Becker, A., F. Di Girolamo, and C. Rho. 2023. Loan Pricing and Biodiversity Exposure: Nature-Related Spillovers to the Financial Sector. *JRC Working Papers in Economics and Finance.* European Commission.

Bellemare, M. F. and C. J. Wichman. 2020. Elasticities and the Inverse Hyperbolic Sine Transformation. *Oxford Bulletin and Economics and Statistics*. 82 (1). pp. 50–61.

Bergant, K., F. Grigoli, N. J. Hansen, and D. Sandri. 2023. Dampening Global Financial Shocks: Can Macroprudential Regulation Help (More than Capital Controls)? *Journal of Money, Credit and Banking*. 56 (6). pp. 1405–38.

Boldrini, S., A. Ceglar, C. Lelli, L. Parisi, and I. Heemskerk. 2023. Living in a World of Disappearing Nature: Physical Risk and the Implications for Financial Stability. *European Central Bank Occasional Paper*. 333.

Bong, A. and G. Premaratne. 2019. The Impact of Financial Integration on Economic Growth in Southeast Asia. *Journal of Asian Finance Economics and Business*. 6 (1). pp. 107–19.

Boz, E., C. Casas, G. Georgiadis, G. Gopinath, H. Le Mezo, A. Mehl, and M. T. Nguyen. 2020. Patterns in Invoicing Currency in Global Trade. *International Monetary Fund Working Paper.*

Brondizio, E. S., J. Settele, S. Díaz, and H. T. Ngo, eds. 2019. *Global Assessment Report on Biodiversity and Ecosystem Services of the Intergovernmental Science-Policy Platform on Biodiversity and Ecosystem Services*. Intergovernmental Science-Policy Platform on Biodiversity and Ecosystem Services Secretariat.

Buckley, R. P., E. Avgouleas, and D. W. Arner. 2020. Three Decades of International Financial Crises: What Have We Learned and What Still Needs to Be Done? In B. Susantono and C. Y. Park, eds. *The Future of Regional Cooperation in Asia and the Pacific.* Chapter 9. Asian Development Bank.

Burbidge, J. B., L. Magee, and A. L. Robb. 1988. Alternative Transformations to Handle Extreme Values of the Dependent Variable. *Journal of the American Statistical Association.* 83 (401). pp. 123–27.

Calice, P., F. Diaz, K. Nepomuk Dunz, and F. Miguel. 2023. Biodiversity and Finance: A Preliminary Assessment of Physical Risks for the Banking Sector in Emerging Markets. *Policy Research Working Paper.* 10432. World Bank Group.

Caporale, G. M., A. D. Sova, and R. Sova. 2023. Financial Integration and Economic Growth in Europe. *Brunel University London Working Paper Series.* No. 2316.

Chen, C. and Y. Kim. 2023. Financial Integration and Economic Growth: Directional Heterogeneity and Threshold Effect. *Digital Economy and Sustainable Development.* 1 (21). pp. 1–12.

Cheng, G., T. Ehlers, F. Packer, and Y. Xiao. 2024. Sovereign Green Bonds: A Catalyst for Sustainable Debt Market Development? *BIS Working Papers.* No. 1198.

Chia, S. Y. and M. G. Plummer. 2015. *ASEAN Economic Cooperation and Integration: Progress, Challenges and Future Directions.* Cambridge University Press.

Chinn, M.D. and H. Ito. 2006. What Matters for Financial Development? Capital Controls, Institutions, and Interactions. *Journal of Development Economics.* 81(1). pp. 163-192.

———. 2008. A New Measure of Financial Openness. *Journal of Comparative Policy Analysis.* 10 (3). pp. 309–322.

Coqueret, G., T. Giroux, and O. D. Zerbib. 2024. The Biodiversity Premium. *SSRN.*

Deutz, A., G. M. Heal, R. Niu, E. Swanson, T. Townshend, Z. Li, A. Delmar, A. Meghji, S. A. Sethi, and J. Tobin-de la Puente. 2020. *Financing Nature: Closing the Global Biodiversity Financing Gap.* Paulson Institute, The Nature Conservancy, and Cornell Atkinson Center for Sustainability.

Eichengreen, B., P. Gupta, and O. Masetti. 2018. Are Capital Flows Fickle? Increasingly? And Does the Answer Still Depend on Type? *Asian Economic Papers.* 17 (1). pp. 22–41.

Fry-McKibbin, R., C. Y. L. Hsiao, and V. L. Martin. 2018. Global and Regional Financial Integration in East Asia and the ASEAN. *North American Journal of Economics and Finance.* 46. pp. 202–21.

Gardes-Landolfini, C., W. Oman, J. Fraser, M. M. de Oca Leon, and B. Yao. 2024. Embedded in Nature: Nature-Related Economic and Financial Risks and Policy Considerations. *IMF Staff Climate Notes.* 2024 (002). International Monetary Fund.

Garel, A., A. Romec, Z. Sautner, and A. F. Wagner. 2024. *Review of Finance.* 28. pp. 1151–86.

Gelos, G., P. Patelli, and I. Shim. 2024. The US Dollar and Capital Flows to EMEs. *BIS Quarterly Review.* https://www.bis.org/publ/qtrpdf/r_qt2409d.pdf.

Giglio, S., T. Kuchler, S. Johannes, and X. Zeng. 2023. Biodiversity Risk. *National Bureau of Economic Research Working Paper.* 31137.

Global Association of Risk Professionals (GARP). 2024. *3 Key Areas for Understanding Nature-Related Risks.* https://www.garp.org/risk-intelligence/sustainability-climate/three-keys-nature-risk-240404.

Gopinath, G., E. Boz, C. Casas, F. J. Díez, P. Gourinchas, and M. Plagborg-Møller. 2020. Dominant Currency Paradigm. *American Economic Review.* 110 (3). pp. 677–719.

Han, B. 2022. The CMI and CMIM. In H. E. Khor, D. C. Guinigundo, and M. Kawai, eds. *Trauma to Triumph: Rising from the Ashes of the Asian Financial Crisis.* Chapter 30. ASEAN+3 Macroeconomic Research Office.

Hoepner, A. G. F., J. Klausmann, M. Leippold, and J. Rillaerts. 2023. Beyond Climate: The Impact of Biodiversity, Water, and Pollution on the CDS Term Structure. *Swiss Finance Institute Research Paper.* No. 23-10.

Hofmann, B., I. Shim, and H. S. Shin. 2020. Emerging Market Economy Exchange Rates and Local Currency Bond Markets amid the COVID-19 Pandemic. *BIS Bulletin*. 5. Bank for International Settlements.

Huang, Y., A. Creti, B. Jiang, and M. E. Sanin. 2024. Biodiversity Risk, Firm Performance, and Market Mispricing. *SSRN.*

Institute of International Finance (IIF). 2024. *Global Macro Views—The Fed Easing and EM Capital Flows.*

International Monetary Fund (IMF). 2023. *Global Financial Stability Report: Safeguarding Financial Stability amid High Inflation and Geopolitical Risks.*

Kawai, M. and P. J. Morgan. 2014. Regional Financial Regulation in Asia. In M. Kawai, P. J. Morgan, and P. B. Rana, eds. *New Global Economic Architecture: The Asian Perspective.* Chapter 6. Asian Development Bank Institute.

Khor, H. E., D. C. Guinigundo, M. Kawai, and J. Choi. 2022. ASEAN+3 Regional Financial Cooperation in Retrospect. In H. E. Khor, D. C. Guinigundo, and M. Kawai. *Trauma to Triumph: Rising from the Ashes of the Asian Financial Crisis.* Chapter 30. ASEAN+3 Macroeconomic Research Office.

Lee, J. W. and C. Y. Park. 2011. Financial Integration in Emerging Asia: Challenges and Prospects. *Asian Economic Policy Review.* 6 (2). pp. 176–98.

Lee, Y. and W. N. Kring. 2024. Regional Financial Cooperation and Regional Financial Arrangements. In P. De Lombaerde, ed. *Handbook of Regional Cooperation and Integration.* Chapter 5. Edward Elgar Publishing.

Lim, C. H., B. Ritu, Y. Carriere-Swallow, K. Kashiwase, M. Kutlukaya, M. Li, E. Refayet, D. Seneviratne, M. Sy, and R. Yang. 2024. *Unlocking Climate Finance in Asia-Pacific: Transitioning to a Sustainable Future.* International Monetary Fund.

Menon, J. 2012. *Regional and Global Financial Safety Nets.* Presentation for the Conference on The Evolving Global Architecture: From a Centralized to a Decentralized System. 26–27 March.

Milesi-Ferretti, G. M. 2024. The External Wealth of Nations Database. The Brookings Institution. Based on P. R. Lane and G. M Milesi-Ferretti. 2018. The External Wealth of Nations Revisited: International Financial Integration in the Aftermath of the Global Financial Crisis. *IMF Economic Review.* 66. pp. 189–222.

Montanes, R. L. and S. L. Schmukler. 2018. Financial Integration in East Asia and Pacific: Regional and Interregional Linkages. *World Bank Malaysia Hub Research & Policy Briefs*. No. 15.

Morgan, P. and B. Huang. 2021. Fintech in ASEAN+3 and Implications for Financial Inclusion and Financial Stability. In D. Guinigundo, M. Kawai, C. Y. Park, and R. S. Rajan, eds. *Redefining Strategic Routes to Financial Resilience in ASEAN+3.* Chapter 4. Asian Development Bank.

Mühlich L., B. Fritz, and W. N. Kring. 2022. No One Left Behind? Assessing the Global Financial Safety Net Performance During COVID-19. *Journal of Globalization and Development.* 13 (1). pp. 123–47.

Ong, L. L., T. L. Quách, H. N. Nguyen, A. L. Tang, Y. F. Ho, P. Pande, and C. Y. Choo. 2023. Opportunities and Challenges of Financial Digitalization: A New Perspective on ASEAN+3 Regional Financial Cooperation. ASEAN+3 Macroeconomic Research Office (AMRO) Policy Position Paper.

Park, C. Y. 2011. Asian Financial System: Development and Challenges. *ADB Economics Working Paper Series.* 285. Asian Development Bank.

Park, C. Y., P. Rosenkranz, and M. C. Tayag. 2020. Financial Integration in Asia and the Pacific: Challenges and Prospects. In B. Susantono and C. Y. Park, eds. *Future of Regional Cooperation in Asia and the Pacific*. Chapter 10. Asian Development Bank.

Park, C. Y. and R. S. Rajan. 2021. Regional Financial Cooperation in ASEAN+3: Taking Stock and Moving Forward. In D. Guinigundo, M. Kawai, C. Y. Park, and R. S. Rajan, eds. *Redefining Strategic Routes to Financial Resilience in ASEAN+3.* Chapter 7. Asian Development Bank.

Pericoli, M. and K. Yilmaz. 2024. Shocks and Global Asset Market Connectedness. In G. M. Caporale, ed. *Handbook of Financial Integration.* Chapter 5. Edward Elgar Publishing, Inc.

Phylaktis, K. and M. Aftab. 2024. Financial Integration and Exchange Market Pressure. In G. M. Caporale, ed. *Handbook of Financial Integration.* Chapter 14. Edward Elgar Publishing, Inc.

Ritchie, H. 2021. How Much of the World's Food Production Is Dependent on Pollinators? https://ourworldindata.org/pollinator-dependence.

Sanchez-Bayo, F. and K. A. G. Wyckhuys. 2019. Worldwide Decline of the Entomofauna: A Review of Its Drivers. *Biological Conservation*. 232. pp. 8–27.

Scheid, B. 2024. *Magnificent 7 Stocks Stumble, Boosting Peak Views.* https://www.spglobal.com/marketintelligence/en/news-insights/latest-news-headlines/magnificent-7-stocks-stumble-boosting-peak-views-82765994.

Schoenmaker, D. 2011. The Financial Trilemma. *Economics Letters*. 111 (1). pp. 57–59.

Selvarajan, S. K. and R. Ab-Rahim. 2020. Financial Integration and Economic Growth: Should Asia Emulate Europe? *Journal of Economic Integration*. 35 (1). pp. 191–213.

Taghizadeh-Hesary, F., T. M. P. Nguyet, H. T. H. Hanh, and T. C. Vu. 2019. Does Financial Integration Matter for Financial Development? Evidence from the East Asian and Pacific Region. *Journal of Economic Integration.* 34 (4). pp. 591–618.

te Kaat, D. M. and A. Raabe. Forthcoming. Nature Financing: Investment Funds and Biodiversity Risks. ADB Working Paper.

Volz, U., J. Beirne, N. A. Preudhomme, A. Fenton, E. Mazzacurati, N. Rhenzi, and J. Stampe. 2020. *Climate Change and Sovereign Risk*. SOAS University of London, Asian Development Bank Institute, World Wide Fund for Nature Singapore, and Four Twenty Seven.

Volz, U. 2022. Climate-Proofing the Global Financial Safety Net. *Journal of Globalization and Development.* 13 (1). pp. 1–30.

World Economic Forum (WEF). 2024. Labelled Bonds for the Net-Zero Transition in South-East Asia: The Way Forward. White Paper.

World Wide Fund for Nature. 2024. *Living Planet Report 2024 – A System in Peril.*

Xin, W., L. Grant, B. Groom, and C. Zhang. 2023. Biodiversity Confusion: The Impact of ESG Biodiversity Ratings on Asset Prices. *SSRN*.

Yadav, I. S., P. Goyari, and R. K. Mishra. 2019. Financial Integration and Macroeconomic Volatility: Evidence from Asia. *Journal of Economic and Administrative Sciences*. 35 (2). pp. 94–112.

# 5 Movement of People

## Migration

### Cross-Border Migration Has Provided Opportunities for Economic Mobility and Higher Welfare

Between 1970 and 2021, international migrants had tripled in number from 84.5 million to 282 million, a moderate yet sustained increase heralding the greater movement of people in tandem with the global economy's pursuit of the freer exchange of goods, services, and capital (Figure 5.1).[42] The intensity and volume of migration have been influenced by various factors. The evolution of the industrial structure and systems of production, the availability of cross-border employment and advancements in transportation and communications, and the pursuit of greater economic gains, along with key global conflicts, have all impacted the cross-border movement of people.[43]

**Figure 5.1: Number of International Migrants**

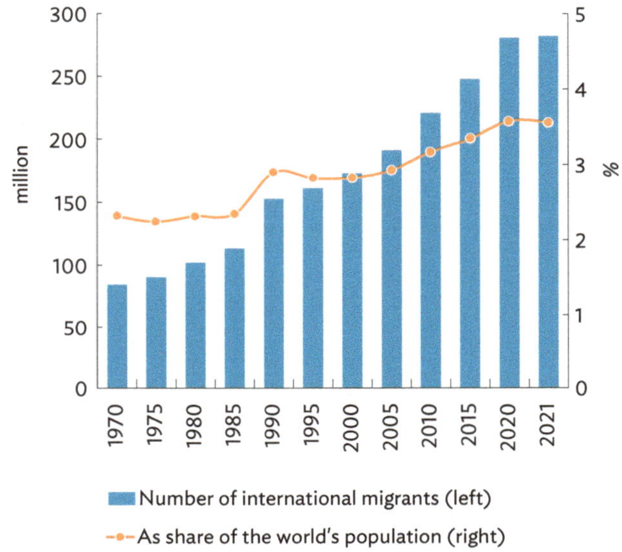


Sources: ADB calculations using data from McAuliffe and Oucho (2024); and United Nations. Department of Economic and Social Affairs, Population Division (UN DESA). International Migrant Stock 2020. https://www.un.org/development/desa/pd/content/international-migrant-stock (accessed May 2024); World Bank Group. Global Knowledge Partnership on Migration and Development (KNOMAD). KNOMAD/World Bank Bilateral Migration Matrix 2021, December 2022. https://prosperitydata360.worldbank.org/en/indicator/WB+KNOMAD+MIG (accessed July 2024); and UN DESA. World Population Prospects 2024. https://population.un.org/wpp/ (accessed September 2024).

#### Migration has been integral to the development of Asia and the Pacific.

Cross-border migration is a major component of Asia's development journey. From 1990, out-migration from Asia grew by about 91% to 95 million in 2021, with one in three global migrants originating from the region (Figure 5.2). Another notable feature is that outbound migration from the region is increasingly directed toward destinations outside Asia. In 1990, economies outside the region hosted about 53.6% of Asian migrants (Figure 5.3). By 2021, this had gone up to almost 65%, with the Middle East, as major host, to about 57% of Asian out-migrants.

42 Throughout this section, references to migrants in the context of frameworks, agreements, conditions, and movement refer to international economic migrants or international migrant workers, unless otherwise specified.

43 For instance, at the turn of the 20th century, people in the agriculture sector mass-migrated from Europe to the Americas and to other lands with temperate climates (Nayyar 2000). The introduction of passports and other border control documents in 1919 to 1939 dented cross border movements only to pick up again after World War II, with the United States (US) and Latin America as primary destinations.

**Figure 5.2: Outbound Migrants from Asia and the Pacific**

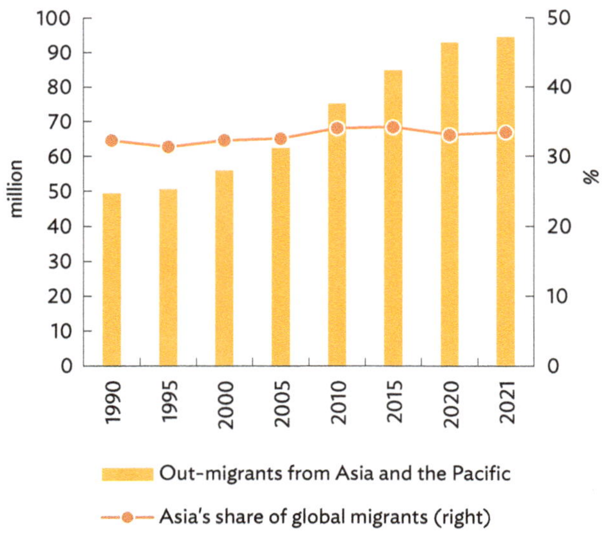


**Figure 5.3: Asian Migrants by Destination Regions** (%)

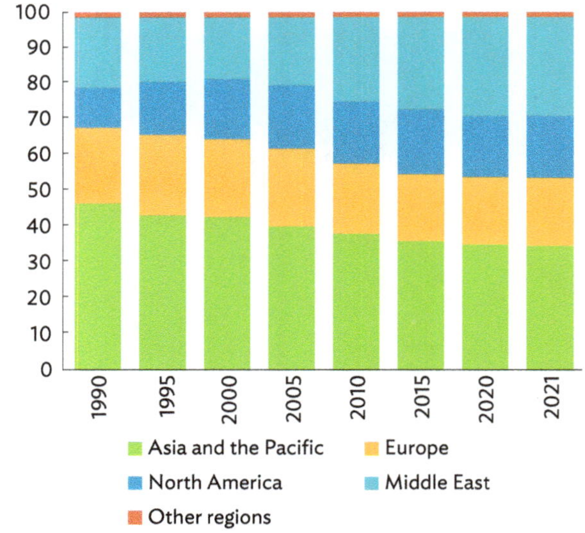


Source: ADB calculations using data from United Nations Department of Economic and Social Affairs, Population Division. International Migrant Stock 2020. https://www.un.org/development/desa/pd/content/international-migrant-stock (accessed May 2024); and World Bank Group. Global Knowledge Partnership on Migration and Development (KNOMAD). KNOMAD/World Bank Bilateral Migration Matrix 2021, December 2022. https://prosperitydata360.worldbank.org/en/dataset/WB+KNOMAD (accessed September 2024).

## Out-migration from the region was led by South Asia and Southeast Asia.

South Asia accounted for nearly half of total Asian out-migrants (Figure 5.4). Among the top 10 migrant-sending economies from the region in 2021, migrants from four South Asian economies comprised 36.6% of the total out-migrants. Southeast Asia has also been gaining ground as a key source subregion. Led by the Philippines, Indonesia, and Viet Nam, the share of Southeast Asia as a source subregion increased to 25.0% of total out-migrants in 2021, from 15.6% in the 1990s. Saudi Arabia, the US, and the United Arab Emirates figure as the top destinations for Asian migrants, especially those from South Asia and Southeast Asia. Relative to 2019, the outflow of Asian migrants slowed when the pandemic struck in 2020 but has since resumed (Figure 5.5).

## Asian migrants have increasingly sought more opportunities beyond the region.

Asian migrants have gained more presence in the Middle East and North America (Figure 5.6). From 2000, their number has increased by 16.7 million in the Middle East and by 6.8 million in North America. This increase was caused, in part, by the influence of international labor agreements that sending economies in Asia and major host economies entered into within bilateral or regional frameworks. Middle Eastern destinations also offer more opportunities for workers from different skills categories, while some migrant employment programs in major destinations such as North America provide permanent residency possibilities (Kikkawa, Gaspar, and Park 2019).

## Asian subregions exhibit diverse profiles in intraregional migration patterns.

The intraregional migration share remained at 39.5%, on average, from 1990 to 2021. Oceania, East Asia, and Southeast Asia were the leading subregions in intrasubregional migration (Figure 5.7). Around 48% of migrants from Australia and New Zealand migrated between these two economies, while about one-third of migrants from East Asia and Southeast Asia went to economies in their respective subregions. Central Asia's strong ties with the Russian Federation explain why at least 90% of its migrants are in non-Asian economies. Within the region, Australia, Thailand, Malaysia, and

**Figure 5.4: Sources of Asian Out-Migrant Stock by Subregion** (% share of total)

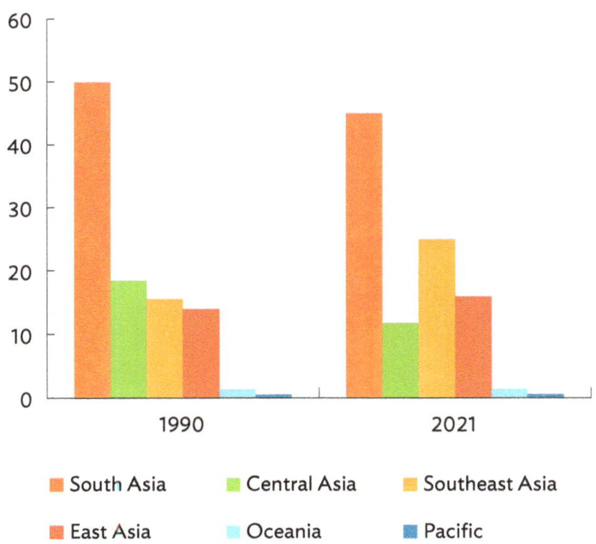


**Figure 5.5: Outflow of Migrant Workers from Selected Asian Economies** (2019 = 100)

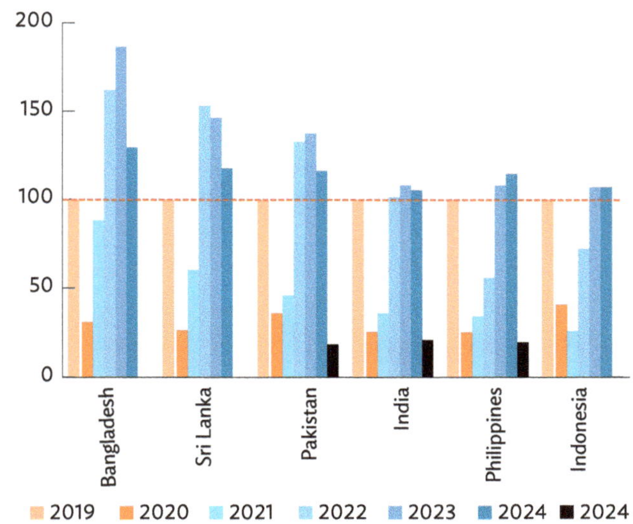


Note: The 2024 data are up to October for Sri Lanka.

Source: ADB calculations using data from Central Bank of Sri Lanka. https://www.cbsl.gov.lk/en/statistics/statistical-tables/external-sector (accessed March 2025); Government of Bangladesh, Bureau of Manpower, Employment, and Training. http://www.old.bmet.gov.bd/BMET/stattisticalDataAction (accessed March 2025); Government of India, Ministry of External Affairs. Performance Smartboard. https://meadashboard.gov.in/indicators/15 (accessed March 2025); Government of Indonesia, Migrant Worker Protection Agency (Badan Pelindungan Pekerja Migran Indonesia). https://bp2mi.go.id/ (accessed March 2025); Government of Pakistan, Bureau of Emigration and Overseas Employment. https://beoe.gov.pk/reports-and-statistics (accessed March 2025); Government of the Philippines, Department of Migrant Workers. https://dmw.gov.ph/statistics/overseas-employment-statistics (accessed March 2025); United Nations Department of Economic and Social Affairs, Population Division. International Migrant Stock 2020. https://www.un.org/development/desa/pd/content/international-migrant-stock (accessed May 2024); and World Bank Group. Global Knowledge Partnership on Migration and Development (KNOMAD). KNOMAD/World Bank Bilateral Migration Matrix 2021, December 2022. https://prosperitydata360.worldbank.org/en/dataset/WB+KNOMAD (accessed September 2024).

**Figure 5.6: Major Extraregional Hosts of Asia and Pacific Migrants in 2021** (million)

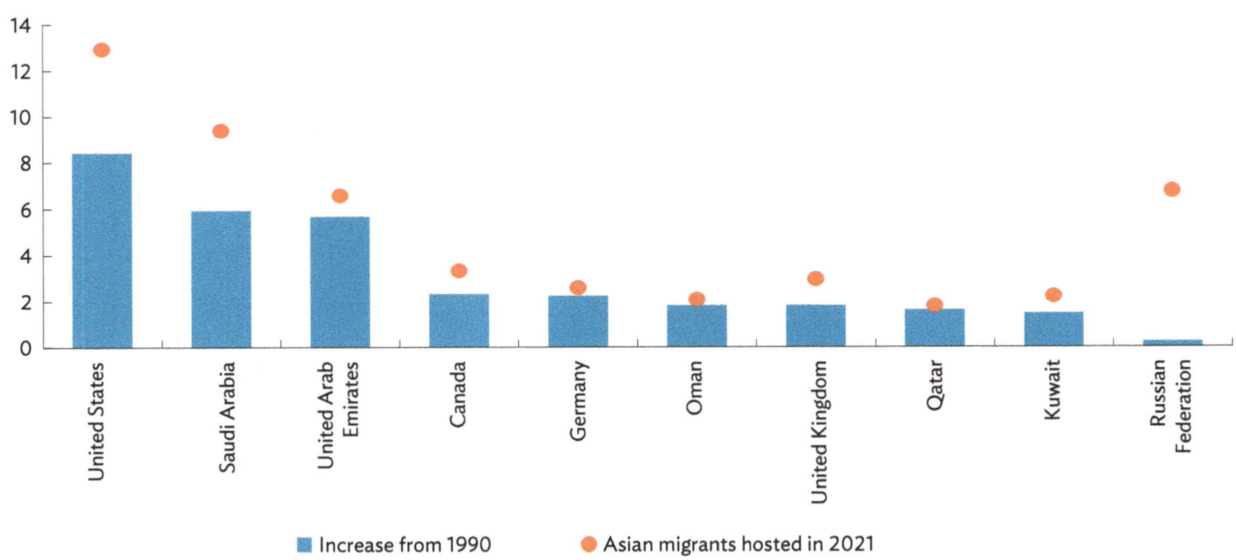


Source: ADB calculations using data from United Nations Department of Economic and Social Affairs, Population Division. International Migrant Stock 2020. https://www.un.org/development/desa/pd/content/international-migrant-stock (accessed May 2024); and World Bank Group. Global Knowledge Partnership on Migration and Development (KNOMAD). KNOMAD/World Bank Bilateral Migration Matrix 2021, December 2022. https://prosperitydata360.worldbank.org/en/dataset/WB+KNOMAD (accessed June 2024).

Pakistan figure as major destinations of Asian migrants. Pakistan hosted migrants from Indonesia, the People's Republic of China (PRC), and Sri Lanka. Thailand mostly hosted working migrants from the neighboring Lao People's Democratic Republic (Lao PDR) and Cambodia. Meanwhile, Malaysia hosted migrants mostly from Indonesia and Nepal. Whereas absolute numbers put Australia as a key destination for migrants from the PRC, the Philippines, and Viet Nam, the majority of migrants to Australia are from the United Kingdom (UK).[44] Among Pacific developing economies, migrants from Fiji, Samoa, and Tonga account for 84.8% of migrants in Oceania.

**Figure 5.7: Intraregional Migration by Asian Subregion** (%)

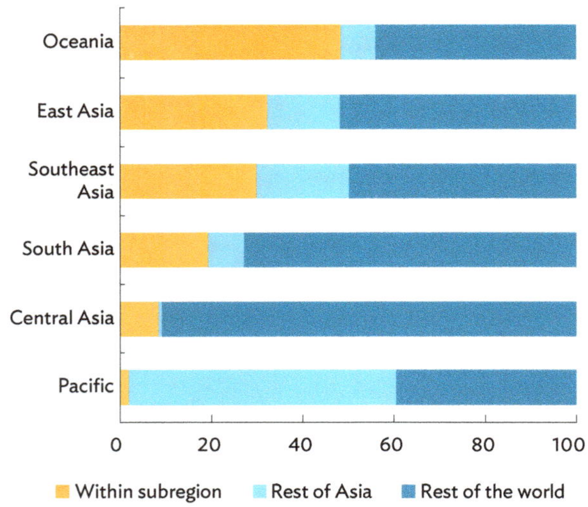


Source: ADB calculations using data from United Nations Department of Economic and Social Affairs, Population Division. International Migrant Stock 2020. https://www.un.org/development/desa/pd/content/international-migrant-stock (accessed May 2024); and World Bank Group. Global Knowledge Partnership on Migration and Development (KNOMAD). KNOMAD/World Bank Bilateral Migration Matrix 2021, December 2022. https://prosperitydata360.worldbank.org/en/dataset/WB+KNOMAD(accessed June 2024).

## Migration and Regional Cooperation and Integration

Over the past 2 decades, bilateral cooperation among governments on migration has intensified. It spans the entire spectrum of mobility governance from highly formalized to informal cooperation—from fully-fledged formal mobility frameworks and trade-related agreements that include migrant mobility components to economic cooperation frameworks that only facilitate specific aspects of mobility, or informal migration dialogues (Frankenhaeuser, Huss, and Frelak 2018). Meanwhile, the Global Compact for Migration (GCM), adopted in December 2018, promotes safe, orderly, and regular migration while emphasizing human and worker rights. The GCM provides broad principles to guide national and regional migration policies.

**International labor agreements can be treaties between economies or economic groups, as components of regional trade accords, or as ways to promote the mobility of highly skilled labor.**

### *Bilateral Labor Agreements*

A bilateral labor agreement (BLA) is an accord between two economies concerning the movement of workers for migration and employment, often focusing on low-skilled labor. Although BLAs often take the form of a memorandum of understanding (MOU), their structure can be adapted to the specific needs of certain groups of migrants. Ideally, both sending and receiving economies share the resources and burden of ensuring adequate conditions for migrants, monitoring migrants, regulating intermediaries (i.e., recruitment agencies), and managing pre- and post-migration processes. Often, migration flows between economies already exist through informal channels and private recruitment agencies before a formal BLA is established.

While the agreement is mutual, the motivations and benefits to sending and receiving economies vary. Economies hosting economic migrants aim to address the labor needs of various industries, manage regular and irregular migration, and promote cultural and political ties with their cosignatories (Blank 2011; Go 2007). Meanwhile, migrant-sending economies aim to maintain access to labor markets while ensuring to protect

---

44 Active migration between the United Kingdom (UK) and Australia is driven by historical and cultural ties. Modern factors include trade agreements like the Australia–UK Free Trade Agreement, which eases labor mobility through working holiday visas and mutual recognition of professional qualifications.

migrant workers' rights, ease unemployment pressures at home, increase capital flows as remittances (Blank 2011; Go 2007), and encourage repatriation of migrants, while mitigating brain drain effects (Oh 1977; Ozden and Schiff 2006).

Most BLA elements cover governance and information exchange, with varying emphasis on migrant worker protection and development aspects. The most commonly addressed topics in these agreements include defining clear responsibilities between parties, such as designating responsible line ministries for implementation (66.8%) and the exchange of information between economies (61.5%), highlighting the importance of structured management and effective bilateral communication in labor migration (Figure 5.8). Notably, provisions for the transfer of savings and remittances (17.8%) and the recognition of skills and qualifications (10.1%), which are key factors in migration and development, have limited inclusion.

**Since 1990, the proportion of BLAs involving at least one Asian economy as a signatory has increased, underscoring the growing role of Asia as both a source and destination for migrant workers** (Figure 5.9). More Southeast and South Asian economies entered into treaties with partners from the Middle East and East Asia. Australia, New Zealand, and the Republic of Korea have also increasingly engaged in BLAs such as the Republic of Korea's Employment Permit System, New Zealand's Recognized Seasonal Employer initiative and Seasonal Worker Program, and Australia's Pacific Labour Scheme with selected Pacific countries. East Asia and Southeast Asia are very active in engaging in intrasubregional BLAs, while Oceania engages in BLAs only with the Pacific and Southeast Asia. These developments suggest that regional economic integration and the potential for greater cooperation on labor issues could lead to more standardized labor practices and improved protections for migrant workers within the region.

**Figure 5.8: Specific Provisions in Bilateral Labor Agreements**

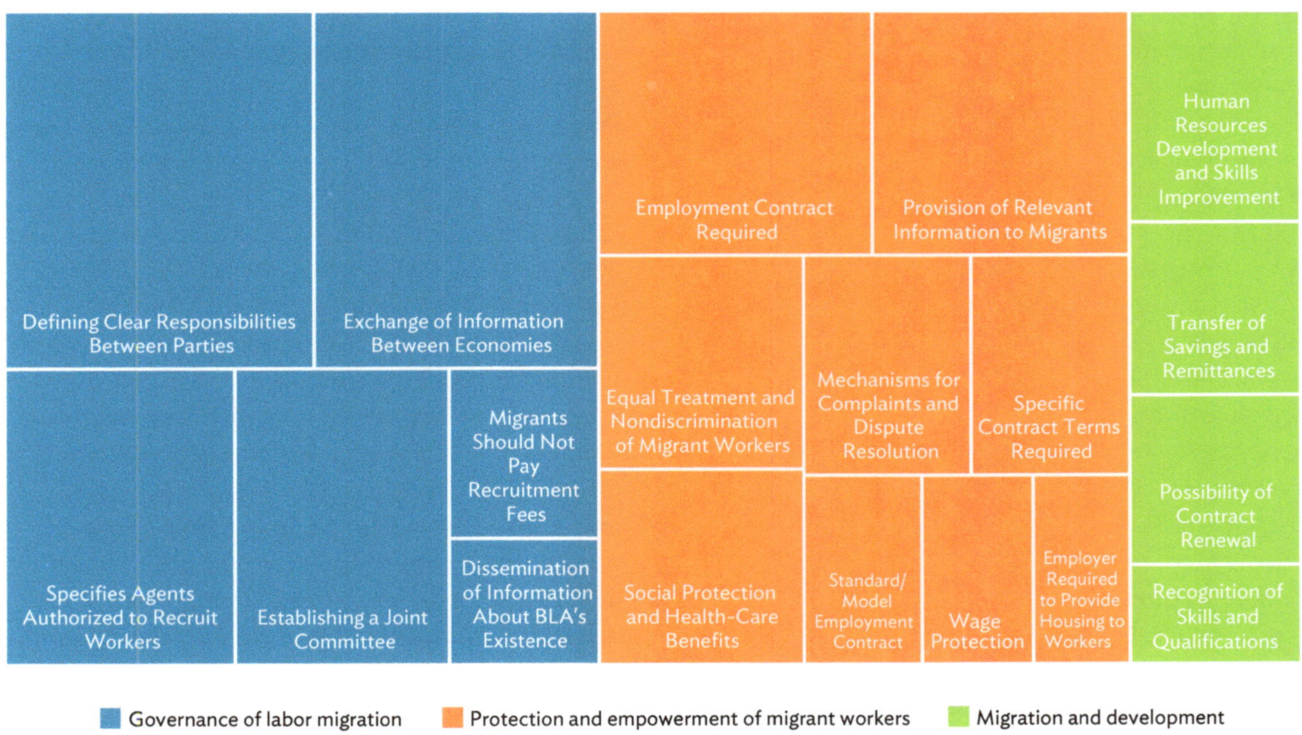


BLA = bilateral labor agreement.

Note: Data refer to BLAs signed since 1990, where Asian economies participate.

Source: ADB compilation based on Chilton and Woda (2022).

**Figure 5.9: Number of Bilateral Labor Agreements**

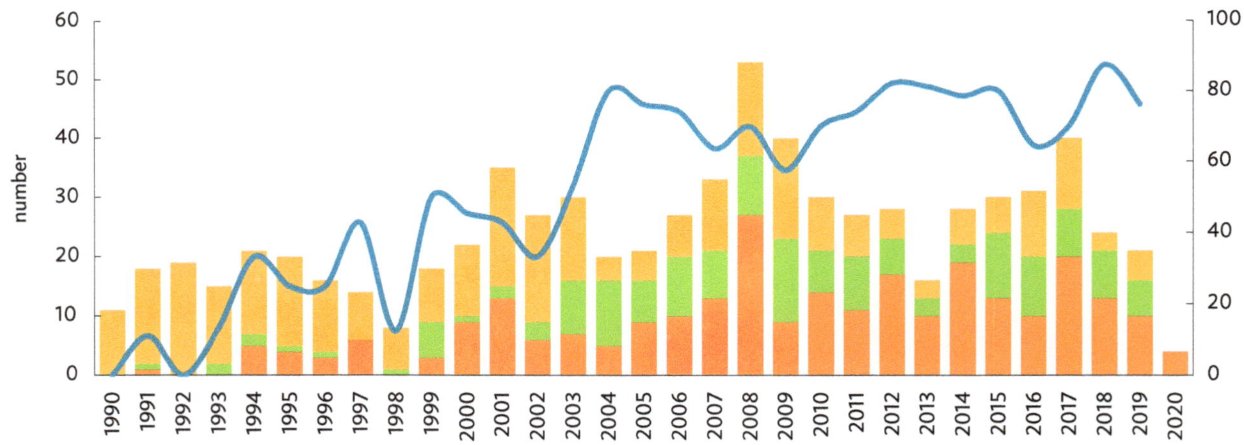


Sources: Chilton and Woda (2022); Chilton and Posner (2018); and Peters (2019).

**Despite the positive association between the presence of BLAs and the migrant stock, the literature shows mixed findings on the causal impact of the agreements on facilitating labor migration.** Early studies on the impact of BLAs on migrant flow indicate that most coincided with an increase in migrant flows on the year of the agreement and the year after (Battistella and Khadria 2011). Studies using global data sets in the recent decade indicate that signing BLAs could increase migrant flows. For example, a global data set of 582 BLAs from 1945 to 2015 revealed that economies with such agreements experienced higher migration (Chilton and Posner 2018), while Peters (2019) found BLAs to be correlated with an average increase in migrant flows of between 7% and 200% within 5 years. Agreements covering a broader set of industries also generated more migrant flows than those with limited or targeted sectors. However, this positive association did not explain causation, suggesting extraneous factors were at play and contributed to the increase in migrant flow. Some other studies found little to no relationship. For instance, O'Steen (2021) found no empirical evidence that the participation of the Philippines in BLAs effectively promoted labor mobility.

**The solid structural framework of BLAs still allows ample room to address the economic and personal welfare issues of migrants.** Homelessness, health outcomes, poverty, and access to education are just some of the issues that continue to challenge the viability of migration, depending on conditions in the destination economy. Migrant workers in the Middle East face work-related risks, such as labor exploitation, legal and social discrimination, physical and mental health issues, especially during the pandemic (International Labour Organization 2016; Ali, Al-Khani, and Sidahmed 2020; Karasapan 2020; Kikkawa et al. 2022; Jamil and Dutta 2021). In Australia, 11% of migrants lived in crowded housing in 2021, compared to the 7% national average.[45] In terms of affordability, around 28% of migrants spent 30% of their household income on rent while another 30% spent it on mortgage repayments. About 8% of skilled migrants in Australia accessed unemployment benefits compared to 13% for the national level. Meanwhile, Tsai and Gu (2019) found no significant difference between the lifetime adult homelessness rates of foreign-born (1%) and native-born workers (1.7%) in the United States (US), one of the top destinations of Asian migrants. However,

[45] Australian Bureau of Statistics. Migrant Settlement Outcomes. https://www.abs.gov.au/statistics/people/people-and-communities/migrant-settlement-outcomes/latest-release#data-downloads (accessed August 2024).

migrants were less likely to have mental health and substance abuse issues. They were also less likely to receive welfare and lifetime incarceration. However, this was not the case in Japan where mental health was affected by trouble in communicating in Japanese , being female, and lack of support (Miller et al. 2019). Migrant poverty is also a concern. Gilleland, Lurie, and Rankin (2016) found 22.3% of immigrants in the US to be living in poverty, compared to 13.2% of the US citizens.

**As demand for Asian migrant workers rises in the post-pandemic period, BLAs are likely to become increasingly more important.** Under these agreements a significant rise in inbound migrant flows occurred to major host economies such as the Republic of Korea, New Zealand, and Australia, driven by labor shortages in low-skilled sectors and the challenges from declining working-age populations in host economies (Figure 5.10). By helping to ensure that host economies have the necessary workforce to operate efficiently, BLAs have become even more crucial in the context of demographic challenges and post-pandemic growth goals.

**Figure 5.10: Number of Labor Migrants in Major Host Economies in Asia Under Bilateral Labor Agreements**
(2019 = 100)

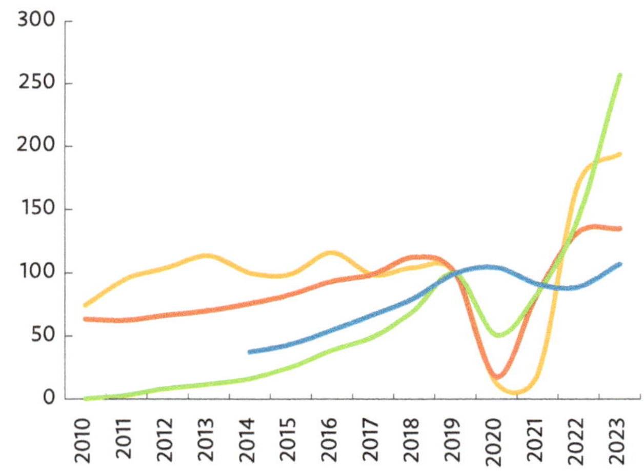


EPS = Employment Permit System, PALM = Pacific Australia Labour Mobility, RSE = Recognised Seasonal Employer, SWP = Seasonal Worker Program, TITP = Technical Intern Training Program.

Notes:

(i) For the Republic of Korea, the EPS is mainly for manufacturing, agriculture, and construction; numbers include those under E9 visas; up to 4 years and 10 months.

(ii) For New Zealand, the RSE is mainly for agriculture (horticulture and viticulture); up to 7 months.

(iii) For Australia, the SWP is mainly for agriculture and accommodation sectors; in 2022, SWP was replaced by the Temporary Work visa (subclass 403; stay up to 9 months under a short-term contract or up to 4 years under a long-term contract) under PALM; and SWP and the Pacific Labour Scheme were consolidated and replaced by PALM.

(iv) For Japan, the TITP is mainly for manufacturing, construction, and agriculture; up to 5 years.

Sources: ADB calculations using data from Australian Government, Department of Employment and Workplace Relations. Pacific Australia Labour Mobility Scheme. https://www.dewr.gov.au/pacific-australia-labour-mobility-scheme; Korean Statistical Information Service. Statistical Database. https://kosis.kr/eng/; New Zealand Immigration. Recognised Seasonal Employer (RSE) Scheme Research. https://www.immigration.govt.nz/about-us/research-and-statistics/research-reports/recognised-seasonal-employer-rse-scheme; and Statista. https://www.statista.com/ (all accessed August 2024).

## *Regional Trade Agreements with Labor and Migration Provisions*

**Regional trade agreements (RTAs) are often used to incorporate labor provisions to ensure compliance with labor rights and standards for workers, regardless of their nationality.** As of March 2024, labor provisions or chapters were found in 33% of all RTAs in force since 1990. This is equivalent to 115 RTAs that contain labor provisions in trade agreements spread across three categories—obligations, monitoring and cooperation, and dispute settle mechanisms (Corley-Coulibaly, Postolachi, and Tesfay 2021).[46] RTAs with labor provisions are more common between non-Asian economies (Figure 5.11a). Among Asian economies, Australia and New Zealand are the primary players. Thematic areas that are mostly covered in trade agreements with labor provisions include child labor (68 out of 115), occupational safety and health (63), and forced labor (57) (Figure 5.11b). However, the lower participation of developing Asian economies in such agreements may limit their impact on facilitating labor migration, particularly for Asian workers.

[46] Labor obligations are domestic and international commitments in labor standards made by signatories of the trade agreement. Monitoring and cooperation are mechanisms to promote labor obligation compliance through dialogues and cooperation activities. Dispute settlement mechanism relates to the resolution of noncompliance issues through processes agreed by stakeholders.

**Figure 5.11: Regional Trade Agreements with Labor Provisions**

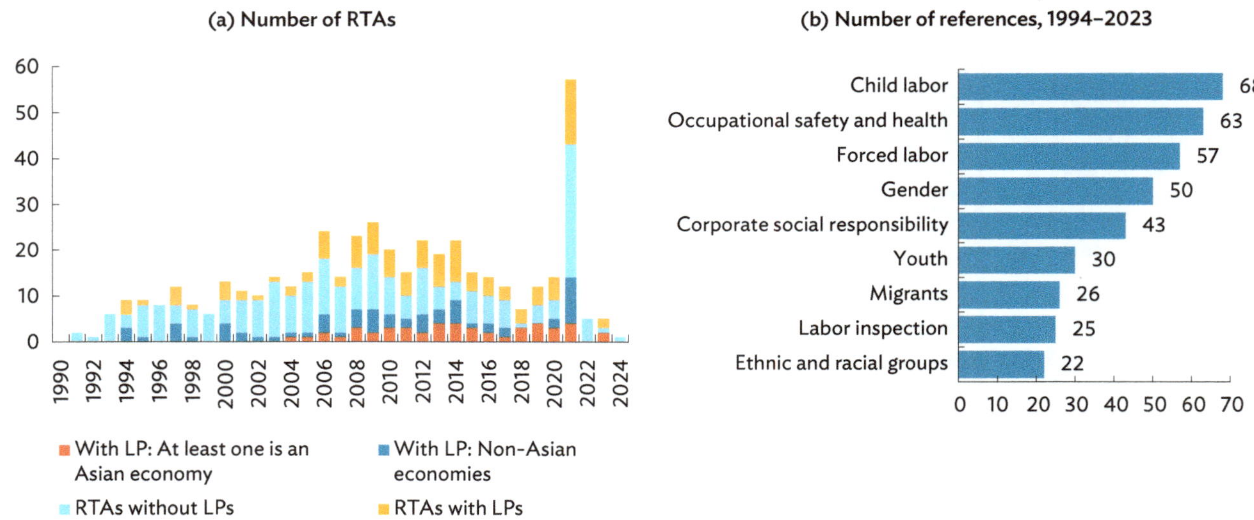


LP = labor provision, RTA = regional trade agreement.

Source: International Labour Organization. Labour Provisions in Trade Agreements Hub. https://webapps.ilo.org/LPhub/ (accessed June 2024).

**Trade agreements also function as platforms to facilitate the temporary movement of highly skilled workers.** Migration provisions within these agreements are designed to enable the mobility of individuals involved in trade in goods, the supply of services, or the conduct of investment, all in relation to the agreement's objectives. Since the 2000s, the inclusion of such provisions has been steadily rising, often involving at least one Asian economy as a signatory (Figure 5.12a). The migration of professionals and skilled workers is primarily facilitated through mechanisms such as reduced processing fees, mutual recognition agreements, and expedited procedures (Figure 5.12b). Studies find that provisions on visas and asylum can be effective in facilitating bilateral migration flows (Orefice 2015; Figueiredo, Lima, and Orefice 2015; and Levelu, Mayda, and Orefice 2023).

## *Mutual Recognition Arrangements*

**Mutual recognition arrangements (MRAs) aim to promote labor mobility of professionals by recognizing their qualifications across borders.** MRAs enable the qualifications of services suppliers, recognized by the authorities in their home economy, to be mutually recognized by other economies who are signatories to the MRAs.[47] Examples of MRAs are those in the Asia-Pacific Economic Cooperation (APEC) and the Association of Southeast Asian Nations (ASEAN). The ASEAN Framework Agreement on Services, signed on 15 December 1995, recognizes the importance of MRAs to facilitate deeper services trade integration in ASEAN. Meanwhile, the APEC MRAs are part of the APEC Services Competitiveness Roadmap (2016–2025) that supports the "cross-border mobility for professionals, building on initiatives such as the APEC Architects and Engineers Registers to facilitate mutual recognition arrangements."

[47] MRAs can be established through various means, for example, regional trade agreements such as the Comprehensive and Progressive Agreement for Trans-Pacific Partnership (CPTPP) and ASEAN Framework Agreement on Services; bilateral free trade agreements (FTAs) (Republic of Korea–Canada); multilateral agreements (the Washington Accord; APEC MRA); and bilateral agreements (Trans-Tasman Mutual Recognition Arrangement).

**Figure 5.12: Regional Trade Agreements with Migration Provisions**

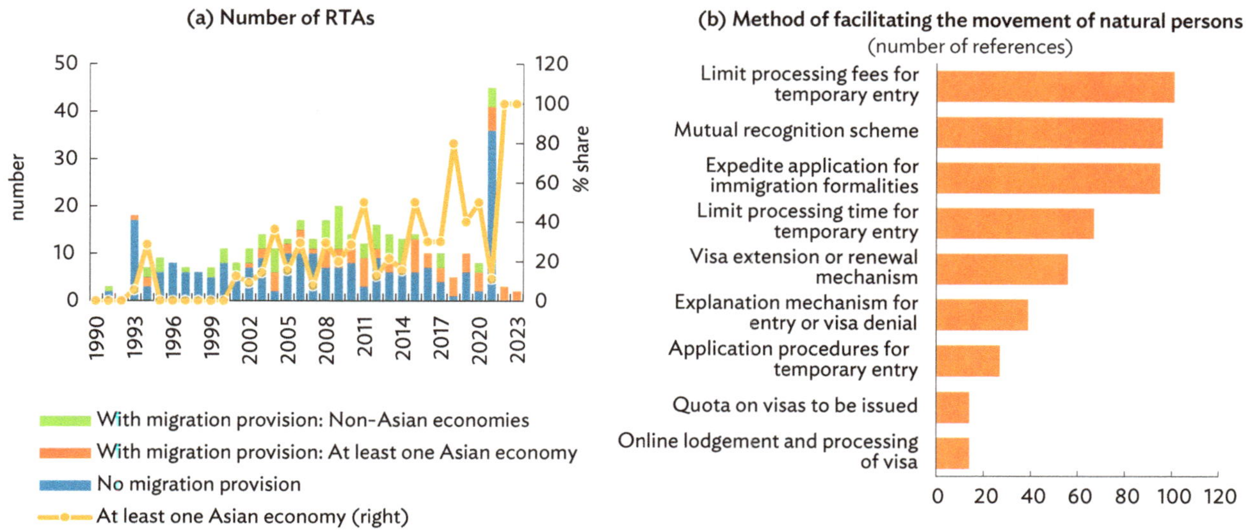


RTA = regional trade agreement.

Notes: Panel (a) is based on labor provisions typology by Corley-Coulibaly, Postolachi, and Tesfay (2021) for the obligations category of RTAs. Panel (b) refers to the top 10 provisions in 400 RTAs using the Visa and Asylum subsection of the Deep Trade Agreements Database.

Source: ADB calculations using data from World Bank. Deep Trade Agreements Database. https://datatopics.worldbank.org/dta/table.html (accessed July 2024).

**MRAs have expanded, but participation among economies remains uneven, and the range of occupations covered is limited.** APEC's Inventory of Mutual Recognition Agreements for Professional Qualifications and Licensure lists 210 MRAs that involve at least one APEC economy. There were 15 agreements enacted in the 1990s, 41 in the 2000s, and 97 in the 2010s—80% of these are bilateral single-profession MRAs, while around 20 are multilateral single-profession MRAs (APEC Secretariat 2024a). About half of the member economies have entered into 10 or fewer MRAs, while five are engaged in 40 or more. About 80% of MRAs in APEC cover professions for engineers, accountants, surveyors, actuaries, and architects. ASEAN has concluded and signed MRAs in several professions: (i) engineering services (December 2005); (ii) nursing services (December 2006); (iii) architectural services and surveying professionals (November 2007); (iv) medical practitioners; (v) dental practitioners (February 2009); (vi) accountancy services (February 2009 and November 2014); and (vii) tourism professionals (November 2012).

**Implementation of MRAs is often complex and resource intensive, and their effectiveness varies significantly across sectors and regions.** Full implementation of MRAs requires clear processes for mutual recognition and registration, but national barriers slow progress (Mendoza and Sugiyarto 2017). Many MRAs focus on recognizing formal qualifications rather than on-the-job experience, limiting their effectiveness (Mendoza et al. 2017). Harmonizing training standards requires significant investment, and decentralized enforcement complicates compliance. Whereas MRAs in technical fields like engineering and accounting are common, their impact on mobility is limited (APEC 2024a). In ASEAN, health care-related MRAs have shown limited outputs because of stringent national regulations, whereas unregulated sectors like tourism professions have achieved more (Hamanaka and Jusoh 2018). In contrast, the experience of the European Union (EU) shows that mutual recognition has facilitated trade in services and improved intra-EU mobility, particularly in health and education (Nordas 2016). As digital economies expand, domestic regulations could become major barriers to cross-border digital services (mode 1), similar to challenges in movement of individuals (mode 4). Embracing digital credentialing may be a key step toward professional recognition in a more digitally connected world (ADB 2022).

### *Labor Mobility Partnerships*

**Labor mobility partnerships (LMP), also known as skill mobility partnerships, are emerging frameworks that go beyond BLAs by encompassing labor market policies and development objectives** (Box 5.1). These connect issues on skills and training placements, mutual recognition of professional qualifications, and circular migration to ensure the fair distribution of benefits (Huckstep and Clemens 2023). LMPs require support from both governments of the origin and destination economies and close collaboration with the private sector to share the benefits of labor migration. This type of partnership is an important component of the European Union's Global Approach to Migration and Mobility.

**However, fully implementing LMPs presents significant challenges related to costs, skills recognition, and coordination.** Issues arise regarding the cost-sharing structure of training programs and pilot projects and the insufficient transfer of resources to origin economies. These cost challenges limit the scalability of labor mobility partnership programs and projects (OECD 2018). Training programs conducted at destination economies, which are intended to benefit home economies through return migration, often have insufficient recognition and few opportunities to utilize these skills at home. Another challenge is enhancing the participation of employers in both economies to better satisfy employer requirements on worker skill levels and training program reliability and timeliness. Employers may be more focused on immediate training needs and labor gaps and may be unwilling to invest in building long-term skills (IOM 2023). Involving multiple stakeholders presents its own set of coordination challenges. The negotiations required to design and implement programs that cater to specific national contexts and sector requirements make scalability a major hurdle (European Migration Network 2022).

## Policy Considerations

Moving forward, labor migration is likely to play an increasingly vital role in the global economy as a declining working-age population in major host economies intensify the demand for foreign labor. Many advanced economies are experiencing aging populations and shrinking workforces, driving the need for migrant workers to fill labor gaps across various sectors. At the same time, the growing impacts of climate change are expected to accelerate migration from vulnerable regions, with individuals and communities seeking new livelihoods and safer environments (Box 5.2).

In the context of the rising importance of labor migration, it is equally critical to ensure that the benefits are shared among all stakeholders—origin economies, host economies, and migrant communities. This section explores key national and international policy considerations to ensure that labor migration delivers inclusive and sustainable benefits for all parties involved.

**Integrate the vital role of international migration into the development policy.** To maximize migration's development impact, models like Skills Mobility Partnerships, which are designed to benefit all stakeholders—migrant workers, origin and destination economies—could promote net gains from labor migration. Incorporating development aspects, such as remittance facilitation, into bilateral labor agreements could enhance positive outcomes, including greater financial inclusion, in origin economies. National and regional migration policies, for both source and host economies, could take guidance from the Global Compact for Migration to promote safe, orderly, and regular migration.

**At bilateral and regional levels, aiming for more extensive labor migration agreements with practical mechanisms for enforceability and monitoring** could ensure a better flow of migrants and better reduce skills mismatches and labor shortages, the protection of migrant rights, fair recruitment, and the portability of social security benefits. Creating a multiagency support structure for labor mobility partnerships could

**Box 5.1: Examples of Labor Mobility Partnerships**

Several models of labor mobility partnerships have been tested, including the Global Skill Partnership model proposed by Clemens (2015). The European Union (EU) Talent Partnership Initiative is another example of labor mobility partnerships that seek to broaden the legal pathways for migration to the EU while engaging partner economies on migration management. Cooperation is tailor-made according to the labor market and skills needs of both the destination and origin economies, and direct assistance is provided by EU partner economies to support vocational training programs and professional exchange schemes. Other labor mobility partnership models include Skills Mobility Partnerships by the International Organization for Migration, Skills Mobility Schemes by the Organisation for Economic Co-operation and Development (OECD), and Transnational Skills and Mobility Partnerships by the Bertelsmann Foundation. These models often differ on the form of engagement (memorandum of understanding, trade-related agreement, migration partnership), the type of migration encouraged (short term, longer term, circular, or permanent), the skill level being developed (low, mid, or high), the location of the skills training (home or destination economy, or both), and the funding structure (public, private, international organizations, foundations, or mixed) (IOM 2023). The box table provides a brief overview of some programs that have been designed and piloted as labor mobility partnerships.

**Labor Mobility Partnership Projects**

| Project Name | Features | Actors |
|---|---|---|
| Australia Pacific Training Coalition (APTC) | • Home economy-based skills and vocational training (automotive, construction, electrical and manufacturing, health and community services, hospitality and tourism)<br>• Embedding APTC programs into Pacific technical and vocational education and training (TVET) systems | Australian and Pacific governments, regional government organizations, Pacific TVET systems, industry peak bodies, individual employers |
| PAM (Partnership Approaches to Development-oriented Training and Labor Migration) | • Full vocational training in Germany<br>• Internship placement for trainees<br>• Training in economy of origin | German Ministry for Economic Cooperation and Development (BMZ), Deutsche Gesellschaft für Internationale Zusammenarbeit GmbH (GIZ) |
| THAMM (Towards a Holistic Approach to Labour Migration Governance and Labour Mobility in North Africa) project | • Taking up skilled employment<br>• Full vocational training in Germany | GIZ; ZAV (Federal Employment Agency); European Union; BMZ; Moroccan Ministry of Employment and Professional Integration; Agency for Employment and Self-Employment in Tunisia (ANETI); Egyptian Ministry of State for Emigration and Egyptian Expatriates Affairs (MoSEEEA) |
| tQMP Bau (Transnationale Qualifizierungs- und Mobilitätspartnerschaften - Bau Academy) Bau | • Vocational training at Bavarian State Association of Bavarian Construction Guilds (LBB) member companies<br>• VET partnership—Bau Academy in Kosovo | Kosovo Ministry of Labor and Social Welfare (MLSW), Bavarian State Association of Bavarian Construction Guilds (LBB), GIZ |
| Triple Win Nurses | • Taking up skilled employment<br>• Adaptive qualifications to receive skills recognition | ZAV (Federal Employment Agency); GIZ; employment agencies in the partner economies (Bosnia-Herzegovina, India (state of Kerala), Indonesia, Jordan, Philippines, Tunisia) |

Sources: Government of Australia, Department of Foreign Affairs and Trade (2017); World Bank (2024); and Sauer and Volarević (2021).

provide the required push for the actual take-off of mutual recognition of skills arrangements, while helping to address the key challenges of the cost-sharing structure in training programs and pilot projects between sending and destination economies. More important, the inclusion of remittance-related provisions in all labor migration agreements would underscore the vast development potential of migrants' remittances, contribute to data infrastructure on remittances, and complement existing remittance initiatives.

**Box 5.2: Migration, Aging Populations, and Climate Change**

**Migration and Aging Populations**

Population estimates by the United Nations indicate that the number of people aged 60 years or over is projected to increase from 13.4% in 2020 to 21.8% in 2050. By the mid-2030s, those aged 80 and over will outnumber infants (1 year of age or less), and that by the late 2070s, the global population aged 65 and older will exceed the number of children under 18. Asia is undergoing rapid demographic changes which pose challenges and opportunities for cross-border migration. These shifts will influence labor market dynamics, economic growth potential, and migration flows across the region.

Central Asia, South Asia, and Southeast Asia are expected to experience an increase in their working-age populations, while East Asia is expected to see a quickening pace of decline (box figure 1). South Asia will add 116 million by 2030 and 302 million by 2050. Relative to 2023, Pakistan's working age population is expected to grow by 18.7% in 2030 and 70.9% by 2050 (box figure 2). In Southeast Asia, the working age population of the Philippines will first increase by 11.8% in 2030 before ballooning further to 39.0% in 2050, while Indonesia's will grow by 6.2% in 2030 before increasing to 10.7% in 2050. East Asia, on the contrary, anticipates a decline in its economically active population by as much as 14 million in 2030 and 246 million in 2050. The People's Republic of China accounts for the majority of this decline (21.3% in 2050 from 0.7% in 2030), followed by Japan and the Republic of Korea.

**Migration and Climate Change**

The World Bank estimates that by 2050, around 216 million people will flee their homes due to sudden onset disasters like flooding and slow-onset changes such as rise in sea levels and low crop yields because of drought (Clement et al. 2021). Although most people displaced or migrating as a result of climate impacts stay within their economies of origin, the accelerating trend of global displacement related to climate impacts is also increasing cross-border movements.

Asia is one of the regions that is hardest hit by climate change. Some of its economies are experiencing greater cumulative climate change impacts than others. Low-lying regions in South Asia are among the most vulnerable. Estimates warn that one in every seven people in Bangladesh will be displaced by climate change by 2050 (Environmental Justice Foundation (2018)). Inhabited parts of some Asian economies are under threat of disappearing under water or being totally uninhabitable because of ecological disasters including Indonesia, Maldives, Pacific economies, and the Philippines (International Organization for Migration (IOM) 2022; McConnell 2022; Missbach and Palmer 2018; Parsons 2023; Uddin 2024; United Nations Framework Convention on Climate Change (UNFCCC) 2017; and World Bank Group 2022).

Although the migration-climate change nexus has gained policy attention in recent years, there are still significant knowledge gaps in determining a clear relationship between climate-induced environmental changes and their effects on migration flows. Numerous empirical studies have explored the potential link but results indicating any specifically direct, monocausal connection between environmental or climate change and migration remain seriously lacking.

**1: Changes in Working-Age Population from 2023, by Subregion** (million)

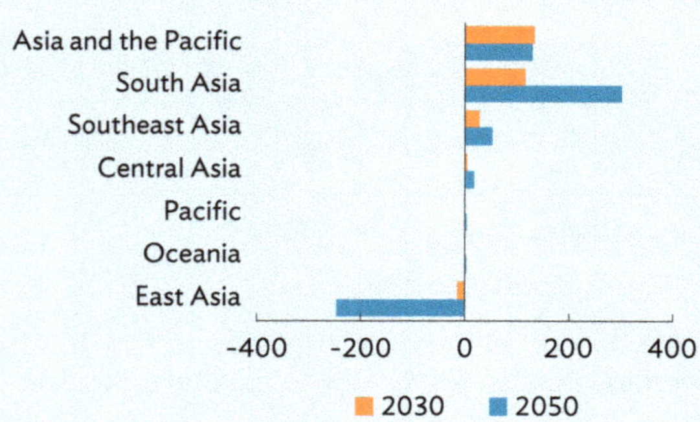


**2: Percent Change in Working-Age Population from 2023, by Economy** (%)

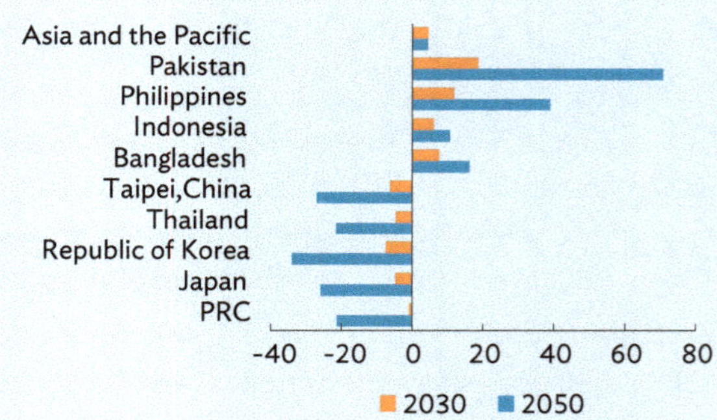


PRC = People's Republic of China.

Source: ADB calculations using data from United Nations Department of Economic and Social Affairs, Population Division (UN DESA). https://www.un.org/development/desa/pd/ (accessed July 2024).

Sources: ADB calculations using data from UN DESA. https://www.un.org/development/desa/pd/ (accessed July 2024); Clement et al. (2021); IOM (2022); McConnell (2022); Missbach and Palmer (2018); Parsons (2023); Uddin (2022); UNFCCC (2017); and World Bank Group (2022).

**Promote greater temporary labor mobility by reducing the costs associated with migration.** Job search, recruitment, deployment, and the attainment of additional financial literacy skills add to the total cost of migration. Interventions at each phase of the migration cycle could reduce the overall cost of cross-border movement of workers and boost the net development effects of migration. Migrant-sending economies will benefit in the medium term to long term by implementing active labor market policies, promoting access to education and employment opportunities, and putting in place better skills matching mechanisms. Destinations could benefit by encouraging the migration of workers skilled in fields that are in critical demand and facilitating migrant inclusion, while addressing the effects of rising migration on the social fabric of their economies.

## Remittances

### Remittance inflows, bolstered by migration, have gained increasing economic significance in the region over the past few decades.

Remittance inflows to Asia have accelerated over the past 3 decades, alongside the growth in labor migration from the region. From 1990 to 2024, these inflows increased 35 times, making remittance inflows the largest and most stable source of external financing for many migrant-sending Asian economies (Figure 5.13). In 2024, remittance inflows to Asia increased by 7.5% to $392.1 billion, up from $364.9 billion in 2023, and make up 43.3% of global remittances. Strong labor markets in major OECD migrant host economies, especially the US, bolstered remittances to the region (Ratha, Plaza, and Kim 2024).

### Remittance flows to Asia have proven resilient, rebounding strongly after periods of crisis.

For instance, inflows to the region contracted by 17.3% in 1998 because of the Asian financial crisis, followed by growth of 11.5% in 1999. The global financial crisis, which caused global remittance inflows to drop by 5.3% in 2009, was made up for by an 8.1% increase in global flows in 2010. Despite the 1.1% contraction in global inflows in 2020, remittances still exceeded foreign direct investment and official development assistance in low- to middle-income economies (Collins 2023). Inflows to the region slowed by 1.9%, but this was followed by a 3.7% recovery in 2021 and a subsequent leap of 11.4% in 2022. The resilience of remittance flows can be partly attributed to migrants' altruism, as highlighted by various studies (Hagen-Zanker and Siegel 2007; Shimada 2011; Bettin, Presbitero, and Spatafora 2017; and Kim, Kikkawa, and Endriga 2022).

**Figure 5.13: Remittance Inflows to Asia and the Pacific, and the World**

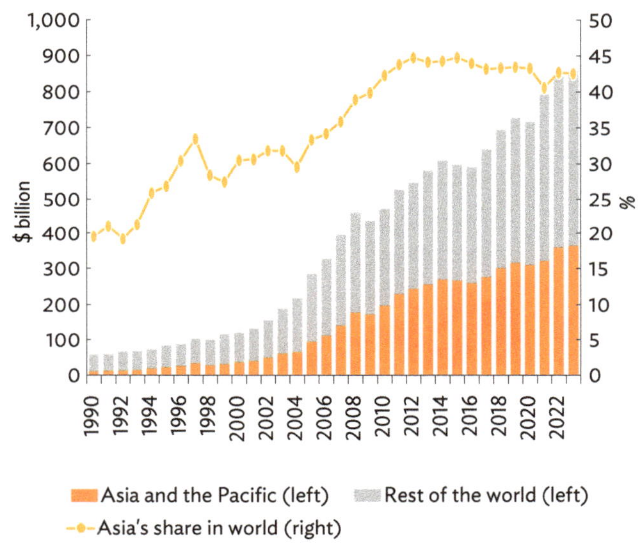


Note: Data for 2024 are estimates.

Source: ADB calculations using data from Ratha, Plaza, and Kim (2024).

**In 2024, remittance inflows continued to grow in South Asia (11.8%) and Southeast Asia (3.6%), as migrant outflows from these subregions continue the prepandemic pace.** (Table 5.1). Inflows to Central Asia bounced back 12.5%, from a 14.2% contraction in 2023, as transfers from the Russian Federation normalized. This led to a $3.7 billion more inflows in 2024 over $29.5 billion in 2023. Significant increases in inflows to Tajikistan ($1.3 billion), the Kyrgyz Republic ($370.5 billion), and Georgia ($210.1 billion) more than offset the combined reductions of $564.1 million for Armenia, Azerbaijan, and Kazakhstan. Remittances to Central Asia in 2023 remained above the $18.4 billion annual average in the 5 years prior to the Russian invasion of Ukraine (Box 5.3). Gross inflows to East Asia, of which around 80% go to the PRC, have been on a decline since 2020, as rising average income in the PRC and an aging population have slowed the pace of less-skilled out-migration (World Bank Group 2023).

**Major recipients from South Asia and Southeast Asia top the list for total remittances in 2024.** For instance, the Philippines received $40.2 billion, Pakistan inflows totaled $33.2 billion, while $26.6 billion flowed into Bangladesh, and $15.3 billion to Indonesia (Figure 5.14a). Relative to GDP, remittances are important to some Central Asian economies, especially Tajikistan (45.4%), the Kyrgyz Republic (23.7%), Uzbekistan (16.9%), and Georgia (13.4%) (Figure 5.15b). Among the Pacific developing economies, inflows are significant to Tonga (38.2%) and Samoa (25.9%). These two Pacific economies rely significantly on inflows from Oceania, where 43,828 Tongans and 91,895 Samoans reside.

**Figure 5.14: Top 10 Remittance Recipient Economies in Asia and the Pacific, 2024**

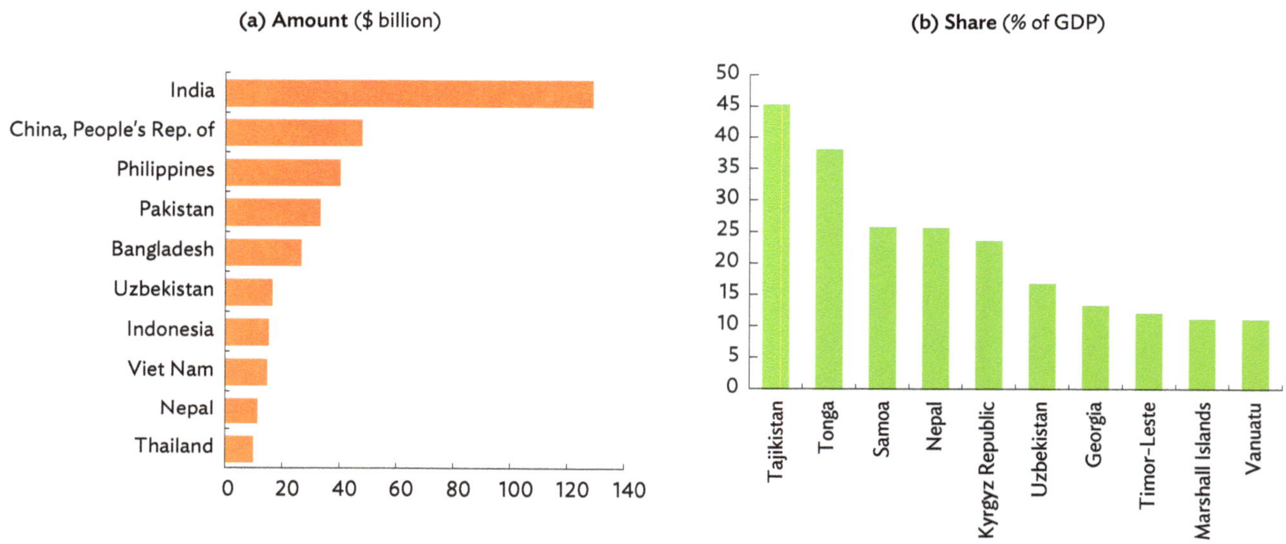


Note: Data for 2024 are estimates.

Source: ADB calculations using data from Ratha, Plaza, and Kim (2024).

**Table 5.1: Remittance Inflows to Asian Subregions**

| Region | Share of Total, 2024 (%) | Remittance Inflows ($ billion) | | Growth (%) | | Level Change ($ billion) | |
|---|---|---|---|---|---|---|---|
| | | 2023 | 2024 | 2023 | 2024 | 2023 | 2024 |
| South Asia | 52.9 | 185.5 | 207.3 | 5.1 | 11.8 | 8.9 | 21.8 |
| Southeast Asia | 22.0 | 83.3 | 86.2 | 5.2 | 3.6 | 4.1 | 3.0 |
| East Asia | 15.6 | 62.7 | 61.3 | -3.6 | -2.2 | -2.3 | -1.4 |
| Central Asia | 8.5 | 29.5 | 33.2 | -14.2 | 12.5 | -4.9 | 3.7 |
| Oceania | 0.7 | 2.5 | 2.6 | 34.9 | 3.3 | 0.7 | 0.1 |
| Pacific | 0.3 | 1.3 | 1.3 | -0.3 | 0.6 | -0.0003 | 0.01 |
| Asia and the Pacific | 100 | 364.9 | 392.1 | 1.8 | 7.5 | 6.5 | 27.2 |

Note: Data for 2024 are estimates.

Source: ADB calculations using data from Ratha, Plaza, and Kim (2024).

**Box 5.3: Recent Trends of Remittance Inflows and/or Money Transfers to Central Asia**

The Russian Federation is the primary destination economy of most Central Asian migrants, serving as a source of foreign exchange through remittances and money transfers, as well as foreign direct investments. As a result, the Russian Federation's economic performance is closely correlated with remittance inflow to Central Asia. In 2022, what was initially expected to be a challenging time for remittance inflows to Central Asia because of the Russian invasion of Ukraine turned out to be a record year as money transfers surged. This increase was driven by capital migration from Russian firms and the relocation of Russians to former Commonwealth of Independent States economies. A strong Russian ruble also boosted remittances to Central Asia.

In 2023, remittances to Central Asia fell sharply by 14.2% from a high base in 2022, as money transfers from the Russian Federation slowed and the depreciation of the Russian ruble (39%) against the United States dollar decreased the value of money transfers from the Russian Federation. The slowdown of money flows from the Russian Federation in 2023 also led to a decline in remittances to Azerbaijan and the Kyrgyz Republic, which are highly dependent on Russian Federation remittances.

**Growth Rates of Remittance Inflows to Central Asian Economies (%, year-on-year)**

| Remittance Recipient Economy | 2020 | 2021 | 2022 | 2023 | H1 2024 | 2023 | |
|---|---|---|---|---|---|---|---|
| | | | | | | Amount ($ billion) | From the Russian Federation (%) |
| Central Asia | −10.5 | 24.1 | 61.9 | −14.2 | 12.0 | 29.5 | 71.2 |
| Armenia | −13.2 | 17.3 | 30.5 | −28.5 | −13.7 | 1.4 | 69.3 |
| Azerbaijan | 10.0 | 8.8 | 158.7 | −51.6 | 1.9 | 1.9 | 55.3 |
| Georgia | −6.6 | 25.3 | 45.8 | 9.0 | −17.7 | 4.2 | 34.8 |
| Kazakhstan | −26.0 | −17.2 | 55.2 | −36.8 | −26.2 | 0.3 | 34.9 |
| Kyrgyz Republic | −2.5 | 14.5 | 7.1 | −11.6 | 6.4 | 2.9 | 93.3 |
| Tajikistan | −5.8 | 33.6 | 83.0 | −13.3 | 56.0 | 4.6 | 80.0 |
| Uzbekistan | −17.1 | 31.0 | 67.2 | −8.7 | 25.0 | 14.2 | 78.0 |

H1 = first half.

Notes: Armenia, Kazakhstan, and the Kyrgyz Republic benefit from visa-free access to Russian Federation labor markets due to their membership in the Eurasian Economic Union.

Sources: ADB calculations using data from Asia-Plus (2024); Daryo (2024); IFAD (2024); Ratha, Plaza, and Kim (2024); and respective central banks.

Source: ADB.

## Facilitating remittances through lower sending costs can contribute to inclusive and sustainable growth.

**Reducing the cost of remittances is crucial because it directly increases the amount of money received by beneficiary households.** The average remittance is about $200 to $300 every 1 or 2 months, but the value and frequency of remitting depends on the migrant's situation and location (IFAD 2024). For example, a World Bank survey of Pacific migrant workers of labor schemes across Australia and New Zealand indicated these migrants send a significant proportion of their wages—with averages ranging from $330 to $500—either every week or every fortnight (Doan, Dornan, and Edwards 2023).. In the Pacific, achieving the United Nations (UN) Sustainable Development Goal (SDG) target of less than 3% per transaction would mean an additional A$79 million annually to households in Fiji, Tonga, and Vanuatu (Collins 2023).

**However, the cost of sending remittances to Asia remains above the SDG 3% target.** As of the second quarter of 2024, the average cost of sending $200 anywhere in the world was 6.7%, which remains above the UN SDG target of 3% by 2030 (Figure 5.15a). In Asia, the cost is lower, at 5.9%, but there are variations across subregions, from 5.5% in South Asia to 8.4% in the Pacific. South Asia, a major migrant-sending subregion, had relatively lower remittance costs than other subregions. The average total cost of remitting to South Asia had also progressively declined from 2018 until mid-2022. Meanwhile, remittance costs in the Pacific have historically been higher than the global average. The continuous trend of derisking and the severance of correspondent banking relationships have kept costs in Pacific remittance corridors at the highest among Asian subregions, although the Pacific's average costs have gradually declined from 11% in 2017 to about 8.4% in the second quarter of 2024.

**Remittance prices vary by service provider and payment instrument.** Banks remain the most expensive followed by regulated money transfer operators (Figure 5.15b). Cash-to-cash remittance transactions—a migrant sends cash sent to a remittance service provider and the recipient collects the proceeds in local currency cash—are the most expensive, averaging 6.4% in Asia. Remittance transactions to the region cost much more if sent through banks (10.1%) than money transfer operators (5.1%). The most affordable sending option, and the closest to the 3% SDG target, is mobile money, which is fully digital end-to-end, and costs around 4% to 5% to send. However, despite the convenience of digital technology, the uptake of digital remittance in Asia and the Pacific remains low, at about 20%, indicating significant room for improvement, particularly in reducing barriers such as the regulatory burdens for cross-border digital remittances (ADB 2024a).

## Another Benefit of Remittances Is Their Potential to Enhance Financial Inclusion

**The intersection between remittances and the finance sector can be a gateway to other financial services, significantly deepening financial inclusion.**

**Figure 5.15: Average Total Cost of Remitting $200** (% of transaction value, as of Q2 2024)

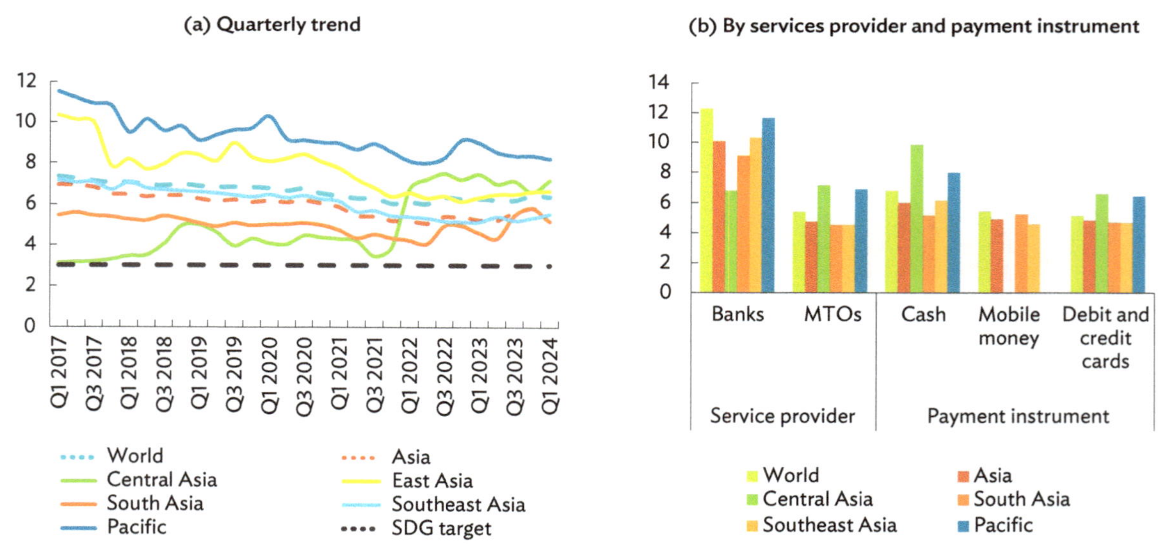


MTO = money transfer operator, Q = quarter, SDG = Sustainable Development Goal.

Source: ADB calculations using data from World Bank. Remittance Prices Worldwide. https://remittanceprices.worldbank.org/ (accessed September 2024).

The goal of financial inclusion is to provide accessible financial products and services to those previously reliant on informal finance or lacked access to traditional banking channels (Box 5.4). Remittances act as a crucial link between migrants and their families, often facilitated by employers or labor programs that require migrants to open deposit accounts for receiving wages. From these accounts, migrants can send funds back home, integrating them into the formal financial system.

**The literature generally shows that remittances strengthen financial inclusion, though some studies suggest an insignificant or negative association, particularly for credit use.** Many studies highlight that remittances help families access formal financial markets by increasing the likelihood of opening bank accounts and improving credit access in various economies (Aga and Peria 2014; Anzoategui, Demirguc-Kunt, and Peria 2014; Ambrosius 2016; Ajefu and Ogebe 2019). The impact tends to be stronger when institutional quality is high (Saydaliyev, Chin, and Oskenbayev 2020). However, other studies suggest that remittances may reduce the demand for formal financial services by acting as a substitute for credit (Ambrosius and Cuecuecha 2013; Brown, Carmignani, and Fayad 2013), with the effect varying based on the availability of formal finance for borrowing (Cuecuecha 2013).

## Making remittances more accessible and affordable can also help improve financial inclusion.

While remittances are regularly sent, not all remittances are captured by the formal financial system. Sending money through formal channels—which is generally the first regular interaction individuals have with financial institutions especially in the rural areas—are met by barriers such as high remittance costs, limited accessibility in remote areas, lack of proper identification, and low financial literacy.[48] A significant portion of remittances

**Box 5.4: Financial Inclusion in Asia by Subregion**

Although financial inclusion offers multiple benefits, it remains uneven across Asia. These benefits include promoting sustainable economic development, reducing poverty and inequality, and fostering entrepreneurship. Access to financial services enhances living standards by encouraging savings, enabling efficient payment systems, and helping households manage financial shocks (Dixit and Ghosh 2013; Le and Nguyen 2020). For firms, it secures capital, boosts productivity, and facilitates trade (Chauvet and Jacolin 2017; Nizam et al. 2020). However, in 2021, only 67% of the population aged 15+ had accounts at formal financial institutions, leaving about 33% unbanked, especially in major migrant-sending subregions like South Asia and Southeast Asia (box figure). In contrast, East Asia and Oceania showed higher financial development, account ownership, and account usage. Access to formal credit is also limited—in 2021, only 21% in Southeast Asia borrowed from a bank and only 6.7% in South Asia used a credit card—despite rising remittance inflows.

**Accounts and Borrowings, 2021** (% of the population age 15+)

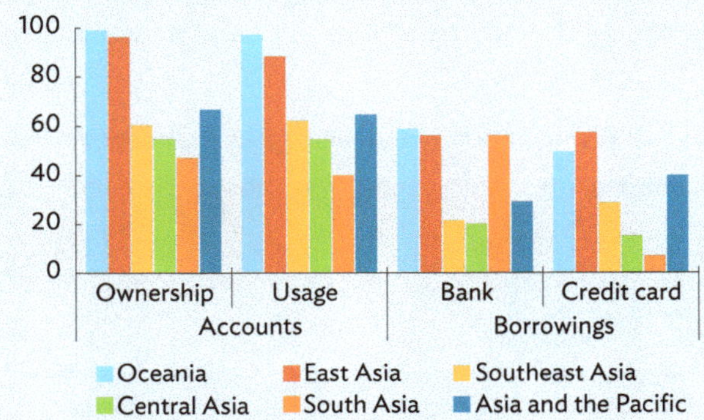


Source: ADB calculations using data from World Bank. The Global Findex Database 2021. https://www.worldbank.org/en/publication/globalfindex/Report (accessed September 2024).

Sources: Chauvet and Jacolin (2017); Dixit and Ghosh (2013); Le and Nguyen (2020); Nizam et al. (2020); and World Bank. The Global Findex Database 2021. https://www.worldbank.org/en/publication/globalfindex/Report (accessed September 2024).

48 According to the International Fund for Agricultural Development (2024), more than 50% of remittances are received in rural areas with limited access to financial services.

is still collected in cash from physical locations in remittance-recipient economies, presenting a major obstacle to financial inclusion (Table 5.2). To overcome these barriers, economies must champion the following:

- **Promoting digital channels.** Encouraging the use of digital channels among migrant workers and their families can significantly reduce transaction costs and improve accessibility. Technologies such as mobile money enable real-time transfers, making remittances faster, cheaper, and more accessible. Also, digital means promote integration into formal finance sectors, further driving financial inclusion by linking remittance transactions to broader financial services.
- **Strengthening the regulatory environment.** Governments and institutions must strengthen laws and regulations that support the inclusion of underserved migrants and their families, and new entrants in the digital and mobile money space. They should integrate domestic and international payment systems, encourage competition among service providers, and protect consumer rights to ensure fair access to financial services.
- **Financial education and digital literacy.** All parties in the remittance services chain must do their part to help educate recipients on the basics of digital finance, the benefits of formal financial services, and expand access to digital services that enhance financial inclusion. By offering additional financial products, such as savings accounts or insurance linked to remittances, providers can improve the financial well-being of remittance-receiving families and contribute to the local economy.

## Advancing Digitalization Can Facilitate Remittances and Promote Financial Inclusion

**Digitalization can reduce the transaction cost of remittances, promote transparency to help comply with Anti-Money Laundering and Combating the Financing of Terrorism (AML/CFT) regulations, and enhance access to the formal financial system for migrants and their families.** It offers significant benefits to both remittance senders and recipients, reducing the cost of remittances, improving the speed of transactions, and providing trackable, secure payment. This adds a layer of certainty to payments and expands access to a broader range of financial services (IFAD 2024).

**Financial technology improves interoperability, enabling seamless cross-border payments and remittances.** For instance, Project Mandala, a collaboration between the Bank for International Settlements Innovation Hub and the

**Table 5.2: Framework for Leveraging Remittances to Enhance Financial Inclusion**

| Status Quo | Challenges | | Enablers | | | Desired Outcome |
|---|---|---|---|---|---|---|
| Regular Remittance Flows | Accessibility | Reliance on Cash | Digital Channels | Regulatory Environment | Financial Education | Financial Inclusion |
| Remittances are sent regularly through formal and informal channels. | Distance, cost of overcoming physical barriers, lack of knowledge, and lack of trust are but some of the barriers hindering remittance senders and receivers from accessing formal finance channels. | Many receivers still prefer to collect their remittances in cash from physical locations. | Advocating for greater usage of digital channels makes remittances faster, cheaper, and more accessible. | Strong and improved laws and regulations foster better risk-based approaches to remittance AML-KYC compliance, and promote security and consumer protection while supporting inclusion of underserved communities. | Educating senders and receivers about the benefits of formal financial services, including digital knowledge. | Remittances function as a "gateway" to establish a long-term relationship with a financial institution. |

AML-KYC = anti-money laundering and know-your-customer.

Source: ADB; and Isaacs and Capal (2024).

central banks of Australia, the Republic of Korea, Malaysia, and Singapore, aims to automate compliance procedures for cross-border financial transactions by embedding regulatory requirements directly into transaction protocols, resulting in regulatory-compliant and more streamlined cross-border payments. Mobile applications from fintech firms in the United Kingdom and Singapore, among others, developed software to launch cross-border digital remittance services, such as Wise (formerly TransferWise) and Nium (formerly Instarem), as well as technological linkages such as Singapore's PayNow, which offers real time payments to Malaysia's DuitNow, Thailand's PromptPay, and India's UPI (Colombu 2023). These services offer the user a much wider range of remittance corridor options than mobile network operator-based mobile money and, in some cases, additional payment services. Through correspondent partnerships, firms such as Wise and Nium are offering almost global coverage.

**In Asia, rapid technological developments are accelerating the adoption of digital payments and remittances.** While overall take-up for digital remittances remains less than 20% (ADB 2024b), the use of app-based remittance platforms is growing quickly thanks to their convenience and safety. A recent Money Travels report from VISA (2024) suggests that 70% to 80% of remittance users in Asia are adopting app-based digital payment options for sending and receiving funds. On average, the share of Asian populations who had sent or received digital payments is 60%, with variations across subregions—from a low of 32% in South Asia to highs of at least 93% in East Asia and Oceania.[49] Digitalization, being less costly than sending cash, has reinforced the adoption of mobile money for remittances, the most affordable among payment instruments, with costs averaging 4.7% in Asia and 5.7% globally, as of the second quarter of 2024.

**The growing adoption of domestic digital remittance services highlights their effectiveness in replacing cash-based transactions, a trend that could similarly reshape international remittances once digital channels are fully implemented.** Between 2014 and 2021, the uptake of electronic accounts in Asia and the Pacific increased by nearly as much as the decrease in reliance on cash. Armenia, Bangladesh, the PRC, Mongolia, Thailand, Viet Nam, and most South Asian economies saw significant increases in electronic accounts usage while reducing dependence on cash payments (Figure 5.16). As digital platforms for cross-border remittances become more accessible, the shift from cash to digital channels is expected to become pronounced. However, challenges such as restrictive national regulations on international payments and the lack of interoperability among network providers remain significant barriers that must be addressed.

**Figure 5.16: Form of Receipt of Domestic Remittances in Asia, 2014 and 2021** (% change of senders and recipients aged 15+)

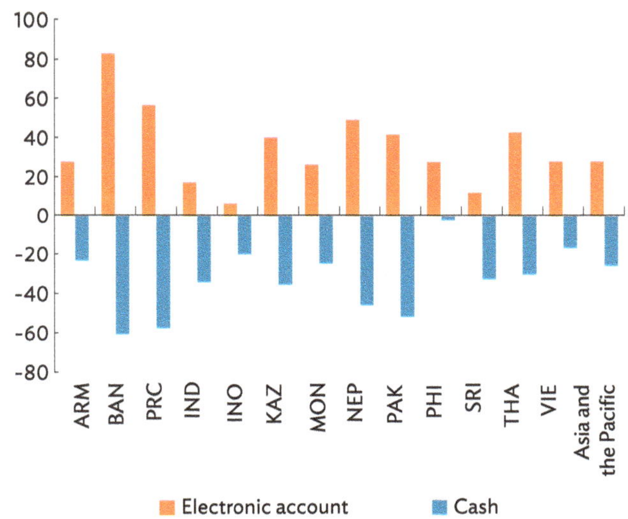


ARM = Armenia, BAN = Bangladesh, PRC = People's Republic of China, IND = India, INO = Indonesia, KAZ = Kazakhstan, MON = Mongolia, NEP = Nepal, PAK = Pakistan, PHI = Philippines, SRI = Sri Lanka, THA = Thailand, VIE = Viet Nam.

Source: ADB calculations using data from World Bank. The Global Findex Database 2021. https://www.worldbank.org/en/publication/globalfindex/Report (accessed September 2024).

## Policy Implications of Remittance Digitalization

**Adequate physical and technological infrastructure is key to digitalization.** Leveraging digital remittance to lower the average cost of sending funds and impact financial inclusion requires secure and efficient payment systems, widespread internet accessibility and affordability, and a

[49] ADB calculations using data from World Bank's Global Financial Index Database. https://www.worldbank.org/en/publication/globalfindex/Report (accessed October 2024).

robust and responsive regulatory and legal infrastructure. Expanding mobile networks is particularly important in rural areas where access to formal finance is limited. Increasing investments in technology and digital infrastructure, through foreign direct investments and public–private partnerships, could encourage remittance service providers to expand and be innovative with services, while aiming for greater client reach at lower cost that is closer to the 3% SDG target. Greater investments in infrastructure could also result in more physical points of access to finance such as ATMs, bank branches, and mobile money providers, thereby potentially improving financial inclusion.[50]

**Legal and regulatory frameworks for digital transactions should address safety and security concerns while fostering innovation and reducing costs.** In Pacific developing economies, for instance, AML and know-your-customer (KYC) compliance and derisking operations of banks since 2013 pushed up costs, reduced the number of operators, and limited the range of remittance services available. While shifting to mobile money still requires compliance with AML and KYC regulations, the process is simpler than opening a bank account. A mobile wallet option could empower people in rural areas or those with little exposure to financial services, many of whom already own a mobile phone, hence enabling access to basic financial services with existing KYC documentation. Digital IDs could also help remittance service providers with an efficient way of verifying identities and complement e-KYC and AML compliance modules.

In addition, regulations to protect consumers and ensure data privacy and cybersecurity will help build trust and safeguard finance sector integrity. The digital environment thrives when access to data is secured, but unimpeded. However, restrictive data localization laws, though well-intentioned, may inhibit the mobile network operators from offering cross-border financial services.[51] Complying with such regulations increases business costs, limits potential for scalability and expansion, reduces the efficiency of mobile money operations, and could even limit the access to technology to mobile money network operations (Global System for Mobile Communications 2024). Harmonization of cross-border data transfer requirements will allow for more efficient business operations across different jurisdictions, increased innovation, and the seamless flow of information for both companies and consumers.

**Financial literacy and knowledge of digital finance are essential for both senders and receivers.** Providing economy-specific education to migrants prior to their departure can help build trust and understanding of financial products. Educating remittance households is just as important as educating the sender—if these recipients can be made to use a transaction account, the funds can be received and accessed securely for daily household expenses, as well as gradually building funds toward saving and investment purposes.[52] Engaging remittance-service providers in the delivery of financial literacy programs could be more effective as this would best showcase the benefits of technology-enabled money transfer services and work in collaboration with community organizations, nongovernment organizations, and migrant network groups.

**Enhanced bilateral, regional, and global cooperation could foster the development impact of remittances to digitalize the remittance environment for greater financial inclusion.** Regional bodies are keeping their cooperation in step with the growth opportunities of remittance and digitalization. For example, the ASEAN launched negotiations for a Digital Economy Framework

50 For every 100,000 adults in Asia, physical access to financial services averaged 44 ATMs and 15 bank branches (Source: ADB calculations using data from G20 Financial Inclusion Indicators Database accessed through World Bank Group. Prosperity Data360. https://prosperitydata360.worldbank.org/en/dataset/WB+GPFI+G20FII (accessed September 2024).) Only 12% of females in South Asia have internet access relative to 72% of females in East Asia and 93% in Oceania. And although 84% of the region's 15+ population have access to a mobile phone, the share is lower among the poorest 40%.

51 For instance, in Pakistan, the National Database and Registration Authority Ordinance 48 and the National Registration Act of 1973 impose limitations on accessing and disclosing information from the National Database. In Bangladesh, laws on data restriction inhibit mobile money operators from engaging in cross-border payments (Global System for Mobile Communications 2024).

52 One example is the Famili i Redi (Family Ready) program launched in Vanuatu in 2022 as a predeparture training program for migrant workers and their families that includes a module on managing finances and remittances. Around the same time, Vodafone Fiji introduced a mobile wallet remittance service from Fiji M-PAiSA to M-Vatu in Vanuatu. Vanuatu has long been underserved in remittance-receiving options, with only a handful of Western Union payout options in urban areas, while workers' families often live in remote rural areas.

Agreement in September 2023 with, among other key priorities, the target of improving how the region cooperates on digital trade, cross-border e-commerce, and digital payments (ASEAN 2023). Currently still negotiated among member states, the digital framework will be completed soon. In Central Asia, the Platform for Remittances, Investment and Migrants' Entrepreneurship Central Asia Initiative was launched in March 2024, in cooperation with the European Union and the International Fund for Agricultural Development, to maximize the socioeconomic impact of remittances in Kazakhstan, the Kyrgyz Republic, Tajikistan, and Uzbekistan (IFAD 2024). In October 2024, APEC finance ministers issued a joint statement which underscored the importance of digitalization, especially digital financial education, and regional cooperation in promoting inclusive finance, reducing digital divides, and building resilient, inclusive and sustainable APEC economies (APEC 2024b).

## International Tourism

### International Tourism Maintained Steady Growth Until 2019

International tourism reached a peak of 1.46 billion global arrivals and generated $1.49 trillion in tourism receipts in 2019. Global arrivals and receipts had been on an upward trend since 1995 except for a slight decline caused by external shocks (i.e., SARS in 2003 and the global financial crisis in 2008). A strong global economy, an expanding middle class in emerging economies, the rise of low-cost carriers, the introduction of new business models, and enhanced visa facilitation fueled the robust growth of tourism (UN Tourism 2019). However, the COVID-19 pandemic halted cross-border travel and caused the deepest drop in both international arrivals and receipts. In 2020, global arrivals declined by 72% and receipts fell by 62%. Among all the regions, Asia and the Pacific suffered the most significant decline.

One in every four tourists in the world visited Asia in 2019, but the following year's inbound tourism flows plunged to 62 million, an 83.1% decline year-on-year. The share of Asia to global arrivals fell to as low as 6.8% in 2021. Asia's combined loss in tourism receipts during the pandemic amounted to $844 billion.

International tourism is gradually recovering. In 2023, 1.3 billion people traveled overseas, while tourism receipts climbed to $1.53 trillion, 3% higher than in 2019. In both international arrivals and tourism receipts, the Middle East led the recovery as it already exceeded its prepandemic arrivals by 16%, and its 2019 receipts by 43%. Meanwhile, Asia was the slowest to rebound. The region hosted 260.7 million tourists, equivalent to 70.8% of its 2019 volume, and generated $320.7 billion or 80.3% of its 2019 level (Figure 5.17).

From 2010 to 2019, international arrivals to Asia grew by an average annual rate of 7.6%, outpacing the global annual average of 5.1%, with the intraregional tourism share increasing from 73.1% to 77.3%. East Asia and Southeast Asia were the key contributors to the region's growth since they drew the largest influx of foreign tourists and generated the highest receipts. Prior to the pandemic, at least 80% of Asia's inbound tourists visited destinations in East Asia and Southeast Asia (Figure 5.18a). While there was a drastic decline in tourist inflows during the pandemic, inbound tourism is slowly going back to normal. By the end of 2023, 38.9% of Asia's tourists traveled to East Asia while 37.6% visited Southeast Asia.

Central Asia's share to Asia's total arrivals increased moderately, from less than 1% in 1995 to 12.6% in 2023 and reflected the subregion's efforts to boost tourism. Meanwhile, arrivals to the Pacific remained consistently small relative to the rest of Asia. Since 1995, the Pacific has accounted for less than 1% of Asia's arrivals and receipts (Figure 5.18b).

Prior to the pandemic, many destinations in Asia heavily relied on outbound travel from the PRC. For instance, around 67% of tourists to Hong Kong, China, from 2015 to 2019 are attributed to arrivals from the PRC (ADB 2024b). In addition, the PRC ranked first followed by Japan as top source markets for the Republic of Korea. The PRC emerged as ASEAN's largest market in 2015,

**Figure 5.17: Tourism Performance by Region of Destination**

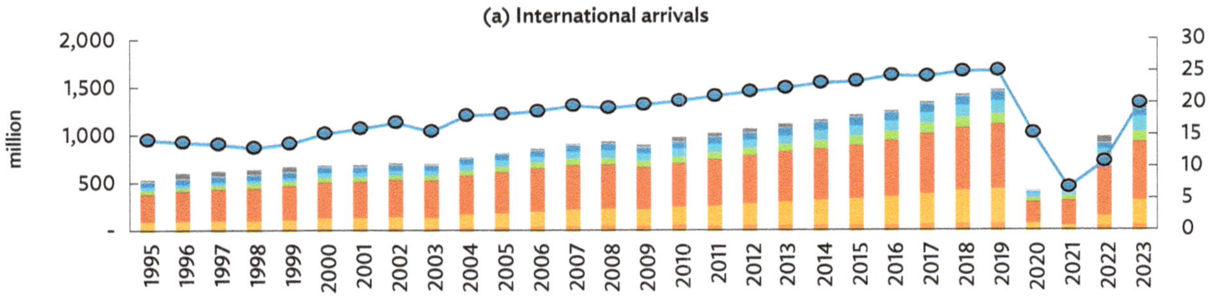


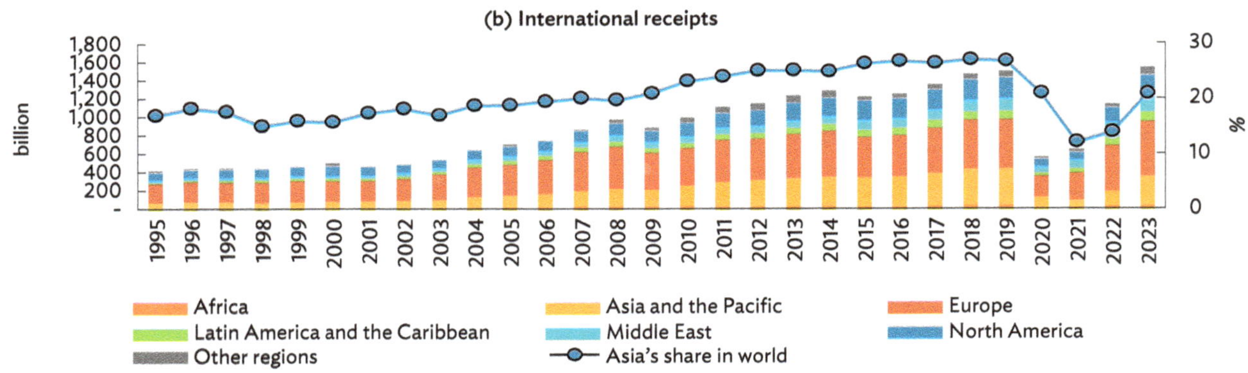


Source: ADB calculations using data from CEIC Data Company (accessed December 2024); UN Tourism. Compendium of Tourism Statistics data set. https://www.unwto.org/tourism-statistics/tourism-statistics-database (accessed September 2024); and UN Tourism. International Tourism Highlights, 2024 Edition. https://doi.org/10.18111/9789284425808 (accessed December 2024).

**Figure 5.18: Tourism Performance of Asia by Subregion**

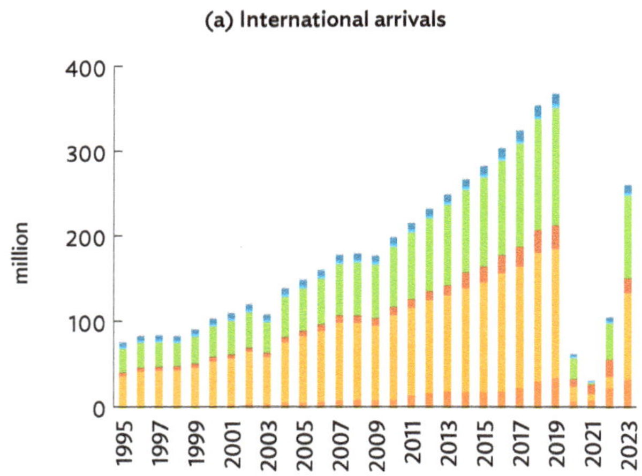


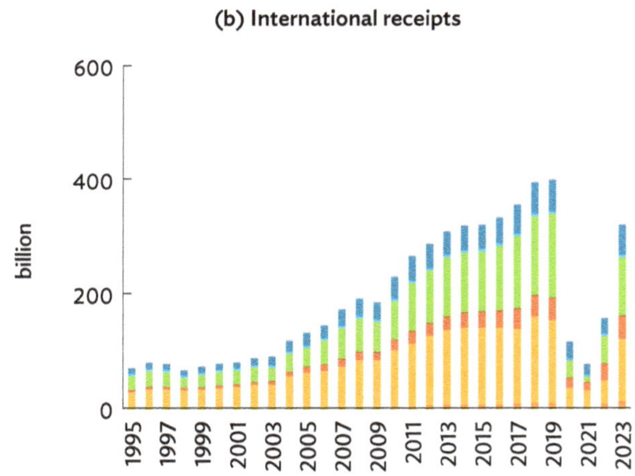


Source: ADB calculations using data from CEIC Data Company (accessed December 2024); UN Tourism. Compendium of Tourism Statistics data set. https://www.unwto.org/tourism-statistics/tourism-statistics-database (accessed September 2024); and UN Tourism. International Tourism Highlights, 2024 Edition. https://doi.org/10.18111/9789284425808 (accessed December 2024).

a strong dependence that has made destinations highly vulnerable to shocks. The pandemic highlighted the need to look for alternative source markets to ensure sustainability and resilience of the tourism sector. Of late, intraregional travel in ASEAN is fast becoming an alternative to many destinations. It accounted for 50% of the total travel in ASEAN in 2022, while only 35% is attributed to arrivals from ASEAN in 2019 (ADB 2024a). ASEAN is increasingly being seen as an important source of tourists for other destinations, such as the Republic of Korea, as well (Box 5.5).

## Unique Tourism Characteristics Can Be Observed in Selected Subregions and Destinations

International tourist arrivals may not automatically translate to high receipts per arrival. While only 3.8% of Asia's international arrivals is attributed to Oceania, the subregion generated 16.8% of Asia's tourism receipts in 2023 (Table 5.3). It earned the highest tourism receipts; at $5,394 per arrival, or more than five times the earnings of East Asia ($1,071) and Southeast Asia ($1,041).

**Box 5.5: Association of Southeast Asian Nations—An Opportunity for the Republic of Korea**

Economies in the Association of Southeast Asian Nations (ASEAN) are emerging as a market for outbound tourism. In 2012, 60.3 million tourists from ASEAN traveled abroad. From 2015 to 2019, that volume increased by an annual average rate of 10.2% and in 2019, 101.3 million tourists from ASEAN visited overseas destinations (box figure 1).

International arrivals from ASEAN used to be concentrated in Southeast Asia, where 68.2% of total ASEAN international trips were made in 2012. In recent years, East Asia has become more popular among ASEAN tourists. Destinations in East Asia welcomed 37 million tourists from ASEAN in 2019, more than a threefold increase from 2012.

From 2015 to 2019, the number of tourist arrivals from ASEAN to the Republic of Korea expanded by 14.7% a year on average, peaking at 2.7 million in 2019. This accounted for 15.4% of the Republic of Korea's total international arrivals, making ASEAN the third-biggest market for the Republic of Korea, after the People's Republic of China and Japan. During the pandemic (2021–2022), ASEAN contributed significantly to the economy's recovery by accounting for 30% of its international arrivals (box figure 2).

ASEAN's notable economic growth, expanding middle class, and a strong interest in Korean culture among the youth have fueled the increase in its tourism flows to the Republic of Korea. Moreover, initiatives and reforms that enhance cross-border travel have been instrumental in facilitating the movement of people between ASEAN and the Republic of Korea.

**1: Association of Southeast Asian Nations Arrivals to the World by Destination** (million)

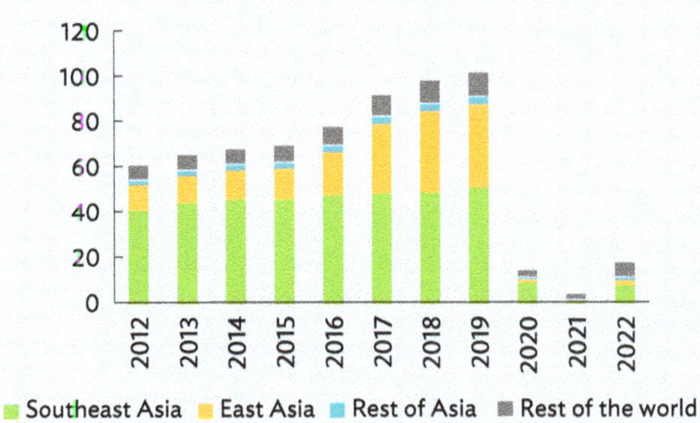


Source: ADB calculations using UN Tourism. Data on Outbound Tourism. https://www.unwto.org/tourism-statistics/key-tourism-statistics. (accessed September 2024).

**2: Share of Association of Southeast Asian Nations to Total International Arrivals in the Republic of Korea** (%)

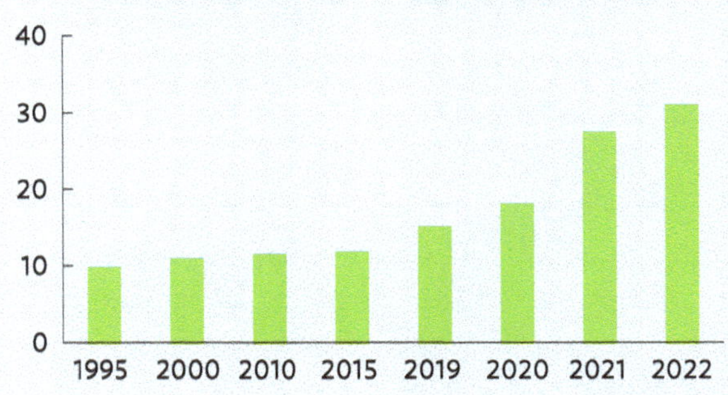


Source: ADB calculations using data from UN Tourism. Data on Outbound Tourism. https://www.unwto.org/tourism-statistics/key-tourism-statistics (accessed September 2024); and UN Tourism. UNWTO Tourism Statistics Database. https://www.unwto.org/tourism-statistics/tourism-statistics-database (accessed September 2024).

Source: ADB (2024a).

**Table 5.3: International Arrivals and Receipts in Asia by Subregion, 2023**

| Subregion | International Arrivals | | International Tourism Receipts | | Receipts per Arrival |
|---|---|---|---|---|---|
| | million | % of international arrivals to Asia | $ billion | % of Asia's tourism receipts | $ |
| Central Asia | 33.0 | 12.7 | 14.1 | 4.4 | 427 |
| East Asia | 101.5 | 38.9 | 108.8 | 33.9 | 1,071 |
| South Asia | 16.5 | 6.3 | 40.4 | 12.6 | 2,444 |
| Southeast Asia | 98.1 | 37.6 | 102.1 | 31.8 | 1,041 |
| Pacific | 1.5 | 0.6 | 1.4 | 0.4 | 912 |
| Oceania | 10 | 3.8 | 54.0 | 16.8 | 5,394 |
| Asia and the Pacific | 260.7 | 100 | 320.8 | 100 | 1,231 |

Source: ADB calculations using data from UN Tourism. International Tourism Highlights, 2024 Edition. https://doi.org/10.18111/9789284425808 (accessed December 2024).

This suggests that Oceania's investments in tourism development have yielded higher nominal returns for every tourist compared to any other subregion in Asia. In contrast, Central Asia receives $427 per tourist, the lowest in Asia.

Across subregional economies, Australia received the highest amount of tourism receipts with $46.1 billion, followed by Japan (Figure 5.19a). It also earned the highest receipts per arrival with $6,410 (Figure 5.19b). The high receipts per arrival can be attributed to the tourists' length of stay and destination's relatively high costs. Compared to tourists in Thailand (9.3 nights) and Japan (6 nights), tourists in Australia (27 nights) stayed longer (UN Tourism 2023). Moreover, compared to other destinations in Asia, Australia's travel costs are more expensive. Its price competitiveness score worsened from 3.5 in 2019 to 2.75 in 2024 (World Economic Forum 2024).

High tourism receipts per arrival can help promote economic growth. Previously, destinations concentrated on attracting more tourists and generating economic benefits that come with tourism such as employment, livelihood, revenues, and foreign exchange receipts. Shifting the destination's efforts to focus on quality tourism as opposed to mass tourism can put less pressure on the destination's natural resources and also help ensure that growth improves local communities' quality of life (World Economic Forum 2019a).

### Tourism's impact varies across economies.

With 63.3% of its GDP in 2023 derived from tourism, Maldives was the most reliant on tourism (Figure 5.19c). Many economies in the Pacific consider tourism as a key economic pillar. Tourism's contribution in the economies of Samoa, Fiji, and Vanuatu were among the highest in Asia. Due to their heavy reliance on tourism, the economies in the Pacific were severely affected during the pandemic. This clearly illustrates the need for tourism-dependent economies to diversify to gain more resilience to external shocks. While tourism activities offer opportunities to other sectors of an economy, it raises merchandise trade because of greater familiarity with products of destination economies (Box 5.6).

## Physical and Institutional Connectivity Are Key Determinants for Tourism

Connectivity enhances the appeal and competitiveness of destinations. The availability and quality of physical infrastructure and institutional policies are essential to facilitate reliable, seamless, and price-competitive tourist movements between or within subregions and to attractions within a destination. Two types of infrastructure connectivity influence international tourism in Asia. The first is cross-border connectivity that includes the transportation infrastructure and institutional air service agreements, motor vehicle transport agreements, and visa policies. The second

**Figure 5.19: Top Recipients of Tourism Receipts**

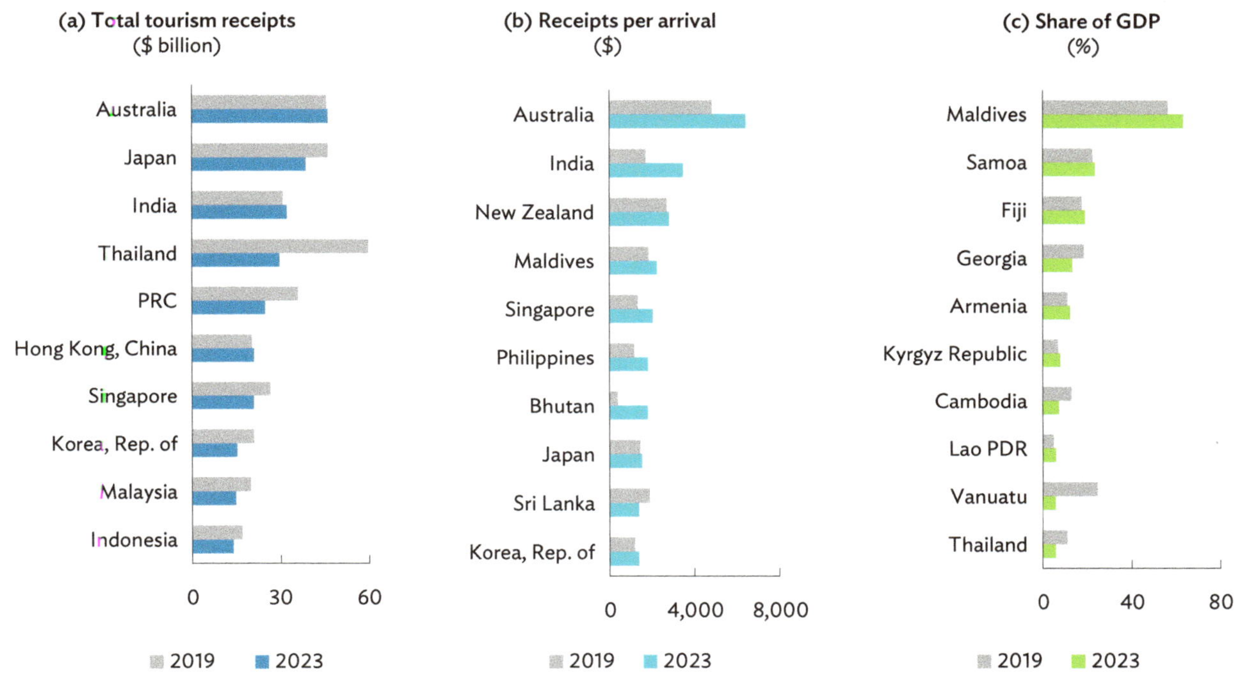


PRC = People's Republic of China, GDP = gross domestic product, Lao PDR = Lao People's Democratic Republic.

Sources: ADB calculations using data from International Monetary Fund. World Economic Outlook Database April 2024. https://www.imf.org/en/Publications/WEO/weo-database/2024/April (accessed October 2024); and UN Tourism. International Tourism Highlights, 2024 Edition. https://doi.org/10.18111/9789284425808 (accessed December 2024).

**Box 5.6: Tourism Inflow Interlinkages with Merchandise Exports—The Case of Pacific Island Economies**

Tourism is an important driver of the economy, especially for economies that heavily depend on tourism receipts. Prior to the pandemic, more than 50% of the total exports of goods and services of the Pacific[a] are attributed to tourism exports. Moreover, tourism mitigates the deficit in merchandise trade. Many economies in the Pacific run a current account surplus because the share of tourism exports to the trade balance is large. The share of tourism exports to the trade balance is more than 100% in the Cook Islands (165.5%), Fiji (135.7%), Solomon Islands (274%), and Vanuatu (108.7%).

High dependence on tourism makes economies in the Pacific susceptible to crises. For example, the goods and services trade deficit in Samoa increased from 13.4% of GDP in 2019 to 40.4% in 2022 due to the absence of cross-border travel during the coronavirus disease pandemic. Thus, to improve resilience, economies in the Pacific need to advance industries that directly benefit from tourism (i.e., food production, handicrafts).

Previous literature shows that trade can push the development of tourism by stimulating the growth of travel (Kulendran and Wilson 2000; Kumar, Prashar, and Jana 2019), and by reducing the costs of market development (Leitão 2010; Santana-Gallego, Ledesma-Rodríguez, and Pérez-Rodríguez 2016). On the other hand, international travel can increase trade by increasing imports of goods that tourists demand (Shan and Wilson 2001; Kumar, Prashar, and Jana 2019) and enable domestic firms to penetrate a foreign market without an expensive marketing campaign (Brau and Pinna 2013). Tourism also helps lessen trade costs since it facilitates understanding of culture and business practices among visitors and host communities

*continued on next page*

*Box 5.6: continued*

(Santana-Gallego, Ledesma-Rodríguez, and Pérez-Rodríguez 2016).

Using an augmented gravity model, the study examines tourist inflows as a determinant of merchandise exports for Pacific economies. The findings reveal that a 1% increase in inbound tourists leads to a 0.17% increase in merchandise trade. This is consistent with existing literature, which shows that international tourist arrivals stimulate a rise in exports through the reduction of trade costs (Santana-Gallego, Ledesma-Rodríguez, and Pérez-Rodríguez 2016). The study also found that the increase in merchandise exports will be higher if international tourists come from source markets that have a common language, free trade agreements, and an enabling visa policy.

Economies in the Pacific can utilize international tourism to develop garments and souvenir-related manufacturing, for example. These products have the potential to be exported if they can be customized to the preferences of international tourists.

[a] The Pacific comprises the Cook Islands, Fiji, Kiribati, the Marshall Islands, the Federated States of Micronesia, Nauru, Niue, Palau, Papua New Guinea, Samoa, Solomon Islands, Tonga, Tuvalu, and Vanuatu.

Source: Gupta et al. (2024).

is domestic infrastructure connectivity such as inland transportation, information and communication technology (ICT), and tourist services infrastructure. Box 5.7 provides an empirical analysis of the influence of infrastructure connectivity on international tourism demand in Asia and the Pacific.

## Cross-border physical connectivity varies based on geography and openness of subregional members.

Air transport is the leading mode of travel in Asia and the Pacific. Travel by land and air are the most prevalent modes of transportation used by tourists. In 2005, 59.2% of total arrivals in Asia traveled by land (Figure 5.20). Over the years, arrivals by air transport have been growing at a faster pace than land transport, and shares to total arrivals have also increased. Visitors traveling by air represented 35% of the region's arrivals in 2005, but in 2019 the share increased to 47.3%. During the pandemic, air travel was the dominant mode of transport as it accounted for at least 60% during 2020–2022.

Among the subregions, East Asia has the most extensive international air connectivity in terms of absolute number of flights and seats, followed by Southeast Asia.[53] Its share of the total flights in Asia increased significantly, from 40.7% in 2010 to 48.4% in 2019. There are more intrasubregional flights in East Asia and Southeast Asia than in other subregions. Both Central Asia and South Asia have limited intrasubregional flights, less than 25% of the total flights in each subregion. Nonetheless, based on the International Air Transport Association's international air connectivity index used in global competitiveness rankings, destination-weighted seats grew faster in the Pacific, South Asia, and Central Asia (Figure 5.21).

Aviation expanded rapidly, driven by the liberalization of bilateral and regional air transport markets that enabled the growth of the low-cost carriers, and expansion and construction of new international gateways through public and private investments (e.g., public–private partnership projects in three airports in the Philippines, and three airports in Cambodia).

[53] ADB estimates using data from the International Civil Aviation Organization data set—Passenger Traffic by City Pair, 2019–2022.

**Box 5.7: The Role of Infrastructure Connectivity on International Tourism Development in Asia and the Pacific**

Infrastructure determines the attractiveness of a tourism destination (Seetanah et al. 2011). Literature review shows the effects of various types of infrastructure apart from factors such as income, population, and distance (Rosselló-Nadal and Santana-Gallego 2022) on international tourism development.

Transport infrastructure "shortens" distance (Gołembski and Majewska 2018) and lowers travel time and costs for tourists (Peng et al. 2015). Meanwhile, high-quality transportation boosts tourism flows and overall competitiveness (Prideaux 2000; Khadaroo and Seetanah 2008). The distance from origin to destination, a proxy for travel costs, influences the mode of transport used by tourists (Thrane 2015). Transport infrastructure is a significant determinant (Seetanah and Khadaroo 2009) on tourist inflows to a destination. The imposition of visa requirements as cross-border institutional connectivity reduces international tourism movements (Rosselló-Nadal and Santana-Gallego 2024).

Information and communication technology (ICT) infrastructure (measured using indicators such as mobile and fixed broadband subscriptions) and accommodation infrastructure, a proxy of destination capacity, both have positive influence on inbound tourism flows and destination income (Lee et al. 2021; Khadaroo and Seetanah 2007).

Using an augmented gravity model, the study investigates the determinants of international tourism flows from global source tourism markets to the destinations in Asia during 1995–2022. The gravity function is specified to include different characteristics of the origin markets and destinations (i.e., origin specific, destination specific, and variables specific to origin-destination). The key variables of interest are the destination transportation stocks as a proxy for the transport modes (air, land, and sea), accommodation and ICT infrastructure, and visa policies. The findings reveal that transportation infrastructure has positive and significant effects on international tourism flows, consistent with the literature, and with air transportation exerting stronger influence, largely because of the distance from the top origin markets. A 1% increase in air transport capital, proxied by international flights, leads to a 0.98% increase in international tourism flows to Asia and a 1.1% increase in intra-Asia tourism. Restrictive visa policies tend to reduce international tourism flows by 52.05% to Asia and by 48.67% in intra-Asia tourism flows.

The availability of common borders and proximity of nearby destinations for multidestination products have positive effects specifically for landlocked economies of Southeast Asia and Central Asia. The impacts of road infrastructure, ports, ICT infrastructure, and accommodation capacities varied across subregions.

Improvements in infrastructure connectivity in the subregions facilitated international tourism flows from 1995 to 2022 (with declines during the COVID-19 pandemic). Nonetheless, empirical data highlighted that reforms in cross-border institutional connectivity, like air service agreements and visa policies in the subregions, facilitated the growth of their air transport infrastructure and international tourism. Investments in physical and institutional infrastructure connectivity particularly in less-developed subregions will help provide more seamless and convenient transfers across modes of transport and increase international tourism growth.

Source: Rodolfo (2024).

**Variation on the prominent mode of transport is observed based on the geographic context.** More than half of tourists in Southeast Asia travel by air. Air transport's share went up from 56% in 2005 to 67% in 2019. Southeast Asia's aviation market grew rapidly, driven primarily by low-cost carriers that accounted for shares of international seats of around 5% in Central Asia and 17% in the Central Asia Regional Economic Cooperation (CAREC) region; 34% in Southeast Asia; 20% in Northeast Asia; and 24% in South Asia (ADB 2024c).

In subregions that share borders (i.e., Central Asia, East Asia), land travel is the dominant means of transportation. For example, 62.4% of arrivals to East Asia traveled by land in 2019. This is heavily attributed to same-day visitors from the PRC to Hong Kong, China. Interregional travel from Southeast Asia to East Asia also increased from 6.5 million in 2015 to 25.9 million in 2019. In the Greater Mekong Subregion (GMS), linkages provided by new transnational highways and bridges between the urban centers have reduced travel times and increased options for visitors to use international tourist coach services and personal vehicles for intraregional travel (GMS Secretariat 2015).

**Figure 5.20: Share of Arrivals by Mode of Travel** (%)

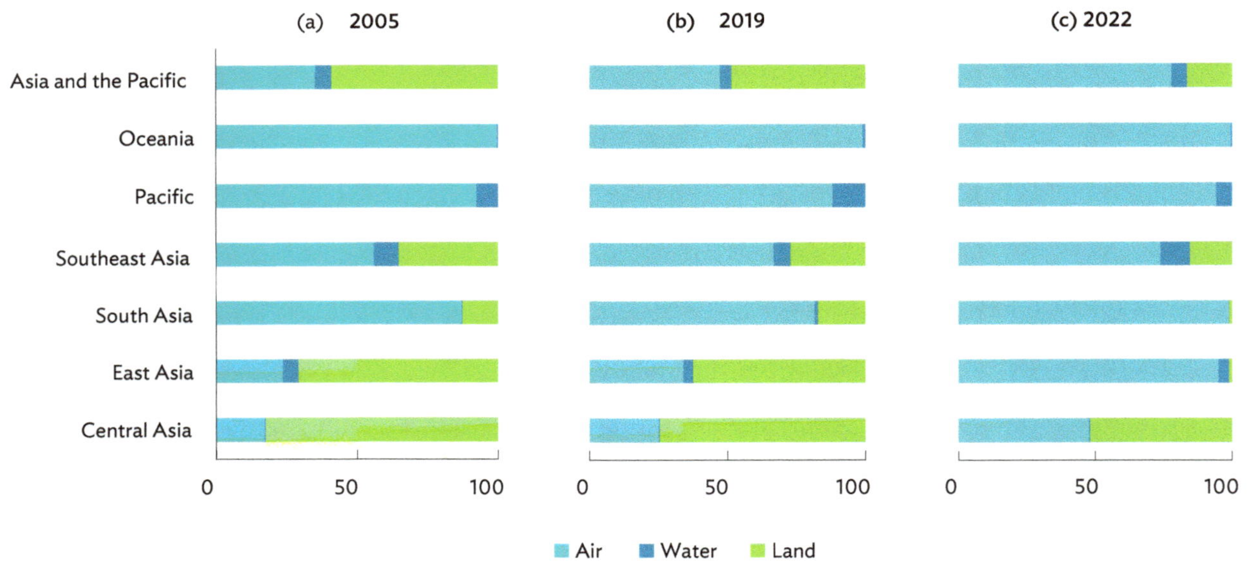


Note: Arrivals include same-day tourists.

Source: ADB calculations using data from UN Tourism. Compendium of Tourism Statistics data set. https://www.unwto.org/tourism-statistics/tourism-statistics-database (accessed August 2024).

**Figure 5.21: International Air Connectivity Growth, 2009–2019** (%)

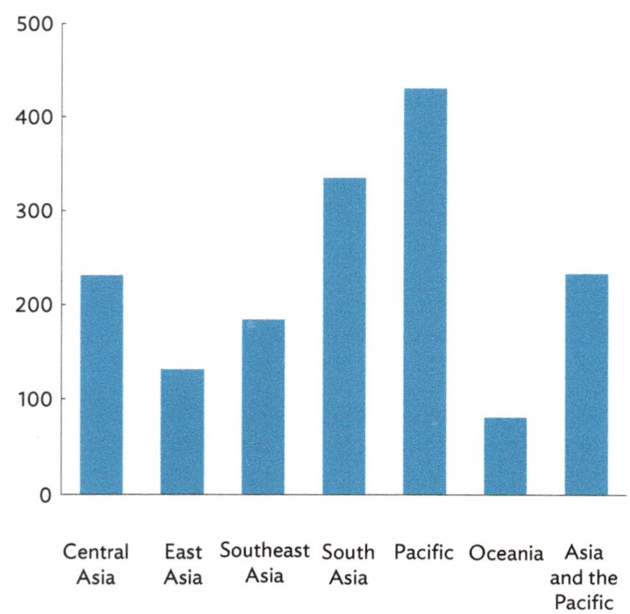


Note: Asia and the Pacific refers to the average growth rate in the region.

Source: International Air Transport Association (2020).

In Central Asia, land transportation represents more than 70% of arrivals to the subregion. Road and rail connections in Central Asia and between the CAREC economies are already used in several regional tour circuits, which ranges from 10 to 120 days, for tourists from Europe to the CAREC region (ADB 2019). Cross-border road transport is the key infrastructure in tourism circuit development in South Asia and in subtourism circuits such as the Great Himalayan Trail in the South Asia Subregional Economic Cooperation (SASEC) region.

The relative shares of arrivals by sea have increased in the Pacific and Southeast Asia, driven by growth of the cruise tourism market. The number of port calls in East Asia and Southeast Asia more than doubled from 2,842 in 2013 to 7,154 in 2019 (Figure 5.22). Apart from Japan and the PRC as dominant ports of call, the home ports of Singapore and Malaysia enabled the growth of intra-ASEAN cruise tourism. The Pacific island economies, with Vanuatu and Fiji as top cruise destinations in terms of passengers handled,[54] expanded their port capacities

[54] ADB estimates using data from UN Tourism. Compendium of Tourism Statistics data set. https://www.unwto.org/tourism-statistics/tourism-statistics-database and reports of National Tourism Organizations (accessed August 2024).

**Figure 5.22: Port Calls in Asia and the Pacific per Year**

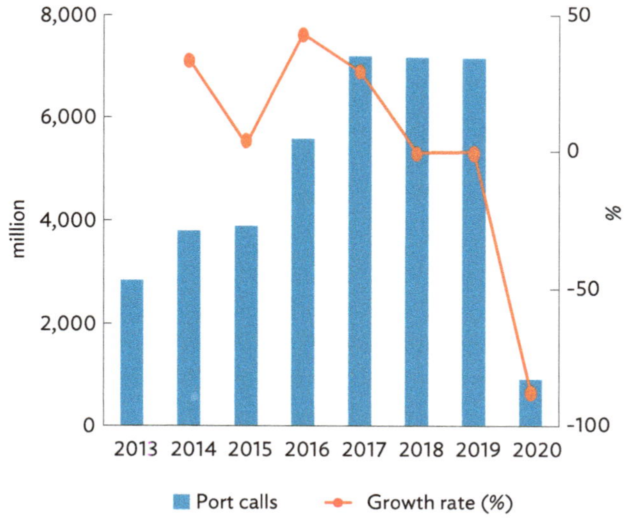


Note: Data include destinations in East Asia, South Asia, and Southeast Asia only.

Source: Cruise Lines International Association (2020).

for regional cruises catering to Australia and New Zealand as major markets. In cruise port development, Royal Caribbean International financed a common-use jetty for passenger transfers on Mystery Island in Vanuatu that accommodated larger vessels and increased economic benefits for the economy (Everett, Simpson, and Wayne 2018). While variations exist across subregions, strong and efficient transport routes that link Asia and the Pacific to its source markets are crucial for improving tourist inflows and the income they generate.

## Progress in institutional connectivity has complemented transport infrastructure developments.

The availability of flights and seats depends on the bilateral air service agreements and their commercial provisions, which limit the number of officially designated airlines, frequencies, type of aircraft and points of entry. Motor vehicle transport agreements define the type of vehicles allowed to cross national borders, the designated border crossing points, and requirements for recognition of licenses among others. Visa regulations, which primarily serve as a security measure, are among the most important government formalities affecting international tourism flows (UN Tourism 2024).

Economies in Asia liberalized their air transport and visa policies using unilateral, bilateral (most common), and regional approaches. Oceania and Southeast Asia are the most open subregions for intrasubregional travel.[55] It has been 2 decades since Oceania formed the Single Aviation Market with the Pacific Islands. In Southeast Asia, low-cost carriers grew rapidly due to the ASEAN Open Skies in 2015 (Bilotkach et al. 2021), which allowed officially designated air carriers of ASEAN member states to mount unrestricted frequencies and seats within ASEAN. ASEAN leveraged the subregion as single destination for industry, trade, and tourism with key partners (e.g., the PRC in 2010) and aviation blocs (e.g., the European Union in 2022). In the case of the Republic of Korea and ASEAN, pending the conclusion of a liberal air transport regime, individual ASEAN member states conducted air talks to amend the commercial provisions of their air service agreements. The amendments cover changes in airline designation (from single to multiple), increase in weekly seats between capital cities, unlimited seats in secondary gateways, and the removal of restrictions in aircraft type. The increase in flights from 17,785 in 2016 to 38,525 flights in 2019 between Viet Nam and Incheon Airport enabled a 120% increase in tourist arrivals from Viet Nam (ADB 2024a).

To promote cross-border road transportation for increased intra and interregional travel and trade, subregions have prioritized and developed motor vehicle transport agreements in the past 2 decades. Examples are the GMS Cross-Border Transport Facilitation Agreement, the ASEAN Framework Agreement on the Cross-Border Transport of Passengers by Road Vehicles signed in 2017, and the BBIN Motor Vehicle Agreement.[56]

[55] Based on ADB estimates of air service agreements using data from the International Civil Aviation Organization. World Air Services Agreements. https://data.icao.int/WASA/ (accessed August 2024); and bilateral visa policies using data from Arton Capital's Passport Index database. https://www.passportindex.org/ (accessed August 2024).

[56] Bangladesh, Bhutan, India, and Nepal.

Ranked as one of the most visa open regions in the world in 2023 (UN Tourism 2024), ASEAN implemented a regional framework in the grant of visa exemption to each other. In relation to extra-ASEAN markets, various categories of visa facilitation procedures emerged—visa on arrival, e-visas, ETA, Evisitor, and use of digital cards. Other visa products, including digital nomad visas and types such as the Muay Thai visa (for boxing training in Thailand) also emerged. These encourage travel by general leisure as well as niche markets, to accelerate recovery and meet national tourism targets. To recover from the pandemic, economies like Indonesia, the Lao PDR, Thailand, and Viet Nam granted visa-free entry to more markets such as the PRC.

## Improved ICT Infrastructure Most Visible Across All Subregions

World Economic Forum Travel and Tourism Development reports have highlighted East Asia as the most competitive and the second-most competitive region in the world (World Economic Forum 2019b), with well-developed cultural and natural assets and exceptional cross-border and domestic infrastructure connectivity and tourist services infrastructure.

While the quality of ground transport infrastructure has improved in Asia overall, it became very visible in the developed economies of East Asia, where high-speed, metro rail, and heavy rail lines serve passenger traffic. From 2010 to 2019, high-speed railways in East Asia grew by an average of 19.47% a year, with the PRC recording the highest increase of 29.64% in line kilometers (km), followed by the Republic of Korea's 19.14%. The metro route railway infrastructure expanded by 9.13% in East Asia and by 7.57% in South Asia.[57] Heavy railway lines dominated the railway infrastructure in Central Asia, South Asia, and Southeast Asia. In 2023, Indonesia launched Southeast Asia's first high-speed rail, to connect Jakarta to the city of Bandung, 142 km east, and reducing travel time from 2–3 hours by conventional railway to just 40 minutes (Medina 2023).

Roads serve as the main transport infrastructure for sightseeing and holiday tours using cars, tour coaches, or public buses. Many tourist attractions are accessible only by land travel and where last-mile connectivity becomes a crucial element of the journey. From 2015 to 2021, physical progress in road transport has been evident across individual member states of subregions such as GMS, South Asian Association for Regional Cooperation (SAARC), SASEC, CAREC, Indonesia-Malaysia-Thailand Growth Triangle, and Brunei Darussalam-Indonesia-Malaysia-Philippines East ASEAN Growth Area. Road length (primary/motorways/highways) in Pakistan, for example, increased by 7.5 times from 5,328 km in 2015 to 40,268 km in 2020. In the GMS, Viet Nam's road length increased from 19,545 km in 2015 to 25,875 km in 2019. The roads emerged as development priority for transport development in the GMS to reduce the connectivity gaps and improve multimodal and intermodal transport projects (ADB 2016). The road infrastructure in Malaysia more than doubled from 19,822 km to 43,093 km between 2015 and 2021.[58]

### A well-developed inland ground transportation system draws private investment into tourist services infrastructure.

An example of a good transportation system attracting investment in tourism is the high-speed rail network of the Republic of Korea, connecting the international airport to the city of Pyeongchang, which hosted of the 2018 Winter Olympics. This catalyzed hotel room investments outside of Seoul (World Travel and Tourism Council 2022). In Asia, destination capacities increased by 1.4 times from 5.3 million rooms in 2010 to 7.3 million rooms in 2022.[59] The hotel room per capita, a measure of intensity, expanded from 0.13 per 100 people in 2010 to 0.17 in 2022. Oceania had the highest room per capita, while the highest average growth rates between 2010 and 2022 were registered in Central Asia (5.8%) and Southeast Asia (4.6%).

57 ADB estimates using data from Asian Transport Observatory (2023). ATO National Database. https://asiantransportobservatory.org/ (accessed September 2024).

58 ADB estimates using data from Asian Transport Observatory (2023). ATO National Database. https://asiantransportobservatory.org/ (accessed September 2024).

59 ADB estimates using data from UN Tourism. Compendium of Tourism Statistics. https://www.unwto.org/tourism-statistics/key-tourism-statistics (accessed August 2024).

ICT infrastructure in Asia expanded significantly from 2010 to 2023 and accounted for the improvements in tourism rankings in World Economic Forum reports. The broadband subscriptions per 100 people more than doubled from 7.07 to 18.67, while mobile phone penetration increased from 68.01 in 2010 to 82.27 in 2023 (Figure 5.23). The economies of Bangladesh, the Lao PDR, and Mongolia registered the fastest average annual growth rates in percentage of individuals using the internet from 2013 to 2022.[60] The growth in ICT infrastructure narrowed the distance between tourists and service providers (e.g., online booking platforms, hotels, tour operators, transport services) and helped reduce the cost of searching for information about prices, facilities, customer reviews, and payment systems. This infrastructure backbone facilitated the adoption of smart applications to manage tourism flows, improve customer experience, and build resilient and smart tourism destinations.

## Opportunities and Challenges

Key opportunities exist to leverage the diverse strengths of the region's tourism assets, human resources, infrastructure advancements, and strong and resilient domestic tourism. First, international tourism in Asia and the Pacific developed rapidly from 2013 to 2019 and is poised to achieve full recovery from the pandemic by 2025. Second, tourism has become an industry of national and regional importance and destinations are intensifying their collaboration initiatives to maximize benefits. Third, the strides achieved in infrastructure development and the ongoing infrastructure projects continue to expand destination capacities for resilient and sustainable growth. Fourth, Asia is home to world-class destinations such as Japan, Australia, and the PRC, which top the global rankings in overall tourism development (World Economic Forum 2024) and provide examples of good practices for the rest of the region. Besides these three, Asian economies made

**Figure 5.23: Number of Subscription to Information and Communication Technology Infrastructure per 100 People**

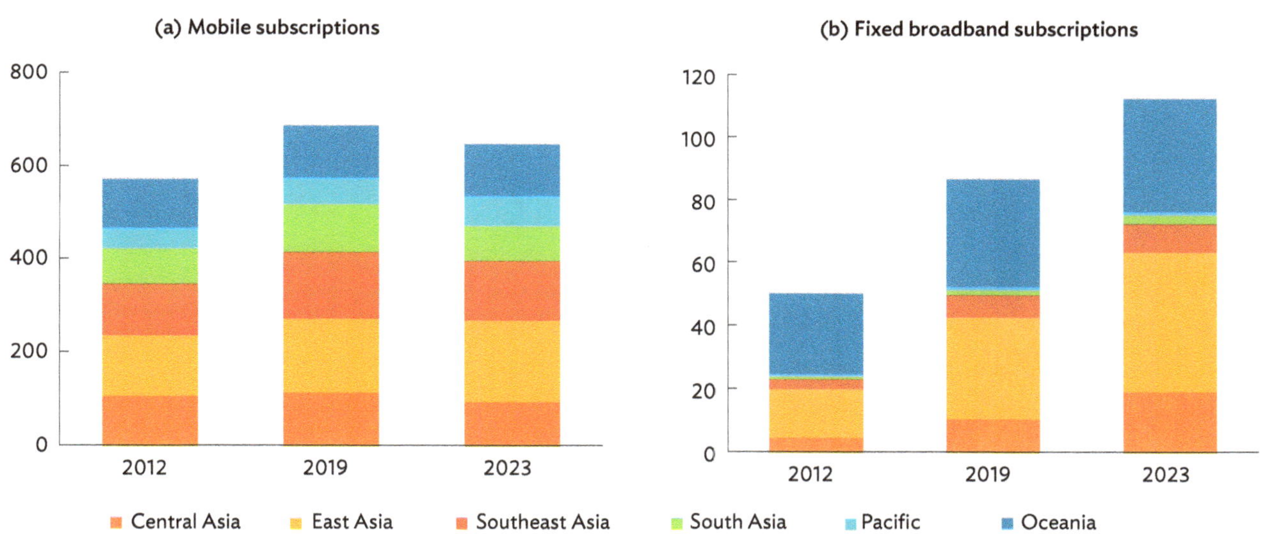


ICT = information and communication technology.

Note: For 2023, the Pacific data for mobile subscriptions per 100 people include only Kiribati and Palau.

Sources: ADB estimates using data from International Telecommunications Union. https://datahub.itu.int/; and World Bank. World Development Indicators. https://databank.worldbank.org/source/world-development-indicators (both accessed September 2024).

[60] ADB estimates using data from International Telecommunications Union (ITU). https://datahub.itu.int/ (accessed September 2024).

it to the list of top 10 performers in air transportation (Singapore) and ground and port infrastructure (Singapore and the Republic of Korea).

A review of subregional tourism strategies, plans, and data highlights key challenges related to infrastructure connectivity and tourism development. First, the limited air connectivity and lingering restrictive visa regimes between subregional economies and international markets are binding constraints on competitiveness. The CAREC region, for example, is constrained from expanding its share of the global business meetings market because of low flight frequencies. Fewer than half of all destination pairs within the CAREC region are served with direct flights, while time-consuming border crossing and visa procedures (including in airports) are the norm (ADB 2020). In Central Asia, economies do not have bilateral air service agreements with each other, while in South Asia only one economy has air service agreements with all subregional partners.[61]

Second, Asia has an extensive network of airports and ports that remain unutilized or underutilized even for subregions with open air access and liberal visa policies. Apart from inadequate airport and port facilities and services, there is a lack of incentive to mount direct flights and make port calls in secondary air and maritime gateways. In the case of ASEAN and the Republic of Korea, while recent policies have opened secondary gateways, ASEAN arrivals are still concentrated in Incheon Airport. Visa policies limit market development further. Only travelers from Brunei Darussalam, Malaysia, Singapore, and Thailand can apply for a Korean Electronic Travel Authorization, while the rest of the ASEAN economies must apply for a traditional visa (ADB 2024a). Outside of the gateways, internal mobility is limited by the lack of last-mile access to tourist attractions, lack of amenities (e.g., rest areas), and ancillary services (e.g., signages) on tourist routes. Developing other gateways can decongest the capital cities' attractions, avoid overtourism, and importantly distribute the economic benefits of tourism to more areas of the economy.

Investments in tourist services infrastructure, particularly in quality accommodation, are needed to meet targets in national and regional tourism plans. While the numbers will matter, the standards and quality of services need to be prioritized as part of quality tourism promotion. In Southeast Asia, for example, up to 55% of the room inventories in some destinations are alternative accommodation units, with limited regulation in safety and quality standards and fair competition (Roth and Schipani 2023). Another challenge in achieving competitiveness is the lack of destination infrastructure (i.e., piped water supply, sanitation services, affordable and reliable energy sources) that reduce the quality of tourist experience and can harm the environment. While ADB is assisting destinations in Asia to address gaps in tourism and infrastructure connectivity (Box 5.8), there are opportunities to further support the growth of tourism and regional cooperation in the region.

## Recommendations for Strengthening Tourism

**Enhance the linkages between tourism and trade in goods to diversify the economic structure and build economic resilience.** The pandemic exposed the vulnerabilities of economies that are highly dependent on international tourism. However, analysis shows that tapping source markets with a common language, free trade agreements, and an enabling visa policy can stimulate merchandise export growth. An example highlighted in this chapter is the Pacific where international tourism can catalyze the development of merchandise goods such as souvenirs and garments that are customized to the preferences of international tourists (Gupta et al. 2024).

**Link infrastructure prioritization, planning, and programming with tourism goals.** National and regional plans should carefully consider tourism in medium- to long-term plans, recognize the role of infrastructure in dispersing tourism benefits to more areas, better manage visitor volumes, and protect destination assets.

61 Authors' estimates using data from the International Civil Aviation Organization. World Air Services Agreements. https://data.icao.int/WASA/ (accessed August 2024).

**Box 5.8: ADB Commitments in Tourism and Infrastructure Connectivity**

The Asian Development Bank (ADB) has a few projects that specifically support the development of tourism. An example is the South Asia Tourism Infrastructure Development Project,[a] implemented from 2010 to 2023. This enhanced infrastructure in tourist sites, including improvements in water supply, sanitation systems, and solid waste management. The project also upgraded airport infrastructure and road networks to improve connectivity to destinations in South Asia. Besides infrastructure development, projects in South Asia have included crafting a tourism strategy,[b] the preservation of cultural sites, and regulatory reforms as part of the investment program.[c]

In Southeast Asia, the first and second GMS Tourism Infrastructure for Inclusive Growth Projects[d] covering Cambodia, the Lao People's Democratic Republic, and Viet Nam are financing the improvement of road infrastructure to decongest urban areas and link secondary towns with tourist sites, the expansion of passenger ports, and the improvement of environmental services such as flood protection and drainage and the management of solid waste. Strengthening institutional capacity for destination management and infrastructure operations and management, and capacity building of stakeholders to implement ASEAN tourism standards are also part of the

**ADB Transport Projects, 2010–2019** ($ million)

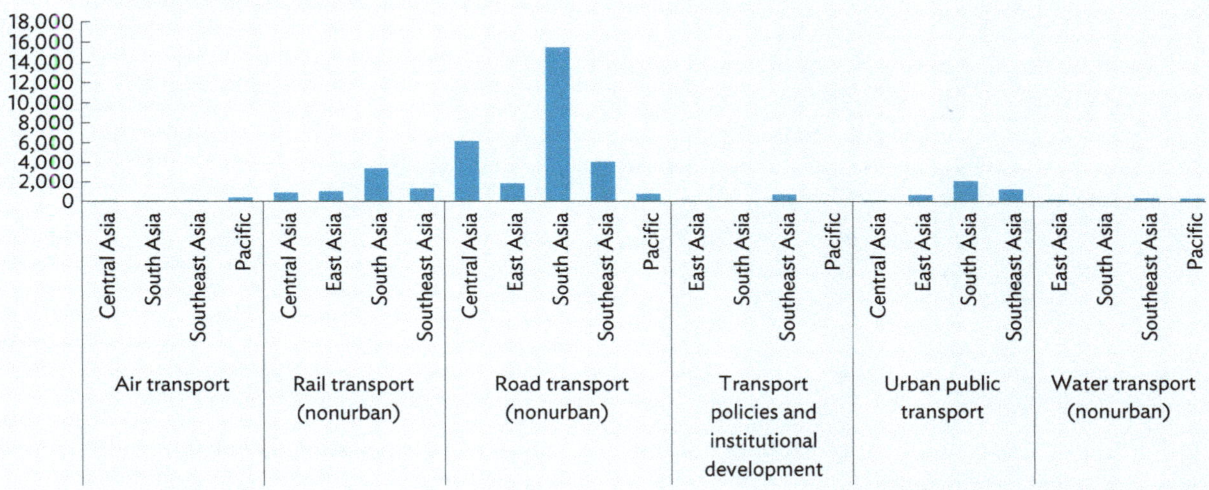


Source: ADB.

Investments in transportation infrastructure will need to be complemented by an increase in access to affordable renewable energy, and water supply and sanitation facilities to build resilient and sustainable destinations. The quality and standards of tourist services infrastructure, including accommodation and ground transport services, should be part of the prioritization process for infrastructure development.

**Invest in the development and utilization of airports, ports, rail, and road corridors to reduce negative effects of route distances.** Significant investments are needed to achieve efficient multimodal connectivity in the subregions that would shorten the distance to remote attractions, make travel more convenient, and promote regional circuit itineraries. To utilize gateways and reduce the development costs of new flights, destinations can provide incentives to charter operators and commercial airlines. Different encouragements come in the form of marketing support and time-bound passenger-based incentives, discounts on airport and port terminal charges, and taxes that are linked with key performance metrics.

*Box 5.8: continued*

projects. In 2021, the Southeast Asia Sustainable Tourism Facility was established to boost the subregion's recovery, stimulate sustainable tourism development, and help local tourism entrepreneurs innovate (ADB 2021).

From 2010 to 2019, ADB invested $41.2 billion in transport projects, of which 68.7% were allocated to road transport (nonurban). Meanwhile, $805.8 million was invested in water transport (nonurban) projects and $546 million (1.3%) was used to finance air transport projects (box figure).

Given the crucial role of aviation in tourism, there is an opportunity for ADB to support projects that help expand domestic and international air connectivity. The intervention is not limited to the construction or upgrading of airport infrastructure. It can also include policy reforms that facilitate the safe, seamless, and efficient movement of people. In the past, ADB supported Nepal in restructuring the Civil Aviation Authority of Nepal to comply with international civil aviation safety standards.[e] ADB also supported Indonesia[f] in strengthening regulatory and institutional frameworks that affect domestic and international connectivity. These have implications for the competitiveness of the economy and its tourism sector.

Most of ADB transport projects finance road infrastructure, with South Asia having attracted most of these investments. Much of the scope of investments and technical assistance is left for other areas such as air transport and institutional measures. Even within road infrastructure, investment for Central Asia needs to be scaled up, as much of the tourism activity in Central Asia happens through cross-border road connectivity. Southeast Asia offers an immense opportunity for investment in air transport as 66% of tourists arrive through international airports. Besides investment in infrastructure, ADB's support for institutional strengthening—through air service agreements, visa policies, and motor vehicle transport agreements—is crucial.

[a] ADB. South Asia Tourism Infrastructure Development Project (Bangladesh, India, and Nepal) - India (39399-013).

[b] ADB. Tripura Urban and Tourism Development Project (53276-001).

[c] ADB. Infrastructure Development Investment Program for Tourism - Tranche 1 (40648-023).

[d] ADB. South Asia Tourism Infrastructure Development Project (Bangladesh, India, and Nepal) - India (39399-013).

[e] ADB. Tripura Urban and Tourism Development Project (53276-001).

[f] ADB. Infrastructure Development Investment Program for Tourism - Tranche 1 (40648-023).

Source: ADB.

Investing in ground transportation infrastructure, a key weakness of tourism in the region, will incentivize the private sector in curating itineraries for overland tourism (cross-border) and creating activities to attract self-driving tourists to new and remote destinations. Ongoing negotiations of motor vehicle transport agreements in the subregions to further liberalize cross-border movements will benefit the development of tourism in landlocked economies. The GMS provides a good benchmark on how investments in road transportation infrastructure, including last-mile connectivity, supported tourism circuit development in subnational areas and enhanced cooperation, both in the subregion and with other subregions.

To address fiscal space issues, governments could pool resources with the private sector. Public–private partnership (PPP) models have been instrumental in the modernization of airports and to some extent ports and land transportation. ADB has provided extensive technical, financial, and institutional support in the development of international airport gateways of the Philippines, which relies on air transportation for 99% of its international tourist arrivals. In 2014, ADB provided financing of $75 million to GMR Megawide Cebu Airport Corporation, the firm that won the PPP contract for the expansion, rehabilitation, and operation of the Mactan-Cebu International Airport, the second-largest gateway in the Philippines. ADB also served as transaction advisor to the Philippine government for the ₱170.6 billion Manila Ninoy Aquino International Airport (NAIA) PPP, the largest such arrangement in the Philippines in nearly 25 years. ADB expertise can also be leveraged to transform more airports and seaports, and increase the value proposition of more destinations in the region. Other areas for PPP include developing amenities and services (e.g., hotels) and transnational tourism routes along economic corridors.

**Liberalize air access and visa policies using regional cooperation arrangements to facilitate travel.** A subregional approach makes negotiations more efficient among like-minded economies. Even if liberal aviation agreements are pursued, the benefits of such policy reform can be reduced by complex border formalities and travel procedures. A package of institutional reforms to reduce institutional connectivity gaps will increase mutual benefits from product and market development programs implemented by tourism organizations and the private sector in the subregions. In the case of the CAREC region, one proposed policy reform is to adopt a more liberal[62] aviation policy, which would allow foreign air carriers to operate intra-CAREC routes, set up bases to increase flight capacities of CAREC airports (ADB 2024c), and devise special visas such as a Silk Road visa (ADB 2019). Based on lessons learned from ASEAN and other regions, a phased approach to Open Skies with specific timelines in a road map can be pursued.

## References

Aga, G. A. and M. S. M. Peria. 2014. International Remittances and Financial Inclusion in Sub-Saharan Africa. *World Bank Policy Research Working Paper Series*. 6991. World Bank.

Ajefu, J. and J. Ogebe. 2019. Migrant Remittances and Financial Inclusion Among Households in Nigeria. *Oxford Development Studies*. 12 February.

Ali, M. A., A. M. Al-Khani, and L. A. Sidahmed. 2020. Migrant Health in Saudi Arabia During the COVID-19 Pandemic. *Eastern Mediterranean Health Journal*. 26 (8).

Ambrosius, C. 2016. Remittances and Financial Access: Is There Really a Link and for Whom? Evidence from Mexican Household Data. *The World Economy*. 39 (7). pp. 964–82.

Ambrosius, C. and A. Cuecuecha. 2013. Are Remittances a Substitute for Credit? Carrying the Financial Burden of Health Shocks in National and Transnational Households. *World Development*. 46 (June). pp. 143–52.

Anzoategui, D., A. Demirguc-Kunt, and M. S. M. Peria. 2014. Remittances and Financial Inclusion: Evidence from El Salvador. *World Bank Policy Research Working Paper Series*. 5839. World Bank.

Asia-Pacific Economic Cooperation Secretariat. 2024a. *Mutual Recognition Agreements for Professional Qualifications and Licensure in APEC: Experiences, Impediments and Opportunities*. https://www.apec.org/docs/default-source/publications/2024/2/224_gos_mutual-recognition-agreements-for-professional-qualifications-and-licensure-in-apec.pdf?sfvrsn=e37207cc_2.

———. 2024b. 2024 APEC Finance Ministers Joint Statement. 21 October. https://www.apec.org/meeting-papers/sectoral-ministerial-meetings/finance/2024-apec-finance-ministers'-meeting.

Asia-Plus. 2024. Unprecedented Growth in Remittance Inflows to Tajikistan Continues. 11 July. https://asiaplustj.info/en/news/tajikistan/economic/20240711/unprecedented-growth-in-remittance-inflows-to-tajikistan-continues.

Asian Development Bank (ADB). 2016. *Review of Configuration of Greater Mekong Subregion Economic Corridors*.

———. 2017. 3,000 People Graduate from Financial Literacy Course Supported by ADB, Australia, PNG. News release. 30 November. https://www.adb.org/news/3000-people-graduate-financial-literacy-course-supported-adb-australia-png.

———. 2019. *Promoting Regional Tourism Cooperation under CAREC 2030: A Scoping Study*.

62 Provision of fifth and seventh freedom rights for intra-CAREC routes for local and foreign air carriers.

———. 2020. *CAREC Tourism Strategy 2030*.

———. 2021. New ADB Facility to Help Southeast Asia Revive Tourism and Boost Sustainable, Inclusive Investments. News release. 17 December. https://www.adb.org/news/new-adb-facility-help-southeast-asia-revive-tourism-and-boost-sustainable-inclusive-investments.

———. 2022. *Asian Economic Integration Report 2022: Advancing Digital Services Trade in Asia and the Pacific*.

———. 2023. *Asian Economic Integration Report 2023: Trade, Investment, and Climate Change in Asia and the Pacific*.

———. 2024a. *ASEAN–Republic of Korea Tourism Cooperation: Fostering People-to-People Connectivity*.

———. 2024b. *Asian Economic Integration Report 2024: Decarbonizing Global Value Chains*.

———. 2024c. *Low-Cost Carrier Opportunities, Air Transport Liberalization, and Post-Pandemic Recovery in CAREC*.

Asian Transport Observatory. 2023. ATO National Database. https://asiantransportobservatory.org/ (accessed September 2024).

Association of Southeast Asian Nations Secretariat (ASEAN Secretariat). 2015. Mutual Recognition Arrangement in Services: Professionals on the Move. https://asean.org/wp-content/uploads/images/2015/October/outreach-document/Edited%20MRA%20Services-2.pdf.

———. 2023. ASEAN Launches World's First Regionwide Digital Economy Framework Agreement. Press Release. 3 September. https://asean.org/asean-launches-worlds-first-regionwide-digital-economy-framework-agreement/.

Battistella, G. and B. Khadria. 2011. Labour Migration in Asia and the Role of Bilateral Migration Agreements: Market Access Facilitation by Informal Means. Presentation for Markets for Migration and Development (M4MD): Trade and Labour Mobility Linkages—Prospects for Development. 13–15 September. https://www.gfmd.org/sites/g/files/tmzbdl1801/files/documents/BattistellaS5.pdf.

Bettin, G., A. F. Presbitero, and N. L. Spatafora. 2017. Remittances and Vulnerability in Developing Countries. *The World Bank Economic Review*. 3 (1). pp. 1–23. World Bank.

Bilotkach, V., J. Caro-Burnett, G. D. Khan, B. L. Sembiring, and Y. Yoshida. 2021. Measuring the Impact of ASEAN Open Skies on International Air Traffic Movements from and to Southeast Asian Cities. *Transport Policy*. 110 (September). pp. 363–78.

Blank, N. R. 2011. Making Migration Policy: Reflections on the Philippines' Bilateral Labor Agreements. *Asian Politics and Policy*. 3 (2). pp 185–205.

Brau, R. and A. M. Pinna. 2013. Movements of People for Movements of Goods? *The World Economy*. 36 (10). pp. 1318–1332.

Brown, R. P. C., F. Carmignani, and G. Fayad. 2013. Migrants' Remittances and Financial Development: Macro- and Micro-Level Evidence of a Perverse Relationship. *World Economy*. 36 (5). pp. 636–660.

Central Bank of Sri Lanka. https://www.cbsl.gov.lk/en/statistics/statistical-tables/external-sector (accessed March 2025).

Chauvet, L. and L. Jacolin. 2017. Financial Inclusion, Bank Concentration, and Firm Performance. *World Development*. 97 (September). pp. 1–13.

Chilton, A. S. and E. A. Posner. 2018. Why Countries Sign Bilateral Labor Agreements. *Journal of Legal Studies*. 47 (S1). pp. 45–88.

Chilton, A. S. and B. Woda. 2022. The Expanding Universe of Bilateral Labor Agreements. *Theoretical Inquires in Law*. 23 (2). pp. 1–64.

Clemens, M. A. 2015. Global Skill Partnerships: A Proposal for Technical Training in a Mobile World. *IZA Journal of Labor Policy*. 4 (2).

Clement, V., W. Chen, K. K. Rigaud, A. Sherbinin, B. Jones, S. Adamo, J. Schewe, N. Sadiq, and E. Shabahat. 2021. *Groundswell Acting on Internal Climate Migration Part II Overview*. The World Bank Group.

Collins, J. 2023. Reducing Remittance Costs in the Pacific Islands. *Lowy Institute Policy Brief*. https://www.lowyinstitute.org/sites/default/files/2023-10/COLLINS%2C%20Pacific%20remittances%2C%20PDF%20v5.pdf.

Colombu, S. 2023. The Future of Cross-Border Transactions in Asia. *RFI Global*. 22 June. https://rfi.global/the-future-of-cross-border-transactions-in-asia/.

Corley-Coulibaly, M., I. Postolachi, and N. Tesfay. 2021. A Multi-Faceted Typology of Labour Provisions in Trade Agreements: Overview, Methodology and Trends. https://www.ilo.org/resource/multi-faceted-typology-labour-provisions-trade-agreements-overview.

Cuecuecha, C. 2013. Are Remittances a Substitute for Credit? Carrying the Financial Burden of Health Shocks in National and Transnational Households. *World Development*. 46 (2013). pp. 143–52.

Cruise Lines International Association. 2020. *2020 Asia Cruise Deployment and Capacity Report*. https://cruising.org/-/media/clia-media/research/2021/oneresource/2020-asia-cruise-deployment-and-capacity-report.ashx.

Daryo. 2024. Uzbekistan Sees 43% Surge in Remittances from USA in 1H24. 25 July. https://daryo.uz/en/2024/07/25/uzbekistan-sees-43-surge-in-remittances-from-usa-in-1h24.

Dixit R. and M. Ghosh. 2013. Financial Inclusion for Inclusive Growth of India—A Study of Indian States. *International Journal of Business Management and Research*. 3 (1). pp. 147–156.

Doan, D., M. Dornan, and R. Edwards. 2023. The Pains and Gains of Working Away from Home: The Case of Pacific Temporary Migrant Workers in Australia and New Zealand. World Bank and Development Policy Centre, Crawford School of Public Policy, Australian National University.

Environmental Justice Foundation. 2018. On the Frontlines: Climate Change in Bangladesh. https://ejfoundation.org/resources/downloads/Climate-Displacement-Bangladesh-briefing-2018-v20.pdf.

European Migration Network (EMN). 2022. Skills Mobility Partnerships: Exploring Innovative Approaches to Labour Migration. EMN–OECD Inform. https://www.oecd.org/content/dam/oecd/en/topics/policy-issues/migration/2022-March-Joint-EMN-OECD-Inform-Skills-Mobility-Partnerships.pdf.

Everett, H., D. Simpson, and S. Wayne. 2018. *Tourism as a Driver of Growth in the Pacific: A Pathway to Growth and Prosperity for Pacific Island Countries*. Asian Development Bank.

Figueiredo, F., L. R. Lima, and G. Orefice. 2015. Migration and Regional Trade Agreements: A New Gravity Estimation. *Review of International Economics*. 24 (1). pp. 99–125.

Frankenhaeuser, M., D. Huss, and J. S. Frelak. 2018. Making the Case for Regional Cooperation on Migration and Mobility. *International Centre for Migration Policy Development—Commentary*. 4 December.

GMS Secretariat. 2015. *Greater Mekong Subregion Tourism Sector Strategy 2016–2025*. https://www.greatermekong.org/greater-mekong-subregion-tourism-sector-strategy-2016-2025.

Go, S. 2007. Asian Labor Migration: The Role of Bilateral Labor and Similar Agreements. Paper presented at the Regional Informal Workshop on Labor Migration in Southeast Asia: What Role for Parliaments, 21–23 September.

Gołembski, G. and J. Majewska. 2018. The Impact of Transport Infrastructure on International Inbound Tourism–A Gravity Model for Poland. *International Journal of Contemporary Management.* 17 (4). p. 135.

Gilleland, J., K. Rurie, and S. Rankin. 2016. A Broken Dream: Homelessness and Immigrants. Homeless Rights Advocacy Project. 1. Seattle University School of Law Digital Commons. https://digitalcommons.law.seattleu.edu/hrap/1.

Global System for Mobile Communications. 2024. Cross-Border Data Flows: Impact of Data Localisation on Mobile Money Services in Africa and Asia. https://www.gsma.com/solutions-and-impact/connectivity-for-good/mobile-for-development/wp-content/uploads/2024/04/GSMA_Oriel_DLR-Report.pdf.

Government of Australia, Department of Employment and Workplace Relations. https://www.dewr.gov.au/ (accessed October 2024).

Government of Australia, Department of Foreign Affairs and Trade. 2017. Australia-Pacific Training Coalition Stage 3 (APTC3): Investment Design Document. DFAT. https://www.dfat.gov.au/sites/default/files/aptc3-design-document.pdf.

Government of Bangladesh, Bureau of Manpower, Employment, and Training. http://www.old.bmet.gov.bd/BMET/stattisticalDataAction (accessed March 2025).

Government of India, Ministry of External Affairs. Performance Smartboard. https://meadashboard.gov.in/indicators/15 (accessed March 2025).

Government of Indonesia, Migrant Worker Protection Agency (Badan Pelindungan Pekerja Migran Indonesia). https://bp2mi.go.id/ (accessed March 2025).

Government of the Republic of Korea, Korean Statistical Information Services. https://kosis.kr/eng/ (accessed October 2024).

Government of Pakistan, Bureau of Emigration and Overseas Employment. https://beoe.gov.pk/reports-and-statistics (accessed March 2025).

Government of the Philippines, Department of Migrant Workers. https://dmw.gov.ph/statistics/overseas-employment-statistics (accessed March 2025).

Government of the United Kingdom. UK-Australia FTA Chapter 21: Labour. https://www.gov.uk/government/publications/uk-australia-fta-chapter-21-labour (accessed November 2024).

Gupta, P., S. Basu-Das, S. Sharma, and M. V. Domingo. 2024. Tourism Inflow Interlinkages with Merchandise Exports: An Augmented Gravity Analysis for the Pacific. *ADB Economics Working Paper Series.* No. 732. Asian Development Bank.

Hagen-Zanker, J. and M. Siegel. 2007. The Determinants of Remittances: A Review of the Literature. *MGSoG Working Paper.* No. 003. Maastricht Graduate School of Governance.

Hamanaka, S. and S. Jusoh. 2018. *Understanding the ASEAN Way of Regional Qualification Governance: The Case of Service Mutual Recognition Agreements.* IDE Discussion Paper No. 722. Institute of Developing Economies, Japan External Trade Organization.

Huckstep, S. and M. Clemens. 2023. Climate Change and Migration: An Omnibus Overview for Policymakers and Development Practitioners. *Center for Global Development Policy Paper.* No. 292.

International Air Transport Association. 2020. Air Connectivity: Measuring the Connections that Drive Economic Growth. https://www.astrid-online.it/static/upload/air-/air-connectivity.pdf.

International Fund for Agricultural Development (IFAD). 2024. Promoting Financial Inclusion Through Digitalization of Remittances. https://www.ifad.org/documents/48415603/49747559/gpfi-report-2024.pdf.

International Labour Organization. 2016. Labour Migration in Asia and the Pacific and the Arab States. https://www.ilo.org/sites/default/files/wcmsp5/groups/public/@asia/@ro-bangkok/documents/publication/wcms_534954.pdf.

International Organization for Migration (IOM). 2022. Climate Action Overview Asia-Pacific. https://environmentalmigration.iom.int/sites/g/files/tmzbdl1411/files/documents/DSPOP_Asia_Pacific%5B99%5D.pdf.

———. 2023. *Skills Mobility Partnerships: Recommendations and Guidance for Policymakers and Practitioners.*

Isaacs, L. and J. Capal. 2024. Movement of People: International Migration and the Relationship Between Remittances and Financial Inclusion. Background Paper for the *Asian Economic Integration Report 2025* Movement of People Chapter. Manuscript.

Jamil, R. and U. Dutta. 2021. Centering the Margins: The Precarity of Bangladeshi Low-Income Migrant Workers During the Time of COVID-19. *American Behavioral Scientist.* 65 (10). pp. 1384–1405.

Karasapan, O. 2020. Pandemic Highlights the Vulnerability of Migrant Workers in the Middle East. Commentary. 17 September. The Brookings Institution.

Khadaroo, J. and B. Seetanah. 2007. Transport Infrastructure and Tourism Development. *Annals of Tourism Research.* 34 (4). pp. 1021–32.

———. 2008. The Role of Transport Infrastructure in International Tourism Development: A Gravity Model Approach. *Tourism Management.* 29 (5). pp. 831–40.

Kikkawa, A., R. Gaspar, and C. Park. 2019. International Migration in Asia and the Pacific: Determinants and Role of Economic Integration. *ADB Economics Working Paper Series.* 592. Asian Development Bank.

Kikkawa, A., K. Kim, R. Gaspar, and P. Sirivunnabood. 2022. COVID-19 and the Deployment of Labor Migrants from Asia: Lessons Learned and Ways Forward. ADB Briefs. No. 223. Asian Development Bank.

Kim, K., Z. Ardaniel, A. Kikkawa, and B. Endriga. 2022. Bilateral Remittance Inflows to Asia and the Pacific: Countercyclicality and Motivations to Remit. *Asian Development Bank Institute Working Paper Series.* No. 1315. Asian Development Bank Institute.

Kulendran, N. and K. Wilson. 2000. Is There a Relationship between International Trade and International Travel? *Applied Economics.* 32 (8). pp. 1001–1009.

Kumar, M., S. Prashar, and R. K. Jana. 2019. Does International Tourism Spur International Trade and Output? Evidence from Wavelet Analysis. *Tourism Economics.* 25 (1). pp. 22–33.

Le, Q. H. and B. N. Nguyen. 2020. The Impact of Credit on Income Inequality in Vietnam. *Journal of Asian Finance, Economics, and Business.* 7 (5). pp 111–118.

Lee, C., M. P. Chen, W. Wu, and W. Xing. 2021. The Impacts of ICTs on Tourism Development: International Evidence Based on a Panel Quantile Approach. *Information Technology & Tourism.* 23. pp. 509–47.

Leitão, N. C. 2010. Does Trade Help to Explain Tourism Demand? The Case of Portugal. *Theoretical and Applied Economics.* XVII. 3 (544). pp. 63–74.

Levelu, A., A. M. Mayda, and G. Orefice. 2023. Deep Trade Agreements and International Migration: The Role of Visa Provision. *Journal of Economic Geography.* lbae014.

McAuliffe, M. and L. A. Oucho, eds. 2024. *World Migration Report 2024*. International Organization for Migration.

McConnell, T. 2022. The Maldives Is Being Swallowed by the Sea. Can It Adapt? *National Geographic.* 21 January. https://www.nationalgeographic.com/environment/article/the-maldives-is-being-swallowed-by-the-sea-can-it-adapt.

Medina, A. 2023. Indonesia Launches Southeast Asia's First High Speed Railway. *ASEAN Briefing*. 5 October. https://www.aseanbriefing.com/news/indonesia-launches-southeast-asias-first-high-speed-railway/.

Mendoza, D. R., D. G. Papademetriou, M. V. Desiderio, B. Salant, K. Hooper, and T. Elwood. 2017. *Reinventing Mutual Recognition Arrangements: Lessons from International Experiences and Insights for the ASEAN Region*. Asian Development Bank.

Mendoza, D. R. and G. Sugiyarto. 2017. *The Long Road Ahead: Status Report on the Implementation of the ASEAN MRAs on Professional Services*. Asian Development Bank and Migration Policy Institute.

Miller R., Y. Tomita, K. I. C. Ong, A. Shibanuma, and M. Jimba. 2019. Mental Well-Being of International Migrants to Japan: A Systematic Review. 2019. *BMJ Open*. November. 9 (11).

Missbach, A. and W. Palmer. 2018. Indonesia: A Country Grappling with Migrant Protection at Home and Abroad. Migration Policy Institute. 19 September. https://www.migrationpolicy.org/article/indonesia-country-grappling-migrant-protection-home-and-abroad.

Nayyar, D. 2000. Cross-Border Movements of People. *World Institute for Development Economics Research Working Paper*. No. 194. The United Nations University.

Nizam, R., Z. A. Karim, T. Sarmidi, and A. A. Rahman. 2020. Financial Inclusion and Firms Growth in Manufacturing Sector: A Threshold Regression Analysis in Selected ASEAN Countries. *Economies*. 8 (80). p. 1–12.

Nordas, H. K. 2016. Does Mutual Recognition of Qualifications Stimulate Services Trade? The Case of the European Union. *Applied Economics*. 48 (20). pp. 1852–1865.

O'Steen, B. 2021. Bilateral Labor Agreements and the Migration of Filipinos: An Instrumental Variable Approach. *IZA Journal of Development and Migration*. 12 (11).

Oh, T. K. 1977. The Asian Brain Drain: A Factual and Casual Analysis. R&E Research Associates.

Orefice, G. 2015. International Migration and Trade Agreements: The New Role of PTAs. *Canadian Journal of Economics/Revue Canadienne d'Economique*. 48 (1). pp. 310–334.

Organisation for Economic Co-operation and Development (OECD). 2018. What Would Make Global Skills Partnerships Work in Practice? *Migration Policy Debates*. 15.

Ozden, C. and M. Schiff, eds. 2006. *International Migration, Remittances and the Brain Drain*. World Bank and Palgrave Macmillan.

Parsons, C. 2022. The Pacific Islands: The Front Line in the Battle Against Climate Change. United States National Science Foundation. 23 May.

Peng, B., H. Song, G. Crouch, and S. F. Witt. 2015. A Meta-Analysis of International Tourism Demand Elasticities. *Journal of Travel Research.* 54 (5). pp. 611–633.

Peters, M. E. 2019. Immigration and International Law. *International Studies Quarterly*. 63 (2). pp. 281–295.

Prideaux, B. 2000. The Resort Development Spectrum—A New Approach to Modeling Resort Development. *Tourism Management.* 21 (3). pp. 225-240.

Ratha, D., S. Plaza, and E. J. Kim. 2024. In 2024, Remittance Flows to Low- and Middle-income Countries Are Expected to Reach $685 Billion, Larger Than FDI and ODA Combined. People Move Blog. World Bank. 18 December. https://blogs.worldbank.org/en/peoplemove/in-2024--remittance-flows-to-low--and-middle-income-countries-ar.

Rodolfo, M. C. 2024. Role of Infrastructure Connectivity on International Tourism Development in Asia and the Pacific. Background Paper for the *Asian Economic Integration Report 2025,* Chapter on Movement of People. Manuscript.

Rosselló-Nadal, J. and M. Santana-Gallego. 2022. Gravity Models for Tourism Demand Modeling: Empirical Review and Outlook. *Journal of Economic Surveys* 36 (5). pp. 1358–1409.

———. 2024. The Effect of Visa Types on International Tourism. *Economic Modelling.* 137. 106757.

Roth, A. and S. Schipani. 2023. Alternative Accommodations in Southeast Asia. *ADB Briefs.* 273. Asian Development Bank.

Santana-Gallego, M., F. J. Ledesma-Rodríguez, and J. V. Pérez-Rodríguez. 2016. International Trade and Tourism Flows: An Extension of the Gravity Model. *Economic Modelling. 52.* pp. 1026–1033.

Sauer, M. and J. Volarević. 2021. *Transnational Skills and Mobility Partnerships (TSMP): Contextual Factors, Conceptual Design and Application.* Bertelsmann Stiftung.

Saydaliyev, H., L. Chin, and Y. Oskenbayev. 2020. The Nexus of Remittances, Institutional Quality, and Financial Inclusion. *Economic Research-Ekonomska istraživanja.* 33 (1). pp. 3528–3544.

Seetanah, B., T. D. Juwaheer, M. J. Lamport, S. Rojid, R. V. Sannassee, and A. U. Subadar. 2011. Does Infrastructure Matter in Tourism Development? *University of Mauritius Research Journal.* 17. pp. 89–108.

Seetanah, B. and J. Khadaroo. 2009. An Analysis of the Relationship between Transport Capital and Tourism Development in a Dynamic Framework. *Tourism Economics.* 15 (4). pp. 785-802.

Shan, J. and K. Wilson. 2001. Causality Between Trade and Tourism: Empirical Evidence from China. *Applied Economics Letters.* 8 (4). pp. 279–283.

Shimada, A. 2011. The Role of Altruism in Sending and Spending Remittances. *Journal of East Asian Economic Integration.* 15 (2).

Thrane, C. 2015. Examining Tourists' Long-Distance Transportation Mode Choices Using a Multinomial Logit Regression Model. *Tourism Management Perspectives.* 15. pp. 115-121.

Tsai, J. and X. Gu. 2019. Homelessness Among Immigrants in the United States: Rates, Correlates, and Differences Compared with Native-Born Adults. *Public Health.* 168 (March). pp. 107–119.

Tu, C. A., N. T. M. Phi, L. Q. Tuan, N. Yoshino, T. Sarker, and F. Taghizadeh-Hesary. 2019. Remittance Inflows, Financial Inclusion, and Economic Development: An Empirical Analysis of the World Sample. *ADBI Working Paper Series.* No. 1000. Asian Development Bank Institute.

Uddin, M. J. 2024. Climate Change, Vulnerabilities, and Migration: Insights from Ecological Migrants in Bangladesh. *The Journal of Environment & Development.* 33 (1). pp. 50–74.

United Nations Framework Convention on Climate Change (UNFCCC). 2017. How Fiji Is Impacted by Climate Change. *News.* 9 February. https://unfccc.int/news/how-fiji-is-impacted-by-climate-change.

United Nations. 2017. Report of the Special Representative of the Secretary General on Migration, A/71/728. United Nations General Assembly. https://www.un.org/development/desa/pd/sites/www.un.org.development.desa.pd/files/unpd_cm15_201702_report_of_srsg_on_migration_-_a.71.728_advance_0.pdf.

United Nations Department of Economic and Social Affairs, Population Division (UN DESA). International Migrant Stock 2020. https://www.un.org/development/desa/pd/content/international-migrant-stock (accessed May 2024).

———. World Population Prospects 2024. https://population.un.org/wpp/Download/Standard/MostUsed/ (accessed July 2024).

UN Tourism. 2019. *International Tourism Highlights, 2019 Edition.*

———. 2023. *Compendium of Tourism Statistics, Data 2017–2021, 2023 Edition.*

———. 2024. *Tourism Visa Openness Report 2023.*

VISA. 2024. *Money Travels: 2024 Digital Remittances Adoption Report.*

World Bank. Remittance Prices Worldwide. https://remittanceprices.worldbank.org/ (accessed December 2024).

———. 2024. Global Financial Index Database. https://www.worldbank.org/en/publication/globalfindex/Report (accessed September 2024).

———. 2024. Labor Migration Schemes, Pilot Partnerships, and Skills Mobility Initiatives in Germany - Background Paper to the World Development Report 2023. Migrants, Refugees, Societies. http://documents.worldbank.org/curated/en/099071024113029746.

World Bank Group. 2022. Philippines Country Climate and Development Report. CCDR Series. World Bank, Washington, DC.

World Bank Group. 2023. Remittances Remain Resilient but Likely to Slow. Press Release. 13 June. https://www.worldbank.org/en/news/press-release/2023/06/13/remittances-remain-resilient-likely-to-slow.

———. Global Knowledge Partnership on Migration and Development (KNOMAD). KNOMAD/World Bank Bilateral Migration Matrix 2021, December 2022 (accessed June 2024).

World Economic Forum. 2019a. *How Global Tourism Can Be More Sustainable.*

———. 2019b. *The Travel and Tourism Competitiveness Report 2019: Travel and Tourism at a Tipping Point.*

———. 2024. *Travel and Tourism Development Index 2024.*

World Travel and Tourism Council. 2022. *Critical Factors to Attract Hotel Investment.*

# 6 Statistical Appendix

The statistical appendix comprises 10 tables of selected indicators on economic integration for the 49 Asia and Pacific members of the Asian Development Bank (ADB). These succeeding notes describe the economy groupings and the calculation procedures undertaken.

## Regional Groupings

- Asia and the Pacific refers to the 49 regional members of ADB.
- Developing Asia refers to Asia excluding Australia, Japan, and New Zealand.
- The European Union consists of Austria, Belgium, Bulgaria, Croatia, Cyprus, Czechia, Denmark, Estonia, Finland, France, Germany, Greece, Hungary, Ireland, Italy, Latvia, Lithuania, Luxembourg, Malta, the Netherlands, Poland, Portugal, Romania, Slovakia, Slovenia, Spain, and Sweden.

## Table Descriptions

### Table A1: Asia-Pacific Regional Cooperation and Integration Index

The Asia-Pacific Regional Cooperation and Integration Index (ARCII) is a composite measure of the degree of regional cooperation and integration in Asia and the Pacific. It comprises eight dimensional indexes based on 41 indicators to capture the contributions of eight different aspects of regional integration: (i) trade and investment, (ii) money and finance, (iii) regional value chains, (iv) infrastructure and connectivity, (v) people and social integration, (vi) institutional arrangements, (vii) technology and digital connectivity, and (viii) environmental cooperation. The construction of ARCII follows two steps: first, the 41 indicators have been weight-averaged in each of the eight dimensions to produce eight composite dimensional indexes; and second, these eight dimensional indexes are weight-averaged to generate an overall index of regional integration. In each step, the weights are determined based on principal component analysis. For more details on the methodology and to download the data, please see Asia-Pacific Regional Cooperation and Integration Index Database. https://aric.adb.org/database/arcii.

### Table A2: Regional Integration Indicators—Asia and the Pacific (% of total)

This table provides a summary of regional integration indicators for three areas: movement in trade and investment, movement in capital, and people movement (migration, remittances, and tourism); for Asian subregions, including Association of Southeast Asian Nations (ASEAN) plus 3 (including Hong Kong, China). Cross-border flows within and across subregions are shown, as well as total flows with Asia and the rest of the world. Table descriptions of Tables A3 and A7 (movement in trade and investment); Tables A5 and A6 (movement in capital); and Tables A8, A9, and A10 (people movement); provide additional description for each indicator.

## Table A3: Trade Share—Asia and the Pacific (% of total trade)

Trade share is calculated as $T_{ij}/T_{iw} \cdot 100$, where $T_{ij}$ is the total trade of economy "*i*" with economy "*j*", and $T_{iw}$ is the total trade of economy "*i*" with the world. A higher share indicates a higher degree of regional trade integration.

## Table A4: Free Trade Agreement Status—Asia and the Pacific

This table shows the number and status of bilateral and plurilateral free trade agreements (FTAs) with at least one of the Asian economies as signatory. FTAs only proposed are excluded. It covers FTAs with the following status: Framework agreement signed—the parties initially negotiate the contents of a framework agreement, which serves as a framework for future negotiations; Negotiations launched—the parties, through the relevant ministries, declare the official launch of negotiations or set the date for such, or start the first round of negotiations; Signed but not yet in effect—parties sign the agreement after negotiations have been completed, however, the agreement has yet to be implemented; and Signed and in effect—provisions of the FTA come into force, after legislative or executive ratification.

## Table A5: Cross-Border Portfolio Equity Holdings Share—Asia and the Pacific (% of total cross-border portfolio equity holdings)

This first two cross-border tables are calculated as $E_{ij}/E_{iw} \cdot 100$ where $E_{ij}$ is portfolio equity holdings of economy "*i*" issued by economy "*j*", and $E_{iw}$ is the total global cross-border portfolio equity holdings of economy "*i*". Calculations are based solely on available data in the Coordinated Portfolio Investment Survey (CPIS) database of the International Monetary Fund (IMF). Rest of the world (ROW) includes equity securities issued by international organizations defined in the CPIS database and "not specified (including confidential) category." A higher share indicates a higher degree of regional integration.

## Table A6: Cross-Border Portfolio Debt Holdings Share—Asia and the Pacific (% of total cross-border portfolio debt holdings)

These shares are calculated as $D_{ij}/D_{iw} \cdot 100$ where $D_{ij}$ is portfolio debt holdings of economy "*i*" issued by economy "*j*", and $D_{iw}$ is the total global cross-border portfolio debt holdings of economy "*i*". Calculations are based solely on available data in the CPIS database of the IMF. ROW includes debt securities issued by international organizations defined in the CPIS database and "not specified (including confidential) category." A higher share indicates a higher degree of regional integration.

## Table A7: Foreign Direct Investment Inflow Share—Asia and the Pacific (% of total FDI inflows)

These foreign direct investment (FDI) shares are calculated as $F_{ij}/F_{iw} \cdot 100$ where $F_{ij}$ is the FDI received by economy "*i*" from economy "*j*", and $F_{iw}$ is the FDI received by economy "*i*" from the world. Figures are based on net FDI inflow data. A higher share indicates a higher degree of regional integration. The bilateral FDI database was constructed using data from the United Nations Trade and Development, ASEAN Secretariat, Eurostat, and national sources. For missing data from 2018 onward, bilateral FDI estimates derived from a gravity model are used. All bilateral data available from 2001 until the latest year available from the data sources were utilized to estimate the following gravity equation:

$$lnFDI_{ijt} = \alpha + \beta 1 lnGDP_{it} + \beta 2 lnGDP_{jt} + \gamma X_{ijt} + \delta_i F_i + \delta_j F_j + \delta_t F_t + v_{ijt}$$

where $FDI_{ijt}$ is the FDI from economy "*j*" (home) to economy "*i*" (host) in year *t*, $GDP_{it}$ is the gross domestic product (GDP) of economy "*i*" in year *t*, $GDP_{jt}$ is the GDP of economy "*j*"at year *t*, $X_{ijt}$ are the usual gravity variables (distance, contiguity, common language, colonial relationship) between economies "*i*" and "*j*", and $F_j$, $F_i$, $F_t$, are home, host, and year fixed effects, respectively, and $v_{ijt}$ is the error term. Data on distance, contiguity, common language, colonial relationship are from the Centre d'Études Prospectives et d'Informations Internationales (the French Research Center in International Economics) and data on GDP are from the World Development Indicators of the World Bank. For more details on methodology and data sources, see Asian Economic Integration Report 2018 online Annex 1: http://aric.adb.org/pdf/aeir2018_ onlineannex1.pdf.

## Table A8: Remittance Inflows Share—Asia and the Pacific (% of total remittance inflows)

These shares are calculated as $R_{ij}/R_{iw} \cdot 100$ where $R_{ij}$ is the remittance received by economy "*i*" from partner "*j*", and $R_{iw}$ is the remittance received by economy "*i*" from the world. Remittances refer to the sum of the following: (i) workers' remittances which are recorded as current transfers under the current account of the IMF's Balance of Payments (BOP); (ii) compensation of employees which includes wages, salaries, and other benefits of border, seasonal, and other nonresident workers and which are recorded under the "income" subcategory of the current account; and (iii) migrants' transfers which are reported under capital transfers in the BOP's capital account. Transfers through informal channels are excluded.

## Table A9: Outbound Migration Share—Asia and the Pacific (% of total outbound migrants)

These shares are calculated as $M_{ij}/M_{iw} \cdot 100$ where $M_{ij}$ is the number of migrants of economy "*i*" residing in economy "*j*" and $M_{iw}$ is the number of all migrants of economy "*i*" residing overseas. This definition excludes those traveling abroad on a temporary basis. A higher share indicates a higher degree of regional integration.

## Table A10a: Inbound Tourism Share—Asia and the Pacific (% of total inbound tourists)

These shares are calculated as $V_{ij}/V_{iw} \cdot 100$ where $V_{ij}$ is the number of nationals of economy "*i*" that have arrived as tourists in destination "*j*", and $V_{iw}$ is the total number of nationals of economy "*i*" that have arrived as tourists in all international destinations. A higher share indicates a higher degree of regional integration.

## Table A10b: Outbound Tourism Share—Asia and the Pacific (% of total outbound tourists)

These shares are calculated as $V_{ij}/V_{iw} \cdot 100$ where $V_{ij}$ is the number of nationals of economy "*i*" that have traveled as tourists in destination "*j*", and $V_{iw}$ is the total number of nationals of economy "*i*" that have traveled as tourists abroad. A higher share indicates a higher degree of regional integration.

**Table A1: Asia-Pacific Regional Cooperation and Integration Index**

(a) Overall Asia-Pacific Regional Cooperation and Integration Index and Dimensional Subindexes—Asia and the Pacific

| | | Dimensional Indexes | | | | | | | |
|---|---|---|---|---|---|---|---|---|---|
| Year | Overall Index | Trade and Investment Integration | Money and Finance Integration | Regional Value Chain | Infrastructure and Connectivity | People and Social Integration | Institutional Arrangements | Technology and Digital Connectivity | Environmental Cooperation |
| 2006 | 0.422 | 0.389 | 0.399 | 0.523 | 0.470 | 0.537 | 0.203 | 0.363 | 0.354 |
| 2007 | 0.422 | 0.348 | 0.389 | 0.531 | 0.467 | 0.538 | 0.207 | 0.377 | 0.357 |
| 2008 | 0.424 | 0.374 | 0.393 | 0.518 | 0.469 | 0.531 | 0.213 | 0.386 | 0.360 |
| 2009 | 0.432 | 0.387 | 0.408 | 0.510 | 0.477 | 0.536 | 0.219 | 0.384 | 0.363 |
| 2010 | 0.437 | 0.399 | 0.415 | 0.516 | 0.477 | 0.541 | 0.222 | 0.417 | 0.359 |
| 2011 | 0.428 | 0.414 | 0.371 | 0.514 | 0.479 | 0.541 | 0.223 | 0.433 | 0.359 |
| 2012 | 0.428 | 0.413 | 0.384 | 0.515 | 0.482 | 0.548 | 0.225 | 0.429 | 0.356 |
| 2013 | 0.445 | 0.393 | 0.441 | 0.519 | 0.484 | 0.531 | 0.227 | 0.463 | 0.358 |
| 2014 | 0.442 | 0.396 | 0.423 | 0.512 | 0.481 | 0.534 | 0.230 | 0.460 | 0.356 |
| 2015 | 0.451 | 0.456 | 0.444 | 0.509 | 0.483 | 0.533 | 0.232 | 0.478 | 0.355 |
| 2016 | 0.448 | 0.412 | 0.419 | 0.532 | 0.480 | 0.528 | 0.233 | 0.478 | 0.360 |
| 2017 | 0.441 | 0.409 | 0.421 | 0.520 | 0.483 | 0.525 | 0.233 | 0.492 | 0.356 |
| 2018 | 0.451 | 0.436 | 0.425 | 0.502 | 0.491 | 0.530 | 0.235 | 0.515 | 0.356 |
| 2019 | 0.452 | 0.411 | 0.419 | 0.507 | 0.503 | 0.538 | 0.234 | 0.523 | 0.353 |
| 2020 | 0.445 | 0.393 | 0.432 | 0.511 | 0.503 | 0.514 | 0.234 | 0.548 | 0.355 |
| 2021 | 0.439 | 0.356 | 0.430 | 0.516 | 0.494 | 0.496 | 0.234 | 0.550 | 0.387 |
| 2022 | 0.449 | 0.397 | 0.417 | 0.531 | 0.505 | 0.502 | 0.236 | 0.561 | 0.384 |

(b) Overall Asia-Pacific Regional Cooperation and Integration Index—Asian Subregions and Subregional Initiatives

| | Central Asia | East Asia | Southeast Asia | South Asia | Oceania | ASEAN | CAREC | GMS | SASEC | IMT-GT | BIMP-EAGA | SAARC | BIMSTEC |
|---|---|---|---|---|---|---|---|---|---|---|---|---|---|
| 2006 | 0.379 | 0.465 | 0.421 | 0.337 | 0.461 | 0.427 | 0.333 | 0.393 | 0.359 | 0.411 | 0.372 | 0.337 | 0.354 |
| 2007 | 0.378 | 0.456 | 0.414 | 0.326 | 0.456 | 0.421 | 0.334 | 0.350 | 0.347 | 0.396 | 0.367 | 0.326 | 0.359 |
| 2008 | 0.378 | 0.462 | 0.414 | 0.305 | 0.462 | 0.420 | 0.346 | 0.345 | 0.319 | 0.414 | 0.373 | 0.305 | 0.332 |
| 2009 | 0.399 | 0.466 | 0.419 | 0.317 | 0.468 | 0.424 | 0.361 | 0.368 | 0.332 | 0.415 | 0.378 | 0.317 | 0.336 |
| 2010 | 0.377 | 0.474 | 0.420 | 0.334 | 0.475 | 0.425 | 0.355 | 0.369 | 0.361 | 0.414 | 0.382 | 0.334 | 0.354 |
| 2011 | 0.372 | 0.457 | 0.406 | 0.358 | 0.456 | 0.410 | 0.352 | 0.366 | 0.388 | 0.414 | 0.379 | 0.358 | 0.377 |
| 2012 | 0.374 | 0.466 | 0.416 | 0.337 | 0.466 | 0.420 | 0.355 | 0.365 | 0.364 | 0.399 | 0.372 | 0.337 | 0.355 |
| 2013 | 0.380 | 0.469 | 0.452 | 0.332 | 0.471 | 0.456 | 0.370 | 0.420 | 0.358 | 0.427 | 0.393 | 0.332 | 0.357 |
| 2014 | 0.375 | 0.476 | 0.431 | 0.327 | 0.460 | 0.435 | 0.375 | 0.414 | 0.350 | 0.414 | 0.386 | 0.327 | 0.356 |
| 2015 | 0.377 | 0.472 | 0.457 | 0.336 | 0.462 | 0.460 | 0.381 | 0.443 | 0.364 | 0.412 | 0.389 | 0.336 | 0.371 |
| 2016 | 0.379 | 0.484 | 0.438 | 0.340 | 0.464 | 0.441 | 0.365 | 0.439 | 0.373 | 0.409 | 0.382 | 0.340 | 0.368 |
| 2017 | 0.383 | 0.472 | 0.425 | 0.323 | 0.456 | 0.429 | 0.378 | 0.414 | 0.346 | 0.399 | 0.378 | 0.323 | 0.342 |
| 2018 | 0.389 | 0.475 | 0.437 | 0.318 | 0.448 | 0.441 | 0.387 | 0.434 | 0.348 | 0.408 | 0.386 | 0.318 | 0.355 |
| 2019 | 0.397 | 0.473 | 0.432 | 0.323 | 0.449 | 0.435 | 0.399 | 0.424 | 0.355 | 0.414 | 0.390 | 0.323 | 0.359 |
| 2020 | 0.404 | 0.469 | 0.453 | 0.329 | 0.457 | 0.456 | 0.392 | 0.432 | 0.360 | 0.425 | 0.391 | 0.329 | 0.364 |
| 2021 | 0.400 | 0.459 | 0.442 | 0.335 | 0.454 | 0.445 | 0.393 | 0.402 | 0.368 | 0.416 | 0.392 | 0.335 | 0.371 |
| 2022 | 0.409 | 0.483 | 0.459 | 0.349 | 0.450 | 0.462 | 0.397 | 0.425 | 0.382 | 0.422 | 0.406 | 0.349 | 0.381 |

## (c) Regional Integration Index—Asia and the Pacific and Other Regions

| | Asia and the Pacific | European Union | Latin America | Africa | Middle East | North America |
|---|---|---|---|---|---|---|
| 2006 | 0.422 | 0.602 | 0.397 | 0.338 | 0.385 | 0.492 |
| 2007 | 0.422 | 0.601 | 0.387 | 0.325 | 0.392 | 0.496 |
| 2008 | 0.424 | 0.597 | 0.385 | 0.335 | 0.381 | 0.511 |
| 2009 | 0.432 | 0.601 | 0.389 | 0.331 | 0.385 | 0.510 |
| 2010 | 0.437 | 0.599 | 0.398 | 0.354 | 0.396 | 0.507 |
| 2011 | 0.428 | 0.599 | 0.394 | 0.351 | 0.402 | 0.512 |
| 2012 | 0.428 | 0.598 | 0.401 | 0.352 | 0.414 | 0.511 |
| 2013 | 0.445 | 0.601 | 0.412 | 0.350 | 0.415 | 0.511 |
| 2014 | 0.442 | 0.599 | 0.392 | 0.363 | 0.399 | 0.515 |
| 2015 | 0.451 | 0.606 | 0.393 | 0.367 | 0.401 | 0.507 |
| 2016 | 0.448 | 0.612 | 0.392 | 0.362 | 0.413 | 0.513 |
| 2017 | 0.441 | 0.608 | 0.398 | 0.352 | 0.414 | 0.510 |
| 2018 | 0.451 | 0.605 | 0.389 | 0.363 | 0.419 | 0.499 |
| 2019 | 0.452 | 0.602 | 0.389 | 0.373 | 0.431 | 0.506 |
| 2020 | 0.445 | 0.614 | 0.400 | 0.374 | 0.428 | 0.499 |
| 2021 | 0.439 | 0.610 | 0.399 | 0.370 | 0.435 | 0.507 |
| 2022 | 0.449 | 0.599 | 0.401 | 0.377 | 0.444 | 0.504 |

ASEAN = Association of Southeast Asian Nations, BIMP-EAGA = Brunei Darussalam–Indonesia–Malaysia–Philippines East ASEAN Growth Area , BIMSTEC = Bay of Bengal Initiative for Multi-Sectoral Technical and Economic Cooperation, CAREC = Central Asia Regional Economic Cooperation, GMS = Greater Mekong Subregion, IMT-GT = Indonesia–Malaysia–Thailand Growth Triangle, SAARC = South Asian Association for Regional Cooperation, SASEC = South Asia Subregional Economic Cooperation.

Notes:

(i) The Asia-Pacific Regional Cooperation and Integration Index (ARCII) for each subregion (subregional initiative) for each year is calculated by averaging the ARCII scores for all the economies in each subregion (member economies in each subregional initiative).

(ii) The economy coverage for subregions and subregional initiatives includes Central Asia (Armenia, Azerbaijan, Georgia, Kazakhstan, the Kyrgyz Republic, Tajikistan, Turkmenistan, and Uzbekistan); East Asia (the People's Republic of China [PRC]; Hong Kong, China; Japan; the Republic of Korea; Mongolia; and Taipei,China); Southeast Asia (Brunei Darussalam, Cambodia, Indonesia, the Lao People's Democratic Republic [Lao PDR], Malaysia, Myanmar, the Philippines, Singapore, Thailand, Timor-Leste, and Viet Nam); South Asia (Afghanistan, Bangladesh , Bhutan, India, Maldives, Nepal, Pakistan, and Sri Lanka); the Pacific (the Cook Islands, Fiji, Kiribati, the Marshall Islands, the Federated States of Micronesia, Nauru, Palau, Papua New Guinea, Samoa, Solomon Islands, Tonga, Tuvalu, Vanuatu, and Niue); Oceania (Australia and New Zealand); ASEAN (Brunei Darussalam, Cambodia, Indonesia, the Lao PDR, Malaysia, the Philippines, Singapore, Thailand, and Viet Nam); CAREC (Afghanistan, Azerbaijan, the PRC, Georgia, Kazakhstan, the Kyrgyz Republic, Mongolia, Pakistan, Tajikistan, Turkmenistan, and Uzbekistan); GMS (Cambodia, the PRC, the Lao PDR, Myanmar, Thailand, and Viet Nam); SASEC (Bangladesh, Bhutan, India, Maldives, Myanmar, Nepal, and Sri Lanka); IMT-GT (Indonesia, Malaysia, and Thailand); BIMP-EAGA (Brunei Darussalam–Indonesia–Malaysia–Philippines East ASEAN Growth Area); SAARC (Afghanistan, Bangladesh, Bhutan, India, Maldives, Nepal, Pakistan, and Sri Lanka); BIMSTEC (Bangladesh, Bhutan, India, Myanmar, Nepal, Sri Lanka, and Thailand).

(iii) The regional integration index for each region (Table A1c) is calculated in the same method as ARCII but is based on worldwide normalization, i.e., normalizing raw indicator values using global minimum and maximum values.

(iv) Estimates for the Asian subregions and subregional initiatives represent intrasubregional and intrasubregional initiative integration, respectively.

(v) Remittance data used in Indicator V-c (Proportion of intraregional remittances to total remittances) was changed to outward remittances.

(vi) Indicator VIII-c (Environmental health score) is revised in the current estimation to ensure compatibility of values across time. It was recomputed using the time series data published by the Environmental Performance Index (EPI) team. Issue categories under the environmental health policy objective which do not have good data coverage from 2006 to 2020 were excluded from the computation (e.g., waste management).

Sources: Asian Development Bank (ADB). Asia Regional Integration Center. Asia-Pacific Regional Cooperation and Integration Index Database. https://aric.adb.org/database/arcii (accessed October 2019); and methodology from Park, C. Y. and R. Claveria. 2018. Constructing the Asia-Pacific Regional Integration Index: A Panel Approach. *ADB Economics Working Papers*. No. 544. Asian Development Bank; Huh, H. and C. Y. Park. 2018. Asia-Pacific Regional Integration Index: Construction, Interpretation, and Comparison. *Journal of Asian Economics*. 54. pp. 22–38; and Huh, H. and C.Y. Park. 2017. Asia-Pacific Regional Integration Index: Construction, Interpretation, and Comparison. *ADB Economics Working Papers*. No. 511. Asian Development Bank.

**Table A2: Regional Integration Indicators—Asia and the Pacific** (% of total)

| | Movement in Trade and Investment | | Movement in Capital | | People Movement | | |
|---|---|---|---|---|---|---|---|
| | Trade (%) | FDI (%) | Equity Holdings (%) | Bond Holdings (%) | Migration (%) | Tourism (%) | Remittances (%) |
| | 2023 | 2023 | 2023 | 2023 | 2021 | 2022 | 2021 |
| **Within subregions** | | | | | | | |
| ASEAN+3 (including HKG)[a] | 43.5 ▼ | 52.7 ▼ | 18.6 ▼ | 16.3 ▼ | 36.2 ▼ | 42.1 ▲ | 30.3 ▲ |
| Central Asia | 9.0 ▲ | 5.1 ▲ | 0.0 ▲ | 0.2 ▼ | 8.5 ▼ | 46.4 ▼ | 3.1 ▼ |
| East Asia | 30.7 ▼ | 63.0 ▲ | 15.8 ▼ | 10.7 ▼ | 32.3 ▼ | 15.4 ▲ | 32.8 ▲ |
| South Asia | 4.7 ▼ | 1.1 ▲ | 0.3 ▼ | 0.0 — | 19.3 ▼ | 5.2 ▼ | 6.7 ▼ |
| Southeast Asia | 21.5 ▼ | 7.8 ▼ | 6.6 ▼ | 8.0 ▼ | 29.9 ▼ | 47.8 ▲ | 10.8 ▼ |
| Oceania and the Pacific | 4.5 ▲ | 26.1 ▲ | 3.5 ▼ | 4.2 ▲ | 52.8 ▼ | 25.5 ▼ | 42.5 ▲ |
| **Across subregions** | | | | | | | |
| ASEAN+3 (including HKG)[a] | 12.8 ▼ | 3.2 ▼ | 3.8 ▲ | 5.5 ▲ | 13.1 ▼ | 6.2 ▼ | 8.7 ▲ |
| Central Asia | 29.5 ▲ | 64.6 ▼ | 7.5 ▼ | 11.5 ▼ | 0.7 ▼ | 0.5 ▼ | 0.2 ▼ |
| East Asia | 22.8 ▲ | 7.1 ▼ | 3.0 ▲ | 7.1 ▼ | 15.8 ▼ | 19.1 ▼ | 15.6 ▲ |
| South Asia | 32.0 ▲ | 53.4 ▲ | 7.4 ▼ | 0.0 ▼ | 7.9 ▲ | 17.5 ▼ | 8.9 ▲ |
| Southeast Asia | 47.2 ▲ | 27.0 ▼ | 28.1 ▼ | 31.9 ▼ | 20.2 ▲ | 19.5 ▼ | 20.2 ▲ |
| Oceania and the Pacific | 70.4 ▼ | 16.9 ▲ | 10.3 ▲ | 16.9 ▲ | 4.6 ▲ | 21.8 ▼ | 5.1 ▼ |
| **TOTAL (within and across subregions)** | | | | | | | |
| **Asia and the Pacific** | **56.1** ▼ | **55.0** ▲ | **21.1** ▼ | **21.6** ▼ | **34.8** ▼ | **44.7** ▲ | **25.5** ▼ |
| ASEAN+3 (including HKG)[a] | 56.3 ▼ | 56.0 ▼ | 22.4 ▼ | 21.8 ▼ | 49.3 ▼ | 48.3 ▲ | 39.0 ▲ |
| Central Asia | 38.5 ▲ | 69.7 ▲ | 7.5 ▼ | 11.7 ▼ | 9.2 ▼ | 46.9 ▼ | 3.2 ▼ |
| East Asia | 53.6 ▼ | 70.2 ▲ | 18.8 ▼ | 17.8 ▼ | 48.1 ▼ | 34.6 ▲ | 48.4 ▲ |
| South Asia | 36.7 ▼ | 54.5 ▲ | 7.6 ▼ | 7.3 ▼ | 27.2 ▲ | 22.7 ▼ | 15.6 ▲ |
| Southeast Asia | 68.7 ▲ | 34.8 ▼ | 34.6 ▼ | 40.0 ▼ | 50.1 ▼ | 67.3 ▲ | 31.0 ▲ |
| Oceania and the Pacific | 74.9 ▼ | 43.0 ▲ | 13.8 ▼ | 21.1 ▲ | 57.4 ▼ | 47.2 ▲ | 47.6 ▲ |
| **With the rest of the world** | | | | | | | |
| **Asia and the Pacific** | **43.9** ▲ | **45.0** ▼ | **78.9** ▲ | **78.4** ▲ | **65.2** ▲ | **55.3** ▼ | **74.5** ▲ |
| ASEAN+3 (including HKG)[a] | 43.7 ▲ | 44.0 ▲ | 77.6 ▲ | 78.2 ▲ | 50.7 ▲ | 51.7 ▼ | 61.0 ▼ |
| Central Asia | 61.5 ▼ | 30.3 ▼ | 92.5 ▲ | 88.3 ▲ | 90.8 ▲ | 53.1 ▲ | 96.8 ▲ |
| East Asia | 46.4 ▲ | 29.8 ▼ | 81.2 ▲ | 82.2 ▲ | 51.9 ▲ | 65.4 ▼ | 51.6 ▼ |
| South Asia | 63.3 ▲ | 45.5 ▼ | 92.4 ▲ | 92.7 ▲ | 72.8 ▼ | 77.3 ▲ | 84.4 ▼ |
| Southeast Asia | 31.3 ▼ | 65.2 ▲ | 65.4 ▲ | 60.0 ▲ | 49.9 ▲ | 32.7 ▼ | 69.0 ▼ |
| Oceania and the Pacific | 25.1 ▲ | 57.0 ▼ | 86.2 ▲ | 78.9 ▼ | 42.6 ▲ | 52.8 ▼ | 52.4 ▼ |

— = unchanged from previous period; ▲ = increase from previous period; ▼ = decrease from previous period.

ASEAN = Association of Southeast Asian Nations; FDI = foreign direct investment; HKG = Hong Kong, China.

[a] Includes ASEAN (Brunei Darussalam, Cambodia, Indonesia, the Lao People's Democratic Republic, Malaysia, Myanmar, the Philippines, Singapore, Thailand, and Viet Nam) plus the People's Republic of China; Hong Kong, China; Japan; and the Republic of Korea.

**Trade**—no data available on the Cook Islands and Niue.

**Equity and Bond Holdings**—based on investment from Australia; Bangladesh; the People's Republic of China; Hong Kong, China; India; Indonesia; Japan; Kazakhstan; the Republic of Korea; Malaysia; Mongolia; New Zealand; Pakistan; Palau; the Philippines; Singapore; and Thailand.

**Migration**—share of migrant stock to total migrants in 2021 (compared with 2020).

**Tourism**—share of outbound tourists to total tourists in 2022 (compared with 2021).

**Remittances**—share of inward remittances to total remittances in 2021 (compared with 2019).

Sources: ADB calculations using data from ASEAN Secretariat. ASEANstats Database. https://www.aseanstats.org (accessed July 2024); CEIC Data Company; Eurostat. Balance of Payments. http://ec.europa.eu/eurostat/web/balance-of-payments/data/database (accessed July 2024); International Monetary Fund (IMF). Coordinated Portfolio Investment Survey. https://data.imf.org/CPIS (accessed January 2025); IMF. Direction of Trade Statistics. https://data.imf.org/DOT (accessed November 2024); United Nations Department of Economic and Social Affairs, Population Division. International Migrant Stock 2020. http://www.un.org/en/development/desa/population/migration/data/index.shtml (accessed May 2024); United Nations Trade and Development. World Investment Report 2024 Statistical Annex Tables. https://unctad.org/topic/investment/world-investment-report (accessed July 2024); United Nations World Tourism Organization. Tourism Satellite Accounts. http://statistics.unwto.org (accessed November 2024); and World Bank Group. Global Knowledge Partnership for Migration and Development (KNOMAD). Bilateral Migration staff estimates (accessed June 2024).

**Table A3: Trade Shares—Asia and the Pacific, 2023** (% of total trade)

| | Partner | | | | | |
|---|---|---|---|---|---|---|
| | | of which | | | | |
| Reporter | Asia and the Pacific | PRC | Japan | EU+UK | US | ROW |
| **Central Asia** | **38.5** | **20.6** | **1.3** | **24.6** | **2.7** | **34.2** |
| Armenia | 24.7 | 9.9 | 1.6 | 12.6 | 3.1 | 59.6 |
| Azerbaijan | 17.4 | 6.1 | 0.9 | 50.0 | 1.8 | 30.8 |
| Georgia | 33.4 | 7.6 | 2.9 | 21.6 | 9.9 | 35.1 |
| Kazakhstan | 39.2 | 22.5 | 1.6 | 28.0 | 2.9 | 29.9 |
| Kyrgyz Republic | 55.7 | 34.2 | 1.6 | 7.1 | 2.8 | 34.5 |
| Tajikistan | 50.0 | 18.2 | 2.0 | 7.3 | 1.7 | 41.0 |
| Turkmenistan | 71.5 | 54.9 | 1.0 | 11.1 | 0.3 | 17.0 |
| Uzbekistan | 45.8 | 23.2 | 0.4 | 10.6 | 0.8 | 42.8 |
| **East Asia** | **53.6** | **13.2** | **4.7** | **12.7** | **11.6** | **22.1** |
| China, People's Republic of | 44.9 | — | 5.3 | 14.8 | 11.3 | 29.1 |
| Hong Kong, China | 78.2 | 48.1 | 3.6 | 7.4 | 5.0 | 9.4 |
| Japan | 55.8 | 20.0 | — | 11.5 | 15.2 | 17.4 |
| Korea, Republic of | 55.3 | 21.0 | 6.0 | 11.6 | 14.7 | 18.4 |
| Mongolia | 69.8 | 63.0 | 2.6 | 3.6 | 1.1 | 25.4 |
| Taipei,China | 69.8 | 27.8 | 8.1 | 9.4 | 13.2 | 7.6 |
| **South Asia** | **36.7** | **11.7** | **2.1** | **15.0** | **10.3** | **38.0** |
| Bangladesh | 47.8 | 16.8 | 3.0 | 24.9 | 9.2 | 18.1 |
| Bhutan | 98.5 | 2.3 | 0.1 | 0.9 | 0.1 | 0.5 |
| India | 34.4 | 10.7 | 2.1 | 14.1 | 10.8 | 40.7 |
| Maldives | 57.3 | 11.0 | 1.2 | 9.1 | 2.3 | 31.4 |
| Nepal | 82.1 | 14.5 | 0.4 | 4.3 | 1.6 | 12.0 |
| Pakistan | 37.6 | 18.4 | 1.5 | 17.6 | 8.5 | 36.3 |
| Sri Lanka | 42.0 | 10.7 | 1.2 | 16.5 | 10.4 | 31.0 |
| **Southeast Asia** | **68.7** | **19.8** | **6.8** | **8.9** | **11.3** | **11.1** |
| Brunei Darussalam | 81.6 | 14.3 | 8.7 | 2.3 | 2.0 | 14.1 |
| Cambodia | 62.6 | 25.1 | 3.7 | 11.3 | 18.7 | 7.3 |
| Indonesia | 73.2 | 26.6 | 7.8 | 7.0 | 7.2 | 12.6 |
| Lao People's Democratic Republic | 92.6 | 30.9 | 2.8 | 3.7 | 2.3 | 1.4 |
| Malaysia | 71.1 | 17.1 | 5.9 | 8.5 | 9.5 | 10.9 |
| Philippines | 74.4 | 20.1 | 10.4 | 8.8 | 10.0 | 6.9 |
| Singapore | 68.4 | 13.8 | 4.5 | 10.2 | 10.8 | 10.6 |
| Thailand | 64.3 | 18.4 | 9.8 | 8.4 | 11.9 | 15.4 |
| Timor-Leste | 89.2 | 17.8 | 4.6 | 2.0 | 2.8 | 6.0 |
| Viet Nam | 64.9 | 25.7 | 6.7 | 9.4 | 16.5 | 9.2 |
| **Pacific** | **82.5** | **18.3** | **9.2** | **9.1** | **2.1** | **6.4** |
| Fiji | 78.3 | 12.0 | 3.1 | 4.9 | 8.9 | 8.0 |
| Kiribati | 86.8 | 7.6 | 3.7 | 2.9 | 4.4 | 5.9 |
| Marshall Islands | 81.2 | 18.1 | 6.1 | 13.1 | 0.4 | 5.3 |
| Micronesia, Federated States of | 37.0 | 6.6 | 4.1 | 0.3 | 13.2 | 49.5 |
| Nauru | 93.3 | 2.5 | 3.8 | 0.6 | 0.9 | 5.2 |
| Palau | 29.8 | 6.8 | 2.5 | 19.8 | 15.8 | 34.6 |
| Papua New Guinea | 88.2 | 20.6 | 15.6 | 6.5 | 1.3 | 4.1 |
| Samoa | 85.0 | 8.9 | 2.7 | 2.3 | 7.9 | 4.8 |
| Solomon Islands | 86.7 | 43.8 | 2.1 | 9.2 | 1.1 | 3.0 |
| Tonga | 85.5 | 11.8 | 7.1 | 2.3 | 8.0 | 4.2 |
| Tuvalu | 93.0 | 1.6 | 1.8 | 1.8 | 1.9 | 3.4 |
| Vanuatu | 75.2 | 6.6 | 8.3 | 2.3 | 1.4 | 21.2 |
| **Oceania** | **74.5** | **30.5** | **10.9** | **10.3** | **7.5** | **7.7** |
| Australia | 75.5 | 31.5 | 11.5 | 9.9 | 7.1 | 7.6 |
| New Zealand | 67.0 | 23.5 | 6.2 | 13.4 | 10.8 | 8.9 |
| **Asia and the Pacific** | **56.1** | **15.1** | **5.2** | **12.2** | **11.1** | **20.7** |
| **Developing Asia** | **55.2** | **14.1** | **5.4** | **12.3** | **10.8** | **21.6** |

PRC = People's Republic of China, EU = European Union (27 members), ROW = rest of the world, UK = United Kingdom, US = United States.

Source: ADB calculations using data from International Monetary Fund. Direction of Trade Statistics. http://data.imf.org/dot (accessed December 2024).

**Table A4: Free Trade Agreement Status—Asia and the Pacific, as of December 2024**

| Economy | Under Negotiation | | Signed But Not Yet In Effect | Signed and In Effect | Total |
|---|---|---|---|---|---|
| | Framework Agreement Signed | Negotiations Launched | | | |
| Armenia | 0 | 6 | 2 | 13 | 21 |
| Australia | 0 | 3 | 2 | 21 | 26 |
| Azerbaijan | 0 | 1 | 1 | 10 | 12 |
| Bangladesh | 0 | 3 | 0 | 5 | 8 |
| Bhutan | 0 | 2 | 0 | 3 | 5 |
| Brunei Darussalam | 0 | 1 | 0 | 11 | 12 |
| Cambodia | 0 | 1 | 1 | 10 | 12 |
| China, People's Republic of | 0 | 9 | 2 | 23 | 34 |
| Cook Islands | 0 | 0 | 0 | 4 | 4 |
| Fiji | 0 | 0 | 0 | 6 | 6 |
| Georgia | 0 | 1 | 0 | 16 | 17 |
| Hong Kong, China | 0 | 2 | 0 | 8 | 10 |
| India | 0 | 20 | 1 | 16 | 37 |
| Indonesia | 0 | 11 | 2 | 17 | 30 |
| Japan | 0 | 7 | 0 | 21 | 28 |
| Kazakhstan | 0 | 8 | 2 | 13 | 23 |
| Kiribati | 0 | 0 | 0 | 4 | 4 |
| Korea, Republic of | 0 | 12 | 3 | 25 | 40 |
| Kyrgyz Republic | 0 | 6 | 2 | 13 | 21 |
| Lao People's Democratic Republic | 0 | 1 | 0 | 11 | 12 |
| Malaysia | 0 | 8 | 0 | 19 | 27 |
| Maldives | 0 | 1 | 2 | 2 | 5 |
| Marshall Islands | 0 | 0 | 0 | 5 | 5 |
| Micronesia, Federated States of | 0 | 0 | 0 | 5 | 5 |
| Mongolia | 0 | 2 | 0 | 2 | 4 |
| Nauru | 0 | 0 | 0 | 4 | 4 |
| Nepal | 0 | 1 | 0 | 2 | 3 |
| New Zealand | 0 | 3 | 1 | 16 | 20 |
| Niue | 0 | 0 | 0 | 4 | 4 |
| Pakistan | 0 | 6 | 2 | 11 | 19 |
| Palau | 0 | 0 | 0 | 4 | 4 |
| Papua New Guinea | 0 | 0 | 0 | 7 | 7 |
| Philippines | 0 | 3 | 1 | 10 | 14 |
| Samoa | 0 | 0 | 0 | 5 | 5 |
| Singapore | 0 | 7 | 4 | 30 | 41 |
| Solomon Islands | 0 | 0 | 0 | 6 | 6 |
| Sri Lanka | 0 | 5 | 1 | 6 | 12 |
| Taipei,China | 1 | 2 | 2 | 5 | 10 |
| Tajikistan | 0 | 0 | 0 | 8 | 8 |
| Thailand | 1 | 10 | 1 | 15 | 27 |
| Tonga | 0 | 0 | 0 | 4 | 4 |
| Turkmenistan | 0 | 0 | 1 | 5 | 6 |
| Tuvalu | 0 | 0 | 0 | 4 | 4 |
| Uzbekistan | 0 | 1 | 0 | 12 | 13 |
| Vanuatu | 0 | 0 | 1 | 5 | 6 |
| Viet Nam | 0 | 2 | 2 | 16 | 20 |

Notes:

(i) Framework agreement signed: The parties initially negotiate the contents of a framework agreement, which serves as a framework for future negotiations.
(ii) Negotiations launched: The parties, through the relevant ministries, declare the official launch of negotiations or set the date for such, or start the first round of negotiations.
(iii) Signed but not yet in effect: Parties sign the agreement after negotiations have been completed. However, the agreement has yet to be implemented.
(iv) Signed and in effect: Provisions of free trade agreement come into force, after legislative or executive ratification.

Source: ADB. Asia Regional Integation Center. https://aric.adb.org (accessed February 2025)

**Table A5: Cross-Border Portfolio Equity Holdings—Asia and the Pacific, 2023** (% of total cross-border portfolio equity holdings)

| | Partner | | | | | |
|---|---|---|---|---|---|---|
| | | of which | | | | |
| Reporter | Asia and the Pacific | PRC | Japan | EU+UK | US | ROW |
| **Central Asia** | **7.5** | **0.1** | **5.1** | **18.5** | **67.9** | **6.2** |
| Armenia | — | — | — | — | — | — |
| Azerbaijan | — | — | — | — | — | — |
| Georgia | — | — | — | — | — | — |
| Kazakhstan | 7.5 | 0.1 | 5.1 | 18.5 | 67.9 | 6.2 |
| Kyrgyz Republic | — | — | — | — | — | — |
| Tajikistan | — | — | — | — | — | — |
| Turkmenistan | — | — | — | — | — | — |
| Uzbekistan | — | — | — | — | — | — |
| **East Asia** | **18.8** | **5.7** | **1.3** | **13.5** | **33.8** | **33.9** |
| China, People's Republic of | 55.2 | — | 1.1 | 8.4 | 20.9 | 15.5 |
| Hong Kong, China | 29.8 | 21.4 | 3.1 | 11.6 | 8.5 | 50.1 |
| Japan | 4.7 | 0.4 | — | 14.6 | 42.0 | 38.7 |
| Korea, Republic of | 10.0 | 1.8 | 3.1 | 18.1 | 63.1 | 8.7 |
| Mongolia | 54.7 | 3.1 | 0.9 | 19.8 | 19.6 | 5.9 |
| Taipei,China | — | — | — | — | — | — |
| **South Asia** | **7.6** | **1.3** | **0.4** | **26.3** | **61.4** | **4.7** |
| Bangladesh | 100.0 | — | — | — | — | 0.0 |
| Bhutan | — | — | — | — | — | — |
| India | 7.7 | 1.3 | 0.4 | 26.7 | 62.4 | 3.3 |
| Maldives | — | — | — | — | — | — |
| Nepal | — | — | — | — | — | — |
| Pakistan | — | — | — | 0.4 | 1.3 | 98.3 |
| Sri Lanka | — | — | — | — | — | — |
| **Southeast Asia** | **34.6** | **8.9** | **4.0** | **13.4** | **25.8** | **26.1** |
| Brunei Darussalam | — | — | — | — | — | — |
| Cambodia | — | — | — | — | — | — |
| Indonesia | 98.5 | 0.0 | 0.4 | 0.0 | 0.2 | 1.2 |
| Lao People's Democratic Republic | — | — | — | — | — | — |
| Malaysia | 44.5 | 6.7 | 4.2 | 19.7 | 27.5 | 8.3 |
| Philippines | 20.0 | 0.1 | 0.0 | 60.5 | 18.2 | 1.2 |
| Singapore | 33.9 | 9.8 | 4.3 | 11.7 | 25.8 | 28.6 |
| Thailand | 15.0 | 0.5 | 0.6 | 30.2 | 28.5 | 26.2 |
| Timor-Leste | — | — | — | — | — | — |
| Viet Nam | — | — | — | — | — | — |
| **Oceania and the Pacific** | **13.8** | **1.7** | **4.1** | **15.2** | **53.6** | **17.5** |
| Australia | 12.4 | 1.8 | 4.2 | 15.8 | 54.0 | 17.8 |
| Cook Islands | — | — | — | — | — | — |
| Fiji | — | — | — | — | — | — |
| Kiribati | — | — | — | — | — | — |
| Marshall Islands | — | — | — | — | — | — |
| Micronesia, Federated States of | — | — | — | — | — | — |
| Nauru | — | — | — | — | — | — |
| New Zealand | 24.8 | 0.6 | 3.1 | 9.9 | 50.1 | 15.2 |
| Niue | — | — | — | — | — | — |
| Palau | — | — | — | — | — | — |
| Papua New Guinea | — | — | — | — | — | — |
| Samoa | — | — | — | — | — | — |
| Solomon Islands | — | — | — | — | — | — |
| Tonga | — | — | — | — | — | — |
| Tuvalu | — | — | — | — | — | — |
| Vanuatu | — | — | — | — | — | — |
| **Asia and the Pacific** | **21.1** | **5.7** | **2.3** | **13.8** | **35.2** | **29.9** |
| **Developing Asia** | **32.2** | **9.7** | **3.1** | **12.9** | **26.7** | **28.2** |

— = unavailable, PRC = People's Republic of China, EU = European Union (27 members), ROW = rest of the world, UK = United Kingdom, US = United States.

Source: ADB calculations using data from International Monetary Fund Coordinated Portfolio Investment Survey. http://cpis.imf.org (accessed January 2025).

**Table A6: Cross-Border Portfolio Debt Holdings—Asia and the Pacific, 2023** (% of total cross-border portfolio debt holdings)

| Reporter | Partner | | | | | |
|---|---|---|---|---|---|---|
| | Asia and the Pacific | of which | | EU+UK | US | ROW |
| | | PRC | Japan | | | |
| **Central Asia** | **11.7** | **1.3** | **2.1** | **14.0** | **49.3** | **25.0** |
| Armenia | — | — | — | — | — | — |
| Azerbaijan | — | — | — | — | — | — |
| Georgia | — | — | — | — | — | — |
| Kazakhstan | 11.7 | 1.3 | 2.1 | 14.0 | 49.3 | 25.0 |
| Kyrgyz Republic | — | — | — | — | — | — |
| Tajikistan | — | — | — | — | — | — |
| Turkmenistan | — | — | — | — | — | — |
| Uzbekistan | — | — | — | — | — | — |
| **East Asia** | **17.8** | **5.0** | **1.9** | **23.1** | **42.1** | **17.1** |
| China, People's Republic of | 31.1 | — | 2.7 | 13.1 | 26.6 | 29.2 |
| Hong Kong, China | 40.5 | 20.9 | 6.8 | 13.9 | 29.4 | 16.2 |
| Japan | 8.0 | 0.9 | — | 28.2 | 48.8 | 15.0 |
| Korea, Republic of | 12.9 | 2.8 | 3.2 | 22.5 | 48.6 | 16.0 |
| Mongolia | 54.9 | 6.1 | 0.6 | 16.8 | 22.9 | 5.4 |
| Taipei,China | — | — | — | — | — | — |
| **South Asia** | **7.3** | **—** | **—** | **3.9** | **82.7** | **6.2** |
| Bangladesh | — | — | — | — | — | — |
| Bhutan | — | — | — | — | — | — |
| India | 7.4 | — | — | 4.1 | 88.4 | 0.1 |
| Maldives | — | — | — | — | — | — |
| Nepal | — | — | — | — | — | — |
| Pakistan | 5.8 | — | — | — | — | 94.2 |
| Sri Lanka | — | — | — | — | — | — |
| **Southeast Asia** | **40.0** | **8.7** | **8.4** | **4.9** | **35.8** | **19.3** |
| Brunei Darussalam | — | — | — | — | — | — |
| Cambodia | — | — | — | — | — | — |
| Indonesia | 85.3 | 1.1 | 0.1 | 0.2 | 11.1 | 3.4 |
| Lao People's Democratic Republic | — | — | — | — | — | — |
| Malaysia | 45.6 | 12.0 | 2.9 | 12.1 | 19.9 | 22.4 |
| Philippines | 39.1 | 2.9 | 1.7 | 6.0 | 37.0 | 18.0 |
| Singapore | 37.7 | 9.0 | 8.5 | 4.6 | 37.9 | 19.8 |
| Thailand | 61.8 | 5.0 | 19.6 | 8.2 | 15.4 | 14.6 |
| Timor-Leste | — | — | — | — | — | — |
| Viet Nam | — | — | — | — | — | — |
| **Oceania and the Pacific** | **21.1** | **3.1** | **5.7** | **28.7** | **31.3** | **19.0** |
| Australia | 20.7 | 3.3 | 6.5 | 30.6 | 30.3 | 18.3 |
| Cook Islands | — | — | — | — | — | — |
| Fiji | — | — | — | — | — | — |
| Kiribati | — | — | — | — | — | — |
| Marshall Islands | — | — | — | — | — | — |
| Micronesia, Federated States of | — | — | — | — | — | — |
| Nauru | — | — | — | — | — | — |
| New Zealand | 23.4 | 1.3 | — | 15.1 | 37.7 | 23.8 |
| Niue | — | — | — | — | — | — |
| Palau | — | — | — | — | — | — |
| Papua New Guinea | — | — | — | — | — | — |
| Samoa | — | — | — | — | — | — |
| Solomon Islands | — | — | — | — | — | — |
| Tonga | — | — | — | — | — | — |
| Tuvalu | — | — | — | — | — | — |
| Vanuatu | — | — | — | — | — | — |
| **Asia and the Pacific** | **21.6** | **5.4** | **3.3** | **20.3** | **40.4** | **17.7** |
| **Developing Asia** | **35.0** | **10.2** | **6.1** | **11.4** | **33.5** | **20.1** |

— = unavailable, PRC = People's Republic of China, EU = European Union (27 members), ROW = rest of the world, UK = United Kingdom, US = United States.

Source: ADB calculations using data from International Monetary Fund. Coordinated Portfolio Investment Survey. http://cpis.imf.org (accessed January 2025).

**Table A7: Foreign Direct Investment Inflow Share—Asia and the Pacific, 2023** (% of total FDI inflows)

| Reporter | Partner | | | | | |
|---|---|---|---|---|---|---|
| | Asia and the Pacific | of which | | EU+UK | US | ROW |
| | | PRC | Japan | | | |
| **Central Asia** | **69.7** | **28.3** | **7.7** | **155.0** | **16.0** | **(140.6)** |
| Armenia | 0.9 | (0.0) | — | (1.5) | 6.9 | 93.7 |
| Azerbaijan | 161.2 | 4.1 | 110.5 | 1,106.7 | 110.1 | (1,278.0) |
| Georgia | 10.5 | 2.7 | 3.7 | 87.8 | 11.1 | (9.4) |
| Kazakhstan | 127.0 | 51.3 | 12.5 | 329.0 | 32.2 | (388.3) |
| Kyrgyz Republic | 85.1 | 57.2 | 0.5 | 22.4 | 3.8 | (11.3) |
| Tajikistan | 281.7 | 268.6 | 2.5 | 24.4 | 11.3 | (217.4) |
| Turkmenistan | 60.9 | 0.7 | — | 3.3 | — | 35.8 |
| Uzbekistan | 20.3 | 16.9 | 0.2 | 2.9 | (0.4) | 77.3 |
| **East Asia** | **70.2** | **13.4** | **2.3** | **11.9** | **5.7** | **12.3** |
| China, People's Republic of | 99.4 | — | 2.8 | 7.1 | 1.4 | (7.9) |
| Hong Kong, China | 41.8 | 35.8 | 0.9 | 10.2 | 5.2 | 42.8 |
| Japan | 45.8 | 5.8 | — | 28.1 | 17.7 | 8.3 |
| Korea, Republic of | 23.4 | 5.1 | 8.6 | 41.1 | 40.4 | (4.9) |
| Mongolia | 24.9 | 8.6 | 3.4 | 115.2 | 4.1 | (44.1) |
| Taipei,China | 28.7 | 9.0 | 6.0 | 1.4 | 0.7 | 69.2 |
| **South Asia** | **54.5** | **2.7** | **9.6** | **26.4** | **13.1** | **6.0** |
| Bangladesh | 46.2 | 6.2 | 3.4 | 39.5 | 11.8 | 2.6 |
| Bhutan | 44.2 | — | — | 6.5 | — | 49.3 |
| India | 56.4 | 0.1 | 11.0 | 25.1 | 13.9 | 4.6 |
| Maldives | 0.7 | (0.4) | 0.6 | 0.9 | — | 98.4 |
| Nepal | 32.0 | 15.7 | 4.3 | 2.9 | 4.5 | 60.7 |
| Pakistan | 67.6 | 37.5 | 4.9 | 31.3 | 11.1 | (10.0) |
| Sri Lanka | 41.9 | 0.8 | 2.2 | 39.7 | 4.6 | 13.8 |
| **Southeast Asia** | **34.8** | **6.3** | **5.0** | **10.8** | **32.7** | **21.7** |
| Brunei Darussalam | 414.7 | (7.7) | 86.9 | (343.3) | 35.4 | (6.8) |
| Cambodia | 84.1 | 50.3 | 7.6 | 2.8 | 1.3 | 11.8 |
| Indonesia | 75.2 | 7.7 | 8.2 | 9.5 | 4.0 | 11.3 |
| Lao People's Democratic Republic | 2.0 | 0.5 | 0.1 | 0.4 | 0.1 | 97.4 |
| Malaysia | 131.0 | 10.3 | 13.9 | (30.1) | (3.5) | 2.6 |
| Philippines | 17.7 | 0.3 | 13.7 | 0.9 | 1.8 | 79.6 |
| Singapore | 25.1 | 4.5 | 3.7 | 14.3 | 45.9 | 14.7 |
| Thailand | 77.5 | 34.5 | 23.3 | 32.0 | 1.8 | (11.3) |
| Timor-Leste | (32.1) | (32.1) | — | 145.3 | — | (13.1) |
| Viet Nam | 5.8 | 1.6 | 0.5 | 1.2 | 0.3 | 92.7 |
| **Oceania and the Pacific** | **43.0** | **2.4** | **20.5** | **50.7** | **4.5** | **1.7** |
| Australia | 23.8 | 1.9 | 20.1 | 53.1 | 2.8 | 20.3 |
| Cook Islands | — | — | — | — | — | — |
| Fiji | 11.8 | 2.2 | 1.9 | 4.4 | 6.0 | 77.8 |
| Kiribati | — | — | — | — | — | — |
| Marshall Islands | — | — | — | — | — | — |
| Micronesia, Federated States of | — | — | — | — | — | — |
| Nauru | — | — | — | — | — | — |
| New Zealand | 142.9 | 1.2 | 19.7 | 21.1 | 19.6 | (83.6) |
| Niue | — | — | — | — | — | — |
| Palau | 7.6 | 1.8 | 4.5 | — | 4.3 | 88.1 |
| Papua New Guinea | (436.9) | (42.7) | (1.1) | (11.6) | — | 548.6 |
| Samoa | — | — | — | — | — | — |
| Solomon Islands | 37.4 | 6.0 | 4.1 | 12.2 | 8.0 | 42.4 |
| Tonga | — | — | — | — | — | — |
| Tuvalu | — | — | — | — | — | — |
| Vanuatu | 140.9 | 38.8 | 35.0 | 101.8 | — | (142.7) |
| **Asia and the Pacific** | **55.0** | **9.9** | **4.7** | **16.6** | **16.0** | **12.4** |
| **Developing Asia** | **56.5** | **10.5** | **4.0** | **14.2** | **16.6** | **12.7** |

( ) = negative, — = unavailable, PRC = People's Republic of China, EU = European Union (27 members), FDI = foreign direct investment, ROW = rest of the world, UK = United Kingdom, US = United States.

Sources: ADB calculations using data from the ASEAN Secretariat. ASEANstats Data Portal. https://data.aseanstats.org (accessed July 2024); CEIC Data Company; Eurostat. Balance of Payments. https://ec.europa.eu/eurostat (accessed July 2024); International Monetary Fund. World Economic Outlook Database, April 2024. https://www.imf.org/en/Publications/WEO/weo-database/2024/April (accessed April 2024); and UN Trade and Development. World Investment Report 2024 Statistical Annex Tables. https://unctad.org/topic/investment/world-investment-report (accessed July 2024).

**Table A8: Remittance Inflows Share—Asia and the Pacific, 2021** (% of total remittance inflows)

| | Partner | | | | |
|---|---|---|---|---|---|
| Reporter | Asia and the Pacific | Middle East | EU+UK | US | ROW |
| **Central Asia** | **3.2** | **2.1** | **7.8** | **2.2** | **84.7** |
| Armenia | 4.3 | 0.5 | 14.8 | 12.3 | 68.1 |
| Azerbaijan | 7.3 | 9.9 | 5.6 | 3.1 | 74.1 |
| Georgia | 9.8 | 4.3 | 21.9 | 5.0 | 59.0 |
| Kazakhstan | 1.3 | 1.2 | 30.0 | 0.9 | 66.7 |
| Kyrgyz Republic | 2.9 | 4.3 | 15.2 | 1.4 | 76.2 |
| Tajikistan | 5.2 | 1.3 | 7.5 | 1.5 | 84.5 |
| Turkmenistan | — | — | — | — | 100.0 |
| Uzbekistan | — | — | — | — | 100.0 |
| **East Asia** | **48.4** | **0.3** | **11.1** | **28.1** | **12.0** |
| China, People's Republic of | 52.8 | 0.4 | 11.1 | 23.9 | 11.8 |
| Hong Kong, China | 39.0 | 0.0 | 12.7 | 22.9 | 25.3 |
| Japan | 23.0 | 0.3 | 16.3 | 44.0 | 16.4 |
| Korea, Republic of | 37.1 | 0.2 | 5.7 | 48.3 | 8.7 |
| Mongolia | 39.2 | 1.7 | 35.4 | — | 23.7 |
| Taipei,China | — | — | — | — | — |
| **South Asia** | **15.6** | **56.6** | **10.6** | **12.8** | **4.5** |
| Bangladesh | 34.7 | 52.4 | 7.2 | 4.2 | 1.4 |
| Bhutan | 85.6 | — | 4.1 | — | 10.3 |
| India | 9.9 | 58.2 | 9.1 | 17.7 | 5.1 |
| Maldives | 73.3 | 0.8 | 18.6 | — | 7.3 |
| Nepal | 49.5 | 36.6 | 4.7 | 8.3 | 0.9 |
| Pakistan | 8.1 | 62.1 | 17.1 | 8.0 | 4.8 |
| Sri Lanka | 21.2 | 46.8 | 19.1 | 2.9 | 10.0 |
| **Southeast Asia** | **31.0** | **19.5** | **11.1** | **30.1** | **8.3** |
| Brunei Darussalam | — | — | — | — | — |
| Cambodia | 69.5 | 0.0 | 8.9 | 18.5 | 3.1 |
| Indonesia | 41.3 | 51.3 | 3.9 | 2.5 | 1.0 |
| Lao People's Democratic Republic | 76.0 | — | 5.1 | 17.3 | 1.6 |
| Malaysia | 88.8 | 0.1 | 4.7 | 4.2 | 2.3 |
| Philippines | 16.5 | 27.5 | 9.0 | 35.0 | 12.1 |
| Singapore | — | — | — | — | — |
| Timor-Leste | 41.4 | 2.1 | 25.6 | 24.1 | 6.8 |
| Thailand | 85.2 | — | 14.5 | — | 0.3 |
| Viet Nam | 35.7 | 0.0 | 13.6 | 43.7 | 7.0 |
| **Oceania and the Pacific** | **47.6** | **0.7** | **22.5** | **19.8** | **9.4** |
| Australia | 27.9 | 1.6 | 46.4 | 16.2 | 7.9 |
| Cook Islands | — | — | — | — | — |
| Fiji | 63.5 | — | 3.1 | 21.6 | 11.8 |
| Kiribati | 90.5 | — | 7.5 | — | 2.0 |
| Marshall Islands | 0.8 | — | 0.1 | 97.4 | 1.6 |
| Micronesia, Federated States of | — | — | — | — | — |
| Nauru | — | — | — | — | — |
| New Zealand | 78.3 | 0.0 | 12.4 | 6.7 | 2.5 |
| Niue | — | — | — | — | — |
| Palau | 13.1 | — | 8.2 | — | 78.7 |
| Papua New Guinea | 93.8 | — | 4.7 | — | 1.5 |
| Samoa | 68.5 | — | 0.8 | 22.5 | 8.2 |
| Solomon Islands | 87.1 | — | 12.3 | — | 0.6 |
| Tonga | 57.0 | — | 0.7 | 40.0 | 2.2 |
| Tuvalu | — | — | — | — | — |
| Vanuatu | 56.9 | — | 16.5 | — | 26.6 |
| **Asia and the Pacific** | **25.5** | **32.2** | **10.7** | **19.5** | **12.2** |
| **Developing Asia** | **25.5** | **32.8** | **10.5** | **19.1** | **12.1** |

— = unavailable, EU = European Union (27 members), ROW = rest of the world, UK = United Kingdom, US = United States.

Source: ADB calculations using data from World Bank. Global Knowledge Partnership for Migration and Development. Bilateral Remittance staff estimates (December 2022). https://knomad.org/data/remittances (accessed August 2023).

**Table A9: Outbound Migration Share—Asia and the Pacific, 2021** (% of total outbound migrants)

| Reporter | Partner: Asia and the Pacific | of which: PRC | of which: Japan | EU+UK | US | ROW |
|---|---|---|---|---|---|---|
| **Central Asia** | **9.2** | **—** | **—** | **16.1** | **2.5** | **72.2** |
| Armenia | 18.4 | — | — | 12.1 | 9.4 | 60.1 |
| Azerbaijan | 13.5 | — | — | 4.9 | 2.6 | 79.0 |
| Georgia | 10.7 | — | — | 21.1 | 4.4 | 63.8 |
| Kazakhstan | 1.4 | — | — | 28.6 | 0.9 | 69.2 |
| Kyrgyz Republic | 3.6 | — | — | 12.9 | 1.1 | 82.4 |
| Tajikistan | 6.2 | — | — | 6.2 | 1.2 | 86.4 |
| Turkmenistan | 1.6 | — | — | 2.9 | 0.9 | 94.6 |
| Uzbekistan | 21.7 | — | — | 3.9 | 3.1 | 71.3 |
| **East Asia** | **48.1** | **2.4** | **8.1** | **11.0** | **27.7** | **13.2** |
| China, People's Republic of | 52.9 | — | 7.0 | 11.3 | 23.3 | 12.5 |
| Hong Kong, China | 38.9 | 20.7 | — | 12.8 | 23.0 | 25.3 |
| Japan | 23.4 | 0.7 | — | 16.4 | 43.2 | 17.0 |
| Korea, Republic of | 37.8 | 6.6 | 20.7 | 5.7 | 47.5 | 9.0 |
| Mongolia | 38.7 | — | — | 34.7 | — | 26.6 |
| Taipei,China | — | — | — | — | — | — |
| **South Asia** | **27.2** | **0.0** | **0.2** | **9.7** | **8.8** | **54.2** |
| Bangladesh | 42.1 | 0.0 | 0.2 | 6.6 | 3.5 | 47.9 |
| Bhutan | 87.7 | — | — | 3.4 | — | 8.8 |
| India | 18.8 | 0.0 | 0.2 | 8.4 | 15.0 | 57.8 |
| Maldives | 75.0 | — | — | 17.1 | — | 7.9 |
| Nepal | 58.2 | — | — | 4.1 | 6.6 | 31.1 |
| Pakistan | 20.5 | 0.1 | 0.3 | 15.2 | 6.4 | 57.9 |
| Sri Lanka | 22.7 | 0.2 | 1.3 | 19.0 | 2.7 | 55.6 |
| **Southeast Asia** | **50.1** | **1.7** | **3.1** | **7.6** | **18.7** | **23.5** |
| Brunei Darussalam | 74.7 | — | — | 13.7 | — | 11.6 |
| Cambodia | 75.8 | — | 0.4 | 7.5 | 14.0 | 2.6 |
| Indonesia | 42.7 | 0.7 | 1.2 | 3.7 | 2.3 | 51.3 |
| Lao People's Democratic Republic | 80.5 | — | — | 4.4 | 13.8 | 1.4 |
| Malaysia | 88.4 | 0.3 | 0.6 | 4.9 | 4.2 | 2.5 |
| Philippines | 17.2 | 0.9 | 4.5 | 9.2 | 33.5 | 40.1 |
| Singapore | 66.0 | — | 0.9 | 17.9 | 10.2 | 5.9 |
| Thailand | 42.7 | 1.1 | 4.8 | 25.5 | 23.2 | 8.6 |
| Timor-Leste | 87.0 | — | — | 12.7 | — | 0.2 |
| Viet Nam | 38.2 | 8.9 | 9.8 | 13.6 | 41.1 | 7.0 |
| **Oceania and the Pacific** | **57.4** | **0.2** | **0.8** | **20.2** | **15.0** | **7.4** |
| Australia | 27.9 | 0.7 | 1.9 | 46.6 | 16.0 | 9.5 |
| Cook Islands | — | — | — | — | — | — |
| Fiji | 64.5 | — | — | 3.2 | 20.4 | 11.9 |
| Kiribati | 91.5 | — | — | 6.3 | — | 2.2 |
| Marshall Islands | 1.2 | — | — | 0.1 | 95.9 | 2.8 |
| Micronesia, Federated States of | 1.6 | — | — | 0.4 | 69.9 | 28.1 |
| Nauru | 96.3 | — | — | 1.5 | — | 2.2 |
| New Zealand | 78.4 | — | 0.5 | 12.5 | 6.5 | 2.6 |
| Niue | — | — | — | — | — | — |
| Palau | 13.0 | — | — | 7.6 | — | 79.4 |
| Papua New Guinea | 93.7 | — | — | 4.8 | — | 1.5 |
| Samoa | 67.6 | — | — | 0.8 | 19.9 | 11.8 |
| Solomon Islands | 88.2 | — | — | 11.1 | — | 0.6 |
| Tonga | 59.0 | — | — | 0.7 | 37.2 | 3.1 |
| Tuvalu | 80.8 | — | — | 3.8 | — | 15.4 |
| Vanuatu | 45.1 | — | — | 13.1 | — | 41.8 |
| **Asia and the Pacific** | **34.8** | **0.8** | **2.2** | **10.4** | **13.7** | **41.2** |
| **Developing Asia** | **34.6** | **0.8** | **2.2** | **10.1** | **13.5** | **41.9** |

— = unavailable, PRC = People's Republic of China, EU = European Union (27 members), ROW = rest of the world, UK = United Kingdom, US = United States.

Source: ADB calculations using data from World Bank. Global Knowledge Partnership on Migration and Development (KNOMAD). KNOMAD/World Bank Bilateral Migration Matrix 2021, December 2022 (accessed June 2024).

**Table A10a: Inbound Tourism Share—Asia and the Pacific, 2022** (% of total inbound visitors)

| Destination | Origin | | | | |
|---|---|---|---|---|---|
| | Asia and the Pacific | of which PRC | EU+UK | US | ROW |
| **Central Asia** | **62.4** | **0.2** | **2.9** | **0.6** | **34.0** |
| Armenia | 26.8 | 0.3 | 7.8 | 3.2 | 62.3 |
| Azerbaijan | 18.2 | 0.2 | 4.6 | 0.8 | 76.4 |
| Georgia | 27.7 | 0.2 | 6.2 | 0.8 | 65.3 |
| Kazakhstan | 58.9 | 0.4 | 2.6 | 0.4 | 38.1 |
| Kyrgyz Republic | 88.9 | 0.1 | 0.6 | 0.2 | 10.3 |
| Tajikistan | — | — | — | — | — |
| Turkmenistan | — | — | — | — | — |
| Uzbekistan | — | — | — | — | — |
| **East Asia** | **72.8** | **9.2** | **7.7** | **11.3** | **8.2** |
| China, People's Republic of | — | — | — | — | — |
| Hong Kong, China | 84.5 | 62.7 | 5.6 | 4.3 | 5.6 |
| Japan | 80.5 | 4.9 | 7.0 | 8.4 | 4.1 |
| Korea, Republic of | 63.7 | 7.2 | 9.9 | 17.2 | 9.2 |
| Mongolia | 34.4 | 3.9 | 4.9 | 3.0 | 57.7 |
| Taipei,China | 76.8 | 2.7 | 5.4 | 9.9 | 7.9 |
| **South Asia** | **34.0** | **0.9** | **36.7** | **6.0** | **23.3** |
| Bangladesh | — | — | — | — | — |
| Bhutan | 71.0 | 0.8 | 12.4 | 11.6 | 5.0 |
| India | — | — | — | — | — |
| Maldives | 26.9 | 0.8 | 41.5 | 4.8 | 26.8 |
| Nepal | 56.1 | 1.6 | 22.2 | 12.6 | 9.1 |
| Pakistan | — | — | — | — | — |
| Sri Lanka | — | — | — | — | — |
| **Southeast Asia** | **70.5** | **2.8** | **10.7** | **6.7** | **12.1** |
| Brunei Darussalam | — | — | — | — | — |
| Cambodia | 84.7 | 4.7 | 8.4 | 4.1 | 2.7 |
| Indonesia | 76.3 | 3.0 | 14.7 | 3.3 | 5.7 |
| Lao People's Democratic Republic | — | — | — | — | — |
| Malaysia | — | — | — | — | — |
| Philippines | 42.0 | 1.4 | 10.7 | 20.1 | 27.2 |
| Singapore | 78.6 | 2.1 | 9.7 | 5.1 | 6.6 |
| Thailand | — | — | — | — | — |
| Timor-Leste | — | — | — | — | — |
| Viet Nam | 58.2 | 3.0 | 8.8 | 7.5 | 25.5 |
| **Oceania and the Pacific** | **66.9** | **2.0** | **16.2** | **8.7** | **8.3** |
| Australia | 59.6 | 2.4 | 21.1 | 8.8 | 10.4 |
| Cook Islands | 99.1 | — | 0.0 | 0.5 | 0.4 |
| Fiji | 84.3 | 1.0 | 2.3 | 11.6 | 1.8 |
| Kiribati | 82.2 | 8.2 | 2.5 | 15.3 | 0.0 |
| Marshall Islands | — | — | — | — | — |
| Micronesia, Federated States of | — | — | — | — | — |
| Nauru | — | — | — | — | — |
| New Zealand | 73.9 | 1.2 | 11.9 | 7.9 | 6.3 |
| Niue | — | — | — | — | — |
| Palau | — | — | — | — | — |
| Papua New Guinea | 86.5 | 6.2 | 5.4 | 5.7 | 2.3 |
| Samoa | 80.6 | 2.1 | 0.8 | 8.3 | 10.3 |
| Solomon Islands | — | — | — | — | — |
| Tonga | 84.9 | 1.7 | 1.4 | 13.2 | 0.6 |
| Tuvalu | 86.7 | 9.3 | 5.8 | 4.4 | 3.1 |
| Vanuatu | 87.2 | 1.6 | 0.0 | 0.0 | 12.8 |
| **Asia and the Pacific** | **65.6** | **2.5** | **9.1** | **5.1** | **20.2** |
| **Developing Asia** | **64.8** | **2.4** | **8.3** | **4.6** | **22.3** |

— = unavailable, PRC = People's Republic of China, EU = European Union (27 members), ROW = rest of the world, UK = United Kingdom, US = United States.

Source: ADB calculations using data from United Nations World Tourism Organization. Tourism Satellite Accounts. http:/ statistics.unwto.org/ (accessed January 2024).

**Table A10b: Outbound Tourism Share—Asia and the Pacific, 2022** (% of total outbound visitors)

| Reporter | Partner | | | | |
|---|---|---|---|---|---|
| | Asia and the Pacific | of which PRC | EU+UK | US | ROW |
| **Central Asia** | **46.9** | **—** | **31.2** | **0.2** | **21.7** |
| Armenia | 53.6 | — | 3.3 | 0.7 | 42.4 |
| Azerbaijan | 2.2 | — | 88.6 | 0.0 | 9.2 |
| Georgia | 13.3 | — | 12.1 | 0.4 | 74.2 |
| Kazakhstan | 63.5 | — | 1.9 | 0.4 | 34.3 |
| Kyrgyz Republic | 87.9 | — | 0.6 | 0.2 | 11.3 |
| Tajikistan | 87.8 | — | 4.0 | 0.1 | 8.1 |
| Turkmenistan | 18.8 | — | 41.9 | 0.6 | 38.7 |
| Uzbekistan | 83.8 | — | 0.2 | 0.1 | 15.9 |
| **East Asia** | **34.6** | **—** | **14.7** | **10.0** | **40.7** |
| China, People's Republic of | 17.1 | — | 10.3 | 4.0 | 68.6 |
| Hong Kong, China | 42.0 | — | 10.6 | 3.1 | 44.3 |
| Japan | 36.6 | — | 28.4 | 21.1 | 13.9 |
| Korea, Republic of | 52.8 | — | 16.8 | 15.6 | 14.7 |
| Mongolia | 65.1 | — | 1.4 | 5.9 | 27.6 |
| Taipei,China | 63.0 | — | 13.1 | 11.8 | 12.0 |
| **South Asia** | **22.7** | **—** | **12.4** | **10.8** | **54.1** |
| Bangladesh | 23.7 | — | 3.7 | 4.8 | 67.9 |
| Bhutan | — | — | — | — | — |
| India | 28.0 | — | 16.7 | 15.3 | 40.1 |
| Maldives | 46.9 | — | 15.4 | 0.9 | 36.9 |
| Nepal | 52.0 | — | 19.6 | 10.0 | 18.4 |
| Pakistan | 6.7 | — | 5.6 | 3.3 | 84.4 |
| Sri Lanka | 44.8 | — | 5.7 | 4.7 | 44.8 |
| **Southeast Asia** | **67.3** | **—** | **5.6** | **3.2** | **23.9** |
| Brunei Darussalam | 78.4 | — | 0.8 | 1.2 | 19.6 |
| Cambodia | 94.9 | — | 0.5 | 2.9 | 1.7 |
| Indonesia | 45.5 | — | 2.7 | 2.1 | 49.8 |
| Lao People's Democratic Republic | 97.0 | — | 1.7 | 0.8 | 0.5 |
| Malaysia | 71.9 | — | 4.9 | 1.2 | 22.0 |
| Philippines | 41.6 | — | 8.8 | 7.2 | 42.4 |
| Singapore | 71.2 | — | 13.1 | 4.9 | 10.8 |
| Thailand | 82.7 | — | 5.8 | 2.4 | 9.1 |
| Timor-Leste | 99.7 | — | 0.2 | 0.0 | 0.1 |
| Viet Nam | 91.0 | — | 1.4 | 4.2 | 3.3 |
| **Oceania and the Pacific** | **47.2** | **—** | **26.6** | **8.5** | **17.7** |
| Australia | 41.4 | — | 30.4 | 8.7 | 19.6 |
| Cook Islands | 91.7 | — | 3.5 | 0.8 | 4.1 |
| Fiji | 82.1 | — | 0.8 | 12.2 | 4.9 |
| Kiribati | 86.7 | — | 2.4 | 4.6 | 6.3 |
| Marshall Islands | 18.2 | — | 51.9 | 4.3 | 25.7 |
| Micronesia, Federated States of | 8.5 | — | 1.1 | 4.5 | 85.8 |
| Nauru | 93.0 | — | 3.9 | 1.0 | 2.1 |
| New Zealand | 68.5 | — | 12.7 | 8.1 | 10.6 |
| Niue | 84.9 | — | 3.0 | 0.9 | 11.2 |
| Palau | 24.2 | — | 2.9 | 4.0 | 68.8 |
| Papua New Guinea | 96.3 | — | 1.5 | 1.2 | 1.0 |
| Samoa | 87.7 | — | 0.6 | 7.5 | 4.3 |
| Solomon Islands | 87.9 | — | 2.8 | 3.6 | 5.8 |
| Tonga | 87.4 | — | 2.4 | 8.6 | 1.6 |
| Tuvalu | 74.7 | — | 3.3 | 8.3 | 13.8 |
| Vanuatu | 84.9 | — | 2.3 | 1.1 | 11.7 |
| **Asia and the Pacific** | **44.7** | **—** | **19.4** | **5.3** | **30.6** |
| **Developing Asia** | **44.8** | **—** | **18.3** | **4.4** | **32.6** |

— = unavailable, PRC = People's Republic of China, EU = European Union (27 members), ROW = rest of the world, UK = United Kingdom, US = United States.

Source: ADB calculations using data from United Nations World Tourism Organization. Tourism Satellite Accounts. http:/ statistics.unwto.org/ (accessed January 2024).

www.ingramcontent.com/pod-product-compliance
Lightning Source LLC
Chambersburg PA
CBHW041754220926
51847CB00014B/204
* 9 7 8 9 2 9 2 7 7 2 5 1 2 *